The Growth of Cities

The Growth of Cities   edited by David Lewis

WILEY-INTERSCIENCE
A Division of John Wiley & Sons, Inc., New York

FOR AN AND PRIAULX

Sole distributor for the United States
Wiley-Interscience, A Division of
John Wiley & Sons Inc., New York

ISBN 0471 53198-7

Library of Congress Catalog Card Number: 70-171916

© Paul Elek 1971

Published by Elek Books Ltd
54-58 Caledonian Road London N1

Printed by The Garden City Press Limited
Letchworth, Hertfordshire SG6 1JS, Great Britain

Contents

Acknowledgements 6

Notes on Contributors 7

David Lewis — Introduction 9
Hans Blumenfeld — The role of design 14
David Kinsey — The French Z.U.P. technique of urban development 19

Jane Drew — Runcorn 28
Morton Hoppenfeld — The Columbia process: the potential for new towns 34

C. A. Junker — subUrban design 48
Denise Scott Brown — On pop art, permissiveness, and planning 63
Theo Crosby — Ten rules for planners 65
John Turner — Barriers and channels for housing development in modernizing countries 70

Christopher Alexander, Shlomo Angel, Christie Coffin, Sanford Hirshen, Sara Ishikawa — Houses generated by patterns 84

John Turner — A new view of the housing deficit 115
Ann and Gordon Ketterer — The modern Mayan house site 126
David Etherton — Concentric towns: the valley of the Mzab 138
Margrit and Declan Kennedy — The regeneration of Regensburg 150
Constantine A. Michaelides — Observations on three Aegean island towns 173
Julian Beinart — Government-built cities and people-made places 184
Charles Moore and Gerald Allen — Church Street South housing in New Haven 208
Raymond L. Gindroz — Housing and urban growth 217
John Craig — Thamesmead: planning 233
Alexander Pike — Thamesmead: report 242
John A. McCarthy — Thamesmead: transportation planning 252

Acknowledgements

Most of the contributions to THE GROWTH OF CITIES have been specially written and illustrated for this publication. However, as the acknowledgements below show specifically, four contributions were previously published in journals and are reprinted without change, while two others have been completely rewritten or radically expanded on the basis of previous more abbreviated published forms; and in all cases, except *On Pop Art, Permissiveness and Planning* by Denise Scott Brown, much new and previously unpublished illustrational material has been included.

Thamesmead Report by Alexander Pike appeared previously in *Architectural Design* (London), Vol. XXXIX, No. 11, November 1969; *The Role of Design* by Hans Blumenfeld appeared previously in the *Journal of the American Institute of Planners,* Vol. XXXIII, No.5, September 1967; *On Pop Art, Permissiveness and Planning* by Denise Scott Brown appeared previously in the *Journal of the American Institute of Planners,* Vol. XXXV, No. 3, May 1969; and *Barriers and Channels for Housing Development in Modernizing Countries* by John C. Turner appeared previously in the *Journal of the American Institute of Planners,* Vol. XXXIII, No. 3, May 1967. A previous and shorter version of *The Valley of the Mzab* appeared in the *Journal of the Royal Institute of British Architects,* November 1969; and a previous and shorter version of *The French Z.U.P. Technique of Urban Planning* appeared in the *Journal of the American Institute of Planners,* Vol. XXV, No. 6, November 1969. The editor and publishers of this book wish to thank the editors of these journals and the respective authors for their kind permission to reprint these contributions.

Houses Generated by Patterns by Christopher Alexander, Shlomo Angel, Christie Coffin, Sanford Hirshen and Sara Ishikawa is excerpted from the report of the submission of the Center of Environmental Structure to the Proyecto Experimental de Vivienda competition for housing, and prepared for this book by Barbara Schreiner Alexander. *A New View of the Housing Deficit* by John C. Turner was a paper delivered at the Developing Economy Conference at the University of Puerto Rico in 1967 and was subsequently distributed in the report of that conference, *The Economics of Housing Policy for a Developing Economy,* a Study of the Social Science Research Center, edited by Charles A. Frankenhoff.

The editor wishes to thank The American Institute of Architects for permission to reprint four recent publicity posters drawing attention to urban ecological, social and pollution problems; the Board of Directors of Chatham Village, Inc., Pittsburgh, for permission to use photographs used here in *The Role of Design* and *subUrban Design;* and the M.I.T. Press, Cambridge, Massachusetts, for permission to use the illustration of Babel IIB by Paolo Soleri from his book *The City in the Image of Man,* 1970.

The editor wishes to thank David Grove of the Greater London Council for his assistance with the Thamesmead material; also Jane Davis Kolts who has been valiant and without despair throughout the two years of putting THE GROWTH OF CITIES together; and in addition he wishes to thank his publisher's editors, Moira Johnston and Janet Haffner.

DL

THEO CROSBY—architect, industrial designer; for some years was technical editor of *Architectural Design* (London) and editor of *Uppercase;* author (with Monica Pigeon) of *Houses,* 1961; *Architecture: City Sense,* 1966; *The Necessary Monument* 1970; in private practice he won the Gran Premio at the Milan Triennale, 1964, for his design of the British Pavilion; he designed the interior of the British Pavilion at the Montreal Expo, 1967; and he was recently visiting professor of architecture at Washington University, St. Louis, USA.

JANE DREW—architect; with husband Maxwell Fry she has designed universities in West Africa, collaborated with Le Corbusier at Chandigarh, and is now in practice in London; recent President of The Architectural Association, London; author (with Maxwell Fry) of *Architecture for Tropical Countries.*

DAVID ETHERTON—architect; presently teaching at the University College of Nairobi, Kenya.

RAYMOND L. GINDROZ—architect; partner of Urban Design Associates, Pittsburgh, USA; also teaches at Yale University.

MORTON HOPPENFELD—architect and planner; head of planning team for Columbia New Town, Maryland, USA; presently vice-president, the Rouse Company.

C. A. JUNKER—architect and planner; in practice with M. Ueland in Philadelphia, USA; winners of a *Progressive Architecture* award for their Montgomery County suburban studies.

MARGRIT and DECLAN KENNEDY—German and Irish architect/planners; members of an in-depth study team for the conservation and rehabilitation of Regensburg, sponsored by the Cultural Circle of the Federation of German Industry, to be published shortly by Karl Kramer Verlag; now living in the USA.

ANN and GORDON KETTERER—architects; their urban design studies of the ancient Mayans in Mexico were carried out with a Fulbright Fellowship.

DAVID KINSEY—planner; graduate of Dartmouth College, 1969; graduate studies at Woodrow Wilson School of Public and International Affairs, Princeton University, 1970-71; Administrative Assistant in the New Jersey Department of Community Affairs, USA; worked in Caen, France, 1969-71.

DAVID LEWIS—Andrew Mellon Professor of architecture and urban design, Carnegie-Mellon University, Pittsburgh, USA, 1963-68; taught at Yale 1969 and 1970; author (with Hansmartin Bruckmann) of *New Housing in Great Britain,* 1961; editor, *The Pedestrian in the City* (1965) and *Urban Structure* (1968); founder-partner, Urban Design Associates, USA.

JOHN A. McCARTHY—traffic and transportation planner, Greater London Council.

CONSTANTINE A. MICHAELIDES—Associate Dean of Architecture, Washington University, St. Louis, USA; author of *Hydra: A Greek Island Town,* 1967; his recent studies of urban form and growth in the Greek islands will form the basis of a new book.

CHARLES MOORE—Chairman, Department of Architecture, Yale University, USA; in private practice, architect of several internationally known buildings including Sea Ranch, California.

ALEXANDER PIKE—architect; teaches at Cambridge University, England; writes regularly for *Architectural Design* (London).

JOHN TURNER—English architect; research associate, M.I.T., USA; worked in Peru, 1957-65; UN consultant on uncontrolled urban settlement; Joint Center for Urban Studies, USA, 1965-67.

CHRISTOPHER ALEXANDER—English architect, planner, mathematician; Director of the Center for Environmental Structure, Berkeley, California, U.S.A.; author of *Notes on the Synthesis of Form,* 1964; (with Serge Chermayeff) *Community and Privacy: Toward a New Architecture of Humanism,* 1963; also wrote the prize-winning essay *A City is not a Tree,* 1966.

GERALD ALLEN—architect; currently working in the office of Charles Moore Associates, USA.

SHLOMO ANGEL, CHRISTIE COFFIN, SANFORD HIRSHEN, SARA ISHIKAWA—members with Christopher Alexander of the Center for Environmental Structure team for the Proyecto Experimental de Vivienda competition, Lima, Peru.

JULIAN BEINART—South African architect and planner; professor of architecture and urban design at M.I.T., USA; formerly Dean of City and Regional Planning, University of Capetown, South Africa; his work has appeared in several international journals including *The Architectural Forum, Perspecta* (USA), *Architectural Review* (London) and *Edilizia Moderna* (Italy).

HANS BLUMENFELD—consultant planner; professor of urban and regional planning, University of Toronto, Canada; author of *The Modern Metropolis,* 1967, writings edited by Paul Spreiregen.

DENISE SCOTT BROWN—partner, Venturi & Rauch, architects and planners, Philadelphia, USA; has taught at the University of Pennsylvania, University of California (Berkeley), University of California (Los Angeles), Rice University, and Yale.

JOHN CRAIG—city planner and chartered surveyor; in the Department of Planning and Transportation, Greater London Council.

INTRODUCTION

DAVID LEWIS

9   At first sight the collection of essays in this book—as in the two collections preceding it, *The Pedestrian in the City* (1965) and *Urban Structure* (1968)—might appear to have been thrown together without theme. I make no apology for that. The reverse, in fact. These books are about the city, 'man's most intricate artifact,'[1] his largest, most contradictory, complex, and most organic and incremental expression, the place to which the majority of mankind is drawn and where increasing millions of people struggle for individual levels of meaning in their lives.

In the face of the enormous and potent complexity of cities these essays are small things. In a many-sided world, they too are fragments. If a collection of such fragments has in itself a common value, it is probably that it reflects what cities themselves are, namely accretions, huge enigmatic montages, in the noise and filth and tragedy of which are embedded incredibly potent markers, intense and sometimes majestic evidences of the dialogue, commitment and being of citizens. Thus the things in this book are offered for what they are, the thoughts, notes, criticisms marginalia of working architects; architects who are also citizens.

Once Frank Lloyd Wright was asked what he as an architect would do with Pittsburgh, USA; and from a high promontory, so the story goes, he surveyed the river valleys filled with steel mills and pollution and ghostly skyscrapers in the soupy fog and the encrustments of small houses terraced on the hills' slopes above the valleys, and he said 'abandon it'. But the architects in this book have not abandoned the city. Nor have the people. They have, on the contrary, found a world in all of that far richer, more profound, more humorous, joyful, zany, and more agonizing and challenging than any that they, or Frank Lloyd Wright, could singlehandedly invent. Like William Blake whose Jerusalem rose out of Paddington and who saw heaven in a wild flower the architect-writers in this book have not left the streets of the cities they inherit; they see in the industrial pollution, in the shacks of the *barrios,* in the sprawl of suburbs, in inherited Victorian or medieval fragments, the very materials-at-hand with which the complex forces of investment, politics, technological knowledge, historicity and individual human passion and expressiveness play, and out of which contemporary processes the future of cities 'poised uneasily between affluence and oblivion'[2] must evolve.

From time to time, particularly during the last hundred years, not only Wright but many other architects have been tempted to abandon the old cities, permeated with their crises, and invent new ones. An example is Paolo Soleri, who worked in Frank Lloyd Wright's studio some twenty-five years ago, and whose huge, magnificent and frightening drawings of visionary cities, to be located in the deserts of Arizona, have recently been exhibited at the Whitney Museum in New York. I illustrate one of them over, Babel IIB, which appears to be located in a canyon and below an airport. Among the footnotes is Paolo Soleri's description of this city.[3] I have chosen Babel IIB, not for its originality, but for its typicality. Clearly it owes something to Sant' Elia in theory as well as to Wright in form, and it also has a relationship to recent Plug-in Cities. Assuming that cities fundamentally are systems, he develops his own layered system of thought and design which he calls arcology ('a passenger liner is the closest ancestor of arcology'[4]). Arcology is presented as the only sane alternative to an urban and suburban laissez-faire sprawl which is foreseen as responding to projections of unchecked population growth and covering the face of the earth like a spreading growth and clogging weed. For this urban sprawl, an urban 'map of despair', Soleri describes his arcological alternative as follows. '*One hundred to five hundred layers of performance will grossly produce a shrinkage of ecumenoply to one-hundredth of its suggested size.* Instead of a stagnant and far too extensive layer of pseudo-urban environment, there would then be fibres of dense vitality running over continents and seas, ribbing the surface of the planet. They would actually be urban rivers whose core would serve for transportation and communication, whose top would be an endless airport, and the sides the actual urban substance. In the foundations and around them, the producing plants would be cybernetically organized. Taking off from the urban rivers, or coming to them, would be urban systems of smaller dimension ending or taking off from large modular cities. *The material presented here is a schematic reference to modular urban systems that find full coherence as appendices and as origins of the urban rivers, carriers of the bulk of civilizations.*'[6]

Cities, of course, closely reflect in their forms the social, technological, economic and political processes within them. Soleri is as aware of this as anyone else. He attacks 'megalopolis,' 'ecumenopolis,' and laissez-faire suburban sprawl as the products of 'speculation' and of a 'materialism (which) is foreclosing man's destiny.' And if in megalopolis 'there is no mention of segregated minorities, of slum clearance, of exploiter and exploited, of tax unfairness, of bossism, of children killed by delivery trucks, of skid-row peripatetics, of "pets not allowed," of profit incentives, of self-help, it is because one assumes that in time the skill of man will take care of them all. *The foundation of equity is thus granted.* There is then happy man with the full-fledged "coordination" of city and suburban expanse. Megalopoly stretches over the continents from top to bottom, from left to right, emerging victorious and shiny above an unending and felicitous suburbia.'[7] Without necessarily quarrelling here with Soleri's view of laissez-faire suburbia but simply turning his searchlight on his own recommendations, what is revealed is not only frightening but typical of the simple-minded arrogance of those architectural and planning utopians who believe that they can sit down and re-invent the total and evolving intricacy of cities of several millions of people. Even admitting that Soleri's drawings, like Babel IIB, are intended as 'guidelines' rather than as concrete proposals, the political, economic and social authoritarianism which they imply is nevertheless awesome: the abandonment of our existing cities, with all their historicity and continuous warp and weft of man's changing culture; the mass movement of people into huge *and already completed* shells; and subscription to social, and even spiritual, management systems the basis of which is mechanical and disciplined rather than human.

'The organization of man's life, subtly directed by the machine which is organization, is going to reach forms

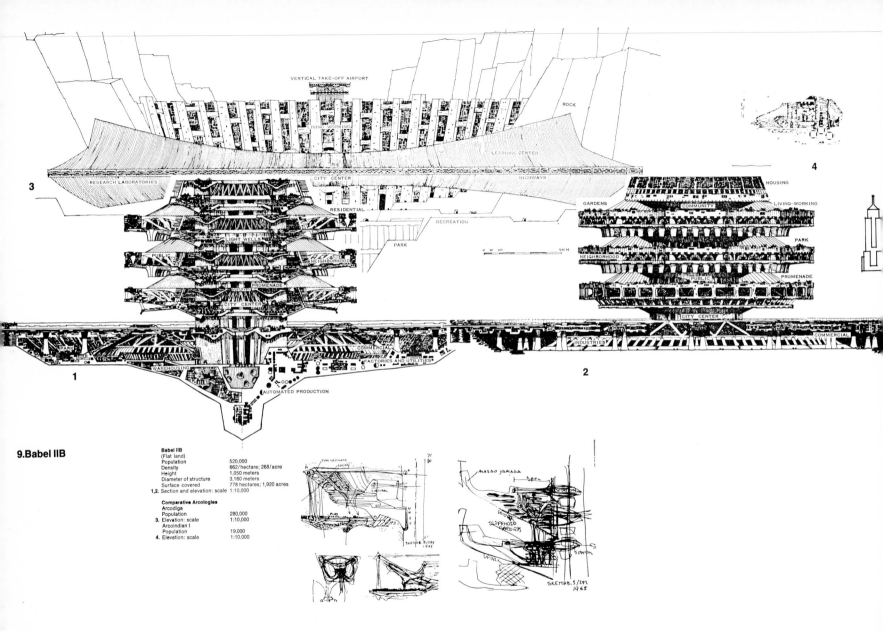

9. Babel IIB

Babel IIB
(Flat land)
Population	520,000
Density	662/hectare; 268/acre
Height	1,050 meters
Diameter of structure	3,160 meters
Surface covered	778 hectares; 1,920 acres
1,2. Section and elevation: scale	1:10,000

Comparative Arcologies
Arcodiga
Population	280,000
3. Elevation: scale	1:10,000
Arcoindian I
Population	19,000
4. Elevation: scale	1:10,000

Paolo Soleri, Babel IIB, from *The City in the Image of Man.* (MIT Press)

11

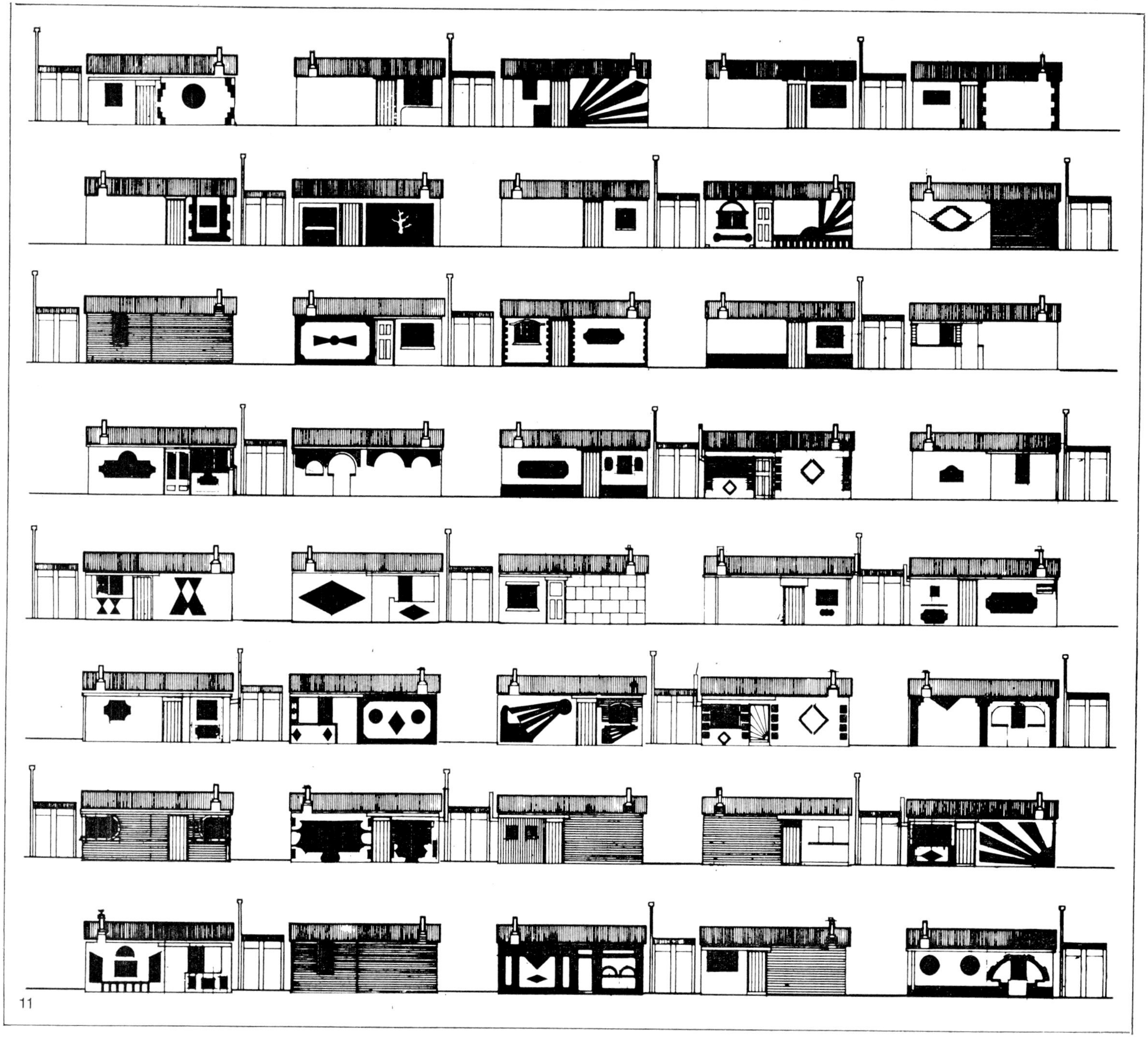

unheard of. *Hour by hour, minute by minute, man will be on a track which his freedom will be "travelling." Mentally as well as physically, he will abide by schedules computed for efficiency.* If this pattern is only temporary and made obsolete by greater sophistication in cybernetics (and discarding the intervention of evil), it will still be with us for more than one generation. What is more, it will be, and is already, conditioning man to a generalized form of non-responsibility and non-will which is very hard to overcome. (The illusion of the profit incentive through free enterprise is on a dead limb.) *The organized freedom promised by progress will conquer the contradiction inherent in itself only if instrumentally contained.*[8] It is hardly comforting to hear that Soleri really intends to be gentle. *'Care is a first-person undertaking. The care of the citizen is the sap of the city. But one can care only for that which one loves. Lovableness is the key to a living city. A lovely city is not an accident, as a lovely person is not an accident.'*[9] One is reminded, with Herbert Read, of Marie Louise Berneri's remarks about utopias. 'There are few utopias of the nineteenth century which can be read today without a feeling of utter boredom, unless they succeed in amusing us by the obvious conceit of their authors in thinking themselves the saviours of mankind. The utopias of the Renaissance contained many unattractive features yet they had a breadth of vision which commanded respect; those of the seventeenth century presented many extravagant ideas, yet they revealed searching, dissatisfied minds with which one sympathizes; but, though we are in many ways familiar with the thought of the utopias of the nineteenth century, they are nevertheless more foreign to us than those of the more distant past. In spite of the fact that these utopias were no doubt inspired by the highest motives, one cannot help "feeling bitter about the nineteenth century", like the old man in *News from Nowhere*, bitter even about the love these utopian writers lavished on humanity, for they seem like so many over-affectionate and over-anxious mothers who would kill their sons with attention and kindness rather than let them enjoy a moment of freedom.[10] The basic view presented in this book is that we cannot and should not abandon our cities, but instead we have to face up to the fact that they are what we are; and that the reason why we continue as architects and as citizens to inhabit them, for all their crises, and continue to work on them and modify

Previous page Western Native Township, Johannesburg. Facades, as recorded by Julian Beinart. (Edilizia Moderna)

them, is because in the profoundest sense they have a past and a future, a continuous and definable evolution, which is not just theirs but ours. Thus the furthest contrast to Soleri's utopia is perhaps the example of the people of the Western Native Township whose transformation of a planned workers' settlement outside Johannesburg, South Africa, into a coherent and unique place is reported in these pages by Julian Beinart. From them we may learn how a process of coherent environmental re-making can occur through each person having the courage to seize his freedom to act out and symbolize a sense of community and belonging very different from the government's planned intention for these people: so different and unforeseen and subsuming, in fact, that the government first penalized and ultimately broke up and dispersed the community. A resident of twenty years in the Western Native Township is quoted by Beinart, '. . . originally we were handed these houses in their base and barren construction and structures, in consequence of which all of us started from scratch, plastering, pounding the floors and pulverizing the walls, as well as applying some paintings . . . this incredible decision of "penalizing" the Natives against compensations in that WE HAVE MADE USE OF THE GROUND AND DERIVED COMFORT OF THESE IMPROVEMENTS.'

The compulsion in the Western Native Township to achieve an identity of neighbours—of belonging to each other, to a street, and to a city—a community of people who were thrown together by external and uncontrollable circumstance but found each other and made for themselves a distinct and contemporary place, symbolized by the joyful invention and free acceptance of a family for forms and hard-line urban images, is surely related to the enforced migration of the Ibādites to the Valley of the Mzab where intricate accretions of buildings and courts and alleyways, of sunlight and shadow and penetration of surface, compile the unselfconscious but exact physical language of a people, a community, a way of life, and a position in their world.

A less obvious relationship perhaps is to the growth of the *barrios* in South America, to the mood of revolt which underlies their incredibly rapid development from shacks to cities as shown by John Turner, and also to the mood of revolt among people in major US and European cities. For underlying the wall reliefs which transformed the Western Native Township from an anonymous camp of spiritual and physical imprisonment into 'an intensely personal piece of city-building' in which the spirit soared free was revolt, and similarly underlying the development of the

Above Town of Ghardaia in the valley of the Mzab. (Photo: David Etherton)

barrios, with their carefully thought-out and equitable social frameworks, is more than the provision of much-needed housing, of amenity; it is a spirit of revolt, the passionate and instinctive uprising of people—anonymous people—against impersonal authority and the impersonality of 'an inevitable unfolding of history,' which has no means to achieve respect for the spontaneity, the passion, and the dialogue of the individual.[11] Thus beneath the apparently chaotic unequalness of the development of the *barrios,* where every family makes its own way and its own image at its own speed, emerges a unity of combined purpose which, in turn, is not too far removed from the revolt which lies behind the incredible success and achievement of Co-op City.

In many cities in the US and Europe a 'neighbourhood' phenomenon is emerging more and more strongly, a spirit of revolt among relatively compact and coherent communities of people, an insistence on 'rights,' on a public participation and discretion in the political and planning and architectural processes which affect the quality of their personal lives. Often these are communities of the urban poor. But their coherence is not broadly political, nor is it one of general insurrection. Rather it is addressed to particular issues: and it is the need to take direct action, to make a direct and personal and creative expression, around which people freely cluster. Thus the mood of revolt takes many forms, the civil rights struggles of minorities, the rebellions of the young against the universities, establishment careers, Vietnam, and the suburbs; and thus coalescing around issues, identity is expressed not so much in a monument as in commitment.

It might well be that the process of contemporary history is a necessary dialogue of two simultaneous histories, the scientific and technological history which is impelled by rationalism to utopian universals and 'betrays a distressing tendency towards authoritarianism'[12] and that of the parallel insurrection of individuals. The words of that great modern sociologist, Karl Mannheim, in a letter to Herbert Read more than thirty years ago seem to be strangely prophetic of the situation now developing in modern cities. 'Although I do not think that the principle of anarchism in its unhistoric form will work in a society of modern social techniques, because planning without a relatively great amount of centralization seems to me to be impossible, the task of this philosophy is still to teach mankind again and again that the patterns of organizations are manifold, and the organic ones should not be and need not be overridden by rigid organization. The natural forces of self-adjustment in small groups produce more wisdom than any abstract thinking and so the scope for them within the plan is more important than we can guess.'[13]

In spite of the still almost unanimous condemnation of the architectural and planning professions of Co-op City compared with an equally strong approval for Thamesmead, the former as community-building is far stronger in the *barrio* sense of people coming together freely to live in the way they want to and not in the way architects want them to. Similarly, as Robert Venturi points out, is not the suburban commercial strip of a Route 66, so deplored by architects and planners everywhere, almost O.K.? 'The seemingly chaotic juxtapositions of honky-tonk elements express an intriguing kind of vitality and validity, and they produce an unexpected approach to unity as well.'[14] And are there no lessons for Runcorn and other

totally planned new towns in the incremental forms of investment and settlement demonstrated at Columbia? It is hardly surprising that for Venturi the historicity of architects should be akin to T.S. Eliot's poet whose historical sense compels him 'to write not merely with his generation in his bones, but with a feeling that the whole literature of Europe . . . has a simultaneous existence and composes a simultaneous order.'[15] The problem is that we, as architects, persist in turning deaf ears to the things we do not want to hear, and seem to forget that the urban accretions from the past from which we draw sustenance, the growth of cities like Hydra, or Ghardaia, or Regensburg, described in these pages, were not the work of architects and planners at all, but of people, ordinary anonymous citizens, who were in direct dialogue with the historical and environmental processes and pressures and crises of their time. These cities too are accretions; they were built up in fragments, by individual thought and action, in time as well as in space; and the result was, and is, a culture, a unity of form and life. It is our mistake, and also our conceit, if we believe that citizens are any less capable of discretion now than they were in the past. The present context has changed, but has the process? Our revolt must be to work against the conceit of authoritarianism, of remote planning. It must be to work with the evolution of cities, not in intellectual and spiritual conditions removed from their essential pulses of life, but in direct dialogue and citizenship. The culture of cities is a coherence of human and physical fragments. To abandon them is, in a profound sense, to abandon ourselves.

Notes

[1] Theo Crosby, *Architecture: City Sense;* Studio Vista (London) and Reinhold (New York), 1965.

[2] Crosby, *op. cit.*

[3] 'A hyperstructure over 1 kilometre high and 2 kilometres in diameter at the bowl base. Vertical shafts carry (1) the vertical transportation system, elevator batteries, and continental, transcontinental air transport "sleeves"; (2) form-grounds of the city; (1) at the periphery, the residential spaces; (2) in the medial belt, the gardens and waste processing plants; (3) towards the centre, civil facilities and work. The top platform-ground is for cultural institutions: schools, labs, studios, theatres, libraries.

'At the ground is a system of parks, gardens, and playgrounds. Under the ground level develops the automated world of production (and research) in an atmosphere of vacuum, fire, cold, gas, radiation, water, pressure . . . the fusion (or equivalent) power

plant at the core. Energy is served radially to plants, to the technological "city" and to the totality of the arcology, including the grounds and the atmospheric dome in which the arcology is contained. Babel IIB floats on a mineral bed. One third of it is scooped out of the ground. From the centre the hollow trunk rises 1200 metres into the air. Four major topographies ring the trunk, partly suspended. On each topography (township) is an annular park separating the outer belt of residences with the inner belt of public facilities. The light reaches deep into the core of the city, vertically from the axial well and obliquely between the four topographies. The whole bowl could be weather-controlled by means of heat-sensitive screens.

'For a structure of this size and structural organization, symmetry along the vertical axis is mandatory. The centre of gravity of the whole system is located exactly on the axis of symmetry.

'The city could well work as a major airport with aircraft taxiing on the outer rim of the bowl within minutes' time from anywhere in the city.'

Paolo Soleri, *Arcology: The City in the Image of Man;* The MIT Press (Cambridge, USA and London, England), 1970, p. 62.

[4] Soleri, *op. cit.*, p. 14.

[5] Constantine Doxiadis, *Ekistics,* Book 3, Chapter 9, Oxford University Press, New York and London, 1968.

[6] Soleri, *op, cit.,* p. 2,

[7] Soleri, *op. cit.,* p. 1.

[8] Soleri, *op cit.,* p. 25.

[9] Soleri, *op. cit.,* p.7. In all cases, italics are Soleri's.

[10] Marie Louise Berneri, *Journey Through Utopia,* Routledge & Kegan Paul, London, 1950, pp.218-9, quoted in Herbert Read's *Anarchy And Order,* Faber & Faber, London, 1954, p. 22.

[11] Attention is drawn to Le Corbusier's project at Pessac, the first planned development of the 'white architecture' of the twenties, where the inhabitants have 'remade' the environment in an apparently wilful way, cutting new windows, adding half-timbering, inserting niches for madonnas, constructing extensions, altering rooflines, and colour-washing, until a new and highly personal *place* has emerged. One recalls Le Corbusier's apocryphal remark, the architect was wrong, the people are right.

[12] Herbert Read, *op. cit.,* p. 12.

[13] Herbert Read, *op. cit.,* p.14.

[14] Robert Venturi, *Complexity and Contradiction in Architecture;* M.O.M.A., New York, 1966; p.102.

[15] T. S. Eliot, *Selected Essays,* 1917-32; Harcourt, Brace & Co., New York, 1932, pp. 3-4; quoted in Robert Venturi, *op. cit.,* p. 19.

HANS BLUMENFELD

14

What is Design?

In its broad sense, the term 'design' means the same as 'planning' – the mental anticipation of a combination of means to achieve a goal, or a set of goals. In this discussion the goal will be defined more narrowly as a modification of the physical environment and design as the creation of the form of city and country. Form is a container; it presupposes a content. The content of 'environmental form' can only be the life of men in the society which lives in the environment.

However, men modify this environment not only, and not primarily, by design. The men who overcropped and overgrazed the western plains did not 'design' the dust bowl. The men who make, sell, and drive automobiles do not 'design' traffic jams and air pollution. They just happen.

It is the planner's task to foresee what will happen as a consequence of human actions and to guide these actions in such a way that they help rather than hinder each other in achieving their goals. Patrick Geddes coined the term 'synopsis' – together-seeing. He used it to denote the seeing together of the interaction of all the factors which determine the life of society, its content. But he used it also, and inseparably, as a seeing together of all the elements of the physical environment, as the perception and conception of form.

How far have American planners attempted and succeeded in designing form in the past? What may they do in the future?

Paradise found and lost

The American autochthones had an image of their environment as the sacred land of the tribe, and an image of their settlements, reflected in the forms created by the mound dwellers of Ohio or by the Navajos in the Southwest. The work of the mound dwellers had only an ephemeral continuation into later culture in the oddity of Centerville. The Navajo village community, antedating the distinction between public and private space, with the roofs of the family dwellings serving as the village streets, may regerminate in the concepts of 'traffic architecture'.

The European invaders brought a different concept from their shores. In Europe too the land had once been the sacred domain of the gods and their peoples, entrusted to the divinely sanctioned king. But the king had conveyed the land to his feudal retainers and the lords had made their fiefs private property. The people who toiled on the land wanted themselves and the land to be free of them. The greatest minds of Europe shared that dream. Goethe's Faust found fulfilment of his lifelong search in 'dwelling with free folk on free land', and his Wilhelm Meister ends his devious journey by organizing a group of men and women to settle in America.

America became the fulfilment of Europe's dream. It was 'The Land of the Free' because the land was free. It was free to take – and to sell and buy. It was free to be subjected, appropriated by whoever had the power to buy. Land was no longer sacred, it was a commodity, 'real estate'. Divinity was exiled to the heavens and had no connection with the business of real estate: God in his heaven, and Mammon on this earth.

In order to be appropriated, the land had to be subdivided, and, just as Sesostris had done 5,000 years before in Egypt, the young Republic divided its territory by geometry into rectangular lots. America was not conceived as a land of sacred mountains and streams, as ancient Greeks and Chinese had conceived their country, but as a subdivision of continental dimensions. Surveyors were its high priests; their lines went straight over hill and lake, regardless of natural form. As colonists have done at all times and places, the American colonists used their system of rural subdivision also to allocate sites in their towns. As the planners of Manhattan observed in 1810, 'a city is to be composed of the habitations of men, and straight-sided and right-angled houses are most cheap to build, and the most convenient to live in'. Rectangular sites added up to rectangular blocks and the sum of rectangular blocks added up to a city· If more sites were needed, more blocks were added; the frontier of the city could expand to infinity. The grid of the streets, which gave access to the private properties and served for interchange between one private property and the other, was the only public element. The street plan was *the* city plan. What was built on the individual sites, was the business of their owners alone.

True, the earliest settlers, both English and Spanish, had a concept of a community, centred on a common or plaza with the church as symbol and dominant landmark. But with the expansion of the nineteenth century the *res publica* was drowned in a welter of contending *res privatae,* private businesses. *The* church was replaced by churches, which like everybody else, had to find the land they needed in the real estate market as best they could. With few exceptions the common has become a subdivision and the plaza a parking space.

Even weaker was the influence of a younger tradition, the Renaissance ideal of the monumental building dominating the streets which fan out from it. It found a charming realization in Annapolis, and it inspired L'Enfant's plan for Washington – awkwardly superimposed on the ubiquitous grid. From these it was to surface again in the plans of 'The City Beautiful'.

Basically the city of industrial capitalism – in Europe as well as in America, only less consistently – was an assembly of real estate for various purposes, served by various networks. The networks multiplied as the cities grew larger and more complex. To the expanding networks of streets were added other networks for water, sewers, gas, electricity, rail traffic, and telephones. They were designed as citywide systems by engineers. What was built on the sites served by the systems, was not the concern of the city, but of the property owners. The dichotomy between the horizontal and vertical dimensions became complete. The concept of streets and squares as well proportioned containers of the community's life, so highly developed in the eighteenth century, decayed in the Europe of the nineteenth century. In America it had hardly taken root.

The commercial industrial city came into being not as a place for living, but as a place for making a living, a place for 'making money'. Neither God nor man designed it; Mammon did.

Back to Nature

Sensitive spirits rebelled against its inhumanity, on both sides of the Atlantic. 'The intellectual versus the city' is by no means a purely American phenomenon.

'God made the country, but man made the city' was a widely accepted belief.

If God made the country, He could be brought back to the city by bringing the country into the city or the city into the country. The latter was made possible by the development of the railroad and the resulting suburbs. But more important was the movement headed by Frederick Law Olmsted for the creation of large 'natural' city parks. Olmsted's vision extended beyond the creation of parks to the entire city, but only the parks became a reality.

Both the parks and the railroad suburbs were designed by landscape architects. Both had their contemporary counterparts in Europe, but only in America did landscape architecture become the mother of city planning.

The City Beautiful

Wealthy Americans travelling abroad were impressed by the magnificence of European capitals, and their pride stimulated them to rival and surpass them. The great example was the Paris of Haussmann, the creation of the Second Empire which had replaced the revolutionary battle cry *liberté, égalité, fraternité* by the slogan *enrichissez-vous*. Its spirit certainly was not alien to the American business tycoons. However, the drive became popular through the example of the Chicago World's Fair and spread under the banner of 'The City Beautiful', under Daniel Burnham's leadership and vision and in his plans for Chicago and San Francisco. Its concerns extended well beyond civic centres and monumental avenues, but by and large only these were built. Every American city wanted to have its Roman forum, but in most cases the width of the streets and the exaggerated scale deprived them of spatial impact.

What was the content of this grand form? What went on in its centre piece, the city hall? Just at this time, more than ever, it had become a market place for the sale of favours, which Lincoln Steffens branded as 'the shame of the cities'. Not accidentally the nadir of civic responsibility coincided with the zenith of the civic centre. The sham of the 'City Beautiful' was to hide the shame of the cities.

The Reform Movement

Lincoln Steffens was not alone: he gave voice to a reform movement which had been rising throughout the land. Americans were determined to do something about the inhuman and degrading conditions in which millions of their fellow citizens lived. The settlement house and the playground movement laid the foundation for the concept of the urban neighbourhood.

But the housing reform movement which led to the establishment of building and housing codes was to have the most lasting affect on the American city. For the first time the public hand reached beyond the property line to shape the environment of the occupants of private structures.

The housing codes attempted to protect the poor. But the middle-class also needed and wanted protection, protection of their property against incompatible uses. Zoning was established as a property-protection device. But the value of a residential property can be impaired not only by 'incompatible uses', but also by disruption of its visual environment. So prescriptions were made governing height, coverage, and setbacks, and sometimes other features as well. As the zoning ordinance had to conform to the basic concept of 'equality before the law', it enforced monotonous conformity. More than any other public action, the zoning ordinance became – and still is – the main designer and form-giver of American cities. As zoning banned certain uses from certain zones, it had to allot space to them in some other location. Thus zoning became 'comprehensive', and the municipality, for the first time, was forced to look at and to decide on the distribution of the various land uses on its territory.

The Master Plan

From the convergence of the landscape architects' work on residential suburbs and on parks, the architects' work on the 'City Beautiful', the reformers' work on housing and neighbourhood facilities, and the lawyers' work on zoning, the modern American city planning profession was born. It had to find its place alongside the older professions, the surveyors and municipal engineers, who were firmly established within the municipal administration and who continued to make the day-to-day decisions. The main task of the city planner was the design of a 'Master Plan', an image of the future city, picturing the future distribution of land uses and the public works to be carried out by the municipality.

The image which guided the Master Plans generally reflected these four elements from which the planning profession had developed. Some aspects of the plans were carried out, at least partially, but practically nowhere was the comprehensive design realized. The Master Plan might envisage the complete three-dimensional form of the city, but the instruments in the planner's hand could not shape it. His instruments were mainly negative. The zoning map, which was to carry out the land use plan, could prevent the undesirable, but it could not create the desirable.

Moreover, it could not change what was already on the ground.

The positive stimulants were not in the planner's hand. The most powerful elements made their own plans. Railroads or other industries owned most of the harbour sites and determined the fate of the waterfront, a key element in most American cities. Transit, gas and power companies, and other public utilities, while more closely related to municipal governments, also made their own plans. Even the state highway departments and the city's own engineers did not necessarily follow the Master Plan.

The innumerable decisions concerning the development of the many thousands of properties out of which the city was composed, were made by their owners – as they had always and everywhere been made. Inevitably, they were guided primarily by the desire to put their land to the most profitable use – its 'highest and best use' in the terminology of real estate. With the real estate tax as the predominant source of income, municipal governments were dominated by the same motivation. Of necessity, they did (and still do) everything to 'attract assessment'. Where the zoning ordinance or some other element of the Master Plan stood in the way, it was amended or bent out of existence.

The Master Plan had, of course, attempted to foresee and to accommodate these economic pressures. But in a highly dynamic economy, they constantly outgrew its provisions. Quantitatively, the actual city expanded beyond the boundary of the legal city, and new demands and new techniques changed it qualitatively.

The Invisible Hand

So the contemporary American city has, in fact, been designed not by a Master Plan but by the forces of the real estate market – good old Adam Smith's 'Invisible Hand', the hand of Mammon. The Invisible Hand, as Adam Smith discovered with delight, has its own logic and rationale. Its creation is not chaos, as is often alleged, but an order which can be analysed and understood.

Land economists and urban ecologists have explored the design of the Invisible Hand. It can be grasped intellectually, but it remains invisible to the eye – with one exception. Viewed from a plane at night, the American city presents an impressive image: from the profusion of lights at the centre the intensity gradually fades towards the periphery. Coloured lights represent commercial concentrations and the stream of headlights delineates the traffic flows. Three technical achievements of the twentieth century, electric light, the aircraft, and the automobile, have come together to create not only an impression of great sensuous charm, but a genuine form revealing a meaningful content.

From the ground, however, this content, the workings of the Invisible Hand of the market, remains invisible. To make it visible is a still unresolved task of the urban planner and designer. Such 'co-operation with the inevitable' is sometimes referred to with contempt. However, only a fool refuses to co-operate with the inevitable; the question is to determine what is and what is not really inevitable.

The Invisible Hand is the hand of the market, of the transaction between two persons, buyer and seller. However, when the objects of these transactions are the physical elements of a closely interrelated spatial complex, a city, each transaction is bound to affect many other persons, singly and collectively. The buyer and seller, however, cannot and do not consider the resultant benefits and 'malefits' to third persons. Thus, the pursuit by all individuals of their own designs results in a total design of the city which frustrates the designs of every individual.

New Towns

This universal frustration has led many planners to regard existing big cities as being beyond redemption and to concentrate their efforts on the creation of 'new towns', designed by the community so as to harmonize and fulfil all individual designs and desires.

Out of the new town movement have come some of the best achievements of urban design in twentieth-century America: Chatham Village in Pittsburgh and Baldwin Hills in Los Angeles, the 'Greenbelt Towns', and the 'new towns' of Reston, Columbia, and Irvine. They have had a far reaching influence, however diluted, on the design of 'neighbourhoods' and sub-divisions throughout North America and beyond. Even the biggest of these, however, though larger in area and population than most older towns, are not self-contained new towns, but parts of a larger metropolis, on which they are completely dependent. In fact, they are glorified upper- and middle-class suburbs, whose inhabitants largely depend on jobs

Above 1830 map of Pittsburgh, USA, shows the grid street and block layout, and individual property subdivisions, in the downtown section of the city.

Right Pittsburgh's downtown, the 'Golden Triangle', photographed from the south in 1970, showing how the original subdivisions were the forerunners of the modern city.

16

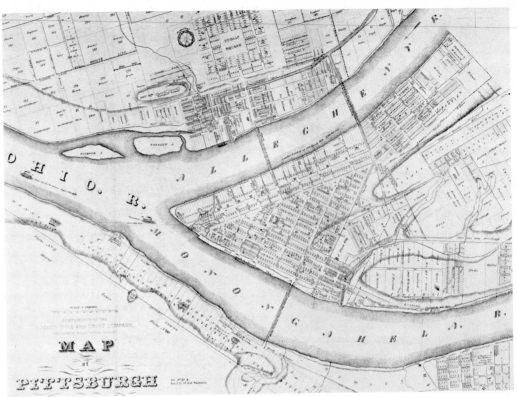

outside the area, and they are often combined with industrial estates, which largely draw on an outside work force.

The New Scale

The form of the historical town could be perceived in two ways: from the outside as a sculptured mass, and from the inside as a system of enclosed spaces, of streets and squares. The spaces and structures were on a human scale. They could be perceived and encompassed by a view from a distance at which a human person could be recognized. All distances could be covered by a human walking on his own two feet. The structures were built by human muscle.

The scale varied from the intimate one of the domestic environment through an entire range up to the monumental one of the symbolic buildings of civic and religious life. But even the grand 'superhuman' scale of gods and kings could be related back to the size of the human being.

The modern metropolis is far too extensive to be perceived from any point as a sculptured mass, or as a system of spaces by walking through its streets. Streets go on to infinity, and movement is primarily by mechanical means. The monuments of gods and kings do not dominate the secular city. There are other and more impressive structures which are neither on the human nor on the superhuman scale: the great bridges, piers, grain elevators, hangars, and, most pervasive, the freeways with their interchanges. They are used not by human beings, but by machines; they are built not by human muscle, but by machines; and they are seen primarily by human beings moving not at their own speeds, but rather at the speed of machines. Their scale is neither human nor 'superhuman'. I have called it 'extrahuman', because it is outside the human being, part of 'outer' nature, like mountains or rivers. These structures are elements of a new metropolitan landscape.

Related to them, but not quite a member of the family, is the most characteristic creation of the American city, the skyscraper. It is not entirely 'extrahuman', because it shelters human beings and its floor heights and windows are determined by their size. It is therefore not surprising that in its early day it was regarded and treated as a new variant of the monumental building on a 'superhuman' scale, as a 'cathedral of commerce'. But increasingly the elements relating it to the human scale, floors and windows, are hidden behind curtains of glass, metal, or marble, assimilating it to the purely technical structures of the extra-human scale.

In either form, the concentration of skyscrapers in the centre has created the characteristic silhouette of the American city. Only in a single case, however, on the tip of Manhattan Island, have the skyscrapers grouped themselves into a sculptured mass. As this was possible only by complete disregard for leaving space open for light, air, and movement, it certainly will never be repeated. Typically, the skyscrapers are too far apart to form a group, too close together to dominate as individual structures, and outside of the central business core their distribution is entirely haphazard.

The vertical extension of the skyscraper – the product of mechanical means of vertical transportation – and the horizontal extension of the metropolis – the product of mechanical means of horizontal transportation – have obliterated the street as a defined space of interrelated proportions. It is not accidental that the utopian images of the two most creative designers of this century, Frank Lloyd Wright and Le Corbusier, both negate the street. In Frank Lloyd Wrights' 'Broadacre City' the buildings, most of them low and rambling with an occasional tower, are scattered broadly over the landscape. But in its apparent opposite, Le Corbusier's 'Radiant City', the emphasis is also primarily on sun, sky, and green. 'But where,' you will ask, 'are the buildings?' Le Corbusier wrote, 'Up there, above the trees, those crystalline prisms.' The forces which those great architects attempted to express in their designs, have been given a less inspiring form by the Invisible Hand. Instead of 'Broadacre City' we have narrowacre suburbs. The houses are, indeed, scattered, too scattered to form a street or any other collective unit, and they are too close together to register as individual units. On the other hand, the 'high-rise' apartment developments and

Below left Chatham Village, Pittsburgh.

Below centre Downtown Pittsburgh at street level.

Below Seagram Building, New York.

17

redevelopments, on or off stilts, are not ethereal visions, but heavily oppressive.

Design for a Motorized World
While both Broadacre City and Radiant City accepted – indeed, enthusiastically welcomed – the automobile, it was not architects or planners, but the Invisible Hand which derived from the automobile America's most significant contribution to urban design, the suburban shopping centre. By the complete separation of pedestrian from vehicular movement, it created anew in its malls and plazas the street and square as well defined outdoor living spaces, and pointed the way for the revival of the human scale in the urban environment. This pedestrian world, however, still exists only as an island in an ocean of parked cars.

When the shopper gets into his car and drives off, he enters a different world on a vastly larger scale, which finds its most complete expression in the freeway. The freeway creates two design problems: the view *to* and the view *from* the freeway. The first is in an urban environment usually best solved by locating the freeway below grade, in a cut or even in a tunnel. But the view *from* the highway requires a location at or above grade. In the wider metropolitan landscape, outside the densely built-up core, such a location can often be found at an edge, where it does not disrupt, but emphasises the natural or man-made structure of the region. The driver's vision in motion can build up a composite memory image of the metropolis comparable to the composite image which was built up by walking through the streets of older and smaller towns. However, with the motor vehicle and other modern means of transportation and communication 'urban' elements spread out further, destroying the traditional image of the countryside and bringing with them pollution of air, water, and soil.

The Revenge of the Gods
Not only the city is disrupting the ecological balance of nature. Practices of farming and logging have an equal share. Typically the American farmer has not been a 'husbandman', not married to the soil, 'mining' it. There is in western thought no counterpart to the ancient wisdom of *Feng-Shui* – wind and water – which has governed Chinese city planning.

The ancient gods of the sacred soil will not tolerate forever the violation of their laws. Man may forget that he is part of nature and treat her merely as a source of 'raw materials' to be utilized and then be thrown away as 'waste', but the waste returns to haunt him. He can continue to live only if he preserves and restores the ecological balance.

This balance is not static. The American landscape is not just 'Oh Wilderness!' It can be a man-made landscape, based on a new and different balance of all its elements, man and his works included.

The Next Fifty Years
The 'design' of the continental landscape of America is perhaps the most challenging task to planners in the next half century. This includes the location of cities; the control of the flow of surface and sub-surface waters; and the design of the shores of rivers, lakes, and oceans, from lonely beaches to the quays of city centres.

On the scale of the metropolis it means articulating its structure by a system of subcentres related to a main centre, making these relations visible by the concentration of tall structures at the focal points. It means giving form to the edges between districts of different character – land and water recreation spaces, various kinds of built up districts – and by unfolding the total image as a sequence of memorable images along the paths of vision in motion.

Within the centres there is the task of separating the realm of the pedestrian from that of the motor vehicle – vertically or horizontally – of shaping pedestrian islands on the human scale and of connecting them with each other. In an age of science the universities, as places for life-long education, may well become the most significant elements of urban centres.

In the vast residential areas the task is to overcome functional and structural sterile uniformity and, in particular, to develop new and richer forms for single-family houses and their groupings.

Technically the means at the disposal of the designer are almost unlimited, and they will become increasingly so, economically as well, in the decades to come. Shall we, as a profession, together with the other design professions, have the creative imagination to use them? Shall we, as a nation, have the will to use them?

A planner recently wrote: 'The people of this nation expect to *provide* security for their capital, and *allow* for their community's physical development'[1] (emphasis mine). Will the people of the United States and of Canada reverse their priorities? Will they want, while *allowing* for security of their capital, to *provide* their community's physical development? That is the crucial design problem of the next fifty years.

Paley Park, New York; a small oasis, with tables and chairs, trees and a waterfall, off Fifth Avenue.

Marina City, Chicago, uses a river, bridges, and a mountainscape of buildings as its panorama.

Note
1 Roger Feinstein in a book review, *Journal of the American Institute of Planners,* XXXIII (March, 1967), p. 126.

THE FRENCH Z.U.P. TECHNIQUE OF URBAN DEVELOPMENT

DAVID N. KINSEY

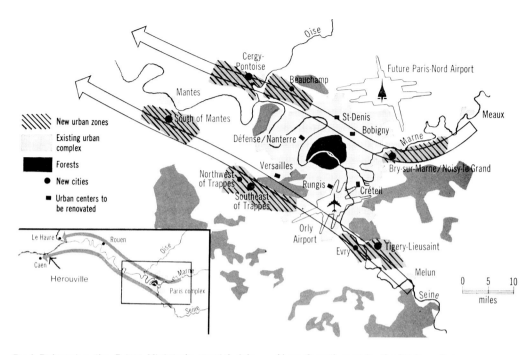

Above Growth axes for the Paris region.

19

An important part of the present French national urbanization policy is the 'Z.U.P.' *(zone à urbaniser de priorité)* or Priority Urbanization Zone. The new town at Hérouville, outside Caen, in Normandy, is an example of this innovative French technique for organizing urban development, using a mix of the public and private sectors. Comparison with British and American new town development suggests that it may be possible to transfer some of the Z.U.P.'s financial and administrative techniques.

French Urbanization Policy

A basic problem of French urbanization stems from the extraordinarily massive concentration of national activities in Paris and the resulting lack of substantial regional development. This can be attributed to the long tradition of administrative centralization initiated by Louis XIV and Napoleon. Continuing rapid growth in the Paris region has not only drawn down development levels in the rest of France, it has also caused a large shortage of housing and public services in Paris.[1]

Present-day French policy for the Paris region, the 1965 *Schéma Directeur d'Aménagement et d'Urbanisme de la Région de Paris,* or Strategic Plan, was prepared by the Délégation Générale au District de la Région de Paris, a special administrative agency directed by

Paul Delouvrier, the Prime Minister's special delegate. Its jurisdiction extends over 5,000 square miles in a 40 to 60 mile radius from Notre Dame. Its primary role is co-ordinating the implementation of its plans for the future of the Paris region. The *Schéma* proposes an axial pattern of growth along a double axis straddling the Seine, from Paris towards Rouen, Le Havre, and Caen[2] (diagram above). The backbones of the double axis are railway lines and expressways. The railways have been electrified to Caen and Le Havre, and the expressways should be completed in the mid-1970s. The banks of the Seine will be protected as a giant recreation zone while new communities are created on both the northern and southern plateaux of the river. According to this plan, Paris will provide the same number of jobs, while the new urban centres will offer new jobs as well as residential facilities. The master plan will prohibit further expansion of today's shapeless dormitory-suburbs and will create along the Seine double axis at least eight completely equipped new towns with populations from 35,000 to 300,000. The plan also calls for renovating several existing urban centres, providing an intensive system of regional transportation, restructuring the region's activity, and satisfying recreational and cul-

tural needs for the region's projected fourteen million inhabitants.[3] The *Schéma* attempts to relieve much of the congestion of the Paris region. It is a decentralization plan, but it recognizes and capitalizes upon the great attractive power of Paris by diverting new growth into the double axis. Caen and its semi-satellite of Hérouville are at the western terminus of the southern axis designated by the *Schéma*.

The Fifth Plan (1966–1970), approved in 1965, proposed a policy of eight *métropoles d'équilibre,* or regional metropolises, to provide a balance to the attraction of Paris and to stimulate economic development in the provinces.[4] These *métropoles* are loosely-defined urban complexes where renovated central cities, new business and housing centres, and selected national investments in key sectors should promote regional growth around that particular centre (diagram opposite).

Caen is not an independent *métropole d'équilibre;* it is too closely tied to Paris. However, Caen is most definitely the regional centre for the sub-region known as Lower Normandy. The *métropole d'équilibre* policy calls for several of these smaller regional centres to

The regional metropolises and their spheres of influence.

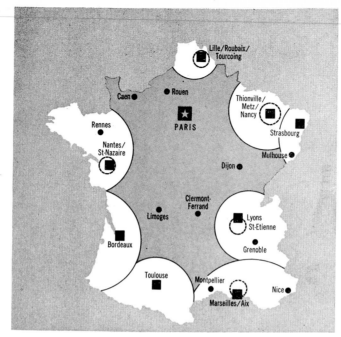

★ Paris
■ Regional metropolis
◯ Urban complex
● Equipped regional relay center

20

be equipped as relay centres between Paris and the distant provinces. Thus, the growth of Caen and centres such as Rouen, Dijon, Limoges, and Clermont-Ferrand will also be encouraged by national investments.

A third segment of French urbanization policy concerns the large cities – such as Caen, Rouen, Le Mans, Tours, Orléans, Reims, and Amiens – in the Paris Basin, the area within 200 miles of Paris. The Basin includes the Paris Region covered by the 1965 *Schéma* and six other administrative regions: Basse-Normandie, Haute-Normandie, Picardie, Champagne, Bourgogne, and Centre. The past growth of these regions and their principal cities has been thwarted by the attraction of commercial and industrial activity to Paris. However, recent decentralization policies have stimulated industrial growth in the Basin, to the extent that the development of regional centres in the Basin has been proposed as an alternative or complementary policy to the *métropole d'équilibre* and *Schéma* plans to check the growth of the Paris region. Such an effort would reduce the net outmigration from the Basin to Paris by attracting people from the rest of France to the Basin itself.[5]

The Sixth Plan (1970–1974) will, it is hoped, specify the relative priorities for investments to be made among: (1) new towns for the Paris Region proposed by the *Schéma*, (2) the eight *métropoles d'équilibre* and their sub-regional centres, and (3) the cities of the Paris Basin. In any case, the satellite city of Hérouville fulfils the two goals of French urbanization policy, decentralization and the development of regional centres, as it contributes to the three alternate or complementary programmes of that policy: (1) it is at the western terminus of the *Schéma's* growth axis, (2) it improves the position of Caen as a sub-regional centre for the *métropoles d'équilibre,* and (3) it greatly strengthens Caen's position as a major centre in the Paris Basin.[6]

The Z.U.P. Technique
The French government, despite its strongly national form, promotes its urbanization policy by stimulating local authorities, not assuming their roles. The national government provides the financial assistance and increased legal powers necessary for planned urban development. The most important French vehicle for structuring such development is the Z.U.P. technique.[7] A Z.U.P., or *zone à urbaniser de priorité,* is a housing zone whose development is entrusted by a commune (the commune is the basic unit of local administration, similar to a township) to a special development corporation. A Z.U.P. can be thought of as a 'semi-satellite', but not a 'new town'. In January 1967, there were 173 such Z.U.P.s in France, covering 59,000 acres with a capacity for 740,000 dwelling units.[8] The purpose of a Z.U.P. is clearly defined in the Z.U.P. legislation:

A decree of the Minister of Construction can designate a Z.U.P. in those communes and agglomerations where the importance of housing projects will necessitate the creation, strengthening, or extension of public services.[9]

Essential public services are schools, roads, utilities, social, commercial, administrative, and cultural centres. Local and national government authorities recognize that they must furnish most of these services sooner or later during the life of a housing project. A Z.U.P. is delimited so that the arrangement of services and dwellings in a new housing zone will be co-ordinated and organized from the earliest planning stages and the life of its inhabitants will be as normal as possible. This concern for quality and variety of life in a new development, the desire to co-ordinate provision of public services, and the wish to avoid disorderly development are the main purposes of the Z.U.P. technique.

A Z.U.P. may be created by the Minister of Construction, acting at the request of an interested commune, or by a decree of the Council of State.[10] If a Z.U.P. is deemed necessary for the development of a particular region, the prefect of the region, an appointed civil servant-governor,[11] may ask a commune to request a Z.U.P. The request may also be initiated by the commune. A Z.U.P. must lie within one commune's borders, otherwise administrative and legal difficulties arise.

Local authorities are given strong development tools by the Z.U.P. legislation. As soon as the decree delimiting the Z.U.P. is published in the *Journal Officiel,*[12] all new construction – financed by the state – of more than 100 dwelling units in that commune must be built within the delimited zone. A developer of housing outside the Z.U.P. may also be refused a building permit if his intended site is not sufficiently equipped with public services and if an equally suitable site is offered to him within the Z.U.P. The existence of a Z.U.P. concentrates housing construction in one sector of a commune so that a comprehensive plan with reasonable costs for necessary public services can be prepared, financed, and implemented. Local authorities are given the right of preemption, similar to 'eminent domain,' for purchase of any ground put up for sale in the Z.U.P. within a period of four years – this may be extended for two years – from the date of the decree delimiting the Z.U.P. If there is no agreement between the landowner and the commune that wishes to exercise its right of preemption, then the purchase price is fixed by regular expropriation procedures. These land acquisition powers limit the land speculation that accompanies any housing project and permit a commune to purchase the land necessary for planned urban development.

Using the Z.U.P. technique to create a viable urban centre is an awesome task for many local authorities. Therefore, the definition, development, and management of a Z.U.P. is entrusted to a specialized corporate body that has the necessary administrative and technical services. This body or authority is either a public establishment or a semi-public corporation dedicated to carrying out projects of public interest or operating public services. The latter is known under French law as a *société d'économie-mixte*.[13] At least 50% of the capital of a *société d'économie-mixte* must be held by local authorities, such as communes or departments (a large territorial unit of government). Specialized public financial institutions and private banks provide

21

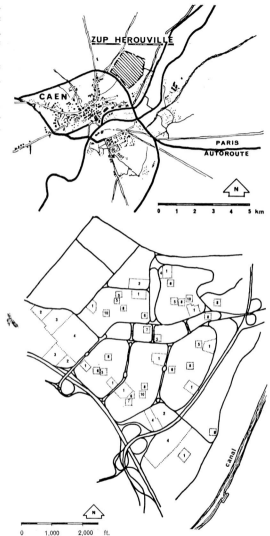

Middle top The Z.U.P. at Hérouville-St. Clair was intended as a shock treatment to promote economic growth in the Caen region. Caen was 75% destroyed in the 1944 invasion of Normandy. However, the city was quickly rebuilt; and its regional plan calls for a peripheral limited-access by-pass to connect several satellite housing and industrial zones, and to join the Paris-Normandy Expressway. The Hérouville Z.U.P. is the largest housing zone in this plan.

Middle below In 1960 the Municipal Council of Hérouville-St. Clair voted to build a Z.U.P. for 35,000 inhabitants. The Master Plan, which was the result of a national competition in 1960 won by the *Union des Architectes Urbanistes* (UAU), includes five main residential neighbourhoods grouped around a central, narrow town centre. Continuous one-way traffic wraps around each neighbourhood.

Top right Model of town centre, October 1967.

Middle right The Belles Portes neighbourhood in August 1967.

Below right A public housing tower in Belles Portes designed by Marc Biass, chief architect-planner of Hérouville-St. Clair. Public housing comprises 36% of the 8,400 dwelling units planned for Hérouville.

1 Elementary School
2 Secondary School
3 High School
4 Sport facility
5 Social Service Center
6 Teen Center
7 Young workers' dormitories
8 Commercial Center
9 Housing for the elderly
10 Churches

from 30 to 40% of the capital, with the rest coming from private and local interests. Activities of these corporations include: markets for agricultural products; express motorways; regional improvement projects; and, of course, town building.[14]

Working under contract with the commune's Municipal Council, the *société d'économie-mixte* defines, develops, and manages the Z.U.P. Construction and financing decisions and plans must be approved by the Municipal Council and the *Conseil Général,* the departmental governing body, giving an opportunity for some political influence in the initial stages.

Financing a Z.U.P.

Z.U.P. status of a development project confers financial advantages on the local government authority. The financial plan for a Z.U.P. must be approved by Committee 2b of the Economic and Social Development Fund (*Fonds de Développement Economique et Social* or FDES) of the Ministry of Finance, before any construction can begin.[15]

Financing options available are: (1) loans from the National Land Management and Urban Planning Fund, *Fonds National d'Aménagement Foncier et de l'Urbanisme* (FNAFU);[16] (2) subsidies from national ministries; and (3) loans from the *Caisse des Dépôts et Consignations* (as described in Table 1).

Table 1
Sources of National Financial Assistance for Z.U.P. Construction

Source	Description
FNAFU	Loans to the commune for land acquisition and infrastructure
Subsidies by national ministries	Direct grants to the commune for public facilities and infrastructure
Caisse des Dépôts et Consignations	(a) Loans to the commune for public facilities and infrastructure (b) Loans for housing construction distributed by: (i) *Caisse des Prêts aux Organismes HLM* for social housing (ii) *Crédit Foncier* for private and co-operative housing

The FNAFU is a special interministry loan-granting fund responsible for land use policy and basic urban infrastructure. It grants loans to local authorities for acquiring land and equipping it with roads and utilities. Loans are made directly to the developing authority, usually a *société d'économie-mixte,* but the commune creating the zone must guarantee the loans. The loans are for two years at 2.5% with a possibility of two renewals totalling six years. These loans are repaid by the developing authority as soon as the land of a Z.U.P. has been acquired, equipped, and its lots sold to builders. FNAFU acts as a powerful catalyst for construction of new urban centres by granting loans for land acquisition and most of the infrastructure.

A second source of general construction money is direct subsidy of particular services by appropriate national ministries. The proportion of these subsidies to the total cost of the particular public service depends on the service and value the national government places on having it included in the Z.U.P. For example, subsidies cover 65% of the cost of schools.

A third major source of loan money is the powerful *Caisse des Dépôts et Consignations,* a specialized nationally owned and managed credit institution which loans money for government-supported operations such as regional development and construction of infrastructure or public services.[17] A commune can borrow from the *Caisse* to finance the local share of public service costs, with loans at 3.25% interest for twenty to thirty years, repaid out of increased local revenues stimulated by population increases from Z.U.P. construction.

Financing land acquisition and infrastructure is necessary so that land can be sold to housing promoters and builders of public facilities. Although

Opposite Aerial view to the south-west in October 1969 shows how Hérouville-St. Clair is a satellite to Caen. Only the by-pass beltway separates them.
(Photos: R. J. Paté)

Top right A playground in a courtyard of public housing in the Belles Portes neighbourhood.

Middle right A central heating plant, designed by Georges Johannet of UAU, provides hot water for all public and multi-family buildings.

Middle right Georges Johannet also designed the 6,000 cubic metre pumping station and reservoir for Hérouville's drinking water.

Right More than 90% of Hérouville's housing construction receives State loans and thus has strict cost limits. Nevertheless its architects have developed inexpensive means of treating the exteriors of large buildings to create diversity.
(Photos R. J. Paté)

23

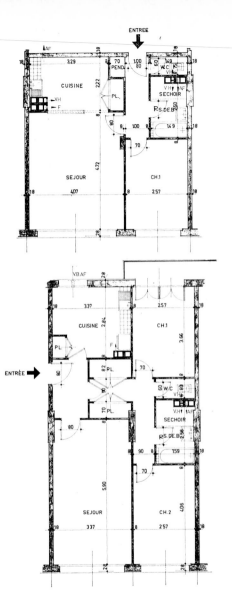

Above Typical apartment floor plans for tall blocks.

Left The 1,500 cubic metre steel water tower designed by Georges Johannet. It is 48 metres high and serves as a symbol for the town.
(Photo: R. J. Paté)

most of these costs should be borne by users of the land in order to develop the land to the point where builders will buy lots, someone must pay for the costs of land acquisition and infrastructure. On the average 75% of initial costs are borne by land users – 25% come from public construction corporations and 50% come from housing. The remaining 25% is evenly divided between direct subsidy from the state and the share assigned to the commune.

French Housing Policy

Because of war damage, age, and increased population, at least twelve million new dwelling units are needed in France in the next twenty years. This is the basic French national housing policy goal.[18] While many of these units are being built in Z.U.P. sectors, there are still three kinds of housing in France: social, private, and co-operative. Social housing, known as 'H.L.M.' or *habitation à loyer modéré* (moderate rental housing),[19] is either publicly or semi-publicly organized and seeks no profits. Private housing, built for profits, may be for rent or for sale as private property, joint property (*la copropriété*), or condominium. Co-operatives, organized to eliminate the profit motive, generally build housing that is superior to most social housing. The national government implements its housing policy by making available several means of financial support (Table 2).

Table 2
Sources of Housing Construction Funds in France

	Principal sector served		
Source	Social	Private	Co-operative
Caisse des Prêts aux Organismes HLM	X		
Crédit Foncier		X	X
Employers' 1% assessment	X	X	X
Private banks, and so on		X	X

There are four main sources of housing construction funds in France. The first is the *Caisse des Prêts aux Organismes H.L.M.*, a public credit institution owned, funded, and operated by the *Caisses des Dépôts et Consignations*. It grants up to 95% of the cost of social housing in forty-year loans at 2.6% interest. The chief source for private housing loans is the *Crédit Foncier*, a semi-public bank that lends funds of the *Caisse des*

Dépôts et Consignations for the national government. Their terms are roughly 4.25 to 5% interest for from ten to thirty years. These loans may cover only 30 to 50% of construction costs. A third source of funds is the *cotisation patronale*,[20] a device requiring all employers of more than ten employees to annually invest in housing a sum equal to 1% of the salaries they have paid during the preceding fiscal year. A final source of construction money is private banks which make loans at an expensive interest rate (7.5 to 10%) for twelve to fifteen years.

Implementation: The Z.U.P. Technique at Hérouville

With a basic understanding of the Z.U.P. technique, we can look at its first major trial at Hérouville.[21] In early 1960, the regional prefect decided to create a 'parallel town'[22] or satellite city next to Caen. On 25th March 1960, the Municipal Council of the Hérouville commune, which at the time had a population of 1,300, accepted the prefect's suggestion. On 19th October 1960 the decree delimiting the Z.U.P. at Hérouville was published. A national competition for the master plan was announced in December 1960, and the winners, the *Union des Architectes-Urbanistes* (UAU) of Paris, were chosen in February 1962. The master plan, as defined by the *Société d'Equipment de la Basse-Normandie* (SEBN), a *société d'économie-mixte* which is the development corporation for the Hérouville Z.U.P., and as designed by the UAU, calls for the creation of a completely equipped town for 35,000 people in 8,400 dwelling units on 740 acres of former fields. There will be eighteen schools for a student population of 11,610, as well as a small commercial centre, a local community centre, and a youth house in each of the five residential neighbourhoods. Churches, dispensary, post office, administrative centre, recreation facilities, dormitories for the nearby university, cinema, regional department store, hotel, cafés, banks, and all kinds of shops and offices are planned in addition to dwellings. Construction began in November 1963; one year later the first families moved in. The final financing plan of the Hérouville Z.U.P. was approved by Committee 2b of the FDES in June 1964. The first school opened in 1965, and by April 1970 the population of the commune had reached 20,000. The Z.U.P. is expected to be completed in 1973. The entire development process has proceeded in an orderly manner with a fair amount of speed. From a bare field and a prefect's idea to a working urban environment for 20,000 people in only ten years is an accomplishment that testifies to the efficiency of the Z.U.P. technique.

Financing the Hérouville Z.U.P.

The total cost of the Hérouville satellite city was an estimated $159 million in 1967. Roughly $90 million, or 56% of the total cost, is contributed by the state as a direct subsidy, a low-cost loan to the commune of Hérouville, or a housing loan. The $13 million infrastructure cost is included in the price of construction lots purchased by public and private builders. However, the state directly contributes 25% of the infrastructure cost through subsidy, loans, and construction of public facilities. The $14 million cost of the publicly financed educational, social, administrative, and cultural facilities will be entirely borne by the state, either as a subsidy or a loan to the commune of Hérouville. The total cost of the 8,400 units of housing is $99 million, resulting in a very low unit cost of $11,800. The state provides about 69%, $68 million, of the housing cost. A miscellaneous category in Z.U.P. cost includes all that is not infrastructure, superstructure, or housing, such as the commercial centres. There is some state participation in this category, but there is none in the privately financed industrial zone. (See Table 3.) The sources of the $90 million national assistance are as follows: (1) direct national subsidies – $14 million; (2) low-cost loans to the commune of Hérouville from the *Caisse des Dépôts et Consignations* – $6.5 million; and (3) loans for housing from the same *Caisse* via the *Crédit Foncier* and the *Caisse des Prêts aux Organismes H.L.M.*–$68 million.

Table 3
National Financial Assistance and the Cost of the Z.U.P. at Hérouville

Category	Total cost (millions of $)	Total assistance (millions of $)	State assistance (%)
Infrastructure	13.0	6.5	50
Public facilities	14.0	14.0	100
Miscellaneous	14.0	2.0	14
Industrial zone	19.0		0
Housing	99.0	68.0	69
Totals	159.0	90.0	56

A Critique of the Z.U.P. Technique

The Z.U.P. technique of urban development has advantages and disadvantages on both national and local levels. Nationally, it permits establishment of

Top A privately owned apartment block. Demand is so great that most buildings are rented before completion. Across the river is a steel works, a major source of regional employment.

Middle A public housing block. (Photos: R. J. Paté)

Bottom Condominiums are a popular way of securing housing. Apartments built for sale in these buildings are similar to those for rental in the privately owned and public blocks, and range from a studio-type to four bedrooms. (Photo: Studio Chauvois)

priorities for government financing of urban infrastructure and choice of sites for new developments throughout France, in short, a *national industrial development and urbanization plan.* This system of priorities is effective in reducing dispersion of new buildings and high cost of public utilities resulting from such dispersion.

One disadvantage at the national level is the problem of allocation of national investments. A fixed amount of national resources, subsidies, and loans is available for distribution to all urban development projects. Since the strikes in May and June 1968 and the austerity measures after the *franc* crises in November 1968 and August 1969, there are fewer resources available for Z.U.P.s, and progress will be delayed.

The state has three alternative policies it can follow: it may (1) concentrate its capital investments in a few Z.U.P. developments to equip them quickly and completely; (2) distribute its capital investments widely and sparsely in order to reach a larger population; or (3) take a middle-ground stance. Politically this is a moot question, and the obvious, predictable choice is the second alternative. However, in a centralized national administration somewhat removed from provincial pressures, economic planners may prevail over politicians. Such was the case at Hérouville. The Z.U.P. at Hérouville was the first major one in France and the first to benefit from a national competition for its master plan. Normandy has the highest emigration in France and greatly needed the economic boost of a well-equipped Z.U.P. A *mystique* about Hérouville developed in Paris, and large subsidies and loans were granted. Other Z.U.P. developments, being financed at the same time, suffered as the state was reluctant to grant more large subsidies because it had overextended itself at Hérouville. By promoting the Z.U.P. technique the state commits itself to financing much new urban development and strains its resources.

Another disadvantage at the national level is an expected lack of strict interministry co-operation and commitment on subsidies. Although Committee 2b of the FDES must approve the financing plan, individual ministries may default on their agreements to subsidize projects. At Hérouville subsidies were actually granted an average of eighteen months later than they had been promised; on some projects the amount of the subsidy was reduced. The development corporation, the SEBN, could do nothing about these delays or changes except wait and hope for the best. As a result, the social centres, youth centres, some schools, and the Z.U.P. centre were not ready for the first residents.

There are many advantages for local authorities in the Z.U.P. technique. Land acquisition is merely an administrative process. The development corporation is given sufficient powers and access to funds to do its work efficiently. The financial plan is coherently organized, and the master plan receives the aesthetic consideration of the *Conseil Supérieur d'Urbanisme et d'Architecture.* Every effort is made to create an environment where the inhabitants will be adequately housed and serviced and happy.

There are, however, disadvantages at the local level. A small commune with a Z.U.P. is dependent on the state. Its debt is monumental due to its extensive contribution to infrastructure and public facility costs. In the future it can expect increased operating costs — balanced, however, by increased tax receipts. It has no real flexibility and cannot break away from national control because of financial limitations. In order to receive a national subsidy to cover municipal budget deficits, the commune must make economies in its local operations, according to dictates of the state. However, despite these disadvantages, the Z.U.P. technique does work. A Z.U.P. is a strange combination of: (1) public initiative that creates the zone; (2) public capital that finances infrastructure, public facilities, and housing loans; (3) private capital that seeks profits; and (4) various organizations that construct the new urban centre. Unquestionably it is an example of a modern mixed economy.

Comparison with American Experience

American planners are sufficiently aware of Swedish and British development techniques,[23] but French methods are less known. A comparison of French Z.U.P. technique with American experience at Columbia, Maryland, may reveal Z.U.P.'s utility as a means of structuring urban development.[24] In the Columbia case, one finds that: (1) there was no applicable national urbanization policy; (2) land acquisition without expropriation powers was expensive and had to be very secretive; (3) the Rouse organization was effective as a developing authority but had no help from the national government; (4) relations with local authorities of Howard County were good because of the skill of the Rouse organization; (5) Columbia was adequately financed, again with no credit due to the national government; and (6) the human environment was well-planned and is succeeding. However, Columbia is the exception rather than the rule in the USA.

The Hackensack Meadowlands Development Commission, created in January 1969 by the state of New Jersey, is another American approach to the challenge of urban development.[25] Nearly 18,000 acres of vacant meadows lie in the heart of the New York metropolitan area, north of Newark, New Jersey. Problems of low elevation, tidal flooding, conflicting ownership claims, political fragmentation, pollution, and garbage have impeded development for many years. The Hackensack Meadowlands Development Commission has the strong planning, title-settling, tax-sharing, and financial powers necessary to solve these problems and coherently develop the valuable Meadowlands. This commission's development technique is much like the Z.U.P. methods. It, too, is a combination of public initiative, public capital and bonds, and private capital. However, this commission is a unique approach to a unique problem. It is too early to see how well it will work. Nevertheless, its general principles: (1) tax-sharing and regional planning to supersede political fragmentation; (2) independent financial capability; and (3) strong land-use and development controls, are applicable in other situations as the Z.U.P. technique is applicable throughout France.

An encouraging note on the part of the federal government is Title IV, 'Land Development and New Communities', of the Demonstration Cities and Metropolitan Development Act of 1966, which expands the Federal Housing Administration (FHA) mortgage insurance programme for privately financed land development by (1) authorizing the Secretary of the Department of Housing and Urban Development (HUD) to insure mortgages to finance 'new communities', and (2) increasing the maximum amount of mortgages permitted. There is, however, a low ceiling of $50 million on any single guarantee per development. Total guarantees may not exceed $250 million

Below A view looking south (August 1969) shows the Grand Delle neighbourhood in the foreground, university dormitories in the town centre, and the Grand Parc neighbourhood above.
(Photo: R. J. Paté)

each year.

As of early 1970, only one planned new community, Jonathan, near Minneapolis-St Paul in Minnesota, had received such a HUD mortgage guarantee.[26] The Z.U.P. technique is far superior to the minimal American efforts to encourage new town development.

Given the differences between US and French economic and social settings, is the Z.U.P. technique a feasible prototype for structuring urban development in America? The French setting is a modern welfare economy with strong capitalistic and socialistic tendencies.[27] The American setting has produced limited socially oriented legislation in spite of the residual belief in the conventional wisdom of American laissez-faire capitalism. We do have considerable experience with a mixed economy. Yet the Z.U.P. technique, depending as it does on extensive national financial commitments through direct subsidies for public services and massive loans from national credit institutions, is *not* directly applicable in the American setting until several changes are made. Since 1937, it has been generally conceded that the federal government is primarily responsible for promoting the general welfare.[28] If the federal government finally takes vigorous action in meeting that responsibility, by providing direct subsidies for educational, social, community, administrative, cultural, health, youth, and recreational facilities and by a strong financial commitment to a national housing policy, then American success with the Z.U.P. technique is possible. The Z.U.P. technique could be best used for concentrating development in new urban centres such as Columbia, Maryland, as opposed to allowing unguided growth to occur around metropolitan areas. For example, a modification of the Z.U.P. technique could be used to implement construction of the hundred new communities proposed for the United States by the year 2000 by the National Committee on Urban Growth Policy.[29]

Conclusion

In short, the Z.U.P. technique is a well-organized administrative and financial formula for structuring urban development. National priorities and urban investments are organized; land acquisition is facilitated; strong development corporations are created; and complete financing is arranged on generous terms at the national level. Unless politically-motivated funding delays impede the progress of a Z.U.P., development can proceed quickly while guaranteeing that new housing projects will be served by the public facilities necessary to permit growth of a complete city.

Notes

1 In 1947, Jean-Francois Gravier, a young geographer working for the Ministry of Reconstruction, published *Paris et le désert francais* (Paris: Flammarion, 1947, 1958), the book that conclusively demonstrated the all pervasive nature of this tradition of centralization in Paris of education, transportation, banking, government, culture, business, industry, and mass media. Gravier demanded a vigorous policy of decentralization to reorient French life and give more effective power to the provincial centres.
See also, Peter Hall, *The World Cities* (New York: McGraw-Hill, 1966), pp. 59–80.

2 Hall describes the previous (1960) plan that called for four great suburban development nodes, pp. 82–92.

3 For a detailed explanation, see, France, Délégation Générale au District de la Région de Paris, *Schéma Directeur d'Aménagement et d'Urbanisme de la Région de Paris* (Paris: 1965).

4 SS *Urbanisme,* No. 89 (1965), a special issue devoted to the *métropoles d'équilibre.*

5 See *Urbanisme,* No. 96–97 (1966), a special issue devoted to the Paris Basin.

6 For a complete discussion of French national and regional planning, see Niles M. Hansen, *French Regional Planning* (Bloomington: Indiana University Press, 1968) and Niles M. Hansen, 'French National Planning Experience', *Journal of the American Institute of Planners,* XXXV (November 1969), 362–8.

7 Another technique, Z.A.D. (*zone d'aménagement défféré*) or Zone for Delayed Development, reserves land for later purchase at a price corresponding to the value of the land one year before the Zone was created see, France, Decree No. 62–848, *Journal Officiel,* 27th July 1962.

8 Gerard Bélorgey, *Le Gouvernement et l'Administration de la France* (Paris: A. Colin, 1967), p. 356.

9 France, Decree No. 58–1464, *Journal Official,* 4th January 1959.

10 France, Law No. 62–842, *Journal Officiel,* 27th July 1962, and Decree No. 58–1464 (See note 9), are the base legislation on the Z.U.P. technique.

11 Since 1959 France has been divided into twenty areas for regional action. For a discussion of prefects and regions, see Lawrence D. Mann and George Pillorge, 'French Regional Planning', *Journal of the American Institute of Planners,* XXX, No. 2 (May 1964), 56.

12 A French publication that combines the functions of the *Federal Register* and the *Congressional Record.*

13 See, J. E. Godchot, *Les Société d'Economie-Mixte et l'Aménagement du Territoire* (Paris: Editions Berger-Levrault, 1958).

14 For a brief survey of the concept of a *société d' economie-mixte,* see, John and Anne-Marie Hackett, *Economic Planning in France,* (Cambridge, Mass.: Harvard University Press, 1963), pp. 253–4.

15 For a complete discussion of the FDES, see, Hackett, *Economic Planning in France,* pp. 66–7.

16 France, *Code de l'urbanisme et de l'habitation,* Article 80.

17 Hackett, *Economic Planning in France,* pp. 83–4.

18 For a concise, complete discussion of French housing policy, see, Bélorgey, *Le Gouvernement et l'Administration de la France,* pp. 346–9. For a quick description of the present housing situation in France, see, Henry W. Ehrmann, *Politics in France* (Boston: Little Brown and Co., 1968), p. 41.

19 The complete handbook on HLM housing is E. Crivelli and J. Bouret, *Les H.L.M.* (Paris: Editions de l'Actualité Juridique, 1965).

20 France, Decree No. 53–701, *Journal Officiel,* 9th August 1953.

21 Data in this section are based on personal research done at Hérouville in the fall of 1967.

22 *L'Architecture d'Aujourd'hui,* No. 101 (April 1962), is a special issue on new towns and urban centres in which the idea of parallel cities is elaborated.

23 See, United Nations, Department of Economic and Social Affairs, *Planning of Metropolitan Areas and New Towns* (New York: UN, 1967); Kell Astrom, *City Planning in Sweden* (Stockholm: The Swedish Institute, 1967); H. Wentworth Eldredge, 'Lessons Learned from the British New Towns Programme', in H. Wentworth Eldredge (ed.), *Taming Megalopolis* (New York: Doubleday and Co., 1967), pp. 823–8; British Information Services *The New Towns of Britain* (London: BIS, 1964).

24 See, Mortin Hoppenfeld, 'A Sketch of the Planning-Building Process for Columbia, Maryland', *Journal of the American Institute of Planners,* XXXIII, No. 4 (November 1967), 389–409.

25 For further information, see, 'The Hackensack Meadowlands–1968', *Jersey Plans,* XVII, No. 2 (Summer 1968), 5–23.

26 *The New York Times,* 14th February 1970.

27 For a further discussion of the French economic and social setting, see, Ehrmann, *Politics in France,* pp. 31–42.

28 See the discussion of the 'Implications of the New Federal System', in Charles Abrams, *The City Is the Frontier* (New York: Harper and Row, 1967), pp. 211–53.

29 Donald Canty, ed. for the National Committee on Urban Growth Policy, *The New City* (New York: Praeger, 1969).

RUNCORN

JANE DREW

Residential.

Proposed Industry.

Industrial Area with Special Control.

Existing Industry.

Town Centre and Local Centres.
Secondary Schools.

Expressway.

Rapid Transit Route.

Diagrammatic Master Plan.

Runcorn is being developed as a New Town of 90,000 to 100,000 to provide new housing and employment for the North Merseyside area. It is an overspill town for Liverpool and its undulating site of 7,250 acres ($3\frac{1}{2} \times 4$ miles) is only fourteen miles from the centre of the city. Virtually an island site, bounded by water and roads, it is well related to national and regional communications, in particular the M.6 Motorway, the electrified Liverpool/London railway line, Liverpool airport and the Manchester Ship Canal. Its parameters are known, its further expansion limited.

Its solutions are unique in that a real attempt has been made to create separate reserved routes for public rapid transport and private transport within the town, and new limits have been set for a pedestrian network; but it is the clear thinking in planning that makes Runcorn important, the design of truly separated means of communication to suit differing patterns of movement.

The town cannot be considered as self-contained, few towns are; and the proximity of Liverpool and other centres of employment has meant that considerable 'flow' has been designed for.

Nevertheless the structure of the town is mainly concentric, and a figure-of-eight reserved rapid transit route passes through the local community centres

linking them with the main town centre and the major industrial centres. Thus, since shops, schools, etc., are linked to the sub-centres and main centre, it is really convenient for Runcorn people to use this system for their diurnal round, though having cars for their special journeys where they travel on roads which lie outside this network. In fact the motorist who uses his car for the daily round is wasting his time and petrol.

In order that the pedestrian does not have too far to walk to his rapid transport, very thorough walking studies have been made. Taking age, slope, weight

and convenience into account, studies of all the different kinds of walking — children with parents, shopping, walking to work etc. — have been made.

These studies found that five minutes' walk was the maximum people will do happily in the North of England. Had the study been done in New York the period might have been even shorter.

These walk-routes within the residential area are, so far as possible, weather protected and separated from cycle tracks. They cater for the concentrated movements of population within the community; being either integrated with the housing, or provided

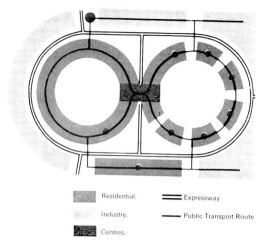

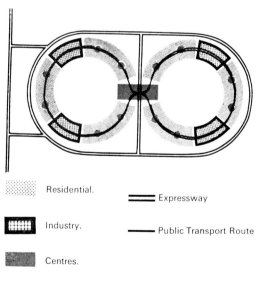

Residential.

Industry.

Centres.

Expressway

Public Transport Route

Above top Diagram of town structure

Above Theoretical town diagram

Right Sketch plan of an 8000 community adjoining the town centre showing an interpretation of the diagrammatic proposals.

29

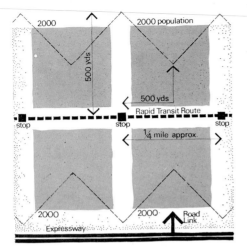

Above Subdivision of 8000 population community into 2000 population neighbourhoods. The catchment areas within 500 yards walking distance of the principal and intermediate stops on the rapid transit system are indicated by dotted lines.

Below Diagrammatic community structure

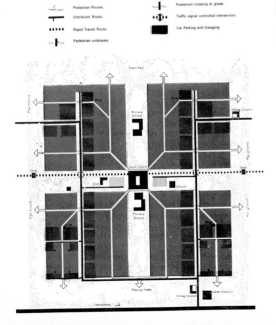

as separate covered ways, and of course they lead to the bus stops and local covered centres. The same convenience is possible at the factories, schools and work centres.

The accent on transport facilities in Runcorn is new in its completeness. It has meant that the general order of priorities has been altered. Housing in Runcorn provides for 1.5 cars, and in the future possibly two cars per family, but inevitably not all attached to dwellings. If each dwelling had an attached garage, this would have imposed access roads and a rigidity of layout in residential areas which is not conducive to the reasonably free movement of pedestrians and would make difficult the social grouping of housing around communal greens, courtyards and squares. The philosophy maintains that all dwellings, whether flat, maisonette or house, require both a private and communal space available nearby, with play areas not so near as to make a disturbance: 400 yards has been used as the farthest possible distance.

I have started by writing about the traffic plan because this is a fresh approach. I have little criticism

Below Astmoor flatted factory development showing pedestrian walkways and landscaping

of the planning or of the social thinking behind it. There are other 'with it' facets. There are stations measuring air pollution and steps are taken to counteract it; definite smoke control areas; on the creative side plentiful open parks; and housing at relatively low average density of fifty-three persons per acre in the whole new town, though the actual density is higher nearer the edges of the greens. Landscaping has been considered throughout, both the formal landscape in parks and the town centre and the more rustic landscaping of the surrounding areas.

Immigrants and emigrants have been taken into account in an attempt to create varied but still balanced communities and second generation marriages have been foreseen.

To give all the figures and arrangements in an article would be boring but the ideas contained in the Runcorn plan are fairly new to town planning. We in England have so concentrated on social and economic factors of the obvious kind that we have forgotten to consider some of the most disruptive forces of our society, such as colour prejudice and teenage needs; and what measures must be taken to create a stable community.

In Runcorn residential communities of 8,000 persons

have been chosen as a typical social grouping, with primary schools placed so as to be convenient for a reverse flow pedestrian movement, and secondary schools to offer social facilities centrally located.

The residential areas have also been carefully designed to accommodate different types of households; expanding, stationary and contracting. Some under-occupation in the beginning has been accepted, creating stability in a new community, and catering for the older persons who should have priority in their location. The balance between 'thing orientation' and 'people orientation' has been kept. Higher buildings should form an edge for parks to give them a form but should not be so high as to destroy privacy. This is sensible because more people get a good prospect, and enjoy the amenity of open space and really fresh air.

Beyond all this is, of course, the question of employment and the need for industry to thrive. The thinking about factories in Runcorn is again quite new so far as I know, and totally successful. Chemical and electrical engineering are the biggest industries but are not labour-intensive relative to their size; so component manufacture in flatted and new growth industries is being encouraged. Accommodation for these is rigorously standardized, offering growth possibilities either by extension or re-option.

The fact that one unit can be taken at the outset, but a two- or three-unit factory obtained should the business flourish, is a good system and takes a worry off industrialists' shoulders. So far as I know no other industrial estate has offered so complete a service with such rigorous conditions of acceptance, and industry, so far from feeling restricted, has welcomed the discipline and recognized the benefits.

The rapid transit system passes through the centre of the Astmoor Industrial Estate; thus pedestrians using the rapid transit system compete with motorists, a convenience which means an economy in the land required for car parking, although multi-storey car parks for visitors and executive staff are provided near the factory entrances, as are access ways for commercial vehicles. These secondary service roads cross the rapid transit road at traffic-signal controlled points which give priority to the rapid transit. Normal car parkers will not cross the rapid transit road.

In addition to the space for major industries, fifteen acres of land in or adjoining the new residential area have been reserved for light industry in compact areas associated with each community, sited at the local centres or on the link road from the expressway. Together these will provide employment for 2,385 workers. Much else can be mentioned about Runcorn: the greenways linking the communities to the public parks, thus allowing a continuity of open space and pedestrian movement from private garden to the largest public grounds; the inclusion of new type corner shops in residential areas; the distance which the main distributor traffic road, with its noise and fumes, is kept from all residential development; and the use of the waterways in and around Runcorn as sports and pleasure ways. The urban renewal problem covering the unlovely existing centre is also well handled, but *the* primary innovation at Runcorn is its logical but humane treatment of the full hierarchy of transport from shanks's pony to the container-monster.

Now let me reflect on the town as built. It is interesting that Runcorn, a town originally conceived as an overspill New Town of 100,000 people for Liverpool, has had as its architect Master Planner Arthur Ling, a socialist *avant-garde* architect whose beautiful but simple office for the town is in The Rows, Chester.

The atmosphere round Cheshire is quite other than that of Lancashire: it is a 'good' address, a simple historical fact, a social snobbism if you like, but a great draw as effective as town planning in creating an idea of moving up when moving out of Liverpool.

Chester was laid out by the Romans, but the Middle Ages produced the elevated walkways called 'The Rows', where shopping and pedestrians are separated from traffic both in plan and section. Today much of the elevational treatment is fake, but the philosophy is there.

Runcorn has some of this element: the separate roads for fast transport and high level shopping, and even the patio planning of Chester. But the scale and method are different — the early residential developments are 'villagy': a black and white colour scheme is generally adopted and the grouping ranges from tiny groups of pitched forked houses at the 'Brow development', round winding narrow country lane quality roads and lay-bys for two or three cars which serve also as play places in beautifully landscaped intimate spaces: to larger scale courtyard plans such as Halton Brook development with more or less typical Radburn plans.

The newer developments are moving forward to complete very large scale industrialized building. Castlefields and now the 'James Stirling area' are huge

31

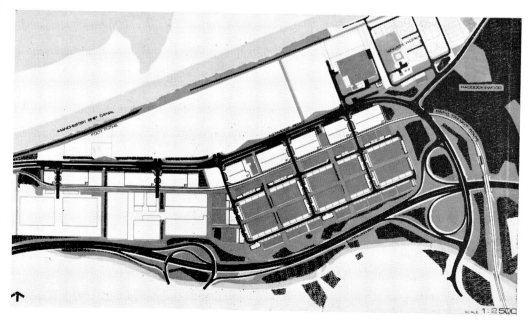

Right Astmoor Industrial Estate

regimented long blocks, grouped again in squares and terraces with very ingenious sections. In Castlefields the access street serves flats on all five levels. In the James Stirling development two maisonettes with their own terraces are topped by flats with their own terrace — levels of site are exploited in both and parking is below. Squares of green are public and used for communal services and low rise housing or gardens in both.

What is happening? The Tower Block is rejected. Private small terraces or gardens are in; standardization is in on a scale rarely seen before. All the general social facilities are well placed: schools; clinics; pubs; community centres; local shops etc.; and housing varies in size to suit families.

Is all now perfect? It is certainly much better. I think of the good and the bad parts of New York, Philadelphia and London. I visit Chester – and I suddenly realize that to become yet better there must be more poetry and more variety, possibly through owner participation or renter participation. The joy of our old towns is, from medieval times, the non-conformism of certain buildings; and from Georgian times it is in the different details in a standard square which give interest: the door knockers, fanlights, front doors which personalize. The phrase 'Filing cabinets for the working classes' cannot be levelled at the low rise development of Runcorn; but as the family walk down the long, long corridor-covered streets to their 'home' in Castlefields, to find their own door, they will feel unlike a suburban dweller whose very front garden identifies his nest and himself.

I think the scale of the larger mechanized housing of Runcorn is reaching the outer edge of tolerability. There is every sign that the engineer mentality is winning, and for me the first proof that the new architect must be more than a good town planner and a good industrial designer is that he must know where and when it is important to do something different with the machine.

In Castlefields — the huge industrialized housing development at Runcorn — all the blocks are straight, and a nasty junction occurs between two angled straight blocks. This junction highlights a problem — that repetition of parts cannot make a whole. In nature we know this to be true — leaves may seem the same wherever they are on the tree but they are not so arranged. The top leaves of any branch are very different in position, often in form.

Above Housing at Brow estate

Left Housing at Castlefields estate

32

Runcorn is beginning to show the defects of both arithmetic architecture and of the 'let's turn the digit round and pretend it's different' approach.

It has faced but has not solved the problems of standardization and mechanization in its building and the conceptual plan is far superior to the implementation — the whole leaves the mark of different philosophies unresolved. The Town consists of parts which do not add up to more than the sum of the parts and one senses that the master planner and the architects were different people. The main shopping centre is certainly complete in itself and, like the commercial centre, should give a considerable city 'feel', and be a pleasant experience to be in. The flatted factories are splendid, but the engineering industry, ICI, with its very low labour intensity and its form dominated by absolute engineering needs, with no apparent concessions to human experience, seems to be a more viable statement about tomorrow; a rather awful tomorrow where the factory is a place where few are employed, no more than seven persons per acre; a place where wages are made but not life lived. This problem of work for people, work and living which gives them an identity, is not solved at Runcorn — convenience is there, and the hard nut of traffic problems appears to have been solved. Social convenience is there, but the housing is getting more and more mass-factory-built. There is a pathetic attempt by private developers to build. There was an idea that 50 % of the town should be privately developed but it is clear that such developers have a very hard job against subsidized housing, and that individuality is almost priced out. There are no signs of private housing thriving at Runcorn; golf addicts (there are private sites near the course) and possessive persons may buy them, but there is no rush at present.

Runcorn lacks greatness in its interpretation. It has avoided the worst faults of other towns. High blocks of flats for families and piecemeal development — only splendid landscaping and trees will humanize it. I sigh for the time when design can go beyond its present parameters and be more conceptual and less pragmatic.

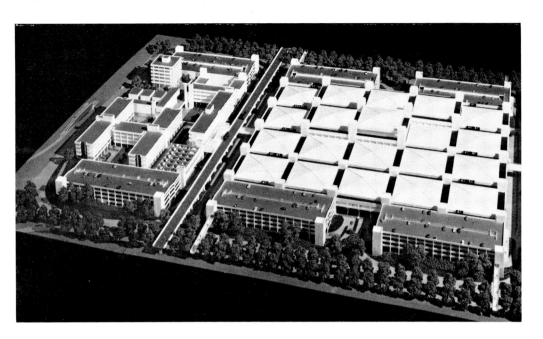

Above Town centre showing commercial offices and shopping development

Right Town centre showing connection between rapid transit routes and shopping; and shopping and walkway to pedestrian area

THE COLUMBIA PROCESS:
THE POTENTIAL FOR NEW TOWNS

MORTON HOPPENFELD

Ours is the first generation of men which might believe it practical to build a nation whose benefits can be available to all of its citizens.

Should we consciously decide to pursue this dream, the task will prove to be consuming and difficult, embracing all aspects of life. To build better cities is to work at the heart of civilization. But we cannot even hope for success if we give priority to other competing tasks; it is diversionary to wage war; it is diversionary now to explore space – unless as a last gasp for survival, to find an alternative habitable place.

We cannot assume that it is possible for a nation to continue to wage war and, simultaneously, make habitable the world we live in. These are contradictory goals. To make peace, we must work at it. The best possible alternative to making death is in the conscious, rational building of a humane environment for life to flourish.

At present there simply are not enough qualified and dedicated people working at building such a civilization, such cities. We need to turn people on to the idea. We need a new way of thinking about city building.

For the last seven years, together with many dedicated people, I have been working at the process of building a new city in the United States. This city in process is called Columbia.

I see the inevitable emergence of a new kind of industry, analogous in scale and organization to our current array of major industries in which all the parts are known to each other and operate interdependently. Within each industry will be major corporate components. Each of these will be large enough to include, under one aegis, the talents knowledge and skills necessary to produce the product, market it, manage its use over time as appropriate, receive feedback from the user world and continually improve overall processes of design and production.

Undertaking to build the city of Columbia has led The Rouse Company into becoming what I consider to be an emerging prototype for a new American city building industry. In that light, the process by which we are learning to build Columbia is significant. It is critical that the planning, design, and other professions reassess and revise their traditionally separate advisory status, and join wholeheartedly in the city building process with the worlds of finance, construction, and social organization. Using the new town of Columbia as an example, I will attempt to describe some of the implications of this new way of working, where the concept of professionalism is not jeopardized by personal commitment and involvement in the private sector of development. It is a description of a multi-disciplinary approach to planning and building, viewed as parts of the same process rather than separate activities, and it is aimed more at illustrating the evolution of a process than at describing the plans and now emerging fact of Columbia.

The very concept of planning per se has changed to become merged with that of building and the evolution of a community. The Columbia planning-development team spans every field of ability concerned with urban development interests. It included at the outset, on a continuing basis, urban planners and designers, economists, mortgage bankers, real estate developers, architects, landscape architects, marketing and scheduling professionals, as well as experts on nursery schools and day care centres, housing, recreation, health, and the rôle of the church.

This team forms and reforms into groups working simultaneously to organize and relate myriads of data and ideas, and establish criteria necessary to attain the community's physical and social goals. Within realistically set economic limits, a delicate balance must constantly be struck between efficient engineering practice, evoking positive sensual response, and maximum market acceptance. Planning for and managing the building of Columbia is being done 'in house' by this kind of integral team where a vital part of the planning-building process is the daily feedback and continuity, from concept to the concrete realities of construction, occupancy and community response.

This comprehensive approach to the complexities of community building is indicative of the demands that will be put on all professionals in the latter part of this century if we are going to build and rebuild enough communities to provide for the growth of this nation.

Motivating values for Columbia

The traditionally detached rôle of the professional as consultant advisor tends to discount the need for personal value statements and commitment. Some of our past failures reflect the fact that skills and technique alone are not sufficient to sustain the human qualities of the city as it grows through the rigours of the building process. The success – the real success – of any project of this scope depends on having a point of view, a sense of values, and a way of thinking that is reflected in thousands and thousands of decisions, large and small, that are made throughout the development process and well into the establishment of management policies. It does not depend on a rigid plan. It does not depend on a set of written policies. It depends on people who share, regardless of their individual capacities and interests, a certain general common intent. That intent, although sometimes stated in broad terms, mostly grows, evolves, unfolds, and develops as the development process itself continues. Certain shared, implicit assumptions underlie the decision-making process, and to the extent that they are genuinely shared, the decision-making process is that much simpler and that much more coherent. The following statement by James W. Rouse, the founder of Columbia, before a committee of Congress in support of the New Communities Section, Title II of the Housing Bill for 1966, expresses a real personal commitment on the part of the principal decision-maker in the effort to build a better city; his values are shared by the entire Columbia staff.

'Our cities grow by accident, by the whim of the private developer and public. . . . By this irrational process, non-communities are born – formless places, without order, beauty or reason, with no visible respect for people or the land. . . . The vast, formless spread of housing, pierced by the unrelated spotting of schools, churches, stores, creates areas so huge and irrational that they are out of scale with people – beyond their grasp and comprehension – too big for people to feel a part of, responsible for, important in . . . .

'I believe that the ultimate test of civilization is whether or not it contributes to the growth and improvement of mankind. Does it uplift, inspire, stimulate, and develop the best in man ? There really can be no other right purpose of community except to provide an environment and an opportunity to develop better people. The most successful community would be that which contributed the most by its physical form, its institutions, and its operation to the growth of people.'

Three fundamental goals for Columbia were set: first, to create a social and physical environment which would work for people, nourishing human growth; second, to preserve and enhance the qualities of the land as we build; and third, as a venture of private capital, to make a profit in the development and sale of land. Certainly, as the bits and pieces of today's enormous urban expansion are put together, however accidentally, profits accrue to many. Should not the organization of these building forces into a co-ordinated city-building effort turn an even greater profit by increasing value and minimizing waste and duplication? The fundamental purpose of business should be service to its community. Profit would accrue to those providing the best services. Should not the creation of an obviously better environment, a better choice for the consumer, be consistent with the profit motive? Therefore, are not the two goals essentially supportive?

A good urban environment is not one only with high levels of sensual satisfaction and functional efficiencies, it is also essentially a place of optimum choices where many of the needs and amenities of contemporary life are freely accessible. On this premise and some modest analysis the minimum size for this city was determined to be approximately 100,000 people. This population would adequately support a necessary and varied job base, as well as the usual array of social systems with regard to health, education, recreation, and consumption of goods. Thus our goal is a truly balanced community; a job opportunity for every residence; a dwelling for every job situation: houses and apartments in a wide variety of size and cost, and a chance to live, work, shop and play in the same place, i.e. a new living style, aimed at the current market – one out of ten from the one million people who in the next fifteen years will seek to live in the Washington-Baltimore corridor. It is essential to note here that Columbia was never conceived to be self-sufficient. It is in every way fundamentally integrated into the socio-economic life of its political base in Howard County and the broader metropolis of Washington, D.C. and Baltimore. It is expected to become a third or major nucleus midway between the two major cities. This strategic location in one of the nation's fastest growing urban corridors makes Columbia an extremely attractive alternative for work or living. The specifics of Columbia's arithmetic, its densities

and form are a product of this market, this place, and this time. (See Appendix 1.) Sensitivity to the market as discipline is not only required for economic success, but, however incomplete, is a way of assessing immediate human response. With a given amount of money and freedom of access, what will people choose from among a given set of alternatives as represented in the entire Washington-Baltimore area? Columbia was designed to be attractive to that majority segment of the population which is economically viable and in the market now.

As a venture of private capital, Columbia will be unable to reach and affect some of the gut social problems of American urbanization. These are essentially problems of poverty and racism involving major national decisions concerning the distribution of wealth and the provision of jobs and adequate environment for currently 'uneconomic' families. Columbia is in the jurisdiction of Howard County, where today there is no adequate programme for subsidizing housing for families, or for the provision of full employment or income supplements. The passage of time will inevitably see the full range of publicly supported institutions and facilities found in most cities, blended into the life of Columbia. The evolution of this city whose developers seek to balance social goals and private profit should be a valuable social experiment to observe.

Beginning the planning

Given the above conditions, the first planning decision was the location of the city. The present site between Washington and Baltimore was selected because of extraordinary accessibility, the growth rate and development pattern of the region, and the fleeting moment wherein enough unimproved land could be accumulated on the open market.

The process of planning and building this new city began in mid-1962, when the first land was bought in rural Howard County. The purchaser was Howard Research and Development, a corporation jointly owned by Connecticut General Life Insurance Company and Community Research and Development, Inc. (now The Rouse Company). With $23,500,000 of funds loaned to Howard Research and Development by Connecticut General, approximately 15,000 acres of land were purchased (average price $1,500/acre) of which 13,690 were to be included in the initial development. Once the Howard County government granted 'new town zoning' to the project in 1965,

Right Location of Columbia in the Washington-Baltimore corridor.

another $25,000,000 was raised for development costs, with significant investments by Chase Manhattan Bank and the Teachers Insurance & Annuity Association of America.

A truly comprehensive description of the planning process would include at the outset the theory and technique of development financing. Acceptable financing arrangements demand confidence in the ultimate profitability of New Towns and the concept of creating urban values in land. This requires patient money willing to wait for profits. Columbia's financing is sufficiently flexible to allow payment on principal to be deferred and for interest to be borrowed as part of the cost of development. In the very nature of this financial arrangement, there were fundamental inputs to the planning process. The land had to be bought at a reasonable cost to make the whole project economically feasible, since some of the acreage purchased would have to be carried, undeveloped, for periods up to fifteen years, while other acreage would have to be set aside for open space. The necessity of getting reasonably priced land in quantity meant getting land without sewers and water and, as the land purchase turned out, on three watersheds. The design and timing of basic utilities exercises a pervasive influence on what can be done in a physical plan for a new city built on raw land.

Another critical influence on planning, sometimes frustrating, sometimes stimulating, has been what the economists call 'the economic model', a highly complex series of projections and conjectures show-

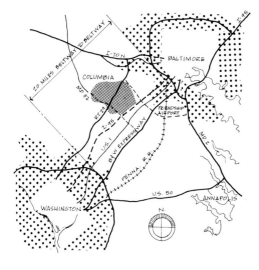

ing when and how the investors are going to get their money back and then make a substantial profit. Economic success is dependent upon the delicate balance of cash outlay and development pace.

As a project the size of Columbia proves economically viable; the big pools of private capital, now found in pension funds, insurance companies, banks and savings and loan institutions, will see the possibility of a competitive return for their investment in large scale participation in urban planning and building. Quite probably, when all is said and done, proof of economic feasibility may be Columbia's most important contribution to American urbanization.

Finally, the very fact that the land was purchased in advance of the basic planning meant that the company was paying carrying charges and taxes on $23,500,000 worth of land while planning was in progress. Suddenly the city builders had become sophisticated land managers. We were the proud owners of the largest farm holding in the county and had to make it pay rather than drag on cash flow. Time was, and continues to be, money, thus giving a sense of urgency to the whole project.

Critical planning decisions were made at an early stage. On the USGS base maps potential lake sites and forested areas were located. Using these basic maps, the existing and proposed highway plans, and the accidents of ownership patterns as guides, over 15,000 acres of beautiful farmland were acquired in more than 140 separate transactions. The process of acquiring so many separate pieces of land in a short period of

COLUMBIA HOLDINGS
FOREST AREAS
RIVERS
INTERCHANGES

Left Major physical determinants.

time required great skill in legal and real estate judgment. Each piece was individually negotiated. Some whose prices were too high were passed over. The ultimate area with which we began to plan was contiguous, but resulted in some significant hold-outs, some as large as 500 acres, others as small as four acres. Extemporaneous 'design' judgments had to be made to establish the critical nature of each piece. Ultimately these decisions became some of the 'givens' around which the plans for development had to be drawn.

One year was allocated to prepare and present an acceptable development plan and financial programme to our partners and to the county. Four months were spent in analysis prior to the first sketch plans. We immediately began to communicate our goals and ideas to the citizens and representatives of Howard County (a now routine and friendly relationship) in anticipation of needed re-zoning. During and after the completion of the preliminary general development plan, the small team which undertook the project (about ten) worked nights and weekends to gain political support. We manned an exhibit on the site and responded to every question with honesty. During this period several plan changes were privately negotiated between neighbours and the new city developers. Plans were altered based on this intimate feedback.

Getting the necessary approvals of planning, zoning, and county commissioners was essential. The cost of carrying the $25 million and ultimately $50 million dollars of land and improvement was about $10,000 a day. Howard County then had primarily a rural population of approximately forty-five thousand. Committed to a 'stop urbanization sprawl' policy, the county accepted Columbia as a desirable alternative and as a part of its own long range development plans. At the final zoning hearing there were no vocal opponents to the plan. Consistent with Maryland laws and tradition, Columbia will probably not incorporate to form a municipality.

Site analysis

An analysis of the land was made to determine all aspects critical to the physical plan. The analysis was taken in just that depth required by the level of design decision at hand: that is, general or specific. During general planning phases it was sufficient to locate tree masses by the acre and to identify land forms by 20 foot contours. Plastic overlays were constructed indicating surface features such as trees, land slopes,

drainage areas, water courses, peaks, ridges, valleys, and lake sites; existing development plans of the county, state, and sewer and water agencies; and property ownership patterns.

These overlays, fundamental tools of physical planning, were developed first from available USGS maps. During the land acquisition phase, secrecy prohibited producing more detailed mapping. The proximity of our business offices to the site allowed for continuous field surveys, and later detailed aerial maps to the scale of 1 inch = 200 feet with 5 foot contours and 1 inch = 50 feet with 1 foot contours served as the basis for 'knowing the land'. This combination of mapped data and personal familiarity began early to reduce the variables in likely design decisions. Choice locations for various activities such as schools, industry, low and high density housing, and lake sites were virtually dictated by the land and the critical economics of 'proper usage' (that is, in harmony with nature).

The same design attitude pervades today: instead of the 5 foot contour suitable for general planning, 1 foot contours are checked in the field; roads are walked before final grades are set in order to minimize cuts or fill; trees to be saved are decided upon by size and species, and a road may bend or bifurcate to save a 30 inch oak.

This careful and realistic design process allowed for reasonable confidence in the development economics and the aesthetic juxtaposition of facilities, roads, and the city's hardware. But it could not give insight into the effects of design decisions on the ultimate quality of life in Columbia. In essence, the questions had to be asked: 'What works best for people? Which arrangements of facilities and institutions will enhance or inhibit the life of the community?'

Social analysis—a break from traditional techniques

At the outset the Columbia planning team was made up of the typical set of 'experts': real estate developers planners, architects, and engineers. Each had his own set of biases about a 'good city', based essentially on his limited experience and reading. None was really objectively or fully aware of the availability of data or enlightening conjecture on the interactions of people and the institutions of the city. Unwilling to act upon our own biases, we set out to gain knowledge of facts and insights into probabilities, to find a satisfactory technique for choosing among the infinite combinations of facilities and systems which would make up the 'physical city' and germinate urban institutions and life styles. We came quickly to the conclusion that there were no easy routes, no few individuals who were the repository of wisdom on urban life patterns. In fact, we chose not to consult those who made such claims. Instead, key ideas lay in many minds in separate fields of interest and often in forms not directly applicable. The task was to bring these traditionally separate disciplines together and discover the richness of their interaction and the pertinence of their discoveries.

The idea emerged of creating a group from a cluster of individuals, each an expert in a generally defined area such as education, health, recreation, and so forth. By their own admission, these were people without firm commitments to 'a way of doing things' but fully aware of their respective fields and prepared to build upon them. Included in the groups were advisors from the fields of government, family life, recreation, sociology, economics, education, health, psychology, housing, transportation, and communication. (A complete list is contained in the appendices). Typically, this 'work group' met for two days and one night (important to sustain a thought pattern in depth).

The meeting took place twice monthly and lasted in disciplined form for about six months through the evaluation of sketch alternatives and the analysis of these by the group. Critical to the successful functioning of the group was the full-time involvement of the psychologist, Donald Michael, to lead the sessions, follow through with correspondence, review and edit tapes, and assign responsibilities for subsequent sessions. In addition to this leadership skill, he represented the one 'field of interest' which is the yeast of the mix, that is, the systems concept and the need for interrelatedness. It was his task not only to identify and articulate the conflicts among competing interests as they were revealed in these meetings but, more importantly, to clarify the benefits and enrichment to community interests which were possible.

Each function was addressed in turn, from individual and community health through libraries, active recreation, and the needs of homebound young mothers, or children, and the aged. The individuals with 'expertise' in a given area prepared to articulate 'optimum' conditions, that is, how it might be when starting anew with no financial or institutional restraints. (These would come into play soon enough in the real world.) These papers served as grist for the interdisciplinary mill, and traditional boundaries crumbled. For instance, the church would serve a need in counselling and become part of the health system. Perhaps the library should sell paperbacks, or private restaurants cater for meals to the school system. No consensus was sought during this process. It was in fact the ultimate responsibility of the principal planners and developers (also acting as members of the group) to put together the pieces of a plan and courses of action. Difficult decisions between 'optimum' goals and existing conditions continued to be made in the light shed by these sessions. While the full group no longer meets, we continue to call on individuals and to create *ad hoc* sessions for exploration of new ideas. A conscious decision was made afterwards not to codify or publish the results of this process. A summary was attempted and it woefully failed to capture the essential value of the group meetings. It is impossible to describe the personal experience of the involved planners in thinking through and living with ideas subjected to the rigours of a systems concept where all parts are interrelated and dogmas and traditional 'standards' are scrutinized. However, this experience still nourishes the decision-making process.

Some concrete results

Fundamental concepts have come out of the work group, been given life, and are now in various stages of transformation and execution, not by the developer, but by those ultimately assuming responsibility for the institutions of the city. For example, the Howard County Board of Education has adopted a new grouping of school grades, altering its previous 6-3-3 arrangement to 5-3-4- (4-4-4 was recommended by the group). The Board enacted substantial changes in curriculum. New schools are being built in Columbia with open plans to accommodate team teaching and individualized programmes. Our relation with the staff and Board of Education is one of mutual respect where good ideas become the focus of attention. The first schools built in Columbia have benefited from this process but, importantly, so have those built and operated throughout the county. This dialogue and recognition of opportunity has stimulated continuous change in the school system.

By proclaiming the significance of continuing education and setting land aside, Columbia is now the site for an exciting new community college and an experimental branch of Antioch College, which uses the community as its campus and setting for a work study programme.

The Johns Hopkins Hospital has joined with the Connecticut General Life Insurance Company to create a new system of pre-paid medical care.

The resulting Columbia Medical Plan is developing a new kind of health system, looking more to preventive and positive health conditions than the traditional diagnostic and cure emphasis of most medical practice. Today they operate a family-oriented out-patient clinic in multi-purpose space tailored to clinical needs. Twenty-five acres of centrally located land are set aside, and plans are now being made for the final phase of a major health facility.

Prime 'corner' sites were not set aside for the highest bidding church. Instead all of the major denominations have joined together into a 'co-operative ministry'. They formed a non-profit corporation to sponsor and build 300 rent-subsidized apartment units for low-income families under the 221 D3 FHA programme. These apartments are distributed in several neighbourhoods in groups of 50 and 60.

Initially the co-operative ministry used the multi-purpose spaces of the community centre and schools. A Religious Facilities Corporation was formed to build the first joint religious facility. Significant savings are resulting from this sharing of facilities and administration. More important are the released efforts to improve the conditions of community and quality of family life. These concrete results stem directly from the original plan process which brought secular and religious representatives together to think as a group about the opportunities in starting a new community.

From the neighbouring cities of Washington, D.C. and Baltimore have come schools for art, music and dance. The national Symphony of Washington, D.C. gives summer concerts in an extraordinary pavilion

Right Diagram of the town.

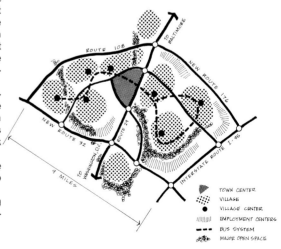

TOWN CENTER
VILLAGE
VILLAGE CENTER
EMPLOYMENT CENTERS
BUS SYSTEM
MAJOR OPEN SPACE

37

seating 5,000 under cover and 2,000 more on the grass in the midst of downtown's 40 acre park.

The obvious conclusion is that the traditional approach of making a plan and then effectuating 'the plan' is archaic. Plans need to be conceived as continually fluid and responsive to the feedback of operating agencies and development processes and opportunities. The sensitivity of the feedback process is essential both to the quality of the plan and its fulfilment.

The essence of our planning techniques is in the continued amassing and refining of a reservoir of pertinent data and knowledge to be applied in the daily need for decision-making at many levels; even the postponement of a choice becomes significant in the process. The plan is at once as general and as specific as the situation demands. It can concurrently consist of the assignment of a broad category of possible activities (land uses) to a piece of land, the detail site plan of a development area, and the specific design of building and landscape.

The first roads, lakes, and buildings have been completed and construction continues at a pace now geared to receive 2,500 families a year. In June 1970, 3,000 Columbia families celebrated a third birthday; but the most critical aspects which affect the quality of urban life, the social systems and institutions, are well advanced. Many people and institutions, independent of the developers' interests, are committed and actively engaged in the creation of life in the new city. The establishment of the work group and process described above was originally conceived to affect physical plan decisions; it served, in fact, to underscore and vivify the basic issues of community life.

Just as the work group could not have predicted such dynamic responses in the fields of religion and comprehensive health care, it is undoubtedly true that the work group did discuss certain potentials which were minimized in further planning, and yet are likely to have significance as the community matures. A great deal of thought, for instance, was given to the problem of communication within the city, with emphasis on Community Antenna Television which would make numerous channels available to every set and for local programming. We turned to a variety of large companies in the electronics field, but none has so far been able to propose a system of communication whose usefulness would warrant the cost.

Nothing is more critical to a community than a communications network which moves ideas, messages, and symbols freely and continuously. Opportunities for local media are already evident and the problems and opportunities of political participation continue to evolve.

Concern was expressed about the social, planning, and even hygienic effects of the automobile. In one of the most euphoric moments of the work group discussions, it was proposed to banish the car from Columbia altogether. More practical market-oriented minds prevailed, however, and the automobile was allowed back into the city. But we have found that applying slightly modified suburban parking standards to urban facilities leads to expanses of blacktop that tend to fragment rather than unify the urban clusters at the village and town centre level. The satisfactory handling of the motor vehicle in compact urban centres, both economically and aesthetically, is still an unsolved problem of urban design and the realities of city building.

In a society where leisure may become increasingly a way of life and where consumership may be the sole economic rôle of an increasing proportion of our population, there is a real need for facilities and programmes in the creative and performing arts. Early work group discussions moved away from the concept of a single agglomeration of bricks and mortar that might serve as a 'cultural centre', and looked instead towards the possibility that the arts, in a variety of forms, might permeate the life of the community with emphasis on spontaneous creation and performance. This has led us to put emphasis on the development of arts and crafts programmes in the villages and the construction of a multi-purpose community centre in each village which will serve the needs of teenagers and adults in a variety of programmes ranging all the way from physical fitness to pottery-making and amateur theatricals.

Below Diagram of a village.

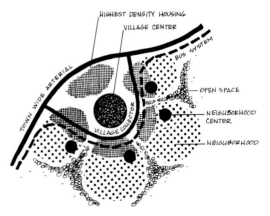

Below Diagram of a village centre.

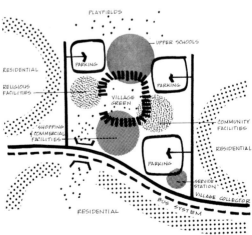

Below Diagram of a neighbourhood.

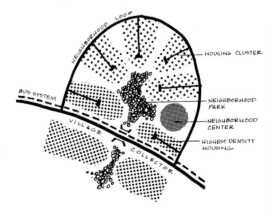

In the downtown area, however, our thinking is moving back towards the creation of cultural institutions to facilitate co-operative efforts by creative and performing artists in theatre, dance, music, and the graphic arts; such projects have not proved feasible in existing urban environments. It is possible that, as the churches have moved out of their denominational entrenchments into a creative relationship, so the various skills and talents in the performing arts may, in the proper friendly environment, be able to join forces. The type of mixed media theatrical presentations now using films, music, and dance in the course of an unfolding drama, suggests the potentials of this kind of interrelationship.

Certain suggestions of the work-group so far have not been achieved. For instance, great stress was laid on a family-life institute which would be concerned with child and family development. Since the work-group deliberations, we have sought counsel from a variety of sources, including the National Institute of Mental Health, but no clear picture of what such an institute might be or how it might function or be financed has as yet appeared. Another interest of the group was in job training and human resource development in relationship to the emergent Columbia economy. Here again, despite some modest successes and a variety of consultations, we are still looking for a way to proceed adequately with this programme.

In praise of a work-group

This process of interdisciplinary confrontation, of

Right The Merriweather Post Pavilion of Music, in the middle of the 40-acre town centre, was the first completed building in the new city.

Below The work-group in session. See Appendix II. (Photo: Robert de Gast)

personal involvement and commitment to the process by planners and developers, and the continued search for social validity is at the crux of Columbia's effort. Design decisions based on aesthetic, engineering, or economic considerations must vie with the test of social purpose.

Following are some of the decisions which gave form to the general development plan. The conclusions are less significant than the process by which they were derived. These are not universal truths; they were not selected from among pat alternatives. Every planner-builder-decisionmaker should simulate the experience of the work-group. Each city building task will vary with location and the unique characteristics of the people involved. Nothing but value can come from the continued repetition of the processes described above. There is no shortcut which can adequately substitute for it.

Plan decisions

Maximum choice and easy accessibility to community facilities and services are valued as fundamental requirements for a good community. Thus the widest ranges of activities and physical environments were sought. Striking the delicate balance between optimizing choice in activities at a given location (critical mass) and maximum participation by members of the community (minimum distance) continues as a planning dilemma. Decisions as to the size and location of activity centres and their resultant service areas created the basic community structure. This balancing of size and accessibility established the size of

schools, shopping and other facilities.

It was this kind of thinking that motivated the decision to create a public transit system. We chose to accept the inevitable use and dominance of the car as a means of getting around, but this still left a significant portion of the population either without access to distant places in the community or beholden to car owners and drivers for their freedom to move about. A bus system frees the young, the old, the less affluent to move about the city. It can reduce the familial stress produced by the chauffering rôle of parents, particularly the mother, in today's spread city and it can permit choice in the expenditures of funds typically allocated for the second car.

Small bus system

After analysis of alternatives, the concept of a small bus was adopted, to travel at relatively low speeds, but with minimum headways. In order to ensure headways and efficient speeds, separation from normal unpredictable auto traffic is required, hence the decision for a separate right-of-way. The choice of bus over other media such as fixed rail was based both on available technology and, more importantly, on the need for flexible routing. However, the minibus is not considered the ultimate solution and evolution of the system over time is anticipated.

The bus system had to be self-sustaining. The choice was made to provide good service to a limited area rather than sparse service to the entire city. This was a fundamental decision resulting in the coalignment of the high density dwelling areas and the bus route. This

40

Top The elementary school is used in the afternoons and evenings for community activities. (Photo: Morton Tadder)

Above Wilde Lake Village Centre.

Above right The library in Wilde Lake Village Centre is rented and operated by the County library service. The play-sculpture is by Pierre du Fayet. (Photo: Winants Bros.)

physical plan decision put approximately 35% of the population within a 3-minute walk to a bus stop (approximately 1,200 feet apart). This choice, coupled with attaining good service to village centres, town centre, and selected employment areas, strongly affected the shape of the city. Along the bus route a single continuous lineal pattern of intense community activities extending through the respective villages was created: villages and neighbourhoods (with their own internal form) overlap and interconnect. The terms of this decision to have a transit system were

fundamental to the form of the city as this factor interacted with decisions on community organization, and the accidents of ownership patterns and topography.

Overlapping communities
The concept of housing cluster, neighbourhood, village and town as a system of overlapping communities was derived from decisions regarding choices in the nature and size of facility clusters, especially the school system. There are many ways to organize a school system to maximum pedagogical and social value. The data available to substantiate one choice over another are at best incomplete. Nonetheless, we asserted that a good learning environment is a basic foundation for a healthy community, and therefore, the maximum access to and use of school plants became a prime objective. We chose (with county school board agreement) to adopt a system of relatively small schools within walking distance to surrounding residents as a focus of communities. In the context of real racial and socio-economic balance within the residential base we believed this to be a desirable pattern.
A neighbourhood centre consists of a K-5 elementary school supplemented by a day care centre, a small store and snack bar, and a multi-purpose meeting room. In addition there are typically a swimming pool, park, and playgrounds. The school and playgrounds are owned by the Board of Education. The neighbourhood centre is seen as a complementary set of facilities and services convenient to the most place-

bound members of an urban community, mothers and young children; with co-operative management, the facilities are used to capacity and maximum value.

Secondary schools form the hub of the village centre, again augmented by other 'non-educational' facilities. This juxtaposition of services and facilities for a residential population ranging from 10,000 to 15,000 represents our judgment of the balance between choice and access.

The architecture and setting of each village centre is different. Each centre will have shopping and other community services different from adjacent centres. The proximity of these centres allows one to use them alternately depending on the individual's choice. The scales of the centre remain similar and engender an apparent sense of identification and association with 'place'. This is clearly the intent. These village centres are completed and in use as the first residents begin to settle a 'village'. Two centres are well established serving 3,000 families (plus adjacent county population) 5 more are in plan and development process. These community centres will serve primarily in the provision of basic facilities and rudimentary services related to home life.

The real community to which individuals belong becomes a function of personal interest and identification. Sometimes it will correspond to the 'physical community' of their neighbourhood or village, but at other times, for families and individuals at different stages in life, it will cut across service areas resulting in 'community patterns' as complex and overlapping as in every living city. Freedom of movement and access to community facility centres via transit and car throughout the city should enhance and foster the sense of real community, based on choice. The concept of clustering facilities is based on the simple assumption of synergistic interaction among the varied activities and the people engaged. Both school and library benefit by proximity as do library and shopping centre, and so forth. More important than the real savings in cost of facilities and land is the

Top left Each village centre has its own year-round recreation facility, including an olympic swimming pool, ice skating rink, arts and crafts and a multi-purpose physical training centre.

Above left The shopping centre at Oakland Mills includes an air-conditioned mall.

Left Slayton House is a multi-purpose community building adjoining the secondary schools, religious facilities and shopping centre at Wilde Lake Village Centre. (Photo: Winants Bros.)

generation of contact between individuals and institutional operations within a centre complex.

The town centre with frontage on the intercity Rt. 29 (between Baltimore and Washington) serves as a centre for a larger service area of perhaps 250,000 people. The same principles of functional linkages bring the college site next to park and shopping facilities surrounded by office buildings and entertainment. Parking spaces can do double duty because of peak hour phasing and convenience is enhanced. Throughout the intricate planning and design process, countless decisions had to be reached on the nature of the city as a series of centres to serve overlapping communities; then the design task was clear and virtually methodical. A basic pattern of movement systems was established for all needs to move people and vehicles directly with minimum confusion between systems. Roads were designed to satisfy performance criteria of purpose, safety and aesthetics. Conflict is minimized by functional classification; some horizontal separation with vertical separation at a few critical points between pedestrian, bus, and car. No preconceived geometric pattern was applied- the system grew out of the concept of use. The roads are to serve activities and to respect land forms. Aesthetic criteria and the need for continued 'legibility' and orientation as one moves about are fed into every decision. Roads differ in width and curvature depending of capacity and travel speeds desired. Lighting, tree planting and sign location reinforce their role as elements of a visual as well as functional framework. Connection to existing county roads, existing ownership and required access plus overzealous 'engineering safety standards' have significantly compromised the road system. Economic restraints have kept vertical separations to a minimum.

Flexibility

A concept of open-endedness has been influential throughout. The adopted general plan and the New Town Zoning Process allows for considerable freedom in the unfolding details of urban design and functional relationships within major categories (residential, commercial, and so forth). The biggest challenge in design is to create relationships between buildings, systems, and places which can adjust as programme requirements change, based on market assessment and user feedback. No preconceived spatial geometry

Next page The design challenge of the new city's centre is to have it appear complete at every stage of its phased development. The first buildings are nestled along the lake with a waterfront plaza.

or rigid structural formation would allow this. The capacity of community centres to grow and readily accommodate changes in programme without destroying the original concept of a place is a prime criterion.

The economic model

An economic model has been developed at each stage in the plan. Even at inception, when there was only a verbal description of the city with rough qualitative relationships, costs and revenue were worked out in a crude economic model. It was this early model which served as basis for Connecticut General's investment. As plans became refined so the model was refined. This model reflects a pattern of full development, setting parameters for expenditures in time and capital investment and serving as a constant guide to economic viability. No 'design' decision can be made without a cost evaluation.

The economic rationale of Columbia is based on the creation of values in the land through creative planning, zoning, installation of roads, utilities and amenities, and resale of land at a profit, and the development of income-producing properties in Columbia through development subsidiaries for investment. To ensure meeting the profit objective, a system of financial accounts and controls was formalized in the Columbia Economic Model (CEM).

The CEM effectively responds to each of the planning objectives because the profit, and the aesthetic or social objectives cannot be met independently of the other objectives.

The CEM, through separate models, accounts for the development activities of three corporate entities:

The Howard Research and Development Corporation (HRD). HRD is the original landowner and developer of Columbia.
The Columbia Development Corporation (CDC). CDC, a wholly-owned subsidiary of HRD, develops residential, commercial and industrial properties in Columbia.
The Columbia Park and Recreation Association (CPRA). CPRA, a non-profit corporation, ultimately controlled by the community, develops recreational and community facilities, operates community programmes, and provides certain types of maintenance to the community.

The CEM is used primarily as a management tool to:

1 systematically identify and classify projected proceeds and expenditures for the development period;

2 determine the financial requirements of each entity;
3 project the cash flow from land development;
4 project the cash flow from operating properties;
5 account for and discipline the disposition of all land;
6 establish development pace programmes;
7 establish specifications for land development;
8 establish guidelines for the preparation of annual development budgets;
9 establish minimum land prices.

It is also used for income tax planning, project scheduling, estimating staff requirements and marketing strategy. The framework of the model allows the feasibility of alternative development programmes and assumptions to be tested. For example: sales pace and land pricing; the effect of lower prices and therefore a faster sales pace, requiring accelerated development programmes, can be examined. The effect of higher prices and a slower pace can also be tested.

The CEM may also be used in the selection of development areas. Annual development programmes requiring varying mixes of product are not always obtainable from one geographic area. Major facilities costs (roads, sewers and water) represent the major portion of development costs for any area. The model is used to select development areas by identifying the area which gives optimum results in terms of sales pace, development costs and carrying costs, consistent of course with meeting Columbia's social and aesthetic objectives as well. The model becomes the basis from which specific design programmes and schedules are prepared.

The CEM is 'officially' updated quarterly for review by HRD's Board of Directors. Other models are prepared regularly to evaluate alternate development assumptions.

To this management tool we add other control techniques such as CPM and PERT systems to help ensure the meeting of critical deadlines.

With a limited development budget, design is a matter of choosing among values. The criteria of engineering feasibility, aesthetic satisfaction, market acceptance, and community purpose have all to be balanced within the context of a realistic budget. The planning and design process requires the continued interaction, dialogue, and feedback among all these.

Complexity

At the outset of the planning and development process we had brave ideas of being able to accom-

Two views of the new city centre, and plaza, Columbia, Maryland. (Photo: Winants Bros.)

plish all our goals through the efforts of our centralized team. We soon came to realize the true complexity of urban systems, and we accepted an operational principle by which we try to discover the best institutional form to carry out a mission, in order that this separate body may not be dependent for its life on other development agents.

This concept was manifest when enabling legislation, which we put before the State Legislature for the creation of New Town zoning and a special taxing district, bogged down. It became apparent that we could not achieve the new tax district, and that it was jeopardizing the passage of the zoning law. It was tactically necessary to abandon this form, and create the Columbia Park and Recreation Association (CPRA). This is now the quasi-public agency to which every land owner belongs, and is assessed by the convenants on his property. CPRA becomes the alter ego to County government, owning park land, community facilities, running recreation programmes, in short filling the voids unsatisfied by the not yet urban County government. Elaborate processes are set up for the staged transfer of control of this entity from the 'developer' (HRD) to the citizens of Columbia. This is a fascinating conflict between the need for control over fundamental development decisions by HRD, and the incessant desire for community control on the part of the residents.

I could continue to elaborate extensively on the intricacy of relationships between CPRA and HRD. This and other important issues concerning the creation of systems of polity and community services can only be identified here.

A process is in effect requiring all building and renovation proposed for Columbia to be approved by the Architectural Committee. This is a significant effort at finding the meeting-ground between private individual taste and aesthetic judgement, and the broader interests of community design.

Other descriptions of process would elaborate on the decision not to attempt the creation of a separate school district, but instead to work within the existing system. Similarly we explored and abandoned the idea of managing a self-sufficient water and sewer system. There is no room here for description of the important relationships and critical development issues which identify the Columbia Development Corporation (CDC), the Howard County Government and particularly the Planning Commission, the Building Department, the Metropolitan Commission, the State Roads Commission or the countless citizens' groups and other public and private organisations to be dealt with in a continuing fashion.

In short, a city is a most complex organism. To plan and build a city means to recognize its complexity at the outset; to organize and relate the parts; to simplify where possible; to accept as natural the inherent complexity of human settlements. There is an understandable tendency to take simplistic views of the world, to ignore a complex problem by eliminating variables, and then to solve the remaining simplified versions. The planning and design professions have been guilty of this with its professed concern for the physical city only. But this approach can be disastrous to human interests. The simplistic version is unlikely to be sufficient; the problems solved are probably not the real ones.

Similarly, the danger in this brief description of the planning process for building Columbia is in oversimplification and in failing to communicate the subtle interactions and the disciplines of dealing simultaneously with countless variables. An appreciation of this condition, and the ability to work within it, requires a commitment to know and work with people. They are the city.

Below and top right Columbia's policy is to allow as much individual freedom of choice as possible for the home buyer. An urban design group and an Architectural Committee work with buyers, salesmen and architects to create harmonious neighbourhoods and to absorb a wide range of design choice.

Upper right Groups of townhouses which are co-operatively owned form homeowners' associations to plan and maintain common areas. (Photo: Max Araujo)

Lower and bottom right: Columbia's neighbourhoods also provide apartments with rentals adjusted to location and amenities. (Lower photo: Winants Bros.)

The implications for the future

Columbia represents an important experiment in the city building process. The need to discover, articulate, and refine successful processes is critical to our survival as an urban civilization.

Consider that in 1900 there were 19 cities with a population in excess of one million. By 1960, this number had increased to 141. World urban population is estimated to be rising since at a current rate of 6.5% annually, and at this rate of increase will double in eleven years.

To grasp the meaning of change on so phenomenal a scale it is necessary to imagine what would happen if all existing cities—including New York—were to retain their present size; we would have to build a duplicate city for every city of the hundreds that already dot the globe, all in eleven years.

In the light of this apparently irreversible trend to urbanization, the US and other industrialized nations should be engaged in a concerted national effort to build new cities. The reasons are many:[1]

First, it is the best way for the nation to build the housing it needs, on the scale it requires. We shall have to assemble and build on large sites if we are to realize the potential of the technology that is or could be at our disposal; and unless we realize this potential—notably that of industrialized production—we shall not be able to build at the proper scale, let alone at reasonable costs.

Second, only by planning and building at sufficient scale—which, after all, is the generic concept behind the notion of new communities—shall we be able to capture the appreciated values of developed land and recycle them into the costs of infrastructure and essential community services and facilities. And unless we capture and recycle these appreciated values, it is clear that we shall not be able to assemble the monies needed to pay for these costs. Certainly, it is not the mood of the public to provide these costs through direct taxation.

Third, we shall not be able to replan our central cities unless we build new communities at the same time as companions to urban renewal. There is no elbow room left in the current land and obsolete housing stock of our older cities to make any current effort at large-scale rebuilding acceptable to those who must be displaced. Unless there are new communities nearby into which to move, displacement becomes immoral and urban renewal remains socially and politically intolerable. We ought to be absolutely clear on this point: any meaningful policy of rebuilding our cities must necessarily have as a concomitant a policy of new city development.

Fourth, only by the kind of comprehensive planning which new communities generically represent, can we achieve the mix of essential services which are becoming the hallmark of our economy and the measure of quality in our urban existence. I refer here to education, day care, health care, legal and other professional services. In the past, we have allowed these services to emerge singly, haphazardly, or in many cases not at all. Further, important innovations in institutional development and social systems can be tried more easily where there is a minimum of vested interest in existing systems.

Finally, only by building our communities with this sophistication and at such scale can we really attract the entrepreneurial leadership and the social imagination that modern living in this complex society demands. We have built an industrial sector that has grown very rapidly with our society; we have also allowed the industrial sector to develop the revenue and resource flows and the banks of executive talent and skills to flourish in this enlarging, mobile society. We have not put the same challenge or given the same resources to that part of our society which is responsible for building and rebuilding our communities. New community building, defined as a matter of scale and process, is an essential part of the overall development process. New communities must be built systematically and continually as parts of existing metropolises and as the nuclei of new ones.

Lessons learned

Following is an attempt to distil from the Columbia experience some ideas which we believe to be crucial to success.

The assumption of risk. Risk is involved: risk in capital, risk is reputation, risk in being wrong or just not as right as one might wish.

It is often said, that we do not know enough or that the urban system is too complex. We shall never know 'enough'; nevertheless we must be prepared to act, to build, to venture new systems and new institutions based on the best available knowledge. We need to rigorously articulate our goals, assumptions, and hypotheses, and follow them through with discipline. Only then can we learn from each effort, from both success and failure. We need continuing research, but not at the cost of inaction. Urban development and renewal must be conceived as the proper laboratory. We shall learn as we build so long as we make the feedback connection between hypotheses and actual development.

The need for wholeness. Wholeness is a necessary condition if we are to be successful in building an urban community. There are two aspects to the concept of wholeness. One is related to size and the need to create opportunity and choice. A city is made of overlapping, interlocking layers and sets of communities: communities of place and of interest. A good city should be able to provide sufficient activities and opportunities to enable each person to pursue his own goals, and to satisfy his own interests and develop his potential. The US is a pluralistic society. If the varied interests which compose American society are to come together and live in cities, the traditional concept of consensus or majority rule will have to shift to that of alternative cultures and varied life styles, brought together by social and physical environment and enabled to co-exist, overlap, and thrive. If a community or city is sufficiently whole, individuals and groups might find the opportunity for fulfilment without fear of isolation or shortage and the resultant need to constrict or restrict others.

The other aspect of wholeness revolves around the concept of systems. An urban community needs to encompass the natural parameters of the systems which serve it. To have a healthy community one needs to affect the whole health system, wherever it extends across traditional geographic or jurisdictional boundaries. In addition, where the concept of health is at issue, it must be possible also to include the necessary connections to related institutions and systems such as housing, education, employment and law. We are too accustomed to dealing with fragments. Only by thinking in terms of function, process, and optimum conditions are we likely to reconceive the life-support systems of the city. We need to begin by conceiving each sub-system as it might be if all related systems were as they should be, and then set out to get there from here.

Physical development plans. The planning process we are engaged in rejects as archaic the traditional approach of making 'the plan' and then effectuating it. Plans need to be conceived as continually fluid and responsive to the feedback of operating agencies and development processes and opportunities. The sensitivity of the feedback process is essential both to the quality of the plan and its fulfilment. In fact, one key criterion of a 'good' plan must be its potential for being implemented.

Social development plans. Physical development plans grow out of social and institutional development plans. The built environment must be conceived as a way of making possible the activities and well-being of people. Before we can plan adequately for building, we should understand purpose. We should know the characteristics of the activities to be accommodated. The criteria of success must be in terms of their effect on the ultimate user; the individual or the community. The leverage which physical development offers for institutional change is significant if it is perceived as that kind of opportunity.

New ways of learning, new systems delivery of social services should become possible as social and physical development efforts are joined. It is necessary systematically to relate institutions to each other, and capital investment to operating programmes. The planner/builder, when operating in a sound community context and with sufficient knowledge, needs to understand and accept the rôle of 'change agent'. The professional can no longer merely advise and consult if he expects to be effective. He is inevitably involved in value-judgements and political behaviour. He must try always to understand the basis and motivation for his actions or proposals.

Planning development: one process: Planning must be linked to development. The discipline and opportunity of actual development must guide the plan. It is a continuous process which should not be segmented arbitrarily by separate responsibilities. The word *development* should carry the implicit prefix *physical* and *social*, since these are inseparable in life. From project to project the emphasis will change, i.e. predominately physical or social, and this should be explicit.

Too many plans are made by public or private interests only to gather dust. Either because of fanciful flights to unreality or by uninspired concepts, plans fail to attract public or private investment or commitment. Plans need to be ambitious but based on reality and able to excite people to action. The very linkage of planning with building process creates credibility and expectation. The feedback which is built into the link triggers change when it is necessary for a plan to remain vital.

Value is in the doing. Actual or even sometimes vicarious participation in the processes of planning and development are as vitalizing to those involved as experiencing the completed environment might be. Professionals have long realized this but have unconsciously and, at times perhaps, selfishly kept the excitement to themselves. Individual and community health seems to thrive during the development process. Those engaged are building their own environment, expressing the power to create, and are

growing as a result. A broad sense of ownership of the goals and participation in the development process is a time-consuming but necessary condition for a healthy community. Under these circumstances, the community is likely to remain fluid and adaptable to change and growth. The fully completed environment is a dubious goal. A plan and 'completed' project at best should remain open and evoke the sense that change is possible and the people of the community should know how to go about it.

The culture of teams. By definition, planning and building the city is complex. To build well no one person or small group of elite professionals can be sufficient. But professionals are essential to perform design and development rôles across the spectrum of interests and disciplines required.

We shall now need to put together teams of people who see the world first from the vantage point of their differing professional disciplines (law, education, engineering, etc.). In part, this is desirable. But if our city building efforts are to work, these different ways of seeing and thinking about the city must be joined in a co-ordinated effort. Much talk exists about the desirability of interdisciplinary teams. This kind of integrated team will not be formed easily or, once formed, will not guarantee effective work over time. The very process of voluntarily grouping, re-grouping and co-operating over time is alien to our culture except under crisis conditions. In fact, I propose that one of the characteristics of the new city should be of constant organizational change, consistent with the tasks and recources available. The result would be very different from the bureaucracy we struggle with today.

Significant effort must be made in team building and organizational development. The city building team will be complex and ever-changing as the plan/development process continues. New participants from the fields of systems design and management must be added to the normal array of urban expertise. Most important is the need to build on the theories evolved by men like Bennis, Beckhard, Bass and others as concepts of organizational development have been tested in American industry. An investment in organizational development must be made. A team development responsibility should be conceived as an essential management rôle and come to be recognized as a critical part of the process from inception through operation.

Model of the future. The word *model* has come to have a new meaning. Traditionally a plan was flat, a model

three dimensional, and operations were something that happened afterwards. We think of models now as a way of simulating life experiences, of what happens to the system as it gets built and is used over time. The most obvious model is the economic one: the sets of accounts which identify costs, income and cash flow and allow for playing out alternatives. A plan process is incomplete without this capability.

The concept of simulating the future needs to be extended beyond the physical environment and the rigours of economic concern into the patterns of social structure and institutional behaviour. While we have barely scratched the surface beyond economic modelling, we shall be able to identify trade-off actions and potential success or failure better than we do today before the expenditure of human resources that often are more limited than cash.

Critical mass of talent. Human resources are the greatest scarcity we have. The question is how to allocate these resources. Today the trend is for people with knowledge and skill to consult together. This lack of identification with a project and its resultant personal involvement prohibits the investment of time and energy required really to build the human relations and processes necessary for success. Consequently no feedback is likely to take place, nor any real advance in knowledge or technique.

Each project requires a critical mass of the 'right' people. These must remain to develop the abilities required. In addition, those who gain the new knowledge and skill must become trainers. It is essential to transmit what we know to new people who, in turn, can commit themselves and participate in other projects.

The new way of thinking. A new culture must be developed among those who will find their life work in the public or private sector of the new city building industry. Participants in building our urban civilization will need the comforting knowledge that only change is constant, that complexity is necessary, that indecision is an art equal only to deciding. The most important of all characteristics necessary for success is belief.

From the Columbia Process, Jim Rouse describes our 'Way of Thinking': 'It is fundamentally focused on people as the purpose of all planning and development. It seeks to identify the circumstances under which man, woman, and family can grow in their individual personality, character, and spirit and then tries to find the way to shape services, institutions, land, buildings and communication systems to create communities that will provide maximum support for the people who live there.

'It believes that people can have a good life and can live together in brotherhood. It looks upon everything short of that as a malfunction to be corrected and not as a condition to be worked around. It proceeds always with the purpose and in the belief that the good life in the good community is available if we build it and that our job is to plan and produce it as a continuing process.

'It believes that these purposes are among the most important of our civilization and that those engaging in them are at work in the most important tasks that can possibly consume their lives.

'It is a way of thinking that is geared to victory, not just to fighting better battles. It understands that important values are created by the most effective interrelationship of all the pieces of "city" and all the processes and institutions supporting life in a community.

'It sets the beginning point of planning at discovering the best that ought to be and then at reconciling the individual pieces into the most feasible solution towards those ultimate goals.

'It asserts that the processes of development and change, while focused on human values, must be undertaken within rigorous disciplines of sound economics, the best available knowledge of development techniques and behavioural science.

'It knows that the creation of these human values produces dividends in new economic values (land, rents, price, etc.), and trade-offs among institutional budgets. It is these increased values that make possible and support many deficit activities, which are essential to the total quality of life in a community.'

Operating each day within this way of thinking, we continue to learn from the successes and failures of the city-building process itself, since there is little real precedent to draw upon.

Footnote

1. Paraphrased from remarks by Paul Ylversaker at a conference at Princeton University.

APPENDIX 1
FACTS ON COLUMBIA

Land Use
Acres:

Total in Columbia	13,700±
Residential land	7,400
Industrial and commercial land	3,100
Reserved for industrial parks	1,800
Commercial/offices	500
Special opportunity sites	800
Permanent open space	3,200
Lakes	500
Parks	1,500
Per village	1,000-1,500

Residential Development
Dwelling units authorized:

Total by 1980	30,000
Single family detached	15,000
Townhouses, garden apts., high-rise apts.	15,000
Per village	2,000-4,000
Village of Wilde Lake	3,000
Per neighbourhood	700-1,200
Projected no. of residents by 1980	110,000
Villages	7 large, 2 small
Neighbourhoods	20-25
Gross residential density	2.5 d.u./acre

Transportation

Miles of roads (approx).	150
Miles to be built during first 18 months	22
Minibus system:	
Miles of minibus route	14-16
Residents within 3-minutes walk	35%

Commercial and Industrial
Square feet of retail space planned:

Downtown (approx.)	1,800,000
Each village centre	30,000-50,000
Village of Wilde Lake	46,000
Projected employment:	
Total in Columbia by 1980	30,000
Industrial primary employment	10,000
Commercial, retail, and services	20,000

Institutional Facilities (partial)
Projected no. of:

Secondary schools	7-9
Elementary schools	20-25
Libraries	4-8
Churches in Columbia	40
Acres reserved for:	
Private college	100
Medical clinic and hospital	25
Acres offered to public community college	100
Acres leased to National Symphony for music pavilion	10

General Information

Projected development period	15 years
Number of land transactions made to assemble tract	175
Average price paid per acre	$1,500
Total estimated population today in immediate vicinity	6,000
Total primary jobs existing in area today in immediate vicinity	3,700
Population of Howard County today	55,000

APPENDIX 2
COLUMBIA WORK GROUP

Public Administration: Dr. Henry M. Bain, Jr., Political Scientist, Chevy Chase, Maryland.

Family Life: Antonia Chayes, formerly Technical Secretary to the Committee on Education, President's Commission on the Status of Women, Washington, D.C.

Recreation System: Robert W. Crawford, Commissioner, Department of Recreation, Philadelphia, Pennsylvania.

Community Structure: Dr. Nelson N. Foote, Sociologist, Consultant, Community Development, General Electric Company, New York City.

Community Structure: Dr. Herbert J. Gans, Sociologist Columbia University, New York City.

Economics and Housing Market.: Robert M. Gladstone, Economist, Washington, D.C.

Education: Christopher S. Jencks, Editor, *New Republic,* Fellow, Institute for Policy Studies, Washington, D.C.

Health Systems: Dr. Paul V. Lemkau, Psychiatrist, The Johns Hopkins University, Baltimore, Maryland. Dr. Leonard Duhl, Chrmn. Board of Technical & Policy Advisors United States Health Corporation San Francisco, California.

Chairman: Dr. Donald M. Michael, Psychologist, Programme Director, Institute for Social Research, University of Michigan, Ann Arbor, Michigan.

Housing: Dr. Chester Rapkin, Professor, Urban Planning, School of Architecture, Columbia University, New York City.

Local Government and Administration: Wayne E. Thompson, The Dayton Company, Minneapolis, Minnesota (formerly City Manager, Oakland, California).

Traffic and Transportation: Alan M. Voorhees, Washington, D.C.

Communication in the Community: Dr. Stephen B. Withey, Psychologist, University of Michigan, Ann Arbor, Michigan.

The Rouse Company members of the Work Group:
President: James W. Rouse.

Vice President in Charge of Project: William E. Finley
Director of Institutional Planning: Wallace Hamilton
Director of Planning and Design: Morton Hoppenfeld

subURBAN DESIGN

C. A. JUNKER

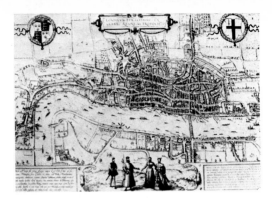

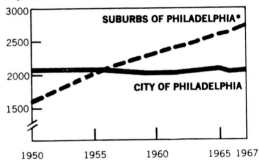

Population in Thousands

3000 — **SUBURBS OF PHILADELPHIA***

2500

2000 — **CITY OF PHILADELPHIA**

1500

1950 1955 1960 1965 1967

*Chester, Montgomery, Delaware and Bucks Counties in Pennsylvania, and Gloucester, Camden and Burlington Counties in New Jersey.

Sources: **U.S. Census of Population, 1950 and 1960, Population Estimates**, series p-25, United States Department of Commerce.

Top Plan of London (Braun and Hogenburg) ca. 1574, showing the walled city and settlement outside the city walls. Note the basically linear quality of the outlying development, following roads and waterways, much as it still tends to do today.[7]

Above Population, Philadelphia metropolitan area, showing stabilization of the city and rapid growth in the suburbs, typical of most cities in the United States today.[8]

Above right 'Habitat', Expo '67, Montreal, Canada, architect Moshe Safdie: architects' vision of future settlement forms.

Right Builders' housing in suburban Maryland, USA; vernacular building in suburbia.
(Photo: Harvey Krasnegor)

48 Suburbs are an ancient phenomenon, and surely every nation in the world must be experiencing their growth today, particularly with expanding personal wealth and improvements in transportation. How many men, given their choice, do not forsake the congested city for more wide open spaces? Yet, despite this popular behaviour, if one opens architectural or planning magazines, or visits schools of architecture and planning in the United States, one will be struck by the vast amount of time and energy spent on the planning and design of central urban areas. Volumes are filled, and walls are covered with master plans, systems designs and magastructures for the urban core . . . while suburbs which contain half the urban population of the nation and are growing at four to five times the rate of central city areas,[1] are barely noticed. At best, a few examples can be seen of improvements in development housing and subdivision design, but fundamental questions concerning the nature and quality of environmental form in suburban areas have yet to be asked.

The very use of the words 'form' and 'suburbs' in the same breath is enough to arouse immediate emotional response in many professional quarters. As every neophyte planning or architectural student *knows,* the suburbs are 'formless' and 'endless sprawl' – the epitome of anti-architecture and anti-urbanism –

while city centres have towering skylines, megastructures, piazzas and all the other exciting urban forms that we have been trained to eulogize.

Efforts have been made to turn the nation's attention to New Towns, twentieth-century cliff dwellings, and other exciting visual concepts, but somehow these 'imported' and sophisticated ideas have failed to catch hold. Families continue to seek out tract homes in suburbia, and local builders keep building and building to meet the demand.

In leading the assault on suburbia, professionals have been so concerned with the familiar and with what seems to be attractive *to them* that they have failed to consider suburbia for what it is, or for what it could be or 'wants to be'. Suburbanization as seen in the United States suggests whole new forms of urban settlement which grow directly out of popular aspirations and the technology of the times. To hope to force suburban growth into a different mould from that which the wealth, space and technology of the nation permits, and the popular will demands, is to lose contact with the main stream of urban life today.

Suburbia must be understood for what it is, and new rules must be developed, if necessary, for dealing with

its environmental problems. In many ways it appears to be a precursor of what the future will hold in the way of world-wide living patterns and settlement forms, and if this is so, there is much to learn from its study.

Robert Venturi once remarked that if a designer feels instinctively repelled by the design of a particular object, it is usually worth his while to attempt to understand what it is that triggers such a strong emotional reaction. The study of what strikes one as being fundamentally wrong can yield many insights, including the discovery of a completely new view of a problem or a completely different frame of values and motivations, all of which would otherwise have been lost or misunderstood. The immediate, strong negative response may be due to the fact that the situation poses a direct challenge to one's current set of values or usual way of thinking, and revaluation could lead to the discovery of entirely new areas of problem solution. Attitudes towards suburban form are a case in point. Most planners and architects in the United States find it easy to criticize suburbia, but difficult to confront it or seek to understand it in a sympathetic, productive way. Yet the fact that suburban living has become the principal mode of living in this country, and promises to be even more marked in the future, makes it imperative that this be done.

The need for architects and planners to confront these issues grows out of their tasks of recognizing emerging forms in the environment, and helping to give them an ordered reality. Suburban areas of today are treated like the early railroad coaches which were made to look like multiple versions of the decorative, horse drawn coaches which preceded them. The railroad car had not yet been seen as an object in its own right, with its own generic form-characteristics, and was forced into the more familiar forms of the past.

Above 'Tom Thumb', an early railroad train built by Peter Cooper in 1830. Like suburbia today, it was an artifact clothed in the forms which preceded it.

The suburbs suffer from a similar kind of neglect on the part of design professionals. Suburbs are criticized as lacking the physical and social qualities of urban or rural living, while little effort is made to understand and appreciate their unique characteristics. The 'forminess' of Italian hill towns and the romance of bucolic life are held up in comparison to demonstrate the wishy-washiness of the suburban environment. What appears to be needed is a 'non-judgmental'[2] examination of suburban life and the suburban environment if suburban form is to be understood and helped to come into its own.

Everyman's dream

In attempting to understand the physical form of suburbia, one must first understand the forces which brought suburbia into being. The history and sociology of suburbia has been well documented and is familiar to most of us. In some ways it is a story which describes an escape from the failures of urban living— from congestion, filth, violence . . . But in a more positive sense, it is the story of the search for the American Everyman's dream: a piece of land to call one's own, fresh air and room to roam . . . And while fulfilment of this dream may be somewhat elusive in the reality of suburbia, the dream is still real enough for the nation to be faced with a strong and persistent desire for suburban living in almost every corner of

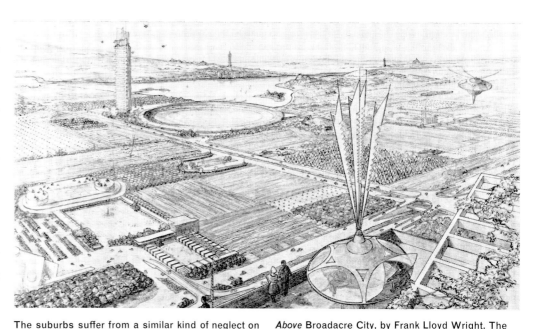

Above Broadacre City, by Frank Lloyd Wright. The American Everyman's dream: an acre of land for every family.[9]

society. Frank Lloyd Wright seems to have understood this. Broadacre City, with its minimum of one acre of land for every family, lives on as a persistent vision and symbol of this dream.

While the dream is real, however, Wright's vision appears today to be simplistic and nostalgic. Massive new development in outlying areas and the magic of instant communications and rapid movement have almost obliterated the rural-urban dichotomy on the American scene. Today one can taste the delights of both city and country life on a daily basis. The romantic vision of a bygone era, of simple cottages and farming plots laid out in neat, small-town fashion, must be superseded by a healthy, dynamic vision which gives recognition to the total complexity and vitality of the new national life-style. And this vision must have its roots in the very nature of the twentieth century suburban phenomena . . . not be a series of warmed-up urban concepts or preconceptions. Suburbia must be looked at very hard, so that its true nature is understood and allowed to become the generator of meaningful suburban form.

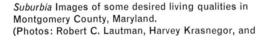

Suburbia Images of some desired living qualities in Montgomery County, Maryland.
(Photos: Robert C. Lautman, Harvey Krasnegor, and Ueland and Junker)

Observations on the sub-urban environment

In our study of suburban Montgomery County in the Philadelphia metropolitan area, our thinking began with the assumption that the environment was founded on a way of life or 'life style' which had been consciously sought out by a majority of the county's residents. Plans for modifying that environment were seen as having to be based on an understanding of the qualities which people sought out and continue to seek in the area. These qualities would have to be enhanced, or at least not discarded, in future planning, unless some strong logic dictated otherwise. This follows from the belief that the first and primary determinants of form under almost any circumstances are the desires and aspirations of those who are to use the

environment being created. These desires are to be understood and respected, or there should be some compelling reasons for doing otherwise.

The study began, then, with the assumption that the environment in question was a legitimate response to the needs and aspirations of the people living in the county. Just *how good* a response it was, of course, was another question. To approach this question non-judgmentally, one had to understand the needs and aspirations of people in the county, and then analyse how well they were being satisfied by the existing environment. Once a grasp of these problems could be made, the matter of 'improved' forms or environmental orders could be considered.

The question immediately arises as to how one can understand the environmental qualities sought by a group of people. Should surveys be made, with questionnaires and visual aids? Or should other more sophisticated techniques be used, such as the construction of alternate environments which are tested after several years of occupancy? Usually none of these methods are useful to the architect and planner. Either they are unreliable due to the impossibility of describing or simulating environments or they are so expensive as to be impractical, as in the case of full-scale test environments.

One very simple way of approaching the problem however, is to observe what has been built, and how people use the existing environment. The premise here is that the existence of a physical phenomenon which is widespread and enduring through time is bound to reflect the needs of its users. Furthermore the degree to which it satisfies or fails to satisfy those needs through time can be observed in the changes and adaptations to the original environment, and in other indications of failure such as commonly expressed enthusiasm or complaints.

Certainly the suburbs have been with us long enough and are widespread enough to be considered fairly reliable evidence of what people who live there are generally seeking.

To apply this simple means of analysis, then, one has only to look carefully at suburbia as it is today, and try to isolate those qualities which are most characteristic of the environment. It is essential, of course, that the look be as objective and non-judgmental as possible if the approach is to succeed. If, for example, one were to look at suburbia through the glasses of the hill-town urbanist or the Sierra Club naturalist, the results would probably be pre-determined from the outset. One has to keep a relatively open mind, and give the millions of suburbanites the benefit of the doubt – at least to begin with – that they live where they do because *they like it* and that they consciously choose to be there for reasons which are very real and important to them.

In a sense, the analyst has to be an 'advocate' for suburbanites, a role most planners and architects are well equipped to fill since they generally come from the same group of people as do most suburbanites—white, middle-class America. Many of the limitations one has to try to overcome in dealing with other social and economic groups are no problem here. One has merely to relax, put aside some of the preconceptions about suburban living which are a standard part of professional education and the professional press, and try to see suburbia for what it is to its users.

What, then, might be regarded as the principal environmental goals of suburban residents, as definable in suburbia today?

One simple but fundamental observation about suburbia is that those who elect to live there generally make a 'both-and', rather than 'either-or', decision regarding the urban-versus-rural question. Most suburbanites do not want to live in a dense area, nor do they want to live alone and isolated in the country. They want to be able to combine accessibility to the city, and all its specialized services and cultural activities, with the qualities of life they associate with countryside and small-town communities. This popular notion is directly opposed to that of many professionals who decry suburban life as neither truly urban nor truly rural. The latter find the lack of 'either-or' clarity in suburban growth disturbing and would like to see dense city forms rising up out of the virgin countryside ... or at least see greenbelts around urbanized areas so that they will know when they have arrived, and when they leave the city. These arguments may have relevance to some, and may even be significant to enough people for government to take action to halt suburban growth, at least in its present form, sometime in the future. For the present, however, the massive and sustained popular movement towards the 'both-and' qualities of suburban living is a fundamental fact to be reckoned with.

Naturally, many factors are included in the basic decision of suburbanites to optimize both urban and rural living qualities. Many people want to own their own home and a piece of land. The air is cleaner and there is room for children to roam. The amount of dwelling and private open space obtainable for one's money is usually greater. Schools and other facilities are generally newer and less crowded. Job opportunities are growing at a much faster rate in the suburbs than in the cities. And in the suburbs a householder can isolate himself and his family from 'undesirables'

and other dangers of life in the inner city. Seen together, these factors have a tremendous force and give some indication of what the urbanist is up against when he speaks of alternatives to suburban living. The solution he proposes must somehow satisfy this set of varied and complex needs to a greater degree than does present day suburbia; or life under his alternative conditions must be made compulsory. The qualities suburbanites are seeking – single family dwellings, home-ownership, private outdoor green space, open countryside, local government, easy access to the city centre ... must somehow become the raw materials of the future environment. These qualities, with all their complexity and seeming contradictions, must not be lost sight of, if new and workable forms are to satisfy the wishes of the people who will use them.

In addition to observations on user choice, a number of observations were made in the Montgomery County Study regarding the nature of 'form' in the suburban context. Traditionally, for example, the physical forms of cities could be understood or perceived as a whole, either through seeing them from a distance or from a mountain top, or by their being simple enough to be retained in the mind as a series of related spatial elements, even though they had to be experienced through time and were not actually observed together as a unified whole at a single instant. Obviously

Below View of Heidelberg, 1645, showing the entire city visible as a single entity.[10]

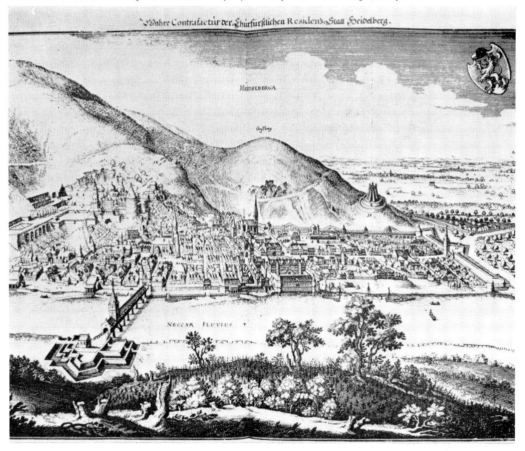

51

the scale, variety and complexity of urbanization today make this experience impossible in the traditional sense, and massive sub-urbanization has played a major role in bringing about this condition. To planners and architects who have been taught to think in terms of 'imageability', 'mega-forms' and the creation of distinct, perceivable physical entities, the twentieth-century urban phenomenon must appear to

Below Aerial view of a portion of central Paris. The plan of main avenues terminating at major focal points creates a simple, 'rememberable' pattern of streets.[11]
Right Aerial view of Washington D.C. from an altitude of 35,000 feet, showing absence of district boundaries and extensive and loosely patterned quality of growth in outlying areas.[12]

be a dismal failure. The pervasive nature of this form, however, and the strength of the forces behind it, must bring about a revaluation of the old design values and the development of a new analytical and design framework suited to these conditions.

Another observation about the suburban environment is that it is not as homogeneous as one might at first assume. Housing tracts are interspersed among older town and village centres which are often appreciated as stabilizing community elements and are well-used by the later-comers. Natural and topographical features, historical structures, parkland, and buildings from earlier eras add to the variety and enrichment of the environment, and the newer 'building blocks' of suburbia – shopping centres, office complexes, colleges, industrial parks . . . add further complexity. While it is true that in many places

Below New commercial centre at recently constructed highway intersection in suburban Montgomery County, Maryland.
Bottom Chatham Village, Pittsburgh, Pennsylvania, 1931-35, Ingham and Boyd, architects, and Stein and Wright, site planners.

52

the natural landscape and important reminders of the past have been obliterated, there are many examples where creative ingenuity has been shown, and the new environment retains a great deal of richness. At close-up view, suburbia is hardly as monotonous and all alike as it is sometimes made to appear, and many opportunities are there for design professionals to operate creatively and effectively within its particular context.

Also, it can be observed that the environmental landscape in suburbia is usually not strongly structured in a visual sense. In a city, for example, one might easily perceive that the location of the highest

Below Apartment tower and smoke stack from suburban freeway: large-scale objects with no particular locational message, except perhaps serving as orientation markers for frequent road users.

Bottom Suburban shopping centre, across parking fields; low visibility, except at close range.

Right 'Fun commercial' on the suburban arterial; you may choose among many places to stop, even one where it is simply fun to be.

buildings is the city centre. In the suburbs, however, size can be meaningless, and hills, water towers, powerlines, television towers, or other large-scale objects can be interspersed erratically throughout the environment. True, some of the traditional rules still appear to hold, such as that which causes shops to be found at major road intersections. People still seem to sense this simple but often unspoken organizing principle in the environment. But low, one-story suburban shops usually have very little physical presence, when seen across their flat hinterland of blacktop parking. Visual prominence and visibility from a distance cannot be counted on as organizing factors in the suburban environment.

A final and important observation has to do with the concept of 'community' associated with this new form-sense. Suburban residents appear to have a multi-dimensional sense of community and use their environment in a correspondingly multi-directional way. In the past, an individual's life was usually centred upon a single community focal-point: his local town or village. Today, however, the automobile gives him greater mobility and ready access to many points in large metropolitan regions. One can

now shop in a dozen different areas, depending on one's needs and tastes. The individual, then, has a multi-level community allegiance spread over wide areas. It could even be said, extending the topic, that television increases his psychological mobility even further and that at times he can feel closer to the 'world tribe' than to his next door neighbour. But the important point here is that the clearly defined, unifocal village structure of the past has little relevance to the suburban environment as it exists today and one must recognize a broader and more fluid concept of 'community' in approaching the question of suburban form.

The foregoing observations, combined with those of certain suburban roadside phenomena, suggest that the key means by which people understand the suburban environment may be through experiences on the road. In suburbia, almost every task which takes one beyond the home must be accomplished in a car. Consequently, one can function effectively only by knowing which road leads to which destination. Roads themselves, then, become the key integrating and organizing factor in the environment, providing essential information as well as a means of movement.

In this context, it is not surprising that the suburban roadscape often takes on a 'strip-development' quality, with all kinds of private and public pieces of information vying for attention. The profusion of roadside graphics may be trying to tell us something: that we are moving about swiftly in a complex, multi-directional environment, with a low level of observable clues to its organization; and that in order to function properly we need certain information about the loca-

Below Sensing 'community' on the suburban arterial Much of the experience of public spaces occurs on the roadway behind the wheel of an automobile. (Photos: Harvey Krasnegor)

tion of things, which must be obtained in one way or another. The most obvious answer to this need is, of course, the simplest form of information known to man, the common sign or symbol. One can see the fundamental role of such information in our lives, and ponder what kind of dry and lifeless (if not unworkable) situation we might encounter if we were to embark upon a programme of 'beautification' resulting in the curtailment or elimination of these basic communication functions.

One might conclude, at this point, since the road system is the key element in the multi-directional suburban environment, that it has to be organized or 'given form' in hierarchical, tree-like, or radial-circumferential systems. Evidence gathered by George Rand[3] would seem to indicate that with respect to perceptual needs, this does not necessarily follow. The average person does not seem to utilize an over-all plan concept in moving about his environment. Instead he appears to learn discreet paths which he knows will take him from one place to another. The necessity for an overall organization or structure to the road system may follow from highway technology or the aesthetic considerations of those aware and appreciative of such things, but it does not appear, from research done to date, to follow from the way-finding techniques of average persons. No doubt a clearly structured road system is helpful in improving the newcomer's comprehension of the environment, and probably increases efficiency in use of the road system for some people. But if the system gains its simplicity by ignoring the complexity and multi-directionality inherent in the environment, then it sacrifices serviceability to arbitrary 'orderliness', and is no longer an expression of what the suburban environment 'wants to be'.

Problems in the suburban environment
A number of problems in the suburban environment have already been mentioned. Certainly suburbia has many examples of the destruction of natural features and historical landmarks. Also, many of the older towns, now engulfed by suburbanization, suffer from many of the same problems besieging larger cities. These problems are very real and important, but most of us are conscious of them already, and public programmes already exist to help in their solution. Other problems, however, are less

Left Information on suburban arterial. All kinds of private and public information vying for attention. (Photo: Harvey Krasnegor)

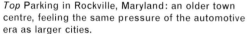

Top Parking in Rockville, Maryland: an older town centre, feeling the same pressure of the automotive era as larger cities.

Above Conflict between automobiles and pedestrians in Silver Spring, Maryland: a problem common to large and small cities alike.

Above middle Housing subdivision showing no attention to the creation of community focal points and public amenities.[13]

clear to us at this time. One area of confusion is in our understanding of what *community* is in the suburban environment, and how this can affect concepts of environmental form, and the design of community facilities and public works. Also, with regard to roads, few efforts have been made to understand the nature of roadspace problems, much less to finance programmes to create solutions.

The new meanings and forms of community described earlier have yet to be understood and given conscious expression in the physical environment. Widespread use of the automobile may have expanded mobility and choice, but it has left the suburbanite with some new difficulties. Many housing subdivisions have little sense of community, owing to an absence of com-

munity focus and public amenity. Local parks or sitting areas are rare, and people must turn either to their own homes and gardens, or to the car and activities outside the neighbourhood, for social life and relaxation. Sidewalks are grudgingly provided, if they exist at all, and usually lead nowhere in particular. Spontaneous and casual meeting at the local level becomes almost impossible.

At the same time, the large new centres of employment, shopping, and high-density dwellings throughout suburbia, while often successful in the design in their internal environments, are fragmentary in what they offer their users. A shopping centre may offer an air-conditioned mall and a variety of commercial services, but usually one must still go elsewhere to browse in a gallery or library, mail a package or pay a tax demand. Similarly in one of the newer industrial parks or office complexes, employees can have an air-conditioned work space and place to park, but must eat at their desks or in the building cafeteria, and spend their noon hours in the building. A secretary cannot stroll out to do some shopping or run an errand at lunch time. Even executives must eat in their roof-top dining rooms, staring at the same faces each day, looking forward to those special times when an important client is visiting, and an excursion can be taken to a nearby roadside restaurant.

Many of the new, high-rise residential developments are similarly isolated: they provide a spacious, modern apartment just off the expressway, with plenty of parking, but once outside the lobby there is no place to walk and enjoy the cool breeze of a summer evening, or meet and chat with other strollers.

While the road is in many ways the key element in the suburban environment, it is also one of its most neglected and least understood. Road design is still the sole province of the highway engineer, whose interests and responsibilities lie in such areas as

Above New suburban apartment blocks which pay little attention to the surrounding environment.

safety, durability and maintenance, with perhaps an occasional foray into roadside landscaping. This is not to say that the highway engineer has not been responsible for notable design and building achievements in his field: the design of expressway structures, including highly-developed road graphics systems, has shown a remarkable and inspiring commitment to the direct expression of industrialized design and construction techniques.

What is most lacking in highway design, however, is an approach which recognizes all of the functions of the roadway, and seeks to unite them into a complex, harmonious whole. Design standards for roads should recognize the environmental requirements of the communities through which the roads pass, as well as their internal movement requirements. Likewise, zoning requirements for sites along the roadway should reflect the many functions and requirements of the road as well as land use and building bulk requirements. A unified spatial concept which recognizes traffic, environmental, and communications requirements must evolve if a positive architecture of the road space is to emerge.

The need for such a new approach is evident when one looks at the existing road environment. Design

Left Structural details and highway signs, Interstate 95, Philadelphia.

Below Home-owners protecting themselves from roadside nuisances.
(Photo: Harvey Krasnegor)

Right Pedestrians in the roadside wasteland: closed curtains in the building at the rear are meant to help provide privacy to occupants.

efforts are generally weak and fragmented, with the engineer's efforts ending at the right-of-way line. Landscaping on arterial roads is rare and usually treated as garnishing, filling up odd-shaped traffic islands unusable for anything else. Zoning requires buildings to be set back, but says nothing about how the space between the building and the road is to be designed. Usually the result is a no-man's land which destroys the continuity and spatial quality of the roadspace, bores the motorist, endangers the pedestrian, and leaves building occupants exposed to roadway noise, nuisances and hazards. Sign controls in building codes often work either to suppress a healthy level of communication and graphic expression, or to permit such a chaos of graphics that individual pieces of information are lost to the receiver.

The price paid for increased mobility and dispersion seems to be a loss in some of the simpler joys of life: spontaneity in movement, and in our encounters with others; diversity and richness in the physical and social environment; the intensity of experience born of many things being experienced at once, with its heightened sense of excitement; the simple pleasures of an attractive, human environment ... Yet many of these pleasures can be recaptured without negating the fundamental purposes of suburbia, if enough creative imagination is brought to bear on the problems.

Thoughts on the Future

The suburban environment has been described as a physically elusive entity, whose occupiers use it in a complex, multi-dimensional way. How can a planner or architect work effectively in this situation, and make a genuine contribution to the evolution of suburban forms?

A first step, it would seem, is to view the needs and aspirations of suburbanites with greater tolerance and understanding; the hackneyed, negative imagery of suburbia must be laid to rest. One must have a positive attitude – even love – for a thing before the efforts of one's full self can be devoted to it.

Secondly, twentieth century suburbanization must be looked upon as a phenomenon of wider significance in terms of the development of urban form. We can continue to think in the same old ways, trying to suppress suburbia, or tolerate it patronizingly, or we can see it as a harbinger of new forms of urban settlement, striving for its own mode of expression and fulfilment. Its great mobility, its woven complexity of forms, its multi-dimensional structure, its dependence on communications... hint of a new kind of form emerging, one which is typically Twentieth-Century and perhaps typically American in style. What is needed is an understanding of the 'rules' of this new phenomenon so that we can gradually hope to work with it in a positive way.

Architecture of the Suburban Community

If preconceived, highly structured images of overall form are no longer possible or relevant in the traditional sense, what physical characteristics must the suburban environment have in order to satisfy the needs of its users and continue to reflect the progress man has made to date in shaping his environment?

In attempting to answer this question in the Montgomery County Study, the term 'Architecture of the Community' was used to emphasize several points. First, the phenomenon of community is still basic to man's existence, though its nature and consequent physical expression may be changing. Second, man's need for a sense of order and environmental quality in his settlements is also fundamental, and the term 'architecture' expresses such a conscious, man-made order as well as an accompanying high level of environmental quality.

The concept Architecture of the Community was given further definition through the analogy of a large, community 'house'. The private rooms of the house are dwellings and places of work. The living rooms are the large public places: plazas, shopping malls, lobbies of large buildings, and so on. Streets and walks form the halls of the house, and as in any good house, they are seen as something more than dark, narrow passages; they should be like pleasantly appointed halls and galleries, with places to sit and enjoy the sunshine, and alcoves where one can enjoy an intimate conversation or a bit of solitude. The 'house' has no particular size limit, and can be as large and intricate as we wish to conceive it, so long as it is comfortable and people can live their lives enjoyably within it.

Since the private spaces of individuals in the suburbs are usually quite commodious and satisfactory to their users, and since they are generally beyond the direct control and immediate concern of public policy anyway, it is the living rooms and halls of the community house which become particularly important in understanding and influencing the public environment. Furthermore, of these common spaces, the corridors – roads and highways – are probably the

places where individuals spend the greatest portion of their 'public' time, and receive their most extensive impressions of the community environment. The design of public spaces, and the roadspace in particular, becomes a key element in the creation of an Architecture of the Community.

As proposed, the physical expression of community in Montgomery County is a continuous network of well-ordered public spaces. Both the overall network and individual areas within it are purposely given individual character. This allows a sense of order and distinct identity at various 'levels' of community, expressing both the uniqueness and connectedness of various parts of the environment.

It was proposed that this be accomplished through a co-ordinated approach to the design of public works which recognizes and brings together the many functions of public spaces, as well as the many factors which go into their design. The architectural order is derived from a careful sorting out and arrangement of functions so as to improve their efficiency and ability to satisfy their users. The use of distinctive graphic themes gives individual identity and variety to portions of the environment, making it easier for a person to identify with a particular place at a given time. At the same time, the basic architectural order and the design of major public elements are held constant to maintain an overall sense of unity and identity. A high level of environmental amenity is sought so as to make the public spaces more pleasant and enjoyable, and create a public environment which gives expression to the highest values and aspirations of the community.

Design of the roadspace, and the 'space of joining':

The roadspace was analysed and three basic components were identified: the cartway or roadway proper, the spaces beyond the right-of-way line where private building takes place, and the 'space of joining' which lies between the two. The principal breakdowns in the roadspace environment usually occur in the space of joining. Here automobiles and pedestrians are seldom isolated properly from one another, and occupants of buildings are exposed to the nuisances of heavy traffic. The absence of consistent design direction in the development of this zone also makes it difficult for a more ordered sense of public spaces to emerge. If we accept the fact, as it appears we must, that most buildings along the roadway will continue to be designed as individual entities with varying degrees of accommodation to overall environmental themes, then the most effective means to create a greater sense of order and

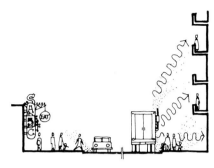

Existing right-of-way

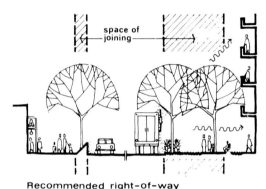

Recommended right-of-way

Above Space of joining; the 'joint' between the roadway and roadside activities is the principal problem in the design of roadspace.

continuity in the road environment is greater co-ordination and control in the space of joining.

The term 'space of joining' is meant to be a reminder of several things. First, this space is a 'joint' between the public and private worlds, and as such requires the co-operation of both individuals and the public at large for its proper design and maintenance. Perhaps one of the reasons why this zone has been so misused in the past is that its ownership and responsibility for its care has been unclear. Yet the quality of this essential link between the individual and the community has great symbolic as well as functional importance. If individuals and the public in general could demonstrate co-operation and inspired action in the creation and care of this important space, it would stand as concrete evidence of true community-

57

spiritness and commitment.

Second, the term is used as a reminder that the space can *join* the world of the motorist and the roadside world together. The simplest solution for eliminating conflicts between automobiles and pedestrians, for example, would be to erect a barrier between them. But this overlooks the possibility that the space can become a positive asset to both worlds, rather than a division between them. A strip of landscaped parkland along a heavily travelled road, for example, can be an amenity to motorists, pedestrians, and the users of roadside buildings alike.

Finally, the term is a reminder that the 'joint' in architecture has always served as an occasion for elaboration and embellishment. Traditionally, many forms of decoration are derived from expression, at the point of juncture, of different architectural elements. As Louis Kahn has noted, the joint is an occasion of great 'celebration'. If we can think in similar terms about elements in the larger environment, new sources of inspiration will open to us. Perhaps we may even lavish some of the care and concern which go into a good building 'joint-detail' on the creation of public spaces of joining.

Above left Expression of the point of juncture; detail of column capitol, the Propylea.[14]

Left Detail of concrete joinery; Salk Institute for Biological Studies, San Diego, California; Louis I. Kahn, architect.

Below left Inadequate buffer zone between an expressway and adjacent housing.
(Photo: Harvey Krasnegor)

Right Combined highway right-of-way and parkland; Meadowbrock Parkway, Long Island, New York.[15]

Below Design of a suburban arterial road and an adjacent centre for shopping, offices, and housing. Montgomery County Community Renewal Programme; Ueland and Junker, architects.

In the Montgomery County Study, the ideas described above were applied to various road types and roadside activities, and a design approach and prototype designs were suggested in each case. Despite dissimilar conditions, a unified architecture of the roadspace was sought through a consistent approach to the design of landscaping, traffic signs, street lighting, and various elements of street furniture. The following discussion and sketches illustrate some of the ideas which were proposed.

Expressways: Expressways were found to be generally well designed, with the exception of instances where the public rights-of-way were too narrow, and adequate distances or landscaped buffer zones could not be provided between the road and adjacent neighbourhoods. These shortcomings could be corrected in the future through the use of more generous right-of-way widths and landscaped areas. Where possible, broad areas of roadside landscaping could also serve as parkland for local communities, as they do on many parkways today.

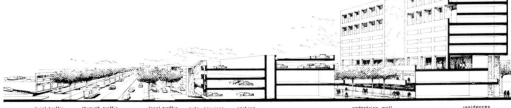

local traffic   through traffic   local traffic   auto services   parking   pedestrian mall   residences

Above The sketch on the preceding page shows a design for a suburban arterial road, while the sketch above shows the design of local roadspace for auto-oriented activities. Montgomery County Community Renewal Programme; Ueland and Junker, architects.

Outlying major roads with commercial frontage: In the areas of the country outside of the town centres, most shoppers and other users of commercial services arrive by car. In some instances shops are located close to the road, with parking provided in the rear, and in others stores are set back farther, with parking areas provided between the road and the store. The accompanying sketches (facing and above) illustrate the re-design of such a road, with both kinds of shop locations shown in the facing sketch. Note that the spaces between the through traffic lanes and the building frontages provide the key to improvements in the road environment.

In the facing sketch, reading from the centre of the road towards the buildings, the following can be seen: through traffic lanes in the centre of the road, with rows of trees separating these lanes from lanes for local traffic to the side; another row of trees comes next, and finally walks or access drives in front of the shops and garages. The local traffic lanes are for the special use of motorists using roadside services, allowing them to cruise more slowly, thereby eliminating the traffic conflicts which normally occur on such roads.

The left hand side of the street illustrates the condition where shops line the roadside. Such shops might be selling furniture, timber, new or used automobiles, or other heavy equipment for which people are likely to make a single, special-purpose shopping trip. These shops therefore relate directly to the road, with no need for pedestrian connections between them. Parking is in the rear, and parking access-drives pass between the shops as necessary. Building design controls are aimed at creating a 'wall' for the public street which is more ordered and continuous than one would probably find otherwise; and where a void might otherwise occur in the wall, a second roadside 'screen' wall might be erected to preserve its continuity. Private advertising signs, while visible from the road, are arranged so as to be oriented primarily toward local traffic lanes. Long-distance visibility and prominence is reserved for the more important public destinations, such as the 'gateway' public parking garage, or some other large centre of development.

The right hand side of the street illustrates the condition where shops are set back away from the street with parking in front, as they are around most suburban shopping centres. In this case more diverse activities such as offices and residences have been added to the older shopping centre, in keeping with current development trends as well as with efforts to expand the diversity of the newer centres discussed earlier. The added activities are built around the existing shops and internal pedestrian mall, and their presence now makes it economically possible to provide parking structures at the roadside, where open parking spaces had previously stood.

The left-hand sketch is a more detailed view of the roadscape within the space of joining. The local traffic lane is in the centre, separated by rows of trees from through traffic lanes on the left, and walks and minor access-drives occur on the right. Entrances to parking structures are visible from a distance through the use of large markers, in this case a garage stair tower with a large 'P' near its top. The location of garage entrances, bus stops, pedestrian pick-up points and major shopping complexes are identified for the driver through a co-ordinated system of markers, signs and symbols. Service-stations are shown located in the ground level of the parking structure, with their signs and advertising prominently displayed.

One of the probable weaknesses in the proposal is its dependence upon the use of trees. Trees take a long time to reach full maturity and are vulnerable to disease and neglect. Man-made elements must also be found which will provide a greater sense of amenity and order to the walls of such important public ways. Unified design of directional signs, lighting, pavements, utilities, and greater control of individual building-setbacks and heraldry may go a long way, but perhaps other possibilities for screening and giving shade and spatial definition will emerge in future studies.

Outlying major streets with residential frontage: Another common condition outside central districts occurs where major roads pass through residential areas. Unlike major commercial roads, where conflicts between local and through traffic require the provision of local service lanes, the principal problem with residential roads is the nuisance and danger which the road presents for the dwellers along it.

The sketch with high-rise housing (over) shows a landscaped space between the road and the buildings with the space of joining once again becoming the key to an improved roadside environment. Public walks, sitting areas and bicycle paths occur beneath the trees. Farther to the right, closer to the building, private walks and access-drives for building residents are located. In this instance the space of joining

the road for residents. Individual driveways do not open on to the highway, and homes face into the residential community. The side of the road functions primarily as a narrow, landscaped buffer zone; since here, unlike the conditions in the high-density residential neighbourhood, private and public open space and recreation areas are assumed to be plentiful within the residential community. In this case, elements in the buffer space are limited to trees, planting, street lights, signs, a small pedestrian walk, and gateway posts marking entrances to residential communities. As in the higher density example, the landscaping serves the visual enjoyment of motorist and resident alike.

Urban commercial streets: In most of the larger town areas in Montgomery County, shops are built in a continuous line alongside the sidewalk, and streets passing the shops carry heavy traffic. Shoppers are confined to a narrow strip of pavement between the shop front and the road, and service and park-

ing takes place both in front and in the rear of shops. In some cases it is possible to create new pedestrian shopping precincts in the middle of blocks, removed from traffic, but in most instances existing shops must remain, and ways must be found to improve the pedestrian environment.

One of the first steps towards improvement under such conditions is the construction of by-pass roads to remove disinterested through-traffic from the

Above Narrow sidewalk in downtown Silver Spring, Maryland.
(Photo: Harvey Krasnegor)

Below Roadspace for low density residential areas.

Above top Roadspace for high density residential areas. Montgomery County Community Renewal Programme; Ueland and Junker, architects.

Above Low density residential development along an arterial road.
(Photo: Harvey Krasnegor)

insulates living areas from road nuisances both through distance and buffer landscaping. It also expands the normal front courts of densely built-up structures into useful, boulevard-like community spaces, and provides pleasant views for residents and motorists.

In the sketch showing low density housing (right), homes are turned away from the main road since major street traffic is not compatible with low-density residential living, and the low volume of local traffic does not justify separate service lanes at the side of

Above Shop-front loading in downtown Silver Spring, Maryland.

Below Renewal of existing roadside shopping area.

Below bottom Detail of roadside treatment in downtown shopping street.

Above right Plan of typical downtown shopping street.

Below right Separation of pedestrians and traffic in densely developed downtown areas. All sketches from Montgomery County Community Renewal Programme; Ueland and Junker, architects.

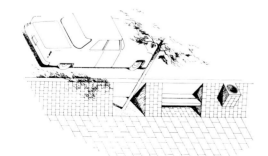

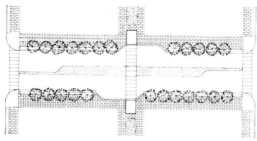

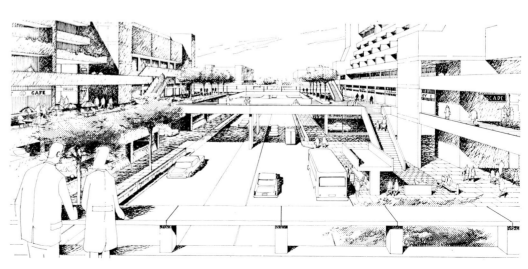

shopping streets. Once this is accomplished, cars on the streets can be slowed down to speeds more compatible with pedestrian activities, and portions of the present roadways can be given over to sidewalks. In the sketches of a typical town commercial street automobiles might have to stop at frequent intervals for pedestrian crossings. The plan shows pedestrian crossings at the corners and at midpoints in the block where they connect to footpaths leading to pedestrian shopping precincts in the block interiors. Special pavings mark the crossings more clearly for the pedestrian and motorist. Bus stops are located mid-way between corners to avoid interference with intersections.

The principal element in the space of joining is a continuous structure at the roadside which serves to provide a sense of protection for the pedestrian, limits street crossings to corners and mid-points of blocks, and eliminates uncontrolled discharge of

passengers from automobiles. The structure helps define the new pedestrian environment, and contains elements of landscaping and street furniture such as trees, lighting, benches and litter receptacles. Even certain utilities such as street lights and power lines are integrated into the structure, as shown in the detail sketch.

A second important public element in the sketch is the bus shelter which extends out over the sidewalk. Bus stops become increasingly important as the use of public transport is expanded to provide frequent town services and local shoppers' 'loops'. The structures provide shelter for people boarding and leaving buses, or waiting for buses to arrive. Because of their importance they are shown as the only structures which are built over public sidewalks. They serve as signposts, signalling points at which buses can be boarded, and provide poster-boards for useful public information.

A further aspect of the large sketch concerns coordination in building design. The shops in the sketch have had a new structure about an arm's length in depth built against their old facades. This simple addition tends to transform the older, individual shops into members of a newer, more unified shopping community. The structures also include sun screens, awnings, lighting and advertising, increasing their usefulness to shop owners as well as enriching the pedestrian environment.

The more densely developed areas in Montgomery County afforded additional opportunities for the solution of environmental problems. In Silver Spring, for example, roadside development is so intense, and traffic volumes so heavy, that multi-level areas of development have become possible in certain areas. In the accompanying sketch, traffic continues to pass through the heart of town development, but pedestrian activities are raised above the motor-ways. Two levels of pedestrian shopping activities occur above several levels of parking. In the foreground, footbridges connect pedestrian levels across the major street, and in the distance, shopping structures are shown spanning the street. The street itself is treated as a strictly automobile, non-pedestrian way, except where pedestrian activities connect with it in 'point' spaces of joining, such as in the bus station and shopping court shown at lower right. Housing, offices, hotels, etc., are built above the shopping levels, and share parking facilities and public open spaces with the shops below.

The Montgomery County Study is probably only a small inroad into what has yet to be understood about suburbia. Yet it afforded an opportunity to realize that many of the things we are fond of theorizing about – new community patterns, high speed movement, environmental information media . . . – already can be seen to exist in microcosm in suburbia. There, if we look, we can see people already dealing with these things, and adapting to modes of living and environmental forms which will become increasingly important in the future.

Architects and planners in this country have overlooked suburbia. In doing so, they have tended to cut themselves off from the major arena of environment-building in the future, and from new and exciting sources of ideas and inspiration. In the American suburb, one can see new prospects and read a whole series of new rules for the creation of the man-made environment. The resulting forms, objectively expressed, can lead to concepts of urban organization and settlement distinctly different from the unifocal and discreetly bounded cities of the past. In contrast to an artificially induced 'New Town' concept of growth through multiplication of separate settlements (with all its inefficiencies)[4] suburbia suggests ways in which our cities might grow as continuous entities fed by high-speed travel which even by conservative estimates will commonly allow fifty mile commuter-sheds in the forseeable future.[5] In these vast urban regions, where man may step into windowless carriers and emerge minutes later many miles away, Euclidian concepts of physical organization

will probably have limited meaning.[6] Instead, much will depend on the design of movement itself, and its systems of information, if people are to understand their environment and move about efficiently within it. We can see in the structure of suburbia, and the suburban road experience, hints of a possible urban environment of the future. If indeed it emerges in this country, it promises to be one hundred per cent American, growing out of the peculiar mobility, complexity and vitality of this nation. It will probably be big and sprawling, but it can be good to be in, too. And if as architects and planners we make an effort, we may even find a part to play in its creation.

Notes

1 Irene B. Taeuber, 'The Changing Population', *Urban Land,* vol. 26, No. 7, July-August, 1967. A recent article in the *New York Times* stated further that 90% of all vacant land in metropolitan areas across the nation available for housing development is outside the central cities, and that 80% of all new jobs in metropolitan areas, and virtually all new blue-collar manufacturing jobs, are in the suburbs. ('NAACP TO FIGHT SUBURBAN ZONING', page 1, 7th December 1969.)

2 This term, as it applies to architecture, has been popularized by Robert Venturi. The reader will recognize other debts to Mr Venturi in references to his ideas on 'complexity and contradiction', and 'both-and' versus 'either-or' solutions to complex problems.

3 George Rand, 'Pre-Copernican Views of the City', *Architectural Forum,* September 1969. Rand found that a sample of taxi drivers in Worcester, Massachusetts could . . . 'reverse routes, interrupt and continue them, over some detours . . . locate a point in space by its closeness to a given intersection without ever being forced to resolve certain blatant contradictions in their understanding of the relative position of places in the city space.' (p. 80).

4 Downs, Anthony, 'Alternative Forms of Future Urban Growth in the United States', *Journal of the American Institute of Planners,* vol. XXXVI, No. 1, January 1970.

5 Fleisher, Aaron, 'The Influence of Technology on Urban Forms', *Daedalus,* vol. 90, No. 1, Winter 1961. pp. 56–69.

6 Rand, *op. cit.,* p. 81. 'As we move into the age of

space-exploration, we begin to sense our own parochialism and rigidity. Travel at 18,000 mph? 240,000 miles? Are these numbers related to life on earth? Or is our conception of life on earth, our way of orienting ourselves in space and time, hopelessly restricted and about to undergo a revolution? How long can we persist in accepting the traditional distinction between illusion and reality? Or in fact, is the 'centre of the United States on its two coasts?' Are the suburbs in fact the city? From a Euclidean point of view these are stupid questions. The centre is the geographical centre. But the miracles of space travel may make such questions more meaningful.'

7 Source: Saalman, Howard, *Medieval Cities,* George Braziller, New York, 1968. illus. no. 22.

8 Source: Epps, Richard E., 'Suburban Jobs and Black Workers', *Business Review,* Federal Reserve Bank of Philadelphia, October 1969.

9 Frank Lloyd Wright, *The Living City,* Horizon Press, New York.

10 Saalman, op.cit., illus. no. 58

11 Source: Blumenfeld, Hans, 'The Modern Metropolis', *Scientific American,* Vol. 213, No. 3, September 1965.

12 Source: Davis, Kingsley, 'The Urbanization of the Human Population', *Scientific American,* Vol. 213, No. 3, September 1965.

13 Source: Tunnard, Christopher, and Pushkavev, Boris, *Man-Made America: Chaos or Control,* Yale University Press, New Haven, 1963, p.100.

14 Source: Le Corbusier, *Towards a New Architecture.*

15 Tunnard, op. cit., p.254.

ON POP ART, PERMISSIVENESS, AND PLANNING

DENISE SCOTT BROWN

Someone has called the nonjudgmental attitude the greatest invention of the twentieth century. Everywhere – in literature, the arts, the social sciences, the humanities, in planning, and now in architecture and urban design – it is making inroads; and in architecture, urban design, and planning it works for the better and is much kinder to people.

Perhaps Freud in our time initiated facing the unfaceable. The words 'nonjudgmental', 'permissive' and 'nondirective' relate first to psychiatry. Merton, borrowing functional analysis from the biologists, suggested that if activities which appear to be 'dysfunctional' continue to exist, they must obviously be functional for someone, ergo closing one's eyes and ordering them to go away won't remove them. Gans in a similar vein has shown how Levittown, hated by architects and berated by the upper classes, is much of what its occupants want, and that architectural diatribes on the uselessness of sociology and the immorality of sprawl won't make it go away. A generation of planners from the social sciences has made this its rallying cry, praising Los Angeles and the 'nonplace urban realm', denouncing the class biases and aesthetic hang-ups of the architecturally trained 'physical planner' and urban designer, and pushing for the reformation of the planning profession in a new image – their own.

The same thought in linguistics produced the 'nondirective' *Random House Dictionary of the English Language,* followed by an uproar from pedants in the name of the maintenance of standards. The movement has hit political science, education, social welfare, and public health, though maybe only at the outer edges; and in literature there are, among others, Gertrude Stein's effort to 'put some strangeness, something unexpected, into the structure of the sentence in order to bring back vitality to the noun,' and Tom Wolfe's attempt to evolve a prose style suitable to the description of Las Vegas.

In the arts the tradition is longer. Francis Bacon said, 'There is no excellent beauty that hath not some strangeness in the proportion'. The frisson that is engendered by trying to like what one does not like has long been known to be a creative one; it rocks the artist from his aesthetic grooves and resensitizes him to the sources of his inspiration. It may be achieved by breaking rules as did the Mannerists. Here the jolt comes from the unexpected use of a conventional element in an unconventional way, the arch with a column under its keystone, the classically detailed room with unclassical proportions. This effect might also come from use of a new and shocking source— Le Corbusier's photographs of western grain elevators and tops of ships managed to *épater* the bourgeois, to blow the minds of the citizens, of several continents for several years. But no longer. The revolution has been lost in its successes over the whole hard face of the metropolis. Today it is the ageing 'modern architects' who 'will not see'. Their neatness compulsion, as they design their multimillion dollar renewal projects or sit in judgment on the work of their colleagues in misnamed 'art commissions', deadens the environment and brings disarray to the lives of many.

In the fine arts a new horror-giving energy source has been discovered: the popular. This too is old. Beethoven doubtless once shocked the *salons* with his themes from folk tunes, but the Beatles have 'made it' into the intellectual elite, and Rauschenberg and Lichtenstein are on the cover of *Time.* Yet we are still outraged if an architect comes out for billboards or if a planner removes the emotion from his voice when talking of urban sprawl. The first has 'sold out to the crassest motivations in our society', and the second doesn't recognize chaos when he sees it. But architects and urban designers are, in fact, Johnnies-come-lately on this scene and can learn from others. From Edward Ruscha, for example. His *Twenty Six Gasoline Stations* are photographed straight: no art except the art that hides art. His *Some Los Angeles*

Good Year Tires, 6610 Laurel Canyon, North Hollywood, California. Photograph by Art Alanis in *Thirty-four Parking Lots* by Edward Ruscha, 1967.

Apartment Houses are the end-of-the-world, bridge-playing, walk-up, R-4, togetherness type, with the Tiki at the doorway and a pool in the patio. Ruscha's *Thirty Four Parking Lots,* photographed from a helicopter, resemble D'Arcangelo paintings: arrowed, tensioned, abstract diagrams where oil patterns on the asphalt reveal differential stress from differing accessibility. His *Sunset Strip,* a long, accordion fold-out, shows every building on each side of the Strip, each carefully numbered but without comment. Deadpan, a scholarly monograph with a silver cover and slip-on box jacket, it could be on the piazzas of Florence, but it suggests a new vision of the very imminent world around us.

Planners and urban designers should be leading the way since this vision is so pertinent to design in the city, but it is the moviemakers – for example, Antonioni in *La Notte,* *Red Desert* and *Zabriskie Point* and more artily in *Blow-Up* – who have investigated the architectural implications of the local scene. TV-commercial makers and billboard designers have stolen a long march on architects in the important area of the mixed use of words, symbols, and forms to reinforce each other for high-speed communication with a moving public.

Years ago, poets and collagists tried mixing high and low sources: Sweeney and Latin, bus tickets and a violin; and the Beatles do it today. But *we* lobby to remove the corner store (or at least the sight of it) from the campus, the gasoline station from beside the public building, and the billboard from the landscape. Our architecture becomes tidy, exclusive, and terribly irrelevant. Even the people, where possible, will scurry in 'urban concourses', underground.

Action painting, the use of the controlled accident, could re-animate urban design, but urban designers who admire the ordered variety of the architecture of the Dogon or the mill town, miss it in Levittown and design it out of Reston, where nothing is accidental, not the decorations in the shop windows, not the graffiti cast into the sculpture, and not the careful vistas which, as surely as the little Kodak arrows in Disneyland, say 'take my picture'.

Architects who buy Op Art should buy Los Angeles. It is the same even, open-ended system with multiple possibilities for the definition and redefinition of focus depending on where you're at. Sometimes the yellows shine brightest, sometimes the blues.

These new, more receptive, ways of seeing the environment, inspired by other sciences and arts, are almost desperately important to architects or planners who hope to stay relevant; and when the artistic fashions move on, we shall still be here because this pop

6565 Fountain Avenue, from *Some Los Angeles Apartments* by Edward Ruscha, 1965.

city, this *here,* is what we have. Despite Ladybird Johnson, it will not be swept under the rug; it needs, rather, a new Patrick Geddes to enter where 'neither Brahmin nor Briton' would penetrate, to document and analyse with loving respect, and to prescribe a conservative surgery based on the belief that there is pattern in the sprawl, order in the chaos.

This is not to abandon judgment, for planned action implies judgment. Judgment is merely deferred a while in order to make it more sensitive. Liking what you hate is exhilarating and liberating, but finally reaffirming for judgment.

Architects and urban designers have been too quickly normative. Where the facts and intangibles are many, a mystique or a system – a philosophy of Man and the Universe or a CIAM grid – may substitute for the collection of facts or for hard thought. This makes them poor scientists and, strangely enough, indifferent artists as well. Social scientists have been the opposite: measuring trends while Rome burns, sniffing at other people's 'values' when they should be recommending new norms for a new society. But all this is coming to an end. Architects and social scientists meet today in many fields, from social protest and advocacy to the analysis of the mass culture and its artifacts. Citizens' groups retain advocate-architects and urban designers as well as advocate-planners, and even in Europe where early

'modern' architectural authoritarianism is still strong, architects and urban designers are learning to put Los Angeles and Las Vegas on their travel itineraries as well as the denser areas of Manhattan, admired by Le Corbusier.

Young architects who confront social issues often abandon both architecture and urban design, frustrated by their irrelevance – as practised by many professionals – to real urban problems. They embrace instead social or systems planning, or projects which demand social and communal concern rather than professional service. This is wasteful and should be unnecessary. For the best thing an architect or urban designer can offer a new society, apart from a good heart, is his own skill, used *for* the society, to develop a respectful understanding of its cultural artifacts and a loving strategy for their development to suit the felt needs and way of life of its people. This is a socially responsible activity; it is, after all, what Gans and the pop artists are doing.

El Paso, Winslow, Arizona, from *Twenty-six Gasoline Stations* by Edward Ruscha, 1962.

TEN RULES FOR PLANNERS

THEO CROSBY

The nineteenth century saw the growth of industry and the adaptation of a rural proletariat to the requirements of technology: cheap, manipulable, stable and interchangeable labour that would also provide a docile market for the resulting products. The materialist philosophies of capitalism and Marxism powered action from both ends of the social scale towards the same goal, a goal precisely in time with the needs of technology.

The years before the first war were the heroic period, savouring the first fruits of technology: electricity, radio, the first airplanes, the great steamships, a worldwide railway network. The rich enjoyed these new luxuries at a moment of perfect balance, in an environment enriched by centuries of civilized endeavour. Noble buildings (for noble men), noble cities, combined at that moment with noble aspirations about the benefits of technology.

The war spread these benefits and pushed technology into the next phase: mass production, centralized control through the growth of massive self sustaining organizations, and an increasingly interventionist role for the State in the daily life of its citizens.

The first war also destroyed the assumptions of a settled, hierarchic society, and opened the way for a new breed of man: meritocrats and adventurers whose loyalties were not to a social order, but to their pro-

ducts, their technology, their sales figures.

All the evil tendencies of big capitalism which were evident in the twenties and thirties (and were noted and attacked by Shaw, Huxley and many others) were greatly reinforced by the massive growth of technology during the second war. Today the effect of the acceleration of technology (and its concentration into ever fewer hands) begins to be visible in every tiny part of our lives: our food, our streets, even in the way we perceive. The exciting adventures of the few in that golden age, the new comforts and the easy travel, are now the normality of the many. On the other hand, things which were once the preoccupation of the masses, such as religious observance, are now nonexistent. The effects of these changes begin now, after a suitable time lag, to work themselves through into the physical environment.

Much of this change is good: the growth of personal income, wider involvements, higher education. The possibility of each one of us being able to grow one's self without immovable material limitations is more real now than at any time in history. The possibility, too, of almost infinite experience (travel, sensation, involvement) is also within almost everyone's grasp. (That is, in Europe and North America, where these technological changes are most fully worked out). Yet there are prices to be paid: the logic of productivity is endless increase, of everything, for ever and ever. The possibility of stabilizing at *enough* seems remote. In terms of material objects in the environment: houses, cars, television sets, there is inevitably endless pressure to buy, or to replace everything, just to keep up the flow of production.

Thus cities, which had grown by the kind of piecemeal adaptation and gradual improvement which was the norm until the twentieth century, find themselves hastily gutted for short-term profits. Present financing and tax arrangements work sharply against the preservation of good buildings and the creation of new ones which can compare with those of the eighteenth and nineteenth centuries. We have all become familiar with the featureless commercial blocks replacing the streets of inventive and humanly scaled houses, which made up our old environments.

These blocks have their origin deep inside the modern movement, which was itself the adaptation of architectural theory to the requirements of technology. The modern movement was born at the turn of the century, in the springtide of industrialization, and it joined the mainstream of social reform and responsibility to the possibilities of technology. Through technology we intended to conquer the social evils of poverty and ignorance. Several generations have dedicated them-

selves to this proposition. Sixty years later we stand surrounded by the evidence of this great theoretical drive and can begin to assess what has been achieved, and to grope for new initiatives.

We can see that the slums are mostly gone (at least in Western Europe); there are schools everywhere (not enough perhaps, but a great many); factories are no longer dark or satanic, through the blessings of fluorescent light. We see around us vast housing estates, hygienic blocks of identical minimum dwellings within which the newly affluent strive to crowd their material possessions. These buildings faithfully follow the diagrams in the Bauhaus primers; their spacing and grouping reflect the reformer's distrust of streets, of the old urbanity with its numberless tempting pubs and shops. They reflect also the necessities

Middle The remains of civilized neighbourhoods in need of protection.

Below We begin to value the lively, complex experience afforded by the 19th-century street, at the very moment of its obliteration by the supermarket and the superblock.

of mass production, and economies of scale so dear to our century. Above all, they reflect an ideal of social equality. Only the trained eye can select those subtle nuances that differentiate the worker's dwelling from that of the rising executive.

This, through the inevitable time lag of the building operation, is a demonstration of a situation already made obsolete by changing technology, and becomes the physical baseline for our present situation. Those splendid housing estates or subdivisions of the fifties and sixties now house a new generation whose violent reactions to them form an entirely new problem. This is primarily a problem of identity: in a world of interchangeable equals one's identity is minimal, and anyway constantly threatened by intangible organizations, all equally faceless and bureaucratic. The reaction to a fantasy world, or rejection of the real, is inevitable in a world without external fantasy, without props or markers. The architects' role in this cultural dilemma is limited. He is the merest creature of the

Zeitgeist, propping his own tweedy identity with fantasies of power and social regeneration. His tried and true programmes, however, prevent the possibility of any radical change, and pressures of economy inhibit experiment. In any case little can be changed through a physical solution.

One

In such a situation we need a tactical holding operation to produce the political, social and economic strategies that might heal the cultural dilemma.

In the environment we must hold to what we have and oppose change brought about simply for short-term profit. The reaction of the public in many countries against the effects of property speculation is the most healthy sign for many years. The preservation of old buildings, of anything that provides an example of another way of life, should be a prime social objective. Such buildings now provide us with much needed elements of identity in a city, but more important, they

Left to right This brief sequence shows how the introduction of superblock scale brings drastic reductions in street amenity. On the left of the third photograph we see the remains of the 19th-century street front; on the right an expression of the scale of the new collectivity.

provide obstacles to the casual obliteration of whole areas that is now technologically desirable. If a planner is presented with a series of untouchable elements his reaction to the situation is inevitably more complex and intelligent than when presented with a clean slate. In the latter case he turns to elementary geometry and current styling. Given a series of old buildings to incorporate he can work within their scales and rhythms, to create that continuity of experience which is the joy of cities.

Rule one: Accept and delight in the past for its disruptive, its poetic, role in the present.

Top The new scale, showing precious little attention to foreground detail.

Middle and below The introduction of the new scale erodes the street.

Two

In those newer areas where technology has run its course, the housing estate now bursting with unplanned-for vehicles, the subdivisions of little boxes on the city outskirts, we shall need to create elements of identity.

Identity grows through variety.

The first need is to create a variety of uses, of ownerships and of involvements outside the communications media.[1] Physical environment is greatly affected by ownership, the pure sensation of possession. A house or object is always more cared-for than something borrowed, given, or hired. Personal identity largely comes from possessions and we must create, in public authority housing projects, the possibility of ownership and community involvement. The experience of Span, the British housing group, is instructive in this context. Given their middle income market, they could not include adequate private gardens for the small houses they provided, because the land would be so cut about with fences as to be impossibly unsightly. They solved the problem by selling 99-year leases, pooling the garden areas and leaving only a tiny patch for each house. Each owner is a member of the committee which is responsible for the maintenance of the gardens and the regular painting of the houses and garages. At a stroke a communal involvement has been created, which also automatically ensures a high level of environmental maintenance.

In such a context the next stage of increasing identity, the individuation of separate groupings, becomes possible. Joint actions can provide communal facilities as they become popular, as a reflection of higher living standards: saunas and swimming pools, party rooms, studios and workshops, sculptures and fountains. Without a communal responsibility and the sense of ownership, these elements are inevitably vandalized out of protest or boredom.

Rule two: Involvement of people in their environment as owners, possessors, is essential to the growth of identity, in the person, and in the place.

Three

While certain areas of technology bring a high return on capital investment, those areas, such as oil, electronics or transport, set the economic tone for a culture. The construction industry, where returns are low,[2] is under enormous pressure to improve productivity. This is done mainly by stringent economies, substitution of cheaper materials, and the elimination of frills. Fortunately the modern movement had a slogan ready for just this occasion, and constantly demanded the elimination of decoration. Buildings based on the ideal of economy ('maximum cover, minimum weight' or 'less is more') result inevitably in anonymity, because they inevitably rely on endless repetition of a single, simple unit. This seldom endears them to their occupants.

Rule three: Posterity will not be grateful for our small economies.

Four

It is a characteristic irony of our time that we have more artists and art schools, more people trained in the visual arts than at any time in history, and that they are quite uninvolved with our daily surroundings. The latter become every year more ugly; cities once famous for their beauty are despairingly accepted as 'ruined'; vast areas of landscape and sea coast have been carelessly despoiled as if by blind giants.

The artists are nicely segregated into the art galleries or put to work on the magazines or in television studios. The advertisements in any issue of *Vogue* contain infinitely more visual expertise than any new town can display, yet the involvement of any of this talent in the environment is never contemplated.

It is largely due to the changing order of patronage. In a highly taxed society the individual is unable to pay for works of art on a public scale. Government and the corporations, by their corporate nature, seldom have the nous or talent for patronage. Besides, they are always pleased to make an obvious economy, and the arts are, in the short term, always expendable. The public and private bureaucracies have thus done very little.

As a result we have bred, for the first time in thirty centuries, a generation of artists who have no experience of public art; who are so conditioned by the requirements of commercial galleries for the bizarre and extraordinary, as to be quite out of touch with the ordinary public. The separating, specializing requirements of technology have thus demonstrably spread over the most precious elements of our whole society. To cure such a primary cultural unbalance requires a large social investment, now.

Rule four: Public art is cultural insurance. Buy now. The artists need the money – and the practice.

Five

City growth is inseparable from general cultural tendencies. While the primary function of cities (conversation, communal enterprise) is undermined by technology we can expect no growth in the same format as in the past. Technology simplifies problems in order to understand them. We have simplified our cities (the 'four functions' of CIAM's Athens Charter:

Above The small-scale elements which once made up our cities.

housing, industry, leisure, transport) and have now discovered that it was the mutual interaction of these, and many other 'trace' elements, which made them work. By taking the organism apart, we have extinguished its life. By forcing 'adequate' areas of open space into overcrowded districts we have often increased social violence, and produced social sterility. Most of the data on open space requirements are therefore many years obsolete, belonging to a period when participation in sport was a mechanism for transcending the barriers of class, or when allotment gardening was considered an adequate weekend occupation for working fathers. Today sport is, like everything else, highly professional and television keeps fathers off the streets and out of the pubs.
Rule five: Grass is the enemy of cities.

Six

The Athens Charter, by raising transport to the level of a major urban activity, at once recognized and sanctified a new, independent and unpredictable force in the city. This first breach in the theoretical wall has allowed the flood of automobiles to sweep us and our cities away. By forcing adequate roads into our city centres, we have destroyed the very places we intend to visit.

Above all the automobile is an obviously primitive and dangerously inefficient vehicle, gulping our oxygen and killing our children on the roads.

We must hold the situation until a more suitable vehicle is produced, silent, non-polluting, and capable of social control. The strategy should be to tax cars, petrol and parking, and spend heavily on sophisticated public transport.
Rule six: The private car must be reduced to the status of a luxury.

Seven

The control of architectural form in cities is governed (in the UK) by plot ratios, light angles and such quasi-scientific methods, which were supposed to liberate the designer. In practice they produce precisely the forms considered desirable by the organizers of the legislation; stumpy blocks camping in a sea of asphalt. At least this misguided legislation has led us to appreciate and revaluate the street, and the mandatory cornice heights and facing materials that were the simple methods of building control in the past. The delusive freedom offered by the current regulations produces vast awkward profiles whose painful presences obtrude on every skyline; they appear everywhere, carelessly spoiling views carefully contrived during the centuries.
Rule seven: Buildings over 20m in height begin to exert effects far beyond the immediate environment. Their position, and above all, their girth should be rigidly controlled.

Eight

In our passion for economy, we have used the various regulations (e.g. permissible distances to fire stairs) as economic determinants. Modern buildings are therefore always as large as possible, to squeeze the maximum advantage from the particular set of rules operating at the moment. Most buildings are thus simply too big for their architects. Where once a street was an encounter with many minds, now a single mind is stretched over a whole block. The technology already available allows a single mind to be spread over several square miles.

In a situation without technological limitation, a civilized society must invent a set of rules for decent behaviour.
Rule eight: the 10 metre rule: no architect should be allowed to deal with more than 10 metres of frontage. This distance contains all the architectural problems; anything more is always solved by mere repetition.

Nine

Those countries with wide land-use controls have undoubtedly benefited enormously in recent times. The British countryside, though ravaged, has not been destroyed, as have large areas of the USA. Negative controls have prevented the worst excesses of speculation and exploitation in the countryside, and retained an asset of immense touristic, social and psychological value.

They must stay.

Positive planning is much more difficult, because local authorities lack finance and know-how to intervene in their own town centres. Thus they are forced to auction off their statutory powers to the highest bidder: the developer whose profits depend on increasingly large-scale operations. Where a small firm might make a significant architectural contribution in a city, the developer wishes to deal only with a giant corporation or supermarket chain which will lease his whole speculative building with the ieast trouble. This administrative convenience carries a heavy price, of boredom and triviality, which is paid by the public.

The basic elements are the cost, the difficulty of acquisition of land, and the very great differentials in city values. Most land is too cheap, and is thus used carelessly. The planner's task is to equalize values. For this he needs access to capital.
Rule nine: Planning without ownership, without direct involvement, is inevitably fragmentary and frustrating.

Ten

No plan can hope to succeed unless those planned are thoroughly committed to it. Plans are easy but implementation is always difficult. Long years of involvement and persuasion are necessary. In areas where compulsion forms an element of the plan (in public authority housing for example) the result is often a diminution of the quality of life, and resentment is externalized in the treatment of the environment. Elegant new housing is often reduced to a shambles, occasionally through no fault of the architect.

He never knows his clients, only the housing committee, and is seldom able to learn anything from them afterwards. The result is the endless repetition of elementary mistakes, of standards methods and forms, for new information seldom percolates into the system.

Yet this is an area where technology is capable of contributing something other than simplification. We are beginning to be able to handle very large quantities of data, and at last the possibility of individual choice in the environment might be considered, rather than the current reliance on statistical averages. We have used our technology always to bring material economies, to reduce individual decisions; and seldom considered the social gains that come from increased involvement, in work and in everything else. *Rule ten:* Someone has to live in it. What if it were you?

Notes

1 US televiewing now averages six hours daily. Milton Eisenhower report 1968.

2 Contracting firms in Great Britain generally make profits of under 5% on the capital involved.

Right The effect of skylines is critical in a street; these are late 19th-century shops.

BARRIERS AND CHANNELS FOR HOUSING DEVELOPMENT IN MODERNIZING COUNTRIES

JOHN C. TURNER

To suggest that planning and building codes designed to improve and maintain modern housing standards have the opposite effect in many parts of the world may seem heretical. While preparing a paper for the United Nations on the subject,[1] however, I found that experience in many developing countries indicates that they do. The planning concepts derived from the experience of modernized countries are frequently inapplicable under circumstances typical in the modernizing countries. It thus is clear that the question should be discussed widely and openly.

The argument, briefly, is that the principle of 'minimum modern standards' is based on three assumptions; that high structural and equipment standards take precedence over high space standards; that households can and should move when their social-economic status has changed so that they can afford to have a larger (above minimum) standard dwelling; and that the function of the house is, above all, to provide a hygienic and comfortable shelter. While these assumptions are valid in the United States, Europe, and the USSR, they do not hold true for such countries as Peru, Turkey, and the Philippines.

Observations of what ordinary families in urbanizing countries do, when they are free to act as they will, show that they prefer to live in large unfinished houses – or even larger shacks – rather than in small finished ones. As Patrick Geddes wrote half a century ago in India: "I have to remind all concerned (1) that the essential need of a house and family is *room* and (2) that the essential improvement of a house and family is *more room*.'[2] The typical family, earning an uncertain wage in an unstable economy which provides little or no social security, depends heavily on property for security – especially while undergoing transition from the status of recently to fully urbanized.[3] For such families, the vast majority in the cities of urbanizing countries, housing is a 'vehicle of social change'.[4] Geographic stability is thus often the agent of social mobility rather than the reverse, which is more generally true in the fully participating sectors of modern society. I have never come across home-building in *barriadas* of the kind described in this article where families were not building for their children and where the builders did not also hope and expect their children to achieve a higher social status.

Charles Abrams, who has observed squatters in every continent, notes that 'when tenure seems secure the foundations are made firmer'.[5] Thus squatters are 'less worried about what they will build than where they will build it and less concerned about initial standards than about initial layout. *Rancho* houses (squatter houses) will improve with time and with better economic conditions if the *rancheros* are given a stake.'[6] Few planners and administrators agree with Abrams yet, but even fewer of the ordinary people would disagree. Secure possession of land where they can live *now* is far more important to them than the promise of a modern house that may never materialize. But given the land and the right circumstances – that is, adequately located, properly planned and the secure title – experience has shown that development to contemporary standards will surely take place, even if slowly.

The imposition of modern minimum standards on popular urban housing in a transitional economy is an assault on the traditional function of housing as a source of social and economic security and mobility. By requiring a heavy financial outlay initially and by leaving little room for the investment of non-monetary resources, modern standards delay the processes of urban settlement and resettlement and aid slum landlords and land speculators. Unattainable standards increase the demand for and the cost of slum housing and worsen slum conditions. By eliminating all low income and many middle income groups from the market, such standards encourage the tendency to invest in unused building land rather than in housing construction.

In cities where the majority of the population live in slums and cannot build needed houses because they cannot afford the costs of land and construction, it is hardly surprising to find that a great deal of urban settlement and resettlement takes place independently of the legislative and commercial systems. The experiences of certain Peruvian cities are typical of urbanizing countries. During the past twenty-five years the population of Lima has trebled from less than 700,000 in 1940 to an estimated 2,100,000 today. In the same period, the squatter population has grown from an unrecorded and relatively insignificant number in 1940 to a conservative current estimate of 25%. As in other urbanizing countries, the situation in provincial cities is even more alarming. In Arequipa, the second largest city of Peru with a population of approximately 200,000, 50% are reported to be living in the *urbanizacions populares,* clandestine lower-middle and working-class subdivisions, almost entirely on marginal desert land belonging to the State. In 1960, on the basis of a fairly thorough analysis of a previous census and a sample survey, I estimated that only 22 to 23% of the urban population at that time was then resident in this kind of settlement.

With squatter settlement growth rates of 12% or more per annum in Mexico, Turkey, and the Philippines as well as in Peru and many other countries – double that of city growth as a whole – it is hardly exaggerating to say that city development is out of control. During the past two decades the major towns and cities of Peru have trebled in area and population; they now represent approximately 30% of the country's total population. Two-thirds of this recent growth, (about 10% of the population or 1,000,000 people) is composed of squatters who have done more city building in terms of settlement than has been achieved during the previous 400 years.[7] So, in spite of the increasing realization of the necessity for urban planning, and the great need for an orderly infrastructure for economic development, city growth in the urbanizing two-thirds of the world is becoming increasingly chaotic.

'This absence of a central concern for the city's role is related to the deepening crisis that cities in all parts of the world are facing; massive unemployment, squatting and squalor in the developing pre-industrial countries; ... Consequently, the city is a poor habitat, not only for man but for industry and trade. Chaotic in form and destructive socially, the mushrooming urban disarray creates a new impediment to economic growth.'[8]

The hypothesis on which the arguments of this article are based is explicit in the claim that the standards required by the authorities (and practised by institu-

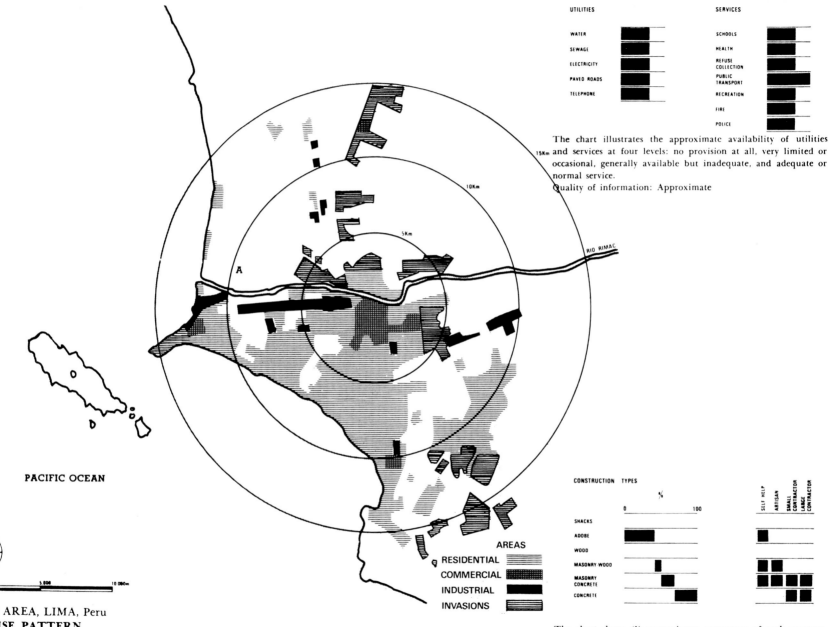

UTILITIES

WATER
SEWAGE
ELECTRICITY
PAVED ROADS
TELEPHONE

SERVICES

SCHOOLS
HEALTH
REFUSE COLLECTION
PUBLIC TRANSPORT
RECREATION
FIRE
POLICE

The chart illustrates the approximate availability of utilities and services at four levels: no provision at all, very limited or occasional, generally available but inadequate, and adequate or normal service.
Quality of information: Approximate

15Km

10Km

5Km

RIO RIMAC

A

PACIFIC OCEAN

AREAS

RESIDENTIAL
COMMERCIAL
INDUSTRIAL
INVASIONS

CONSTRUCTION TYPES

%

0   100

SELF HELP
ARTISAN
SMALL CONTRACTOR
LARGE CONTRACTOR

SHACKS
ADOBE
WOOD
MASONRY WOOD
MASONRY CONCRETE
CONCRETE

RBAN AREA, LIMA, Peru
ND-USE PATTERN
rces: Planos de los Municipios Distritales de Lima y
        Alrededores, 1965
lity of information: Approximate

The chart shows (1) approximate percentage of each construction type within the total number of dwellings and (2) building group that generally produces each type.
Quality of information: Approximate

tional and capitalist enterprise) conflict with the demands of the mass of urban settlers. The loss of administrative control over urban settlement and the frequently chaotic conglomerations of inadequate structures which make up the greater part of contemporary city growth in the modernizing countries are a product of the gap between the values and norms required by the governing institutions and those imposed on the people by the circumstances in which they live. The greater the gap between the nature of the officially recognized supply of housing and the nature of the popular demand, and the greater the demand in relation to the police power exercised by the authorities, the greater is the proportion of uncontrolled settlement.[9]

Case Study of a Barriada: The Invasion

The best and perhaps the only way to illustrate these principles is to describe the situations which have led to their formulation. The following description is a composite case study very largely based on one particular squatter settlement on the outskirts of Lima. Pampa de Cuevas is perhaps the nearest thing to a model *barriada* of its type. Established fairly recently (in 1960), in a more than usually favourable, but otherwise typical location, the settlement has a population of approximately 12,000. Cuevas is one of the type of *barriadas* populated by families moving out of the city slums, where the adults have lived about ten years before moving. Many of them are of recent previous provincial origin, but are not in the lowest income groups and are not without some urban experience.[10] This contrasts with another basic *barriada* type, formed by people with very low incomes and living standards, whether the urban-born poor or rural immigrants, and the commercially established tenement slums which have much higher densities and are almost always located near employment centres. Settlements of these latter types serve as 'bridgeheads' or urban toe-holds, enabling the very poor to live cheaply and to obtain work more easily by living within walking distance of principal markets and employment areas. Cuevas, which is not within walking distance of either, is an unsatisfactory location for down-and-outs or for ambitious but still very poor migrants.

The great majority of its inhabitants are young families with more or less steady incomes. They are poor but represent the average rather than the below average wage-earning sectors and, as the rate of physical improvement of the average dwelling indicates, they have maintained an appreciable rate of upward mobility.[11] I am not, therefore, about to describe

a version of the classic shantytown: '. . . the rudest kind of slum, clustering like a dirty beehive around the edges of any principal city in Latin America' where 'living almost like animals, the *tugurio*'s residents are overwhelmed by animality. Religion, social control, education, domestic life are warped and disfigured'.[12] Cuevas, along with at least two thirds of the *barriadas* of Peru, the majority of the *colonias proletarias* of Mexico City, or of the *Gecekondu* of Ankara, can be more appropriately described as self-improving suburbs than as 'slums'.[13]

The history of a settlement must begin with a description of the original settlers and their motives for settlement. As is now clear, the necessity of squatting may occur in quite different circumstances in the same city or at different stages in the life of the same family: The recently arrived migrant may be forced to squat if unable to find or afford other accommodation or, on the other hand, the wage-earning family that cannot afford tolerable accommodation or that desperately needs the security of home-ownership may also be forced to squat if there is no alternative.[14] The great majority of Cuevas settlers were motivated by the desire to escape the tyranny and insecurity of paying high rents for miserably poor conditions. For the average family of five or six with an average monthly income of about $90 (United States dollars) there are only two legal alternatives: to wait until the family's income has risen sufficiently (or until it has accumulated sufficient savings) to buy and build in the lowest-priced subdivisions, or to wait for the chance to get a subsidized government project house. Many families, for reasons explained below, reject the latter alternative, even when they are among the small minority to whom the opportunity is presented. The great majority prefer the illegal alternative of squatting if the prospects of obtaining *de facto* possession are good, even if very considerable sacrifices must be made to get a plot of land and to build.

The original Cuevas settlers, about 500 adults from different parts of Lima, formed the 'Asociación de Padres de Familia Pro-Viviendo', a community association for housing, in December, 1959. Just how this

Right 'Invasion' sequences.
Above Police throw tear-gas bombs against the first wave of squatters at Pampa el Angel, Lima.
Middle Angel invaders, following ejection by the police, wait while their leaders negotiate below.
Below Cuevas invaders, similarly thrown out, camp on a nearby railroad beneath a banner reading *Union de Madres Necessitades*— 'Union of Needy Mothers'. (Photos: Carretas Magazine, Lima, Peru)

Above Following negotiations with the police, a committee member of the Angel invaders is typing out allocations for the occupation of lots drawn up after surveys and subdivisions by sympathetic engineering students. Already the first primitive shelters, made of straw mats and poles, have been erected.
(Photo: Carretas Magazine, Lima)

Below People receive water rations pumped from a truck while another truck, in the background, brings further supplies of mats and poles.
(Photo: La Prensa, Lima)

particular group was formed I do not yet know,[15] but the case of El Ermitano, adjacent to Cuevas, is typical. The Ermitano association was organized by a self-appointed committee in 1962 which claimed to be the successors of an earlier association that in 1945 had applied to the ministry of Public Works for permission to develop the land the new association intended to invade. Having received no answer, the organizing committee maintained a certain claim to the land, even though it was somewhat tenuous and of a moral rather than legal character. It was enough, however, to guarantee the support of the 'Frente Unico de las Barriadas del Peru' – a confederation of *barriada* associations which commanded some political support and lobbying influence. With moral reinforcement and the probability of some political support, a group with access to a good site and with enough members to provide sufficient funds (to defray expenses and to compensate the organizers for their efforts) would be ready and prepared to invade if no other course is open to them.

The Cuevas invasion took place the night of 17th November, 1960. The police forced them off the land and the invaders, several hundred men, women, and children, camped along a nearby railway embankment while their leaders negotiated with the authorities. The government was particularly anxious to avoid further invasion at that time because it was about to promulgate a law designed to prevent further invasions and squatting by providing low-cost building land.[16] The owner of the adjacent land, a wealthy man with political influence, was also strongly opposed to the invasion which he saw as a threat to his property. Future events justified his fears. The invaders were allowed, however, as a 'temporary measure' to set up an encampment on a part of the land on Christmas Eve, five weeks later.

Either unknown by the authorities, or disregarded by them, the association contracted five topographers (elsewhere reported to have been students of civil engineering) to set out the blocks and individual plots. The plots were to have been 10 by 20 metres (about 2,000 square feet), but the majority were in fact only 8 by 16.5 metres. The association paid about $1,000 for the work, which took two months to complete. Ostensibly, the permission granted to the invaders to camp on the land was strictly temporary and was to allow time for the allocation of an alternative site. Over Christmas it was hardly humane – or even politic – to let so many apparently desperately poor families continue to live in the open. The families themselves, or their leaders, had timed the operation well and had correctly calculated that, once on the land, they would

have *de facto* possession. The invaders, therefore, were prepared to risk their funds for the layout plan and, as soon as it was completed each family transferred its temporary shack (made from woven cane mats wired to a light bamboo frame) to the plot allocated to it by the organizers.

During the first five weeks, the squatters had lived, literally, in the open. Although it was during the summer, when there is no precipitation in the Lima area, camping with no equipment to speak of was a considerable hardship. But, given the hope of a building plot of acceptable size on level land reasonably near the city and adjacent to a public transport route, a large number of people were prepared to sit it out indefinitely, rather than return, defeated and demoralized, to the city slums and high rents from which they had escaped. As soon as the encampment on the site was established, the association organized a school which provided primary education to adults as well as to children, and many set up shops for vermicelli, candles, inca-cola, and other essentials. At first everything, including water, had to be carried up a footpath, but once the families had moved to their own plots an access road was made through the cultivated land which separated the site from the main road, in spite of the landowners' protests. Shortly after the invasion many certainly felt themselves to be far better situated than they had been in the slums.

Even with such primitive beginnings, a major part of their housing needs were satisfied. In the first place, each family had a fair sized plot of land rent free and with little or no fear of eviction. In terms of space, sunlight, and unpolluted air their shacks were a vast improvement over the dark, unventilated, and crowded rooms on narrow, smelly and noisy slum courts. There are hardships and expenses in Cuevas, such as having to buy water from doubtful sources at exorbitant rates (usually about 15 US cents per gallon drum). The lack of electric light reduces the opportunity for social life and study and increases a sense of physical insecurity (although there seems to be far less violence in the *barriadas* than in the city itself). On the other hand, the absence of the extremely inadequate number of poorly maintained communal toilets with which the slum courts are equipped is of little or no disadvantage when there is plenty of space for individual pit latrines. Transportation cost for the family as a whole is generally greater than before but the extra cost rarely surpasses the saving made on rent as long as there are primary schools and basic shopping facilities in or near the settlement itself. So, even for the minority of families whose cash expenditures are slightly greater than before (through having to buy water or spending more on fares) the net gain in improved conditions is generally appreciable and with regard to personal security it is invariably considerable.

Tenure and Community Development

As the security provided by the possession of a home-site is the settlers' first concern, top priority is given to action that will consolidate tenure. If there is no way of obtaining title legally and at short notice, and if the precedents show that, once settled, land of low value is rarely reclaimed, then the surest way of ensuring permanent tenancy is to settle firmly on the land. The squatter associations therefore demand that their members build as soon as they take possession of their allocated plots, so all who can do so, even if it is only to place some foundations. A current anecdote in Lima tells how the government sent bulldozers to clear an invasion of cane matting shacks. The first flimsy shack approached, however, stopped the bull-dozer dead in its tracks. It concealed a solidly built structure of reinforced concrete. Though probably no more than a fable, the moral is nonetheless clear.

Apart from building to consolidate tenure – and invest savings before there are further increases in the cost of building materials – there is, of course, the need for a permanent house. The possible sequences of operations and orders of priority between the components of the dwelling structure[17] will be largely determined by the climate and the economic situation or expectations of the settler. Where there is little or no rainfall, as in Lima, it may be more appropriate to enclose the plot with a perimeter wall than to build two or three rooms with permanent roofs. The perimeter wall provides privacy and an improved micro-climate in which the discomforts of a shack are greatly reduced; the family is no longer pestered by neighbours' dogs and children, it is more secure against pilfering, and has, in effect, a spacious living area, even if the rooms are temporary shacks.

During a discussion of priorities of services and structures, one of the leaders of the Cuevas *barriada* argued forcefully for first maintaining perimeter walls until public utilities were installed, then building a bathroom unit, and only after that, beginning the rest of the structure.[18] This man, the secretary of the *barriada* association, felt that it was important to invest first in the improvement and installation of community facilities, then in public utilities, and finally in individual structures. Most *barriada* settlers, however, would give the dwelling structure – the first few rooms anyway – a higher priority than the installation of public utilities. But judging from the results of a series of conversations held in Cuevas, most settlers evi-

74

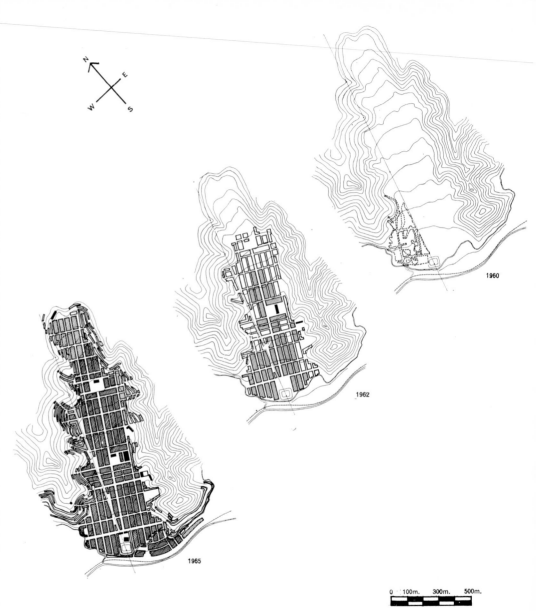

The development of Cuevas from 1960 to 1965

75

dently place as high or even a higher priority on the provision of community facilities or services such as schools, markets, meeting rooms, medical facilities, a parochial centre, and a police post than they do on the completion of their own dwellings. These facilities and services, even more than public utilities (with the possible exception of electricity), are a greater asset than a finished house. Observations of what settlers do in fact agitate for and attempt to install, support the statement of the United Nations Ad Hoc Committee on Housing in its report of 21st February 1962: 'From the family's perspective,... housing is not "shelter" or "household facilities" alone, but comprises a number of facilities, services and utilities which link the individual and his family to the community.' [19]

While the order in which community services and public utilities have been installed – or attempted – has been partly determined by economic, technical, or administrative practicality, there is a close correspondence between the actual programme of operations and the 'practical ideal' formulated by the community housing-group mentioned above. The indispensable components were provided, albeit crudely, at the very start. Even before the settlers moved on to their own plots they had a water supply, public transportation (at the main road), an elementary school, retail facilities, and basic shelter (in the encampment). In 1962, about eighteen months after the invasion, a permanent primary school, a medical post, a police post, and a chapel had been built. (The latter guaranteed regular visits from priests of a particularly active and highly regarded foreign missionary order.) In the following year a secondary school was established and the area became a separate parish with resident clergy. In 1963 the association also contracted with a private entrepreneur for the installation of electricity. The

Above left The first settlement of Cuevas, late 1960.
(Photo: Aerofotografico Nacional, Lima)

Left Cuevas in 1962, see middle map opposite. The preliminary settlement shown in the first photograph is immediately below the camera. In the background, centre, is a plaza with a school and community building, built by the people with the assistance of a group of missionary priests. Another school, on the north-west edge of the settlement, is temporarily built from woven cane mats; and this reappears in the next photograph, rebuilt by the government.
(Photo: Alberto Rojas, Junta Nacional de la Vivienda, Lima)

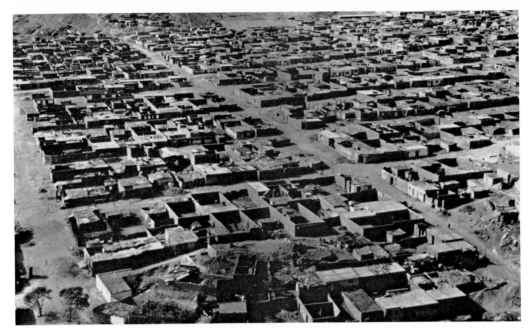

system was installed and put into operation for a short time with generators powered by a second-hand diesel ship's engine. Unfortunately there was a disagreement with the contractor who eventually withdrew his equipment at considerable loss to himself as well as to the inhabitants of Cuevas. Since then the only electricity available has been from small generators installed by individuals who supply current (at about $2.00 per 50 watt lamp per month) to their immediate neighbours. In 1964 the government installed a provisional water supply but this had not yet been put into operation by the fall of 1965. During 1964 and 1965 the government built several additional schools and a private clinic. A land use survey made in June, 1965[20] revealed a total of 218 retail shops (mostly very modest businesses of more social than economic value) and 14 artisan workshops. Dressmakers', dentists', and electricians' signs, among others, can be seen today. A sample of the dwelling structures surveyed showed that permanent construction had been started on 80% of the plots and 42% had walls completed to roof height. Only 9%, however, had a finished first floor structure and only 2% had started second floor structures.

In 1965 Cuevas became the centre of a new municipality incorporating two adjacent settlement areas. In November, 1966 municipal elections were held and, administratively, Cuevas became a fully incorporated part of the city.[21] Physically, however, much remains to be done. No public utilities are operating yet, only a few houses are structurally complete, no roads have been paved, and there is not a single tree because water is not yet piped in.

More serious is the fact that all along the perimeter, creeping up the surrounding hillsides, is a steadily expanding belt of new shacks, many of which are occupied by the poorest sector. This peripheral

Above left Cuevas in March 1964 has reached a point where the construction of permanent housing has advanced considerably, and the government school has been built.

Left This photograph of St. Martin de Porres shows development after eight years, without technical or financial assistance. The houses are at various stages of development. Those with shacks belong to city-dwellers who do not yet have enough capital to begin building, but who allow another family to occupy the site rent-free to prevent it being seized by another squatter family.
(Photos: John Turner)

growth (which in fact started as soon as the area was occupied, probably by those who could not pay the dues or who were late-comers) now threatens the future status and development of the entire settlement. The resident priests estimated that the population of the *barriada* had increased from 9,000 to 12,000 between 1963 and 1965. This is partly accounted for by a normal and healthy increase in the density of the planned area where a proportion of plots remain unoccupied, but part is also due to the ring of 'sub-squatter settlement'. Its existence could well frustrate efforts to bring the rest of the area up to modern standards – which should be only a matter of time – by reducing the status of the neighbourhood and the value of the properties. Those with the greatest expectations and social mobility are therefore likely to leave, further down-grading the area and perhaps leaving it to degenerate into a slum before it can develop its potential. Thus, in spite of the remarkable progress that Cuevas (and many other similar areas) has made to date, its future is by no means assured. What happens now depends very much on the nature and the effectiveness of the aid it receives from the municipal and central government authorities.

Whether the settlement as a whole will down-grade the adjacent and as yet undeveloped urban land, or whether its presence will hold potential development in the area at a low level, also remains to be seen. Presumably, Cuevas' influence will depend on the nature of its development. If the community achieves the level it is at present capable of reaching – that of a working and lower middle class neighbourhood – there is no reason why adjacent land values or development should be damaged. Both the public and private sectors, therefore, as well as the actual inhabitants, have a considerable vested interest in Cuevas' continued development.

Left Cuevas is in the foreground. In the middle distance is El Hermitano, in two stages of development. On the nearer side the disorganized shacks reflect the order in which people arrived in the invasion. On the further side, the lots are laid out systematically according to a plan. In the distance is Lima, about three miles from Cuevas. (Photo: John Turner)

Next page Shacks recently erected on a newly planned settlement. Each lot is clearly marked out with stones picked off the land. Some shacks already have electricity from small, privately owned generators. (Photo: John Turner)

Popular Versus Official Housing Norms

The most striking thing about this type of development is the spontaneous mobilization of human and material resources – spontaneous in the sense that it has taken place independently and even in spite of the public institutions. If governments could induce the same initiative, efforts, and sacrifices for their own housing and urban development policies, both living conditions and the rate of economic growth would be immensely improved.[22] Scarcely less striking is the contrast the spontaneous popular settlement process makes with the 'normal' subdivision and construction procedures required by law and practised by capitalist and state enterprise. If the latter procedures were preferred by squatters and would-be squatters the differences might be dismissed as being the inevitable consequence of the violation of law and the failure of the government to provide low-cost housing. But the more traditional popular procedures are not only a logical response to the economic and social circumstances of modernization, they are actually *preferred* by the great majority of the people concerned.

This fact is less surprising after one has examined the main differences between 'popular' and 'official' norms in the light of the human situations and experience involved. If we start by comparing the typical programmes of operations, the advantages of the popular programme are immediately clear. In a society which does not possess, or which cannot mobilize, the necessary material resources to build complete modern minimum standard units for all who need them, each family must wait its turn. Generally, the wait is very long, the best part if not the entire time that the applicants are parents of young children. The squatter's procedure of occupying his plot as soon as he obtains possession, living initially in any sort of shelter he can manage, allows the family to improve its living conditions and to become far more independent at a much earlier and a more active stage of life.

Even if they have to pay for the land at commercial rates, the typical family will still jump at the chance to follow this procedure (as a recent clandestine sale of building land adjacent to Cuevas has shown).[23] The sequence of operations subsequent to occupation is also radically different. Official norms give priority to residential construction and the installation of public utilities. The popular procedure is to provide community facilities and services before either dwellings or utilities. Since security of tenure is more important than physical comfort (especially in this favourable climate) and since security of tenure is enhanced by a

reduction in the cost of living and the presence of medical and police services, the advantage is clear.

Finally, the disadvantages of orthodox modern 'instant' as opposed to initially primitive 'progressive' development are considerable, both economically and, once again, from the social security points of view. If capitalization takes place at one fell swoop it must be financed on the basis of long-term credit. Credit is very scarce in a developing economy and thus the cost of an instantly built, fully or semi-finished housing scheme is very great. Even if the interest rates are heavily subsidized by the state (greatly reducing, of course, the number of units the state can finance) the cost of the most economic orthodox housing schemes still imposes a long amortization period on the beneficiaries.[24] A long-term mortgage can also greatly reduce the occupants' security of tenure. The official procedure, therefore, is doubly disadvantageous: it forces the great majority to live in rented slums for many of the years when the need to own a home is greatest, and once a home is obtained they are saddled with a long term debt which threatens the very security which they seek through ownership.

The outstanding physical advantage of 'progressive development' over the 'instant development' procedure – apart from an early escape from overcrowded and unhealthy slums – is that the families' living areas are generally much larger at an appreciably earlier stage of construction. The progressive developer often provides much more living space than in the average, low-cost instant development scheme. If given the choice, many of the readers of this article would prefer a living area of 700 or 800 square feet enclosed by cane mats lined with newspapers rather than a brick or concrete house half that size and fifteen times the cost. Besides offering more living space, the great majority of *barriada* dwellings have roofed areas of over 1,000 square feet per floor, and virtually all are designed to take a second floor. In one *barriada* begun some twelve years ago, a large proportion of the dwellings have second floors under construction or already habitable. From an analysis of six typical *barriada* dwellings it is evident that after approximately twenty years of construction without any outside financial assistance, a two-storey house with a total floor area of over 2,000 square feet can be completed for the same outlay that a government sponsored instant dwelling of half the size or less would cost, even when the administrative overheads and credit financing are heavily subsidized.

It has been stressed that the investment programmes

Top Main street of St. Martin de Porres after ten years. The street was paved shortly after this photograph was taken. Already there are metropolitan bus services, and electricity supplied by the Lima Light and Power Company. A mobile unit of a central national bank has been installed, and many houses have a second storey under construction. (Photo: Eva Lewitus, Lima)

Middle A street in the barrio Surquillo. An older working-class district, not settled by invasion, but more likely by clandestine subdivision of land, Surquillo was built up in much the same way as squatter settlements. (Photo: John Turner)

naturally reflect both these differences and the advantage of reducing the need for credit to a minimum or of eliminating it altogether. The other vital economic advantage of progressive development is that it permits and stimulates the investment of non-monetary resources – those that are in most abundant supply in a developing economy. The cause of the great difference in the financial costs of 'instant' and 'progressive' construction (the former costing at least 100% more than the latter) is that the owner-occupier builder provides other resources in the form of initiative, skills, and time. The time, patience, and bargain-

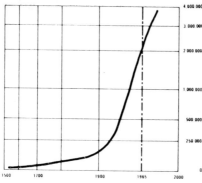

Urban Population Growth
horizontal: dates; vertical: population

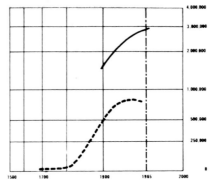

Urban Population Growth
urban area: solid line; city proper: broken line
horizontal: dates; vertical: population

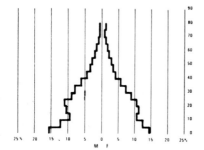

Urban Population Distribution
Census, 1961; population, 1,845,900

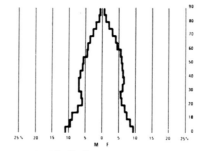

Urban Population Distribution
Census, 1959; population, 2,589,300

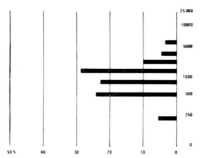

Urban Annual Income Distribution
J.N.V. data 1964; households, 331,000
horizontal: percentages; vertical: dollars

Lima, Peru

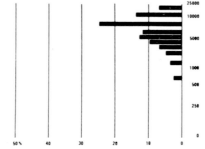

Urban Annual Income Distribution
Census, 1959; households, 640,526
horizontal: percentages; vertical: dollars

Boston, Massachussetts, USA

80

ing skills of most wage-earning families together with the myriad contacts through workmates, friends, and relatives often results in remarkably good value for precious money spent on materials and on hiring skilled labour. This is true in spite of the fact that substantial help from relatives or even neighbours seems to be quite rare as a spontaneous or traditional attribute of these newly forming communities.

An additional 'product' of progressive development is its stimulation of social development through the cultivation and strengthening of the family and of the positive attitudes and relationships to society that the satisfied family acquires. These are qualities which elude quantification but which are, perhaps, the ultimate test of the validity, and value of any activity. Anyone who doubts the reality or existence of such 'products' has only to spend a little time among people who are working in these ways.

A further very serious problem often created by 'instant' housing projects and one that is now receiving the anxious attention of many authorities,[25] is the social stratification and subsequent stagnation of the communities formed. An important difference between the groups formed by officially sponsored projects and squatter settlement communities is that of the criteria and procedures for participant selection. The financial liabilities and socio-political risks of projects which depend on the recovery of capital from people with low and uncertain incomes automatically impose a demand, by those responsible, for the careful screening of the prospective 'beneficiaries'. The taxpayers' representatives are likely to require that accommodation be provided only for those who are either financially able to afford the costs involved, or politically acceptable by being the 'deserving poor' who most need subsidies. The resultant social groups are stratified either way: if selected on the basis of economic capacity they are narrowly lower-middle-class or, if on the basis of need, they are narrowly lower-class.

In neither case will one get the mix necessary for social change and development. Squatter settlement selection is more orthodox in the commercial sense because no attempt is made to match precisely the consumer and the product.[26] Anyone who decides that he would do well by participating in an invasion is free to do so. A midwife, a dentist, or a retailer, for example, might well decide that a livelihood could be ensured by becoming a participant member of a squatter comunity. In this way the initial socio-economic composition of the squatter community is far more likely to include the necessary elements for social and economic balance and development than a screened project community. Furthermore, as long as the squatters, as an auto-selected community, experience a reasonably continuous rate of progress, diversification will increase. In an adequately located progressive *barriada* where the basic land use pattern is sufficiently flexible (as the simple grid-iron systems generally employed usually are) social diversification will be matched by a growth of industrial and commercial activity. The more there is going on and the more people there are with whom one can have contacts, the more opportunities the poor have of improving their status. The policy of limiting the allocation of housing units in specific projects to specific income groups – and of imposing specific housing types – naturally limits the social mix and inevitably increases the administrative costs both in the short and in the long run. The progressive development procedure virtually eliminates the necessity for direct subsidy, however, and therefore eliminates the motives for socio-economic selection.

Contrary to the beliefs and arguments of many opponents of 'progressive' development, the process provides for relatively high urban densities. It is frequently held that progressive development procedures, which demand one-family housing, are uneconomic because of the immense areas required and the consequent increase in the spread and costs of urban services. In the case of Lima, this argument collapses on close examination. In the first place, during the earlier phases of development, the demand and need for urban services are very limited. Initially, sewers and even water mains are unessential. The difference in time for public transportation, if only a matter of minutes, is negligible in cost terms. An efficient bus service requires very little capital and, in any case, is

Below and right The birth of an industry. A privately-owned electric generator and power lines in Cuevas
(Photos: John Turner)

usually a commercial proposition. By the time sewers and water mains are essential the densities are great enough to justify them. The potential density of the average progressive development settlement, like Cuevas, is 160 persons per acre, in single-family dwellings and in structures of no more than two floors. This is assuming that no structures are higher than two storeys and that every purely residential property would house an average of one and a half families, a reasonable assumption considering that the majority of second floors are built for children's families or for rent.

If this development procedure is adopted by the planners, and its administration is given over to local authorities, there is no reason why a proportion of land should not be put in public ownership to ensure some flexibility, particularly the attainment of higher densities when circumstances justified them. In the earlier stages, for instance, a market could be a collection of stalls on an open plaza, later to be occupied by shops and apartments. Similarly, cheap one-storey rental tenements, municipally owned and administered could be later replaced by multi-storey apartments. Land values, in any case, are likely to rise as metropolitan expansion leaves the neighbourhood relatively

closer to the city core.

Normally the walk-up apartment solution imposes a relatively low density, but in fact there is very little difference between the residential densities of typical walk-up apartment projects and the potential and probable future density of Cuevas.[27] Exceptionally, as in the case of the seven-storey walk-up, one-room apartment blocks of Hong Kong, very high densities can be achieved. Only very rarely, however, are such solutions likely to be socially and politically viable. The more orthodox and socio-economically practical 'high-density' developments for families with very low incomes rule out the 'progressive development' procedure. In relation to the incomes and amortization capacity of the beneficiaries, low-rise, relatively high density developments require excessively high initial capital outlays. That the financial economies achieved through a slight – or even appreciable – increase in residential density will be sufficient to compensate for the financial and social economies of the 'progressive development' procedure is very doubtful. The spatial economy of initially high density residential development (for owner-occupiers) rests on the false assumption that the residences must be fully equipped to modern standards, whatever the economic situation and real needs of the inhabitants or, alternatively, on the so far unjustified fears of excessive land consumption by modern growth.

Conclusions

The argument for progressive development and against 'instant' development based on modern minimum standards can best be summarized by considering the priorities between the basic functions of the dwelling environment in relation to the changing life-situations and consequently changing priorities between the physical components of the environment.[28] It has been argued that the order of priorities between the basic components for popular housing – in the wider sense – is the reverse of that required by official standards. The average lower income family seeking a home in an urban environment wants secure land tenure, community facilities, an adequate dwelling, and utilities – in that order. The state offers the exact opposite: a modern (but minimum) house in the first place, some community facilities (generally at later stages), and eventually, title to the property after the mortgage has been paid off. This latter procedure, however, is generally preferred by the middle income groups, whose social and economic security depends far less on home possession than it does on occupation and social status.

Further, in a developing free-market economy, the

middle-income family also has access to insurance as well as to banking services and financial credit seldom available to the lower income sector. Since its socio-economic security depends more on the material status of the dwelling it occupies than on actual ownership of it, the 'progressive development' concept is, understandably, anathema. The unconscious transference of middle-class values to the designs and plans for the lower classes is, undoubtedly, the main reason for the emotionally loaded opposition of most technicians and administrators to the idea of permitting – still less of encouraging – people to live in an only partially completed environment, and of their apparent blindness to its obvious potential.

The significance of the cultural change that takes place over time and in the same *barriada* location not only confirms this kind of dwelling environment as a vehicle for social and economic development, but also points to the connections between the different demands of various social levels. It is clear that the relative priorities and demands of the low-wage earner and those of the high-wage (or low-salary) earner must be different though not as different as the levels compared above. Preoccupation with material status is as evident in the *barriadas* as it is elsewhere. The typical home-building family, for example, may finish the facade and a 'parlour' often to quite high standards and at considerable expense, before the rest of the dwelling is complete. As the family becomes more secure, so will its dependence on the proximity of community services diminish. The pattern of upper-lower or lower-middle income level priorities will be an intermediate link between the lower and the upper-middle priority patterns.[29]

If over-capitalization and the consequent strains on the inhabitants and the state are to be avoided, and if the maximum contribution from the inhabitants is to be obtained in order that the state can serve the greatest number, the interpretation put forward in this article points clearly to the progressive development principles practised by squatters – and city builders from time immemorial – as against the principles governing housing and urban development policies based on the direct construction of minimum modern standard dwelling units. The modern minimum standard concept, which acts as a barrier to development by attempting to prohibit the intermediate stages, must give way to a concept which uses standards as guides towards the progressive achievement of minimum *goals*.

Notes

1 J. C. Turner, *Uncontrolled Urban Settlement: Problems and Policies*, a paper prepared for the United Nations Seminar on Development Policies and Planning in Relation to Urbanization, Pittsburgh, Pennsylvania., Fall, 1966.

2 Patrick Geddes, *Town Planning Towards City Development*, a report prepared for the Durbar of Indore, India, 1918. Vol. I, p. 85.

3 J. C. Turner, *A New View of the Housing Deficit*, a paper prepared for the Seminar on a Housing Policy for a Developing Economy, University of San Juan, Puerto Rico, April 1966, and printed in this volume for the first time.

4 United Nations, *Methods for Establishing Targets and Standards for Housing and Environmental Development*, E/C. 6/31. 1965.

5 Charles Abrams, *Man's Struggle for Shelter in an Urbanizing World* (Cambridge: M.I.T. Press, 1965), p. 53.

6 A report made by the author for the United Nations on the housing situation in Arequipa, Peru, with special reference to the squatter settlements, 1959–60 (unpublished).

7

	1940 Census	1961 Census	Estimated Growth Rate (per acre)
Cities of over 50,000 inhabitants	675,000	2,556,100	6% (own estimate)
Total population	6,208,000	10,365,000	3.2% (1961 census)

8 Ernest Weissmann, United Nations, Economic and Social Council, Social Commission. Statement made at the 403rd meeting, 25th April, 1966. UN bulletin number E/CN 5/L. 313.

9 J. C. Tuner, *Uncontrolled Urban Settlement, op. cit* chap. IV.

10 J. C. Turner's 'Lima's Barriadas and Corralones: Suburbs versus Slums', *Ekistics*, 112 (March 1965).

11 William P. Mangin, 'Urbanization Case History in Peru', *Architectural Design* (August 1963).

12 Sam Schulman, 'Latin American Shanty Town', *New York Times Magazine* (16th January 1966) – a typically misleading generalization from a case study of doubtful worth.

13 Bernard J. Frieden, 'The Search for a Housing Policy in Mexico City', *Town Planning Review*, XXXVI (July 1965), and Granville H. Sewell, *Squatter Settlements in Turkey; Analysis of a Social, Political and Economic Problem*, Ph.D. Thesis, M.I.T., Cambridge, Mass., 1964 (monograph).

14 J. C. Turner, *A New View of the Housing Deficit, loc. cit.*

15 Further information will be provided from the field studies recently carried out under the auspices of the Joint Centre for Urban Studies of M.I.T. and Harvard University.

16 The 'Ley de Remodelacion, Saneameinto y Legalizacion de los barrios marginales' Lima, 1961. This law provided for the improvement of *barriadas* of the 'progressive development' variety and for the relocation of those incapable of improvement. New low-cost subdivisions were to be provided in order to satisfy the continuing demand for building land.

17 The 'components of the dwelling structure' which are subject to different sequences of operations in the construction process in the Lima *barriadas* are: a *cerco* or perimeter wall enclosing the plot: the walls of the first floor (or of the first rooms) with a provisional roof: a permanent (hollow clay tile reinforced concrete slab) roof structure: joinery and metalwork (doors, windows, and window grilles): installations (water supply, domestic drainage, electric light) and fittings; finishes (floor finishes, plastering, and painting): and second storey (repeat of the relevant components).

18 The main source for the interpretations of the basic functions of housing, and the priorities between them, are the minutes of a series of meetings between architects (from the National Housing Agency), a US Peace Corps volunteer, a priest resident in the locality (an Englishman), and an average of three *barriada* leaders. The two items discussed were: 'In what location should the working-class family live, and why?' and 'In the locations selected, what services, utilities, and buildings are required, in what order of priority, and why?'

19 *United Nations: Report of The Ad Hoc Group of Experts on Housing and Urban Development*. (New York: United Nations 1962), p. 1.

20 From a survey carried out by Ralph Pattisson, student of architecture at the University of Newcastle, England, while resident in the *barriada* in 1965.

21 Though the legalization process (the administration of the 'Ley de barrios marginales') is incomplete, the municipal incorporation of the principal *barriada* districts has proceeded and it is now likely that the newly created municipalities will be largely responsible for subsequent development and legalization.

22 'The unutilized talents of their people constitute the chief waste and future hope of the developing countries. Only a small fraction of these populations participate actively in national life today.' United Nations document on *Self-Help*. ST/SOA/53. 'Squatter building is probably the main contributor to the building inventory of the developing nation. It is largely self-help or aided self-help construction. It

is financed without government aid.' Charles Abrams *Squatter Settlements; The Problem and the Opportunity* (Washington, D.C.: Department of Housing and Urban Development, 1966).

23 In July 1965, a large tract of land was bought by an 'Asociación' which, within the space of one month, has sold every plot (reportedly 800) for $500 – 50% cash, the balance in twelve monthly payments – to low-income families with similar status to those who establish the *barriadas*. The plots measure 25 by 60 feet No services or utilities were included in the agreement and no legally valid title could be given as the subdivision and sales are illegal.

24 Mortgage and credit terms for typical low-cost housing generally provide for a twenty-year amortization period and interest rates of between 5 and 10%. Where the loans are made with foreign currencies such low rates (relative to the commercial bank rates generally between 15 and 20%) imply a direct subsidy of about half the financing cost.

25 The 'José Maria Caro' district of Santiago de Chile, with a total low-income population of over 100,000 is an illustrative case. This is discussed in J. C. Turner, *Uncontrolled Urban Settlement.*

26 The typical agency project is 'sold' under circumstances that no free market producer or distributor would dream of imposing: both the buyer and the article are predetermined. Few, if any commercial manufacturers or distributors would care to risk investments on such narrow margins: if the producer wants to decide what to make then he must offer the product on the widest possible market. If he wants to sell to a given sector of the market, then he must produce what that sector demands. Official housing policies commonly attempt to define both and commonly encounter serious consumer problems.

27 Walk-up apartments (one room dwellings) have been built in large numbers in seven-storey structures in Hong Kong and, at 12 square feet per person, have achieved very high densities. A typical 4-storey partment block project in Peru (Tacna) has a planned density of 160 persons per acre – the potential (and probable future) density of Cuevas.

28 J. C. Turner, *A New View of the Housing Deficit.*

29 The very low income sector is not discussed in this article. In J. C. Turner, *A New View of the Housing Deficit*, arguments are put forward to justify the priorities shown on the chart: since the very poor are primarily concerned with feed themselves and of getting employment, it is argued that they are even more dependent than the wage earners on community facilities (and proximity to sources of employment) but that they are consequently less concerned with

stable residence having little or nothing to invest or gain by investment.

Addendum

After this article went to press, my attention was drawn to the US Department of Urban Development publication *The Unfinished but Habitable Home* by William M. Shenkel. This report surveys the existing unfinished house market in the USA – which 'In recent years ... has absorbed a significant share of the housing market' – from 30,000 to 100,000 units a year. The report concludes that the system is economic and should be supported and extended. In principle, it is similar to the procedures discussed in this article, although the savings achieved are proportionately much less – rarely exceeding 25%. 'Unfinished', however, refers mainly to dwellings that lack only the finishes and fittings. On page 73, Shenkel writes: 'Four room houses sold with open stud interiors with no interior walls would probably not conform to the minimum property standards. But it is most doubtful that houses unfinished to this point would be regarded as adequate loan security without some provision for early completion of the dwelling.' Both the potential economy of 'progressive development' and the institutional barriers to its achievement are thus confirmed.

In another very interesting report that has just come to my attention: *A Proposal to Demonstrate Financing and Construction Techniques for Developing Low-Income Housing in Rural California*, by Bellow, Lorenz, Powell and Goldes for the Rural Development Corporation of Los Angeles, the relevance of these principles is further confirmed. Quoting from the 1963 State *Report on Housing in California*, the authors point out that 40% of farmworker families (of the survey sample) own or were purchasing their own homes in spite of average monthly incomes of only $222.50! Having demonstrated that the demand exists, the report goes on to specific proposals for financing, technical assistance, and designs – illustrating the rather advanced 'roof house' and 'core house' concepts derived from experience in the developing countries.

Below Barrios around Lima display all the characteristics of the organic growth of cities; the grid plan of streets, the early housing which in a few short years will have water, power, sewage, bus services, schools, shops, and politics. The parallel with the organic growth of major US and European cities is obvious.
(Photos: Aerofotografico Nacional, Lima)

83

HOUSES GENERATED BY PATTERNS

CHRISTOPHER ALEXANDER
SANFORD HIRSHEN
SARA ISHIKAWA
CHRISTIE COFFIN
SHLOMO ANGEL

Preface: The Proyecto Experimental de Vivienda
In January 1969 the United Nations, working with the Banco de la Vivienda of Peru, asked us at the Center for Environmental Structure, Berkeley, USA, and 12 other architects from various countries to submit competition designs for a community of 1,500 houses. The houses are to be built at a gross density of 37 houses per hectare on a site of 40 hectares, 8 kilometres north of Lima. The site is bounded by two major arterial highways, and crossed by a third; these highways are fixed by the Lima transportation plan. The financial arrangements require that each house be contractor built, on its own land, at a cost ranging from 78,000 to 164,000 *soles* ($1,800–$3,800, £720–£1,520) and that the houses be sold to low-income white-collar workers (empleados) earning between 2,800 and 5,800 *soles* ($65–$135, £26–£54), per month.
We were asked to present our designs in a way which would help the evolution of Peruvian community and house design in the future. We have therefore chosen to present our work in two parts:
In part one we present our *designs*. This part includes a site plan, drawings and construction details for individual houses, and a choice-process which allows the final site and house plans to be formed, in detail, by the idiosyncratic needs of the individual families who buy the houses.

In part two we present some of the 67 general design principles which we call *patterns*. These patterns describe, in an abstract sense, the lessons which a Peruvian architect might learn from our designs, and could re-use, over and over again, in his own designs. We have combined these 67 patterns in one particular way, to form the designs presented in part one. However, in the hands of different Peruvian architects, or in the hands of different individuals designing and building their own houses, these patterns can generate an almost infinitely rich variety. In this sense, these patterns may begin to define a new indigenous architecture for Peru.

PART ONE

The site
The site contains 1,726 houses, at a gross density of 43 houses per hectare. House lots are 5.20 metres wide, and vary in length from 13 to 27 metres.
No two houses are alike. The exact form and length of each house is determined by a choice-process which allows families to fit their houses to their own needs and budgets.
Since the lengths of houses in the final site plan will be based on the choices which families make, and are unknown at present, the current drawing of the site plan is only approximate. Once each family has made its choices, it will be necessary to lay out a new site plan. This new plan will have the same morphology as the one shown, but the exact number of houses of different lengths, will reflect the families' choices. The morphology of the plan is fluid enough to adjust to the new lengths.
The site contains a number of cells Each cell contains 30–70 houses; it is a pedestrian island, surrounded by a sunken one lane road, which feeds small parking lots which surround the cell.

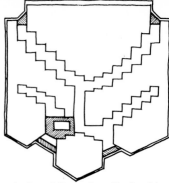

The cell

We have designed the cells with the idea that the particular group of people who live in a cell can make an impact on their cell, can give it a unique atmosphere, created by them, and can then, in a real sense 'take possession of it'.
First, the basic form and circulation of each cell is unique – according to its particular location in the large plan.
Second, during the choice-process, people will be asked questions about the location they want for their house. When they are then located according to these choices, people with similar attitudes and interests will be living in the same cell.
Third, the cells are physically separated, and the pedestrian passes through a physical gateway whenever he enters a cell: this will give each cell a better chance to build up its own unique flavour.
Fourth, at the heart of each cell, there is a small open place, surrounded by an unfinished, roofed arcade. It is our intention that the people who live in the cell will develop this arcade according to those community uses they think most valuable.

Road system

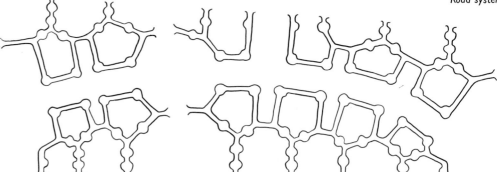

Over and above the cells, the site contains three
major overlapping configurations: the road system,
the pedestrian network, and the community spine.
Vehicles travel on narrow one-way loop roads,
around the cells, with car parking at the entrances to
the cells. There are enough parking spaces to provide
for 50% car ownership. This figure was given to us by
the United Nations: they estimate 50% car ownership
in 30 years, and asked us to work to that figure.
The central spine of the pedestrian system, we call

Central spine

Below The site

1 Primary school
2 Secondary school
3 Technical secondary school
4 Church
5 Cinema
6 Supermarket
7 Market
8 Municipal offices
9 Grove of trees
10 Kindergarten
11 Clinic
12 Dance hall
13 Sports center
14 Parking
15 Outdoor room

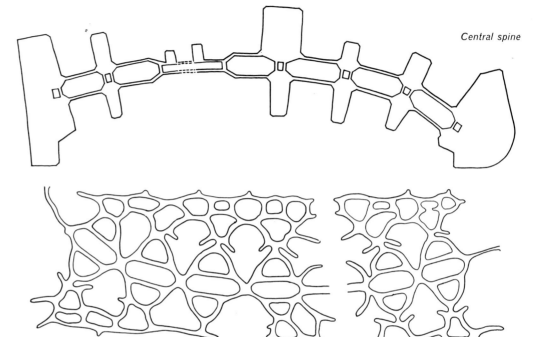

Pedestrian path system

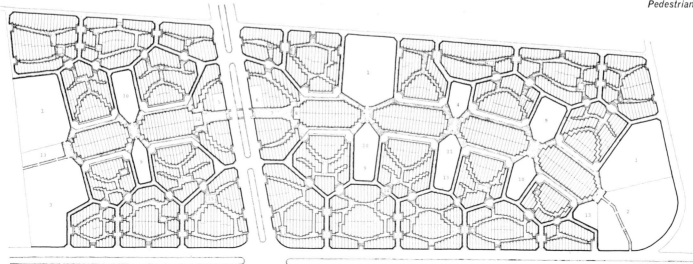

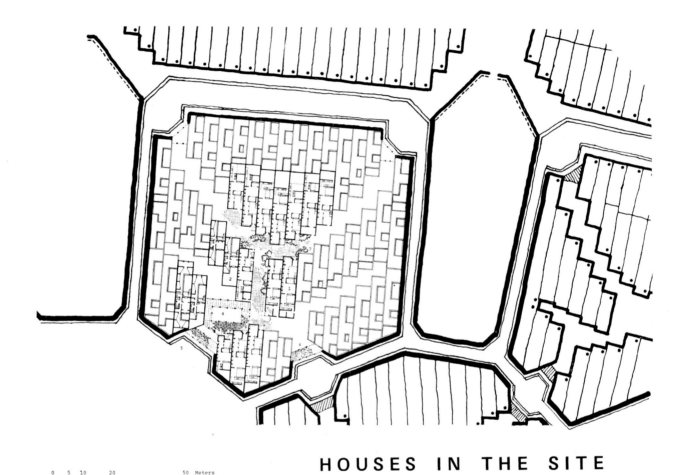

HOUSES IN THE SITE

0   5 10   20   50 Meters

1 First floor of house   5 Parking
2 Second floor of house   6 Cell gateway
3 Shop   7 Garden
4 Outdoor room

the 'paseo'. This name is taken from the Latin American habit of the evening and Sunday stroll (paseo in Spanish). The paseo gives people a high density pedestrian spine of looped paths where a tradition of evening and Sunday walks can develop.

At frequent intervals along the paseo there are 'activity nuclei': small open places, with the community facilities and shops grouped around them. The community facilities are grouped in such a way as to create a special character at each of these activity nuclei.

The peripheral pedestrian paths connect cells to one another, and connect them to this main paseo. Each cell which is large enough, has a pedestrian loop in it: this will help to create the inner character of the cells, since it will become natural for people to take a walk 'around the cell'. All pedestrian paths from the outer parts of the site lead towards one of the eight activity nuclei. The nuclei will always be full of people.

The house
Although the choice-process guarantees that no two houses will be exactly alike, all houses are based on one generic house, see next page.

This generic house is a two-storey house, 5.20 metres wide, and about 20 metres long, which has an alternation of rooms and patios along its length, the rooms connected by deep verandas. This alternation gives every room light and air, and makes the house seem larger. The two main patios are always one behind

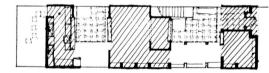

the other in the direction of the breeze (which comes from the south) – so that cool air circulates through the house in summer. In winter, the patios will be covered by dacron sailcloth covers which run horizontally on rods at roof level. They may be controlled from upstairs by cords, and make the patios usable all the year round.

The ground floor of the house contains two parts: a public part and a family part. The main features of the public part are the front patio, and the sala (formal living room or parlour). In Peruvian life there is a strong distinction between members of the family who may go anywhere in the house, and strangers who must be entertained in the sala. The sala is

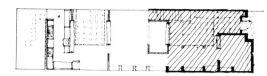

separated from the rest of the house by the front patio which even in the smallest house allows visitors to be treated with proper formality.

The family part of the house centres on the family room (comedor-estar). An alcove (two in large houses) opens off this family room to make a place where children study at night, where women can sew, where people can talk while the TV is on, etc. Behind the family room there is a kitchen, with two service patios, one on either side of it. The one between kitchen and

family room is a pleasant place, where people can eat, and work. The other provides storage for the inevitable building materials, animals, and laundry lines.

Upstairs the house contains a master bedroom, bathroom, and a number of tiny individual bed alcoves. These bed alcoves give each child a small space which is his own, for his own things; very young children may double bunk in a single alcove. Since Peruvians don't like being isolated, these alcoves are clustered around common spaces. There are two clusters; one for boys and one for girls. Every house,

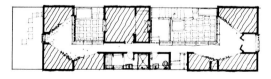

even the smallest, can be extended to make room for as many as eight beds.

Every house can be extended to provide accommodation for a grandmother downstairs near the family room, a sleeping place for a servant, a room at the back which can be rented out, or a small shop. Many low income families try to make extra money by renting out rooms or selling things. These extensions

are much easier if the back of the house opens on to a pedestrian way: those people who are willing to pay for it may select this option in the choice-process. Finally, each house has a very strongly marked entrance, with deep recesses, a seat outside, and a gallery or 'mirador' at the second storey. Peruvians spend a great deal of time street watching: people hang out in doorways, sit on benches outside the doors, and watch the street from windows above. They like to be in touch with the street, but from the seclusion of their homes. Most houses in our site

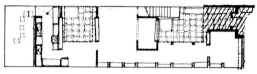

plan command a direct view into the centre of the cell in which they stand, so that activity can be seen from the front window or the door.

Construction
The basic structure of the house consists of a floating slab foundation, load bearing walls, and a light weight plank and beam system. This form is conceptually very similar to traditional construction: but each of the components is a cheaper, lower-weight higher-strength version of its traditional equivalent. The floating slab is laid in large sections by a road building machine. The walls are of interlocking mortarless concrete blocks, reinforced with sulphur, with a cavity for plumbing and conduits. The planks and beams are made of urethane foam-plastic and bamboo, reinforced with a sulphur-sand topping.

All these building components can be produced in Peru today with available resources and skills. Further, the ideas embodied in these methods and products have the potential for long-range development of natural resources. These, in turn, will directly contribute to the economic growth of the people and the country, a vital factor in creating a national housing policy. Sulphur is available in huge quantities in Peru; current estimates show 50,000,000 tons of sulphur waiting to be mined in the Peruvian Andes. The use of urethane foams has been tested in various parts of Latin America; it is a seed industry of great importance, since foams are now used in many different ways, inside and outside the building industry. A urethane plant, once started, would benefit many sectors of the national economy. Bamboo is widely

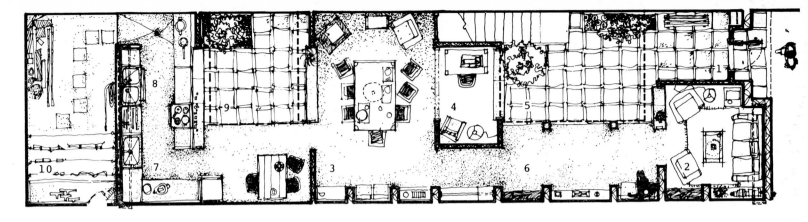

First floor

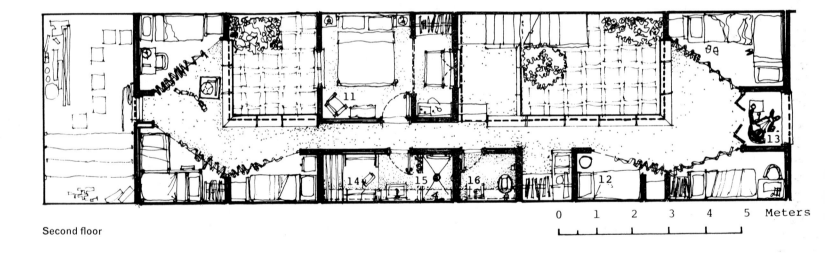

Second floor

	Meters
0 1 2 3 4 5	

1 Entrance
2 Sala (Parlour)
3 Family room
4 Family room alcove
5 Main patio
6 Veranda
7 Kitchen
8 Laundry

9 Kitchen patio
10 Storage patio
11 Master bedroom
12 Bed Alcoves
13 Mirador
14 Clothes drying closet
15 Shower
16 Toilet

THE GENERIC HOUSE

89

available in the north of Peru, and may be imported cheaply from Ecuador. Though it is often thought of as a low-prestige material, it will quickly become a material of great value when used together with high performance bonding agents.

These building materials are especially suited to the local earthquake conditions. The mortarless block has been tested in Mexico under earthquake conditions, and has performed well throughout. Sulphur is now being tested in earthquake zones, and performs as well as steel reinforcing. The floating slab has a long history of success in earthquakes. The urethane-bamboo sandwich is enormously strong – and its very light weight reduces loads during earthquakes.

These are not merely low cost, high performance materials. The yellow diamonds of the block wall, where it is reinforced with spots of sulphur, the warm texture of the bamboo ceilings, the deep polished red of the oil stained concrete slab, and the translucent white of the dacron sailcloth patio cover, combine to create a house which is far more warm and human than the usual heavy grey of low cost construction.

To simplify building construction, all components are prefabricated, on site. They all conform to the 10 cm module. They are assembled dry. This makes them equally suitable for use by the contractor, when the houses are first built, and by the families who live there, when they want to change their houses later.

We have chosen these components with special emphasis on the idea of future do-it-yourself construction. Peruvian families add to their houses, and change them, continually. They can only do this if the components are extremely small in scale, and easy to work with home tools. We have therefore tried very hard to create a system of components that are easy to work, and can be used at the rather low tolerances that correspond to the realities of home construction. In our opinion, this is more relevant to people's needs than a system of highly machined components, which must be built to very fine tolerances. Given the assumption that home construction will always be done rather roughly, with hammer and nails, and fillers where required, our system will allow the homeowner to do almost anything he wants to do.

For example:

On the slab foundation, a new wall can be built anywhere, without needing extra footings. The mortarless block wall can have individual blocks removed or added, at will. The hollow wall makes it easy to add new plumbing fixtures or electrical conduit, cheaply and simply, by taking out a block. A person can make his own blocks, instead of buying them: the block

90

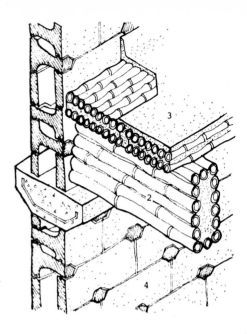

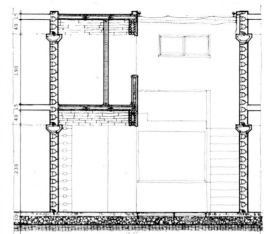

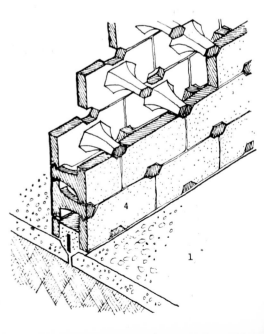

Right
1 Floating slab
2 Bamboo—urethane foam beam
3 Bamboo—urethane foam plank
4 Mortarless block cavity wall

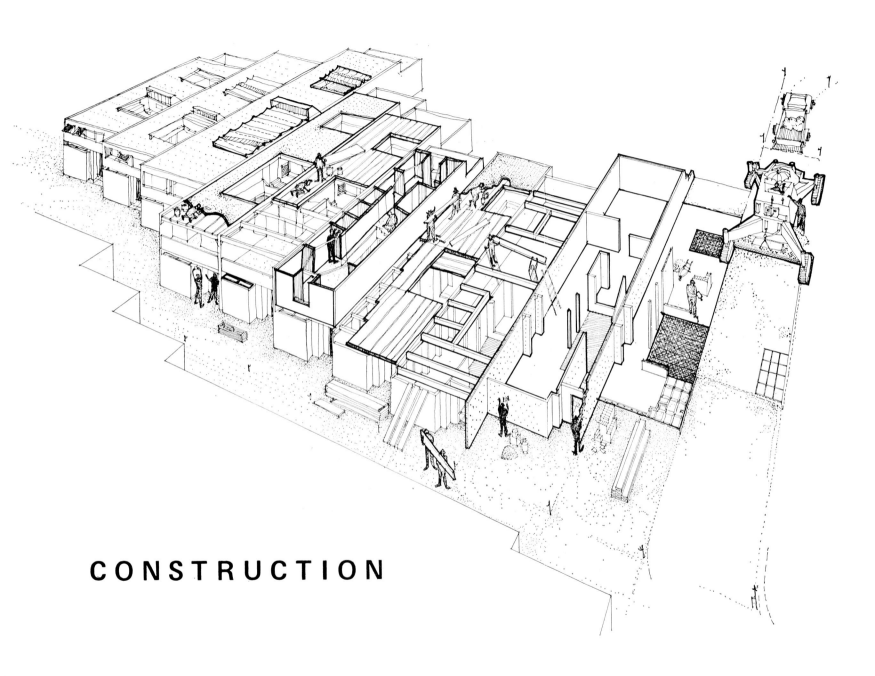

CONSTRUCTION

moulds are designed to be operated by one unskilled person. Extra block columns can be inserted at any point. The sulphur joints, unlike cemented joints, need only to be melted by local application of heat, to loosen; when they cool they harden again. The bamboo foam beams are made in 5 metre lengths which fit across every house; they can sit anywhere along the length, on the continuous impost block. They can be hand cut to frame any desired opening. The bamboo foam planks can also be hand cut to any length and any width. The beams which support the roof are initially designed to carry a minimal live load only: if the house owner wants to make a usable third storey, he may insert extra beams next to the existing ones.

Finally, the components must be easy to get. They will be impossible to obtain on the open market. To make them available, we propose that the community contain a new kind of community service, which we call the Community Building Supermarket. This supermarket will start as the on-site factory needed for initial construction. In its later life, it will manufacture components, sell them, rent out the equipment needed for assembly, provide skilled labour for those aspects of the construction which involve new techniques, and train members of the community who want to learn these techniques for themselves.

The choice process

The people who live in our houses will, because they are all Peruvians, share certain needs and all have similar backgrounds. At the same time, each person, and each family, will be unique. The choice-process tries to do justice to this fact.

The needs which people share led us to the patterns and these patterns led us to the generic house design already presented. But even if all families share the needs which are satisfied by this generic house, they will, because they are unique, also have very different attitudes to the relative importance of these different needs. One family, which tends to be formal, will consider the need for a sala most important of all; another family in which life tends to be informal, may live most of the time in the kitchen. Although both families will want a sala and a kitchen, the first family would prefer a large sala and small kitchen, if they had to choose – and the second family a large kitchen and a small sala. The uniqueness of any family, will, in this way, be reflected by the relative amounts of money they would want to spend on satisfying their various needs.

This is essentially how the choice-process works. We ask each family to decide how much they want to

spend; and then we ask them to divide this money up among the various parts of the house, in the way that best reflects their individual preferences. The form of the house allows its various parts to vary in size, independently of one another; without disturbing the unity of the whole.

Even though no one part of the house can take more than a small number of different sizes, the total number of combinations is extremely large – in the neighbourhood of a million. In a community of 1,500 houses, it is highly unlikely that any two will be the same. This variety is not just visual variety: it reflects the real variety of attitudes to life which will exist among the fifteen hundred families who live in the Proyecto Experimental.

On the following pages we present the choices which a family would have to make, before buying a house in the Proyecto. These choices would, of course, have to be made before construction starts. To help people make the choices, it would be essential to build one or two model houses ahead of time, and allow people to visit them. Otherwise they would probably not be able to grasp the meaning of the choices.

The combination process

The combination process is not unlike the process by which the leaves on a tree are formed. All the leaves are defined by the same morphogenetic rules. The

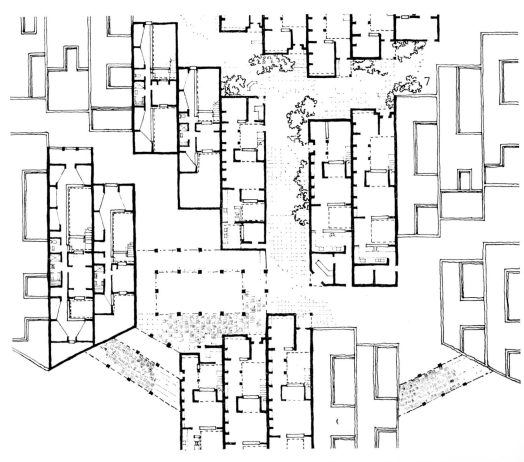

FAMILY CHOICE SHEET

By answering the questions on this sheet, you may decide how big to make the various rooms inside your house. Start by deciding how much money you want to spend on the house, altogether. You may choose any amount between 79,000 soles and 163,000 soles.

When you have decided how much you want to spend altogether, you may start making choices about individual rooms and finishes, and about the location of the house in the community. Each of these choices costs money. To make your choices, you will have to decide which things matter most to you.

The available choices are shown below. The numbers which follow each item, show, in thousands of soles, how much each of the various choices costs. Write the number you have chosen for each item, in the column on the right. When you have finished, add up the numbers on the right. You must be sure that the total is the same as the total price you are willing to pay for your house. Thus, for instance, if you want to spend 95,000 soles on your house, the numbers in the right hand column must add up to 95.

On the pages which follow this one, we give you the detailed explanation of these choices one by one, so that you can understand clearly what you are choosing. You should read these detailed explanations before you try to make your choices.

								Your Choice
SALA	Choose one of these			3	8	14	20	
FAMILY ROOM	Choose one of these	22 24	26	28	32	35		
MAIN PATIO	Choose one of these			18	21	23	27	
KITCHEN-LAUNDRY	Choose one of these					13	22	
BED ALCOVES	Choose one of these		6	9	13	16	19 22	
MASTER BEDROOM	You must choose this						11	
GRANDMOTHERS BED ALCOVE	Choose one of these					0	1	
LAUNDRY-STORAGE PATIO	Choose one of these			6	7	8	10	
CAR HOUSE DISTANCE	Choose one of these					0	3	
RENTAL/BACK DOOR	Choose one of these		0	2	4	8	10	
SHOP	Choose one of these			0	8	10	20	
EXTRAS	You may choose more than one of these, or none. Write the total on the right	1 1	1	1	2	3	5	
FINISHES	You may choose more than one of these, or none. Write the total on the right				1	1	2	

TOTAL:

93

1. SIZE OF SALA

In all houses, the sala is a receiving room, separate from the comedor-estar. The very smallest sala you can have is a tiny alcove just large enough to hold two chairs and a sofa, inside the front door. Or you can have a sala more like an ordinary room.

Choose one:

Tiny sala	COST:	3,000 soles
Tiny sala with option for medium sala later	COST:	8,000
Medium sala	COST:	14,000
Large sala	COST:	20,000

2. SIZE OF FAMILY ROOM

Your family room can have a number of different sizes. All of these rooms have one small alcove off them, where children might do their homework, or a woman might sit and sew. In the smallest one, this alcove is very small. In the larger ones, there is a second alcove.

Choose one:

Small room + one (small) alcove	COST:	22,000 soles
Small room + one alcove	COST:	24,000
Medium room + one alcove	COST:	26,000
Large room + one alcove	COST:	28,000
Medium room + two alcoves	COST:	32,000
Large room + two alcoves	COST:	35,000

As you will see on the next page, the master bedroom size is determined by the family room size which you choose. For this reason the costs of the family room shown here include the extra costs created by larger master bedrooms.

3. MAIN PATIO

Every house has a main patio, which contains the stair, is flanked by the sala, the family room, the entrance, and by a veranda which connects the sala and family room. This patio is covered in winter by a dacron sailcloth. The patio is always 3 meters wide, but its length may vary. Especially if you intend to plant things there, you should choose one of the larger ones.

Choose one:

Tiny patio	COST:	18,000 soles
Small patio	COST:	21,000
Medium patio	COST:	23,000
Large patio	COST:	27,000

4. KITCHEN-LAUNDRY

There are two kitchens to choose from. The small one has no sitting space in it, and has the laundry counter out of doors, in the storage patio. The large one is twice as large, has room for a table in it, and has the laundry counter under cover. Both kitchens contain, as an integral part, a small kitchen patio, which will be covered in winter, and gives you extra room to work, room for children to play, etc.

Choose one:

Small kitchen	COST: 13,000 soles
Large kitchen	COST: 22,000

5. NUMBER OF BED ALCOVES

Every house will have a master bedroom; but this is the only conventional bedroom. All the other beds will be in individual bed alcoves, containing a bed, a dressing space, and storage, and nothing more. These bed alcoves will be arranged in two small clusters, one for boys and one for girls.

At least one of the alcoves will be an extra large one, large enough to hold two bunk beds. If you would like to have two of your children sleeping in bunk beds like this, you may choose a number of alcoves which is one less than the number of children in your family.

You may choose how many individual bed alcoves you want (each alcove costs 3,000 soles), and you may also say how you want the alcoves clustered. Choose one of the following. (The first number is the number in the front cluster, the second in the back.)

Two beds:	2,0	COST:	6,000 soles
Three beds:	3,0 or 2,1	COST:	9,000
Four beds:	4,0 or 3,1 or 2,2	COST:	13,000
Five beds:	4,1 or 3,2 or 2,3	COST:	16,000
Six beds:	4,2 or 3,3 or 2,4	COST:	19,000
Seven beds:	4,3	COST:	22,000

6. MASTER BEDROOM, BATH AND STORAGE

The master bedroom and storage are always above the family room. These rooms can vary in size, but their size must always correspond to the size of the family room you have chosen. In this sense, you have no real choice of sizes here, though it may influence your choice of family room size: the bathrooms are always the same size.

The fixed cost of this room is 11,000. All additional costs are included in the costs of family rooms. For all family rooms the master bed costs are:

Master bedroom	COST: 11,000 soles

7. GRANDMOTHER'S BED ALCOVE

Every house has the possibility of placing a bed alcove, on the ground floor, just next to the family room, for an old person. You may choose to have this bed alcove built today, or you may build it yourself, later.

Choose one:

Grandmother's bed alcove built now	COST: 1,000 soles
Not built now	COST: zero

8. LAUNDRY-STORAGE PATIO

Every house has, at the very back, an extra patio which gives you room for expansion on the ground floor, a place where servant quarters may be constructed, a place to hang laundry, and to store building materials and large objects. If you want to use this patio to build rental space, or a little shop, do not choose the very small patio.

Choose one:

Very small	COST: 6,000 soles
Small	COST: 7,000
Medium	COST: 8,000
Large	COST: 10,000

9. CAR HOUSE DISTANCE

Some houses have parking lots right next to them, others do not. In no case is a house more than 50 meters from the nearest parking lot. If you have a car or if you expect to have a car in the near future, you may want to choose a house near a parking lot. Otherwise you may prefer the quietness and safety of a pedestrian street, especially if you have children who play outside the house.

Choose one:

There is a parking place within 15 meters of your house	COST: 3,000 soles
There is a parking place between 15 meters and 50 meters from your house	COST: zero

10. RENTAL AND/OR BACK DOOR

If you hope to rent out a small room in the future, or if you are particularly anxious to let your servant have a back door which is separate from the front door, you may have a lot which has a back or a side opening onto a walkway. If you choose a lot that has a second entrance, you may have a small room for rental, built there today, or you may leave it unbuilt, and build it yourself later. If you choose a shop you may not choose a rental unit.

Choose one:

Corner lot with second entrance on side and rental space built today	COST: 10,000	soles
Corner lot with second entrance on side	COST: 8,000	
Lot with second entrance on back and rental space built today	COST: 4,000	
Lot with second entrance on back	COST: 2,000	
Lot with front only	COST: zero	

11. SHOP

You may want, now or in the future, to open a small shop. In this case you will want to have a location where a shop can prosper - either next to the main market, or at some corner which many people are going past. If you choose a shop location by the market, you will have the shop built now, automatically. If you choose one of the other shop locations, you may have the shop built now, or you may choose to leave it unbuilt now, and then build it yourself later. If you have chosen a rental space, you may not choose a shop.

Choose one:

Market location, with shop built now	COST: 20,000	soles
Corner location, with shop built now	COST: 10,000	
Corner location, shop not built now	COST: 8,000	
No possibility of building a shop	COST: zero	

12. EXTRAS

If you find that you can purchase adequate space for your family without using all the money that you plan to spend on housing, or if some of these extra features mean more to you than extra space, you may want to choose some of the optional features listed below.

Fiberglass patio covers instead of sailcloth on front patio and middle patio	COST: 5,000	soles
Electric hot water heater, connected to bathroom, kitchen and laundry	COST: 3,000	
Second wash basin for family	COST: 1,000	
Wash basin and WC for servant, enclosed	COST: 2,000	
Colored tiles around the main door	COST: 1,000	
Bench near the main door	COST: 1,000	
5 meter Eucalyptus saplings near front door	COST: 1,000	

13. FINISHES

In Proyecto Experimental the basic finishes are the finishes of the building materials, block and bamboo. If you want to, you can have plaster or white wash in the sala or comedor.

Plastered ceiling in the sala	COST: 1,000	soles
Plastered ceiling in the comedor-estar	COST: 2,000	
White washed block walls	COST: 1,000	

Finally, you may choose where you want your house to be in the larger community. There are two choices: neither has any cost.

14. QUIET AREA OR BUSY AREA

There are two kinds of housing area to live in. In one kind of area there are many people walking up and down the pedestrian way outside the houses. During the day and in the evening, there will almost always be some people on the street. In the other kind of area there are far less people walking through.

Choose one:

Many people going past your house.
Few people going past your house.

15. NEARBY COMMUNITY FACILITIES

The church, market, clinic, parks, kindergartens, schools, secondary school, technical school, evening entertainment, are all fixed positions on the site, and each has a housing area that is particularly closely tied to it. Choose the one which you would most like to be near:

Church
Market
Clinic
Park
Kindergarten
Schools
High school
Technical school
Evening entertainment

95

* * *

individual leaves are formed by the interaction between these rules and the local conditions to which the leaves are subject. As a result, each leaf becomes unique, according to its position in the whole tree; yet in a generic sense the leaves on the tree are all the same. The combination process works in the same way.

All houses are formed by the same sequence of rules, based on the form of the generic house. But each house has to meet certain particular conditions: those imposed on it by the family's choices, and those imposed on it by its position in the site – orientation, the lengths of next door houses, location of nearby footpaths, and so on. Each individual house is formed by the interaction of the local conditions which it has to meet, and the generic rules of the combination process.

For example, in order to make the house-form coherent, the shape of the house entrance must be different for houses with a small sala and houses with a medium sala; it must be different for houses on a corner site and houses on a centre site; it must be different according to the length of the next door house on the eastern side (since the entrance is always on the east). The rules which form the house entrance (Steps 6, 7, 8 below), therefore depend on the size of the sala, the type of site, and the position of the next door house on the eastern side.

It is only this high degree of interaction between the rules of the combination process and the local conditions which guarantees that all houses are internally coherent, and that each house fits coherently into the larger site plan. Like the leaves on a tree, all the houses will be different, yet all of them coherent and all of them the same.

We must stress the fact that the rules of the combination process are almost mechanical, and can be carried out by any trained draughtsman. *The low cost of the houses cannot support any individual design time.* We estimate that a trained draughtsman will need about one hour per house, to translate the family choice sheet into a set of working drawings and specifications for the contractor.

The draughtsman has one master site plan with the house sites shown on it; one file for each family, containing the family choice sheet, and a blank house plan, which shows the side walls only, 5.20 metres apart, for both floors, and no end walls or interior walls. He now builds up the detailed design of each house, by using the following rules, one step at a time:

Step 1

Assignment of houses to cells
Assign each family to a cell in the site plan, on the basis of their answers to questions 14 or 15 on the choice sheet. Location across the site is determined by choice 14. If they want to be in a busy area, place them along the paseo. If they want to be in a quiet area, place them far from the paseo. Location along the length of the site is determined by the community facility they want to be near (choice 15).

Step 2

Determination of house length
Fix the house length as the sum of the lengths of the chosen sala, patio, family room, kitchen and back patio (choices 1, 2, 3, 4, 8).

Step 3

Assignment of houses to sites, within the cell
Within the cell fixed by step 1, assign each house to a lot whose length is as near as possible to the length determined by step 2, and which also satisfies the family's choices concerning shop location, rental/back door, and distance from parking lots (choices 9, 10, 11). (At this point the new site plan will be slightly different from the current site plan – since each house will have a slightly different length. It will now be necessary to make minor changes in layout and arrangement of houses, so that pedestrian paths, loop roads and parking lots still have a coherent form.)

Step 4

Detailed site conditions for each house
Since the house is now fixed within the site plan, the positions of next door houses, positions of adjacent paths and roads, the front end of the house and orientation of the house are now fixed. Transfer these to the drawing of the individual house.

Step 5

Position of patio openings
The patio openings are always on the east side of the house. Sketch in patios for different orientations as shown.

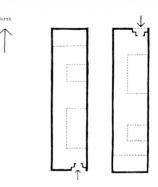

Step 6

General position of front door
The position of the front door is given as a function of patio position (step 5), and the presence or absence of adjacent houses. Sketch entry arrows according to this table.

The arrangements for houses facing north are mirror images of the arrangements for houses facing south. To avoid duplication, all future diagrams will be shown for south facing houses only. Arrangements for north facing houses are obtained by taking the mirror images of these arrangements.

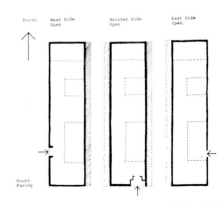

96

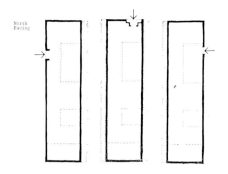

North Facing

Step 8

Detail of front door if at front end
The front door is on the east side of the front end of the house (step 6). Its detailed treatment depends on the position of the house next door and to the east, and on the sala size (step 7). Draw according to this table.

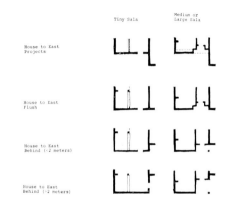

	Tiny Sala	Medium or Large Sala
House to East Projects		
House to East Flush		
House to East Behind (-2 meters)		
House to East Behind (-2 meters)		

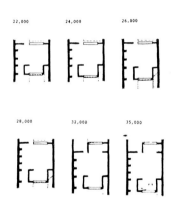

Medium Patio

Large Patio

Step 7

Sala size and position and exact position of front door
The design of sala and front door, in relation to one another, are given as a function of door position (step 6) and the size of sala shown on family's choice sheet (choice 1). Draw sala and entrance according to this table.

97

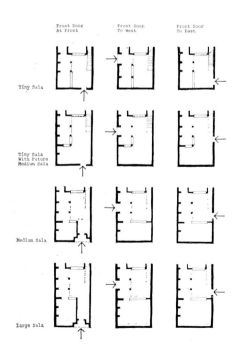

	Front Door At Front	Front Door To West	Front Door To East
Tiny Sala			
Tiny Sala With Future Medium Sala			
Medium Sala			
Large Sala			

Step 9

Size of front patio
The position of the front wall of the family room alcove and veranda column positions are fixed according to the family's choice of patio size (choice 3), and the size of the sala (step 7). Draw according to table.

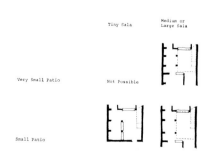

	Tiny Sala	Medium or Large Sala
Very Small Patio		Not Possible
Small Patio		

Step 10

Family room
The family room is fixed directly by the amount the family wants to spend on it (choice 2). Draw as shown.

22,000	24,000	26,000
28,000	32,000	35,000

Step 11

Stairs
The position and size of the stair landing vary according to the size of the front alcove. Draw as shown.

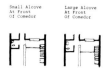

Small Alcove At Front Of Comedor   Large Alcove At Front Of Comedor

Step 12

Kitchen and laundry
The arrangement of the kitchen is determined by the kitchen size (choice 4), by the presence or absence of a second family room alcove (step 10), and by the number of beds in the back cluster upstairs (choice 5). Draw according to table.

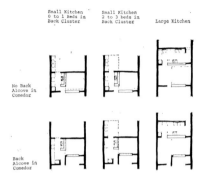

Small Kitchen 0 to 1 Beds in Back Cluster   Small Kitchen 2 to 3 beds in Back Cluster   Large Kitchen

No Back Alcove in Comedor

Back Alcove in Comedor

Step 13

98

Master bedroom and bathroom layout
The layout of the master bedroom is given directly by the length of the family room below (step 10). Draw as shown.

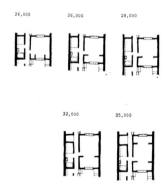

24,000   26,000   28,000

32,000   35,000

Step 14

Back cluster of bed alcoves
The layout of bed alcoves in the back cluster depends on the number chosen by the family (choice 5), and the kitchen size (step 12). Draw according to table.

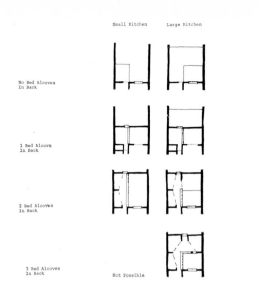

Small Kitchen   Large Kitchen

No Bed Alcoves In Back

1 Bed Alcove In Back

2 Bed Alcoves In Back

3 Bed Alcoves In Back   Not Possible

Step 15

Front cluster of bed alcoves
The layout of bed alcoves in the front cluster depends on the number chosen by the family (choice 5). Draw according to table.

Four front bed alcoves (1)

Three front bed alcoves (2)

Two front bed alcoves (3)

Medium Sala Medium Patio   Medium Sala Large Patio   Large Sala Medium Patio   Large Sala Large Patio

Medium Sala Very Small Patio   Medium Sala Small Patio   Medium Sala Medium Patio   Medium Sala Large Patio

Large Sala Very Small Patio   Large Sala Small Patio   Large Sala Medium Patio   Large Sala Large Patio

Tiny Sala Small Patio   Tiny Sala Medium Patio   Tiny Sala Large Patio   Medium Sala Very Small Patio

Medium Sala Small Patio   Medium Sala Medium Patio

Step 16

Mirador
Front mirador is given by step 15. Side mirador occurs in corner houses only. Draw according to table.

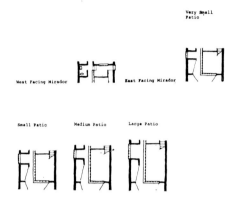

Step 17

Position of windscoop
The windscoop always faces the south wind. It is on the main patio in a south-facing house, and on the kitchen patio in a north-facing house. Draw in positions shown.

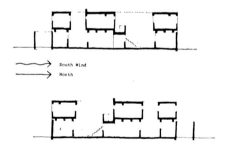

Step 18

Bed alcove for grandmother
If the family has asked for a bed alcove (choice 7) downstairs, it is placed in the kitchen patio, next to the family room. Draw according to table.

Step 19

Position of shop
If the family has asked for a shop (choice 11) the house either fronts on the market, or has a corner lot. The exact arrangement depends on the relative positions of the corner, the sala, the kitchen. Draw according to table.

Shop facing market

Shop at front of house

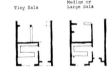

Shop at back of house

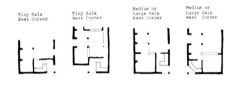

Step 20

Back door and rental space
If the back or the side of the house is open to a pedestrian way, the back door is placed according to the site and the position of the kitchen. If the family has asked for rental space (choice 10) this is built in the position marked R; otherwise this position is left unroofed. Draw according to table.

Costs

The generic house will cost 119,000 *soles* ($2,800, £1,120) as of summer 1969. The smallest house will cost 79,000 *soles* ($1,800, £720), and the largest, with all possible extras, will cost 163,000 *soles* ($3,800, £1,520).

These costs are within 1,000 *soles* of the target set by the United Nations. They give an average of 1,130 *soles* per square metre of interior space (not including verandas or overhangs). This is 25% less than current low-cost construction in Lima.

Our major cost savings have come from the following sources. The foundation slab, without footings, costs 100 *soles* per square metre, compared with the usual price of 200 *soles* per square metre for slab and footings. The mortarless concrete block wall reinforced with sulphur, costs 120 *soles* per square metre, compared with the usual price of 140 *soles* per square metre for a mortared block or brick wall. The long side walls are two-leaf party walls, thus halving the usual cost of individually owned walls. The bamboo-urethane floors and roofs cost 200 *soles* per square metre, compared with the usual cost of 340 *soles* per square metre for reinforced concrete slabs. The finish of the mortarless block wall and the finish of the

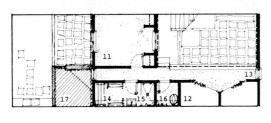

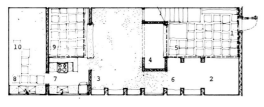

1 Entrance	10 Storage patio
2 Sala (Parlour)	11 Master bedroom
3 Family room	12 Bed alcoves
4 Family room alcove	13 Mirador
5 Main patio	14 Clothes drying closet
6 Veranda	15 Shower
7 Kitchen	16 Toilet
8 Laundry	17 Future bed alcove
9 Kitchen patio	

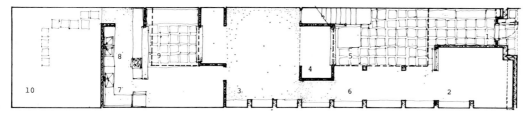

bamboo ceilings make plastering unnecessary, and save the usual cost of 50–60 *soles* per square metre for plaster. The dacron sailcloth cover on the patio, costs 250 *soles* per square metre and saves the cost of windows throughout the house, at a usual cost of 500–600 *soles* per square metre. We have eliminated several doors at a cost of 550 *soles* per door. The ABS accumulator and use of the cavity wall as a vent, saves the cost of several metres of waste pipe, vent pipe, and connections. The fact that our site plan has 1,726 houses, as against the 1,500 expected, saves 12% of the cost of site development.

All costs are for summer 1969. The savings are based on innovations in the building and site development only, since land and financing costs were fixed.

PART TWO

Introduction

We now present some examples of the 67 patterns from which we have built our designs. We do not present these patterns merely to explain our designs, but because we believe that each of them expresses a generally valid principle, which can be used over and over again. *This is the essential point of the patterns: they are re-usable.* Since many of them deal specifically with Peru, we hope that they may be particularly useful to Peruvian architects and builders.

A pattern defines an arrangement of parts in the environment, which is needed to solve a recurrent social, psychological, or technical problem. Each pattern has three very clearly defined sections: *context, solution* and *problem.*

The *context* defines a set of conditions. The *problem* defines a complex of needs which always occurs in the given *context*. The *solution* defines the spatial arrangement of parts which must be present in the given *context* in order to solve the *problem*.

If the needs in the *problem* are correct, and do occur as stated in the given *context,* then this arrangement of parts, or an equivalent one, must always be included in any design for the given *context*. Any design for this context which does *not* include the pattern, is failing to solve a known problem.

This does not mean, of course, that the patterns are absolute. The rightness or wrongness of a pattern is an empirical matter, and as such is always open to further observation and experiment. For this reason, we have tried to state the observations and evidence behind the patterns as clearly as possible, so that they can be checked by others, and rejected when incorrect. The evidence we use comes from three sources: the published literature, our observations in Lima, and our laboratory tests and experiments. We spent a month each living with low income Peruvian families in Pampa de Comas, San Martin de Porras, La Victoria and Rimac (districts of Lima) to better understand their way of life. We built and tested each of the major building components, with supportive testing from professional laboratories. Where our observations are hard to support, we have stated them as conjectures.

Each of these patterns is part of a larger system of patterns, called the pattern language, which we are developing at the Centre for Environmental Structure. When the pattern language is working, as it will be within a few months, it will allow any designer who uses it to draw out all the patterns appropriate to a particular design for any design problem in the city. Even more important, each designer can contribute to the language: he will be able to communicate his design ideas to other designers, by expressing them as patterns.

One final note. The patterns which are presented here were originally prepared for the Proyecto Experimental competition. Each pattern therefore ends with a short statement which explains how the pattern has been realized in the geometry of THE PROYECTO EX-PERIMENTAL. This statement is just an example of the way the pattern was used by *us,* in *our* design. It is *not* part of the pattern itself. The pattern itself always starts with the words THE GENERAL PATTERN IS.

Subculture cells

THE GENERAL PATTERN IS:

Context:
Any urban area which contains more than a few hundred dwellings.

Solution:
The area is made up of a large number of small inward focused residential 'cells'. The cells are separated as sharply as possible from one another; if possible by open land, community facilities, or public

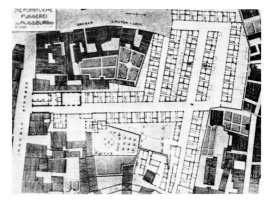

land.
Each cell is intended, in the long run, to sustain a different way of life: a different subculture. A subculture is defined as a group of people (not necessarily friends) who share certain attitudes, beliefs, habits and needs not shared by others; and who may require special environments, local organizations, or services to support these special needs. The community facilities which surround any given cell should reflect the particular interests characteristic of that subculture. All community facilities (including roads, schools, hospitals, churches, parks, industry, commerce, entertainment) are placed in the boundaries between cells.
The arguments which define cell size, are not yet fully clear. At present it seems that no cell should contain more than 1,500 people, or less than 50, with a mean cell population of about 500.

Problem:
People need an identifiable unit to belong to. They want to be able to identify the part of the city where *they* live, as distinct from all others. Available evidence

suggests that the areas which people identify with are *extremely* small – of the order between 100 and 200 metres in diameter. They cannot identify these areas, unless the areas are well differentiated from one another: and studies show that areas will not be strongly differentiated from one another unless they support identifiably different ways of life. This suggests that any urban area should be broken into a number of small 'subculture cells', each supporting an identifiably different way of life.[1]
Psychological arguments lead to the same conclusion. There is strong evidence to suggest that a person cannot develop his own life style fully, unless he does so in an ambience where others share his life style.
In a homogeneous urban area, differences of life style tend to vanish, and ego-strength, self-confidence and character formation deteriorate. This again suggests that the urban area should, as far as possible, support a large variety of strongly differentiated life styles, each supported by a 'subculture cell'.
Ecological arguments help to fix the suitable cell size, and show the need for radical separation between cells. To develop their own life style, the families in a cell must be able to agree on basic decisions about services, community land, etc. Anthropological evidence shows that a human group cannot maintain the face to face relations required to co-ordinate

itself in this way, if its population is above 1,500; many people set the figure as low as 500.[2]
It has also been shown that the group feeling necessary to support a particular unique life style, is greatly strengthened when that group is physically separated from all adjacent groups. This suggests that cells should be inward looking, and wherever possible separated by community facilities.[3]
IN THE PROYECTO EXPERIMENTAL, the community is divided into 43 small residential cells, each containing between 25 and 75 houses. The cells are clearly separated from one another. All houses in a cell face inwards, and the outer cells are surrounded by a narrow road sunken 50 cm below grade, so that these cells are elevated pedestrian islands.
Families choose the cell they want to be in, according to its relative 'quietness', and according to the community facilities nearby. As a result, the families in any one cell will probably share attitudes and interests;

101

we hope that each cell will develop a unique 'character', different from the others.

Looped local roads

THE GENERAL PATTERN IS:

Context:
Any residential area served by local roads.

Solution:
These local roads are narrow one-way 'loop' roads serving a maximum of 50 parking spaces. They need be no more than one lane wide, the surface should be rough. A loop road is defined as any road in a road network placed so that no path along other roads in the network can be shortened by travel along the 'loop'.

Problem:
Through traffic is fast, noisy, and dangerous. At the same time cars are important, and cannot be excluded altogether from the areas where people live. To safeguard these areas, the roads must be laid out to discourage all through traffic – hence the loops. The loops themselves must be designed to discourage high volumes or high speeds: this depends on the total number of houses served by a loop, the road surface, the road width, and the number of curves and corners. Our informal observations suggest that a loop is, and feels, safe as long as it serves less than 50 cars. At this level, there may be a car every two minutes at rush hour, and far fewer during the rest of the day. The number of houses served will vary, according to the average number of cars per house. At $1\frac{1}{2}$ cars per house, such a loop serves 30 houses; at 1 car per house 50 houses; at $\frac{1}{2}$ car per house, 100 houses.
IN THE PROYECTO EXPERIMENTAL, all access to houses is provided by one lane, one-way, loop roads. No one of these loops serves more than 100 houses or 50 parking spaces (at 50% car ownership).

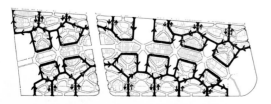

Car – pedestrian symbiosis

THE GENERAL PATTERN IS:

Context:
Any area which contains pedestrian paths and local car roads.

Solution:
The system of pedestrian paths and the system of roads are two entirely distinct orthogonal systems.

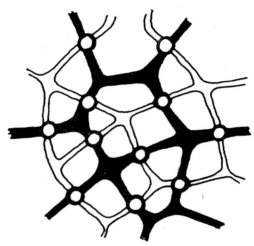

They cross frequently; so that no point on either system is more than about 50 metres from a crossing. Every time they cross, both paths and roads swell out, making room for pedestrian activity and for parking and standing.

Problem:
It is common planning practice to separate pedestrians and cars. This makes pedestrian areas more human, and safer. However, this practice fails to take account of the fact that cars and pedestrians also need each other: *and that, in fact, a great deal of urban life occurs at precisely the point where these two systems meet.* Many of the greatest places in cities, Piccadilly Circus, Times Square, the Champs Elysées, are alive *because* they are at places where pedestrians and vehicles *meet.* New towns like Cumbernauld, where there is total separation between the two, seldom have the same sort of liveliness.
The same thing is true at the local residential scale. A great deal of everyday social life happens where cars

and pedestrians meet. In many low income areas, fo example, the car is used as an extension of the house. Men, especially, often sit in parked cars, near their houses, drinking beer and talking.[4]
Many studies show that conversation and discussion grow naturally out of the communal car lots where men meet when they take care of their cars. Vendors always set themselves up where cars and pedestrians meet; they need all the traffic they can get. Children always play in parking lots – perhaps because they sense that this is the main point of arrival and departure; perhaps because they enjoy the cars.
In Peru, there is a new version of the paseo: the 'autopaseo' – several friends hop into a car, and drive around, visiting their friends, often not even getting out of their cars, but talking from house to car and back.
None of these things can happen in a plan where car roads and pedestrian paths are separated, unless the two meet frequently, and the places where they meet are treated as minor centres of activity.
IN THE PROYECTO EXPERIMENTAL, the car roads

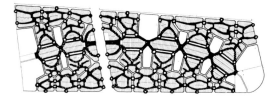

form loops, and the pedestrian paths form a diagonal network which crosses these loops at right angles. Where they cross, there are parking lots, cell gateways, and spaces for pedestrian activity. The two systems form a double gradient: car densities dominate towards the outside of the site, pedestrian densities dominate towards the inside of the site, with a smooth gradient between the two.

Pedestrian 50 cm above car

THE GENERAL PATTERN IS:

Context:
Any area which contains roads with traffic densities of more than a few vehicles per day.

Solution:
These roads are sunk 50 centimetres below all pedestrian paths.

Problem:
In the modern city, the car is king; the pedestrian is made to feel small. This cannot be solved by keeping pedestrians separate from cars; it is in their nature, that they have to meet. But where they meet, the car must be 'put down', symbolically, and the pedestrian world given more importance. This is most easily achieved if the car is physically below the pedestrian. Our experiments suggest that the effect first makes itself felt, when the car is about 50 centimetres below the pedestrian paths. There are two possible reasons for this figure.

Most people's eye level is between 1.30 and 1.60

metres. A typical car has an overall height of 1.40 metres. Although tall people can see over the cars, even for them the cars fill the landscape, since a standing person's normal line of sight is 10 degrees below the horizontal.[5] To get the top of a car that is four metres away, completely below the line of sight, it would have to be standing between 50 and 80 centimetres below the pedestrian.

It may also be that the car overwhelms the pedestrian because of a constant, unspoken possibility that a runaway car might at any moment mount the kerb and run him down. A car can climb an ordinary 15 centimetre kerb, easily. For the pedestrian to feel certain that a car could not climb the kerb, the kerb height would have to be greater than the radius of a car tyre (30–38 cm): thus at least 40 cm, preferably 50 cm.

IN THE PROYECTO EXPERIMENTAL, all local roads are 50 cm below grade. The pedestrian precinct defined by each cell, is an island, floating 50 cm above the road which surrounds it. Where a pedestrian path crosses a local road, there are three steps down.

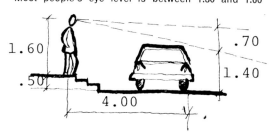

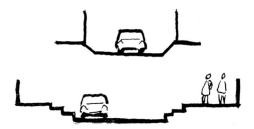

Activity nuclei

THE GENERAL PATTERN IS:

Context:
Any community large enough to support community facilities.

Solution:
The community facilities are clustered round a small number of very small open spaces which we call activity nuclei. The facilities in any one nucleus are clustered in such a way that they co-operate functionally. (See problem statement.) All paths in the community pass through these activity nuclei.

Problem:
One of the greatest problems with new communities, is the fact that the available public life in them is spread so thin, that it has no impact on the community, and is not in any real sense 'available' to the members of the community. Yet studies of pedestrian behaviour make it clear that people seek out concentrations of other people, whenever they are available.[6]

To create these concentrations of people in a community, facilities must be grouped densely round very small public open spaces which can function as nuclei – and all pedestrian movement in the community channelled to pass through these nuclei. These nuclei need two properties.

First, the facilities grouped around any one activity nucleus must be carefully chosen for their symbiotic relationships. It is definitely not enough merely to group communal functions in so called community centres. For example, church, cinema, kindergarten, and police station are all community facilities – but they do not support one another mutually. Different people go to them, at different times, with different things in mind. There is no point in grouping them together. To create intensity of action, the facilities which are placed together round any one nucleus must function in a co-operative manner, and must attract the same kinds of people, at the same times of day.

For example: When evening entertainments are grouped together, the people who are having a night out can use any one of them, and the total concentration of action increases. When kindergartens and small parks and gardens are grouped together, mother and young children may use either, so their total attraction is increased. When schools and swimming pools and football space are grouped together, they form natural centres for school children.

Second, the open places which form the nuclei should be very small indeed. Our observations suggest that 15 × 20 metres is the ideal size; if the space has to be larger, it should be long and narrow, with its short dimension no more than 20 metres.

Our observations in Lima showed, again and again,

that places which are larger look and feel deserted, and discourage activity. The reasons for this recurrent observation are obscure, but the following facts may have something to do with it. A person's face is just recognizable at about 20 metres, and, under typical urban outdoor noise conditions, a loud voice can just be heard at 20 metres.

This may mean that people feel tied together in spaces whose diameter is less than 20 metres, and lose this feeling in larger spaces: perhaps a major factor in the development of activity.

IN THE PROYECTO EXPERIMENTAL, all community facilities open on to one of eight small squares, *and all pedestrian paths in the community* lead towards these eight small squares.

Each of the activity generators is unique, according to the facilities which surround it. The market square is surrounded by small shops, has a supermarket at one end, the artery crossing at the other, and contains market stalls. The evening centre is surrounded by bars, cinema and dance hall, and contains clustered lights for night time activity, and sheltered tables round the edge. The open spaces between kindergartens and walled eucalyptus groves, contain shallow tiled pools, where toddlers can splash and play, with seats around them for mothers. The open space between church and clinic contains flowers,

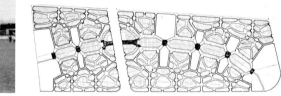

grass and bushes, cared for by the church. The open spaces in front of primary schools, and sports centres, contain a stepped depression, large enough for football in the middle, the steps deep enough to form seats for people who want to watch the games.

Walled gardens

THE GENERAL PATTERN IS:

Context:
Any small park or public garden in an urban area.

Solution:
It is walled, or partly enclosed, yet close to major centres of pedestrian activity.

Problem:
People need contact with trees and plants and water. Their symbolic character is not replaceable. In some way, which is hard to express, people are able to be more whole in the presence of nature, are able to go deeper into themselves, and are somehow able to draw sustaining energy from the life of plants and trees and water.

The small parks and gardens in a city try to solve this problem; but they are usually so close to traffic, noise, and buildings, that the impact of nature is entirely lost. To be truly useful, in the deepest psychological sense, they must allow the people in them to be in touch with nature – and must be shielded from the sight and sound of passing traffic.

In those few cases where there are small walled gardens in a city, open to the public – Alhambra, Morocco, Copenhagen Royal Library Garden – these gardens almost always become famous. People understand, and value the peace which they create.

This is a particularly crucial problem in desert areas like Lima. In the desert, trees and plants are infinitely precious. Gardens are almost like oases – people flock to sit and talk and lie in them, wherever they exist. In such desert areas it is doubly important to keep at least partial separation between the garden

and its surroundings, so that the garden can be fully felt, and the oasis character isn't lost.

At the same time, just because they are so precious, such gardens need to be close to major centres of pedestrian activity, so that people can use them and enjoy them often.

IN THE PROYECTO EXPERIMENTAL, there are three small walled gardens containing grass, seats, paved areas and eucalyptus trees. Each one opens on to one of the activity nuclei along the paseo. The eucalyptus will be a fast growing variety, suitable for Peru, and should reach a height of 25 metres in five years. The gardens will be irrigated by the irrigation water that comes in from the north-east corner of the site.

Multi-purpose Outdoor Room

THE GENERAL PATTERN IS:

Context:
Any local part of a residential community.

Solution:
There is, within view of every house, at least one 'multipurpose outdoor room' with the following characteristics. It is open to the sky, surrounded or at least partly surrounded by a continuous roofed arcade always at least two metres deep, and, where possible, built up against the walls of existing buildings.
The outdoor rooms are left unfinished, with the understanding that they will be finished by people who live near them, to fill whatever needs seem to be most pressing. They may contain sand, or water faucets, or play equipment, for small children. They may contain steps, and seats, where teenagers can meet. Someone may build a small bar in a house that opens into the arcade, making the arcade a place to eat and drink. There may be games for old people, like chess and checkers.

Problem:
In existing modern housing projects, people rarely feel comfortable lingering outside their houses. There are few places where it is 'all right to be'. Yet at the same time, it is clear that almost everyone wants, at some time or another, to linger in some public space. Our observations in Peru show that the men seek corner beer shops, where they spend hours talking and drinking; teenagers, especially boys, choose special corners too, where they hang around, waiting for their friends. And of course these things are not peculiar to Peru – something like it happens everywhere. Old people like a special spot to go to, where they can expect to find others; small children need sand lots, mud, plants, and water to play with in the open; young mothers who go to watch their children, often use the children's play as an opportunity to meet and talk with other mothers.
Few modern housing projects provide for these needs; it is very hard to provide for them. On the one hand, indoor community rooms are too enclosed. When provided, they are rarely used. People don't want to plunge in to a situation which they don't know; and the degree of involvement created in such an enclosed space, is too intimate to allow a casual passing interest to build up gradually to full involvement. On the other hand, vacant land is not enclosed enough. It takes years for anything to happen on vacant land; it provides too little shelter, and too little 'reason to be there'.
What is needed is a framework which is just enough defined so that people naturally stop there, and tend to stop there; and so that curiosity naturally takes

people there, and allows them to stay there. Then, once community groups begin to gravitate towards this framework, there is a good chance that they will themselves create an environment which is appropriate to their activities. Some possible examples of such future developments are given in the solution statement.

We conjecture that a small open space, between 10 and 20 metres in diameter, and surrounded on all sides by an open roofed arcade, may just about provide the necessary balance of 'openness' and 'closedness'. The arcade should be at least 2 metres deep, for the reasons given in 'Two Metre Balcony'.

Even if this conjecture turns out to be correct in theory, it will undoubtedly be very hard to implement. Only detailed experiments, in communities, will show up the finer points that are needed to make this pattern work in practice.

IN THE PROYECTO EXPERIMENTAL, each cell contains one open space about 6 × 10 metres, surrounded by a two metre deep, roofed arcade, and several smaller, non-continuous sections of the same arcade in other places. Each one of these arcades is placed at a node in the system of pedestrian paths. They are left unfinished, with the understanding that community residents may build in games like table tennis, *bochas* or *sapo,* sand-pits, seats, water faucets,

walls, and small shops or bars, according to their needs.

Flowers on the Street

THE GENERAL PATTERN IS:

Context:
Any pedestrian path outside houses.

Solution:
The paths are paved with removable paving stones and it is understood that the people who live in any given house may take up the stones outside their house, to plant flowers, trees and grass.

Problem:
The overall effect of a community, especially in a desert area like Lima, is largely determined by the planting. An area with well kept plants is beautiful; the areas without them seem arid by comparison.

However, the only plants in a community which get looked after, are those which individual people plant, and care for – public planting usually flops – no one takes the responsibility of looking after it, and there is no money for gardeners.

We may thus establish a principle: the planting in a community should be in the form of small gardens, clearly associated with the front of specific individual houses, and planted by the individuals in these houses.

However, only a few of the people in any given community really enjoy gardening. If all the houses are provided with front gardens, three quarters of them will be left unkept – and will very likely end up as dust and weeds. There must be a way of giving gardens to all those people who will look after them, and to no one else. This is easily done. If the footpaths are all

paved with the understanding that anyone who wants to can take up the paving stones and plant things, the only people who will bother to do so will be those who really want a garden.

IN THE PROYECTO EXPERIMENTAL, the pedestrian paths outside houses are paved with large, removable earth-cement paving blocks laid over unfinished earth. It is understood that any homeowner who wants to plant flowers or trees or grass outside his house, may remove these paving stones to do so.

Patios Which Live

THE GENERAL PATTERN IS:

Context:
Any patio intended for active use.

Solution:
1 It has sources of traffic and activity on at least two sides (opposite each other), and functions, at least in part, as a circulation space.
2 It is placed so that you can see out of it, into some other larger space beyond.
3 At least one side of it is roofed, this roofed part being at least two metres deep, and connected to the rest of the building.

Problem:
Many of the patios built currently in modern houses are dead. They are intended to be private open spaces – but often remain unused.

Informal observation suggests that patios are unused for the following reasons:
1 No one ever goes to them when they do not have any natural relation to the activities in the house – this is especially true for those that are dead-ends, off to one side of rooms. To overcome this, the patio should have activities opening off at least two opposite

sides, so that it becomes the meeting point for these activities, provides access to them, provides overflow from them, and provides the cross-circulation between them.

2 They are so enclosed that they become claustrophobic. Patios which are pleasant to be in always seem to have 'loopholes' which allow you to see beyond them, into some further space. The patio should never be perfectly enclosed by the rooms which surround it, but should give at least a glimpse of some other space beyond.

3 They are oppressive. No one wants to sit surrounded by blank walls, disconnected from the house, with a little square of sky overhead. To solve this problem, the patio needs to be partly roofed. This provides a sitting space that is less nakedly exposed to the sky, and, if the roofed position is continuous with the interior of the house, makes the patio seem more like a part of the house, and people will drift more naturally into it.

The veranda formed by this overhanging roof will not work unless it has room for a small table and a couple of chairs, so that people can sit there and talk and drink. This requires at least two metres.

IN THE PROYECTO EXPERIMENTAL HOUSE, both the kitchen patio and the main living patio are

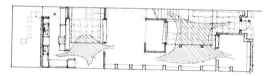

surrounded on three sides by activities, contain a two metre veranda which connects the patio to the house, and are placed so that natural circulation moves through the patio.

Tapestry of Light and Dark

THE GENERAL PATTERN IS:

Context:
Any building where people live during the daytime.

Solution:
Openings and covered areas alternate in such a way that the interior of the building is a tapestry of alternating light and dark spaces, with special emphasis on the boundary areas where dark changes to light.

Problem:
In a building with uniform light level, there are few

'places' which function as effective settings for human events. This happens because, to a large extent, the 'places' which make effective settings are defined by light. People are by nature phototropic – they move towards light, and, when stationary, they orient themselves towards the light. As a result the much loved and much used places in buildings, where most things happen, are places like window seats, verandas fireside corners, trellised arbours; all of them defined by non-uniformities in light, and all of them allowing the people who are in them to orient themselves towards the light.

There is good reason to believe that people need a rich variety of settings in their lives.[7] Since settings are defined by 'places', which in turn seem often to be defined by light, and since light places can only be defined by contrast with darker ones, this suggests that the interior parts of buildings where people spend much time should contain a great deal of

alternating light and dark.

IN THE PROYECTO EXPERIMENTAL, each house has a sequence of alternating patios and rooms along its length.

Intimacy Gradient

THE GENERAL PATTERN IS:

Context:
A house in Peru, or any other Latin country.

Solution:
There is a gradient from front to back, from the most

formal at the front to most intimate and private at the back. This gradient requires the following strict sequence: entry-sala-family room-kitchen-bedrooms.

The most important element in this sequence is the sala (parlour). It is essential that the house contain a sala. If the house is so small that cost rules this out, the house should at least contain a tiny receiving alcove immediately inside the front door.

Problem:
In Latin American countries, such as Peru, friendship is taken very seriously and exists at a number of levels. Casual neighbourhood friends may never enter one's house. Formal friends, such as the priest, the daughter's boy-friend and friends from work may be invited in but tend to be limited to a well furnished and maintained part of the house, the sala. This room is sheltered from the clutter and more obvious poverty of the family which are visible in the rest of the house. Relatives and intimate friends, such

as *compadres,* may be made to feel at home in the *comedor-estar* (family room) where the family is likely to spend much of its time. A few relatives and friends, particularly women, will be allowed into the kitchen, other workspaces, and, perhaps, bedrooms of the house. In this way the family maintains both privacy and pride.

This is particularly evident at the time of a fiesta. Even though the house is full of people, some people never get beyond the sala; some don't even get beyond the threshold of the front door. Others go all the way into the kitchen, where the cooking is going on, and stay there throughout the evening. Each person has a very accurate sense of his degree of intimacy with the family, and knows exactly how far into the house he may penetrate, according to this established level of intimacy.

Even extremely poor people try to have a sala if they can. Many modern houses and apartments in Peru combine sala and family room in order to save space. *Almost everyone we talked to complained about this situation. As far as we can tell, a house must not, under any circumstances, violate the principle of the intimacy gradient.*

IN THE PROYECTO EXPERIMENTAL, there is a strict gradient from formal to informal, front to back.

Each house contains entry-sala-family room-kitchen in that order. Those houses too small to have a proper sala, have a small receiving alcove, just inside the front door, which functions as a sala.

Family Room Circulation

THE GENERAL PATTERN IS:

Context:
The family room (*comedor-estar*) of any low income Peruvian house.

Solution:
The room is relatively long and narrow. The dining table is in the middle; traffic in and out of the house goes through one end, and there are seats or leaning spaces at this end; the TV set is at the other end, in a darkened corner.

Problem:
For a low income Peruvian family, the family room (*comedor-estar*) is the heart of family life. The family eat here, they gossip here, they watch TV here, and everyone who comes into the house comes into this room to say hello to the others, kiss them, shake hands with them, exchange news, gossip. The same happens

when people leave the house.

The family room cannot function as the heart of the family life, unless it helps to support these processes. The room must be so placed in the house, that people naturally pass through it on their way in and out of the house. The end where they pass through it, must allow them to linger for a few moments, without having to pull out a chair to sit down; this requires 'leaning space'. The TV set should be at the opposite end of the room from this throughway; since a glance at the screen is often the excuse for a moment's further lingering. If possible the part of the room for the TV set should be darkened; the family room and the TV function just as much during midday as they do at night.

IN THE PROYECTO EXPERIMENTAL HOUSES, the main part of the family room (not including alcoves), is 3–3.80 metres wide, running across the plot. There is room for a large dining table in the middle, close to the kitchen. Circulation from the front of the house to the kitchen, goes past one end of the table, perpendicular to the room's main axis, and there are seats and leaning niches at this end of the room. The far end of the room is windowless, and contains an electric outlet for TV.

Family Room Alcoves

THE GENERAL PATTERN IS:

Context:
The family room of any house.

Solution:
There are a number of alcoves off the family room (preferably at least two). Each alcove is between one and two metres deep; the alcoves are all narrower than the walls they open from; and their ceilings are

lower than the ceiling of the main room. Each alcove looks at the other alcoves.

Problem:
In modern life, the main function of the family is emotional; it is a source of security and love. But these qualities will only come into existence, if the members of the house are physically able to *be* together, as a family.

In modern life, this is often difficult. The various members of the family come and go at different times of the day; even when they are in the house, each has

108

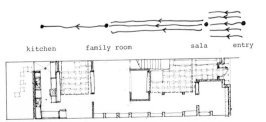

kitchen   family room   sala   entry

his own private interests: sewing, reading, homework, carpentry, model-building, games. In many houses, these interests force people to go off to their own rooms, away from the family. This happens for two reasons. First, in a normal family room, one person can easily be disturbed by what the others are doing: the person who wants to read, is disturbed by the fact that the others are watching TV. Second, the family room doesn't usually have any space where people can leave things and not have them disturbed. Books left on the dining table get cleared away at meal times; a half finished game can't be left standing; naturally people get into the habit of keeping some activities away from the family.

To solve the problem, there must be some way in which the members of the family can be together, even when they are doing different things. This means that the family room needs a number of small spaces where people can do different things. The spaces need to be separate from the main room, so that any clutter that develops in them does not encroach on the communal uses of the main room. The spaces need to be connected, so that people are still 'together', when they are in them: this means they need to be open to each other. At the same time they must be secluded, so that a person in one of them is not disturbed by the others. In short, the family room must be surrounded by small alcoves. The alcoves should be large enough for one or two people at a time: about two metres wide, and between one and two metres deep. To make it clear that they are separate from the main room, so they do not clutter it up, and so that people in them are secluded, they should be narrower than the family room walls, and have lower ceilings than the main room.

IN THE PROYECTO EXPERIMENTAL HOUSES, small family rooms have one alcove opening off them, and the large family rooms have two. These alcoves

are 250 cm wide and between 120 and 160 cm deep. Ceiling height in the alcoves is 2.20 metres (compared with 2.70 in the main part of the family room).

Thick Walls

THE GENERAL PATTERN IS:

Context:
Interior wall, in any part of a building which is intended to be personal.

Solution:
The wall has 'depth', at least 40 cm, which is created by a hand-carvable rigid space frame, in which a continuous variety of niches, shelves, seats, cupboards, leaning posts, and window seats occur at frequent intervals. This hand-carvable space frame is made of materials which are readily available on the retail market, and easily cut, modified, painted, nailed, glued, or replaced by hand, using only tools available at any hardware store. Possible examples are wood, plywood, fibreglass, styrofoam, polystyrene. The space frame is highly redundant structurally: large sections of it may be removed, without weakening it, and pieces or sections may be added in such a way that these sections become continuous with, and indistinguishable from, the original surface.

Problem:
Rooms with large, flat, unbroken wall surfaces almost never have any personal character, and it is very hard for people who live in such rooms to make them personal. A room becomes personal only when the imprint of its inhabitants is clearly visible, the walls crowded with treasures and belongings: presents, pictures of sweethearts and grandparents, flowers, vases, knick-knacks, books, collections; these treasures built integrally into the fabric of the room, and the surface of the room moulded to the character of its inhabitants. If a room has large unbroken wall surfaces, made of unmouldable materials, none of this is possible. It is hard to store things in the open, without cluttering up the room, and it is not possible to build these things in a personal way into the fabric of the room.
Wall surfaces must be deep enough to contain a variety of niches and recesses, where special things can be placed, without being in the way; and the wall must be made of materials which allow these niches and recesses to be adapted to the idiosyncrasies of the things which are to be placed there, and to the habits which go with them.[8]

IN THE PROYECTO EXPERIMENTAL HOUSE, the wall connecting the sala, patio, veranda and family room, has a series of small niches in it, formed by 40 cm stub walls that project at right angles to the main wall. Each niche contains a seat, shelves, cupboard or display.

Entrance Transition

THE GENERAL PATTERN IS:

Context:
Any house entrance.

Solution:
The path from the street into the house passes through a zone where levels, materials, view, light and other qualities change.

Problem:
There is no doubt that houses which provide a graceful transition space between street and house, are nicer than those which open abruptly off the street. If the transition is too abrupt there is no feeling of arrival, and the house fails to be an inner sanctum. The following argument may help to explain it. While people are on the street, they adopt a mask of 'street behaviour'. When they come into a house they

naturally want to get rid of this street behaviour and settle down completely, into the more intimate spirit appropriate to a house. But it seems likely that they cannot do this, unless there is a transition from one to the other, which helps them to lose the street behaviour. The transition must, in effect, destroy the momentum of the closedness, tension and 'distance' which are appropriate to street behaviour, before they can relax completely.

Evidence comes from the report by Serge Bouterline and Robert Weiss, *The Seattle World's Fair*.[9] The authors noticed that many exhibits failed to 'hold' people; they drifted in, and then drifted out again within a very short time. However, in one exhibit people had to cross a huge, deep-pile, bright orange carpet on the way in. Though the exhibit was no better than other exhibits, people stayed. The authors concluded that people were, in general, under the influence of their own 'street and crowd behaviour', and while under this influence could not relax enough to make contact with the exhibits. The bright carpet presented them with such a strong contrast as they walked in that it broke the effect of their outside behaviour, in effect 'wiped them clean', with the result that they could then get absorbed in the exhibit.

There are many ways of marking the transition from street to house: change of view, change of light, change of level, change of surface, change of sound, change of scale; all break the continuity of passage from street to house, and all can be helpful.

IN THE PROYECTO EXPERIMENTAL HOUSE, there is a dark, covered area, immediately inside the front door, and a well lit patio further in. A person entering thus passes through a dark zone, towards the light of the patio beyond, and then enters the house through the main veranda, between sala and family room.

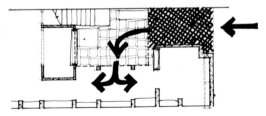

Front Door Recesses

THE GENERAL PATTERN IS:

Context:
Any Peruvian house which has a front door opening directly off a public path.

Solution:
The front door is surrounded, on both sides, by deep recesses, each at least 50 cm deep – if possible by double recesses. The effect of the recesses is helped by an opening in the door, or a dutch door.

Problem:
'Hanging out' is a standard part of Latin culture. People like to watch the street. But people do not always want the same degree of involvement with the street. The process of hanging out requires a continuum of degrees of involvement with the street,

ranging all the way from the most private kind, to the most public kind. A young girl watching the street may want to be able to withdraw the moment anyone looks at her too intently. At other times, girls, young men, and the women of the house, may want to be watching the street, near enough to it to talk to someone who comes past, yet still protected enough so that they can withdraw into their own domain at a moment's notice. At still other times, old men, less afraid of real involvement on the street, will actually sit out, in front of their doorways, and feel secure provided that the seat is still clearly identified with their house.

In the most common kind of hanging out, people lean in doorways, half in, half out. They can see what is happening outside, they can talk to anyone they want to – yet they can withdraw in a moment. To invite this activity, front doors need deep recesses, large enough to hold a person (thus at least 50 cm deep), and, if possible, a way of hanging over the door, like that which a dutch door provides.

IN THE PROYECTO EXPERIMENTAL HOUSE, each front door is surrounded on the outside by one or more deep recesses, according to the exact position of the entrance with respect to other houses. The front doors are of the dutch door type.

Composite Bamboo Foam Beam

THE GENERAL PATTERN IS:

Context:
Short spans and light loads in countries where bamboo is abundant and cheap.

Solution:
Beams may be made of bamboos (pinned and glued with epoxy) to form a box which is filled with plastic foam. Spans may range from 3 to 5 metres with corresponding variation in beam spanning. Allowable loads are shown in the problem statement.

Problem:
Concrete beams are expensive, very heavy, hard to move around, and hard to work. In many buildings, especially those where people will be building for themselves (as in self-help housing) beams need to be lightweight, and easy to work. In earthquake zones, it is also necessary to reduce dead loads as far as possible. If bamboo is locally available and petroleum resources allow local manufacture of urethane foams, then it is possible to make lightweight bamboo/foam beams, with excellent structural characteristics.

We have built three different beams of this type, and tested them. It is clear from our tests that bamboo/foam beams of this type are about as strong as softwood beams of the same size. The most serious problem is deflection. Bamboo is extremely strong in tension, and the urethane foam makes the beam section rigid; but the bamboos tend to slip past each other in horizontal shears.

In the third of the three test beams, we pinned and spotglued bamboos together with epoxy glue and dowels. This test beam was 20 cm wide, 40 cm deep. We tested it over a clear span of 3.50 metres. At a uniformly distributed load of 1,300 kilograms the deflection reached 0.8 cm after an hour, and showed no sign of further creep 24 hours later.

We may use the formula:

$$\text{Deflection}_{Max} = (5/384)WL^3/EI$$

to obtain a value for EI, and extrapolate the following figures for maximum allowable uniform loads, at various spans:

Clear span between supports (metres)	Maximum allowable uniformly distributed load, for beam deflection less than L/360 (kg).
3.00	2200
3.50	1620
4.00	1240
4.50	980
5.00	800

(where the design criterion is L/240, for unplastered conditions, these loads can be increased by 50%)

These beams will cost 100 *soles* per metre (compared with about 200 *soles* per metre for comparable rein-

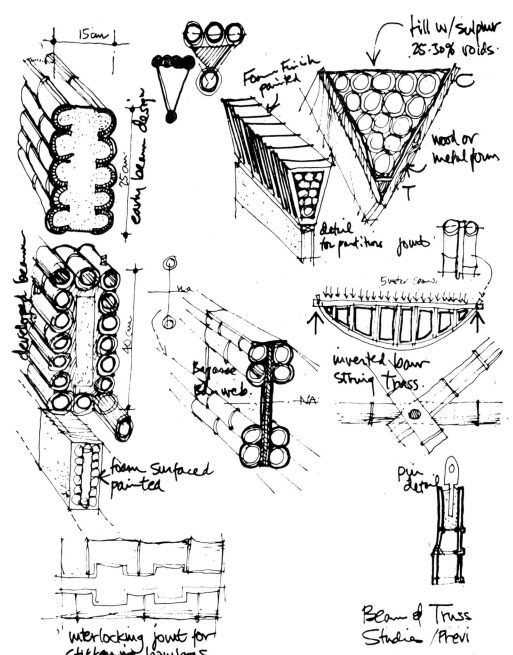

111

forced concrete beams), and weigh about 20 kilograms per metre (compared with 50 kg per metre for a reinforced concrete beam of similar strength). Furthermore, these beams can be cut with simple tools: they can easily be lifted and installed by two men.

It is important to note that the beam type described here is by no means the last word in composite bamboo/foam beams. Much development is needed to try others which use different indigenous materials in place of bamboo, other foams like high-density sulphur foams, and new glues and bonding agents. The sketches illustrate some of these possibilities.

IN THE PROYECTO EXPERIMENTAL HOUSE, all beams are rectangular section boxed beams, 20 cm wide, 40 cm deep, and 5 metres long. The beams are made of 6 cm bamboos, placed over plywood templates, with a core of 2 lb density polyurethane fire-retardent foam, foamed in place. The bamboos are pinned and spot glued together at 50 cm intervals, with epoxy glue and wooden dowels.

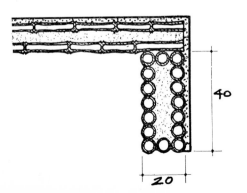

The framing model is shown below. The second storey floor beams are all supported by interior partitions or columns, and have clear spans of 3 metres or less – except in the family room, where they span 4.50 metres between shear walls and impost blocks, and are spaced close together to make up for the long span. The roof beams span the full 4.80 metres between impost blocks, and are spaced at intervals ranging from 1.50 to 2.40 metres.

The second storey floor is designed to carry 200 kg per square metre (bamboo foam plank 15 kg per square metre, sulphur cement topping 45 kg per square metre, second floor partitions 50 kg per square metre and live load 90 kg per square metre). The roof is designed to carry 80 kg per square metre (bamboo foam plank 15 kg per square metre), thin topping 20 kg per square metre and live load 45 kg per square metre). To put a third storey on the house, additional beams will need to be inserted (they can be slipped

Below top first floor ceiling
Below bottom second floor ceiling

on to the impost block easily), and the topping on the roof increased.

At these loads, the beams have a deflection of less than 1/360 of the span, and can safely be plastered. Families who do not like the appearance of the exposed bamboo can plaster them.

Composite bamboo foam plank

THE GENERAL PATTERN IS:

Context:
Short beam spacings and light loads in countries where bamboo is abundant and cheap, compared with other materials.

Solution:
Floor and roof planks may be made from bamboo/polyurethane foam sandwich. Maximum span for this system is approximately 2.50 metres unless panels have additional thickness and reinforcing. Allowable loads are shown in the problem statement.

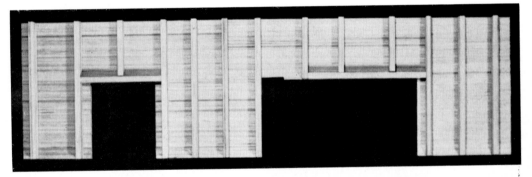

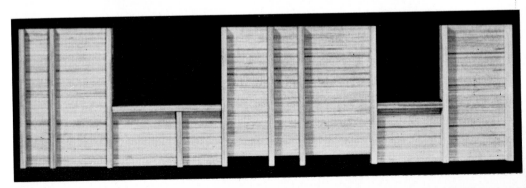

Problem:

Conventional reinforced concrete beam and plank is expensive and heavy. A number of recent experiments have shown that sandwich planks with plywood, gypsum or cement asbestos skins and polyurethane foam cores have enough strength to span 2-3 metres with normal live loads; they have been widely built and tested in many parts of the United States. In a country where bamboo is readily available, and wood expensive, it seems natural to use bamboo as the outer skin of the sandwich instead of plywood.

We built a test plank, with bamboos for the lower

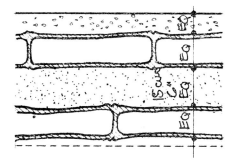

Plank section

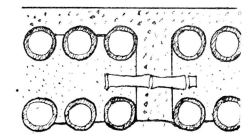

Plank joint

skin, and 3 mm fibre board for the upper skin. This plank performed very well in tests. At final failure the upper skin failed, in shear; the bamboo held. The following table shows the deflection test data.

These figures are for a centre load, on a plank 70 cm wide, over a span of 170 cm.

Load (kg)	Deflection (cm)
45	.25
91	.50
136	.75
182	.95
227	1.15
272	1.30
318	1.50
364	1.70
409	1.90
454	2.10
546	2.55
636	3.00
729	3.50

This rudimentary plank, which has half bamboos in the lower skin, and very little in the upper, is too weak. We recommend a stronger plank, which has whole bamboos top and bottom.

By means of the formula

$$\text{Deflection}_{Max} = (1/48)WL^3/EI$$

we may obtain a value of EI for the weaker plank. Reckoning that the moment of inertia will be tripled in a plank with whole bamboos top and bottom, we estimate that the stronger plank will support the following loads, at the stated spans:

Clear span between supports (metres)	Maximum allowable uniformly distributed load, for plank deflection less than L/360 (kg per square metre)
1.00	200
1.50	590
2.00	250
2.50	128
3.00	74

These planks are extremely light: they weigh about 1.3 kilograms per square metre, they can be hand carried, and laid by two men. Since they can easily be made in long lengths, it is advisable to lay them over several supports, thus getting the benefit of the negative moments. The urethane core gives them excellent thermal and acoustic performance. The foam can also be used as base for applying plaster or

113

can be painted when desired.

Since the plank relies heavily on the use of polyurethane foam, it is important to add a note on the manufacture of these foams: particularly since the countries which are most likely to benefit from the use of bamboo, like Peru, will have to create urethane manufacturing capacity from scratch.

Capital equipment will cost £20,000 to £40,000. The organization of the factory and one year's operation will cost £80,000 to £100,000; with £40,000 of this amount going for the initial inventory of raw materials. At these costs it will be important to use polyurethane foams for other purposes too. They can be used for beams (see Composite Bamboo Foam Beam) e.g. for interior partitions, and in a slightly different chemical formulation, for the manufacture of furniture, bedding and soft seating.[10]

IN THE PROYECTO EXPERIMENTAL HOUSE, the second floor and roof structure are bamboo/polyurethane foam sandwich planks laid over beams. The outer skins of the plank sandwich are made of 6 cm bamboos, and the core is 2 lb density polyurethane. A sand-sulphur topping is poured after planks are in position to form the upper walking surface, and the jointing between planks.

The planks are 15 cm thick (including the topping), 50 cm wide and 5 metres long. They are supported by similarly constructed beams (see Composite Bamboo Foam Beam) spaced at intervals between 1 metre and 2.40 metres, according to position in the structure. Since planks are 5 metres long, they act as continuous members over at least two supports after the topping is poured over them. If families do not like the exposed bamboo, the plank will readily take plaster.

114

Notes

1 See Frank Hendricks, 'A Situational Approach to Residential Environmental Planning: A Research Framework', unpublished report to the US Public Health Service, March 1967.

2 See for example, Anthony Wallace, *Housing and Social Structure,* Philadelphia Housing Authority, 1952; currently available through University Microfilms, Inc., Ann Arbor, Michigan.

3 The full arguments, and empirical evidence for all these points, are presented in Christopher Alexander, *Cells of Sub-cultures,* Centre for Environmental Structure, Berkeley, California, 1968.

4 Clare Cooper, 'Some Social Implications of House and Site Plan Design at Easter Hill Village: A Case Study', Institute of Urban and Regional Development, Centre for Planning and Development Research,

University of California, Berkeley, California, 1966, pp. 39 ff.

5 Henry Dreyfus, *The Measure of Man,* New York, 1959, sheet F.

6 e.g. Jan Gehl, 'Mennesker til Fods (Pedestrians)', *Arkitekten,* No 20, 1968.

7 see Roger Barker, *The Structure of Behaviour: Explorations of its Structure and Content,* Appleton-Century-Croft, New York, 1963.

8 This argument is presented in full, with empirical evidence, in Christopher Alexander, 'Thick Walls', *Architectural Design,* February 1968.

9 Cambridge, Mass., 1963.

10 For a general discussion of urethane foams in building, see *Structural Potential of Foam Plastics for Housing in Underdeveloped Areas,* Architectural Research Laboratory, University of Michigan, Ann Arbor, Michigan, November 1965.

A NEW VIEW OF THE HOUSING DEFICIT

JOHN C. TURNER

The hypothesis that I am putting forward for discussion is that the failures of policies and programmes for popular housing – and for the control of urban growth – are partly due to misunderstandings of the nature of housing. I argue that the common mistake is in evaluating housing quantitatively, in terms of its objective appearance, and that this is unrealistic; instead, the value of a house, or rather of the dwelling environment, is the quality of its response to the life-situation of the person in the family and in the local community. The reality of the dwelling place, in other words, is in its attributes as they are experienced and perceived and not in its material shape or condition.

It follows that the 'housing problem' is commonly misstated in quantitative instead of in qualitative terms so that the targets set tend to be unattainable and, therefore, self-defeating. Further, that the project types most commonly employed to solve the popular housing problem, by failing to respond properly to the life-situations of their intended inhabitants, tend to compound social, economic and political problems rather than solve them. I conclude that the housing problem, as distinct from economic problems such as employment and the distribution of wealth, is a problem of the proper use of resources available for housing – and not in straining all resources indiscriminately for the production of the maximum possible number of modern standard housing units.[1]

I have referred to two ways of seeing – or of defining – 'housing'; one can *see* the *appearance* of the material artifact or *object* and one can *perceive* the *external reality* (as distinguished from appearance) or the *subject* of the attributes perceived. As the appearance of an object, its shape and texture, size and weight and so on, is meaningless without knowledge of its content and purpose, its definition should be based on the attributes of the subject rather than on the appearance of the object.

Three Functions of a Dwelling

Empirically, without any theoretical justification that I have yet been able to discover and, therefore, tentatively, I postulate three essential functions which any dwelling must satisfy in order to become an external reality: shelter, security and location. A house is not a house if it does not provide the minimum of protection from unbearable climate and unbearable people; if the shelter, however excellent the protection it provides, cannot be occupied with a reasonable guarantee of tenure it will be of little or no use; and if the house does not afford access to a suitable environment – if the occupants cannot get to work, to markets, schools and the facilities their lives demand, or if they cannot be with the community to which they belong, the house will be of no practical value whatsoever.

In principle these three functions are constants; they are equally true for any cultural or geographic situation but, of course, the *forms* which houses and 'housing' take vary as climates and cultures vary. In order to understand these variations – in this article I am concentrating on cultural variations in Lima, Peru, at the present time – it is necessary to know how the different functions operate for each social sector. To understand these variations one must view them in terms of the relationship between the person and the total environment (social, economic and physical) in which he lives. For instance, an upper-class executive will be personally connected with and 'at home' throughout a huge, maybe world-wide geographic area; a worker in one of his factories on the other hand will feel at ease only in two or three localities. It is obvious that this difference, along with all those that go along with it, will profoundly affect the ways in which each man's dwelling must function as well as the shape of each man's environment.

Take location: accessibility to those on whom the person depends for society and to the facilities he requires in order to live adequately and to be sociable is essential. The factory worker must live within cheap public transportation distance of his work, and his family must live near markets, schools and so on – and very near friends and relatives if they are to have any real, social life and the community security which goes along with it. For the executive, owner of chauffeur-driven cars and frequent user of jet aircraft, residential proximity to his work or friends is unnecessary while proximity to markets or schools is a nuisance to be avoided. These different cultural situations and the attitudes, values and concepts which go along with them – both shaping the resultant image and being shaped by it – are not unconnected. In modern or modernizing society, whether in Lima or New York, there are no hard and fast frontiers between adjacent sectors and there is a great deal of social mobility between them.

Upper, middle, lower-middle, 'working' or 'blue-collar' classes and 'the poor' are categories recognized both in American-English and Peruvian-Spanish although, scientifically, they may be imprecise and often misleading. The North American situation is especially fluid in the lower and middle ranges, and both the North American and the Peruvian situations are complicated by the presence of important subcultural groups, especially in the lowest ranges. In spite of the criticisms that can be made, I have superimposed these 'class' categories on the graph showing the distribution of the Lima population by income – itself based on estimates which have been challenged though I have reason to believe that they are reasonably accurate. In any case, without the help of an illustration of this kind it would be impossible to explain the hypothesis – the principles of which are independent of the statistical accuracy of the sample used.

I have already described, by way of illustration, why one function – location in terms of proximity to the community and its facilities – should have such very different orders of priority for two different income and class levels. To form a more coherent and complete picture of each 'level': one must interpret the three functions in terms of each life-situation – or, at any rate, in terms of a representative of each level described. The three situations that I will summarize in the following paragraphs do not describe every aspect of contemporary life in Lima – all they attempt to do is to illustrate the typical situations along the line of urban acculturation and social mobility: a sequence which an exceptionally fortunate immigrant family might follow over the course of two or three generations.

The Quest for Security

The necessary attributes of a practical dwelling for the very poor immigrant family, unable to double up with friends or relatives, are straightforward and simple: they must be located as near as possible – within walking distance – to their work-places and the markets where food is cheap; they need shelter for sleeping, eating and leaving their few belongings and a sheltered place to look after children – and, maybe, leave them while both parents are working or looking for work. That the dwelling itself should be very small and that domestic life should overflow into a common courtyard, may be an advantage. The higher the density, the lower the rents and semi-communal living can greatly increase effective living space as well as the safety of children while mothers are working. The only 'security' which the very poor are concerned with – those who have less than necessary for subsistence – is that provided by work and an income which will enable them to climb out of their present situation. Location, in terms of proximity to sources of livelihood – and the support of friends and relatives – is, therefore, by far the most important consideration for the penniless but hopeful immigrant; more important than security – in terms of permanency of residence – and far more important than the quality of his shelter or the 'modernity' of his dwelling.

116

Above A recently-arrived immigrant family living in a rented room: possibly an abandoned mother. The interior is similar to those in the shacks, right.
(Photo: Raoul Becerra)

Middle A young couple, brother and sister, possibly recent migrants, in the central wholesale market (La Parada), Lima. Being young and perhaps without children they have a more cheerful situation.
(Photo: William Mangin)

Above right Shacks in a downtown *corralon* in central Lima. Note the high building in the background and the tricycle in the foreground – the kind used by street vendors. The low-income family in the passageway is typical. The Highland plaits of the woman are similar to the woman in the interior above.
(Photo: John Turner)

Right This aerial of a *corralon* was taken soon after the photograph, above right. This fairly large *corralon* has one entrance, in the upper lefthand corner. The property may have been invaded and squatted upon, or clandestinely rented to the squatters by the owner with a law-suit over the property.
(Photo: John Turner)

117

If all goes well for the penniless immigrant for a number of years, five to ten say, he will have become a fairly regularly employed blue-collar worker earning an average wage; enough to maintain a normal household of five or six at low but locally acceptable standards – and even to save a little. With his changed social and economic situation, the family's housing needs will have changed: with an income sufficient for a modest expenditure on public transportation the family are no longer tied so closely to their sources of livelihood. Financially able to enjoy appreciably better living standards, and with growing children, the family will be much more sensitive about their physical housing conditions. The extremely high densities of the typical slum will no longer have the advantages which they give the very poor or recent immigrant; the physical and psychological health hazards become a major preoccupation, especially for the family dependent on an insecure income. The uncertainty of the wage-earner's income in a society with a high degree of under-employment and no effective provisions for assistance to the unemployed – even when sick – is a dominant factor in most Limenos' lives.

Economic insecurity constantly threatens a family's improved status. A variety of normally minor crises such as illness, a strike, a trade recession or a bankruptcy – all of which are naturally very common in a city like Lima – can push the family back down the slope it has so painfully climbed. Such a demoralizing disaster – often enough to break up a family, especially as so many of these families are emotionally or institutionally unstable to begin with – can easily be precipitated by eviction from rented housing of the type that the family is most likely to be living in at this stage.

Above left A *callejon* or passageway in central Lima. At the far end is a court for hanging out clothes where there may also be some toilets. Other toilets are built into the *callejon* itself, just beyond the water tap. A tailor's sign appears above the second door, right.

Left An aerial view of the inner city, where there are innumerable *callejones*. The large building, upper left, is the central retail market and it attracts much low-income labour. Apart from the *callejones* there are a number of *quintas* – lower middle class rental apartments – a superior version of a *callejon*, lower left. Most *callejones* are adobe one-storey structures. Their construction has been prohibited since the 1930s and few have been built in central Lima since. (Photos: John Turner)

The vast majority of blue-collar households, and many of white-collar employees, who do not live in a *barriada* – a permanent and developing form of squatter suburb – live in *callejones*. The typical *callejon* is a passageway leaving to a small courtyard along and around which there are one- or two-room dwellings. A water faucet and half a dozen latrines will be provided in the courtyard for the thirty or forty families of the *callejon*. As a result of short-sighted and opportunistic legislation – the premature prohibition of the construction of *callejons* and rent freezing – the cheapest available housing is extremely expensive for the newcomer.

Many low-income households, who must spend between two thirds and three quarters of their earnings on food to maintain a poor but locally acceptable diet, are spending between a quarter and one third of their income on rent. If rents are too high – they should not be more than 15% of the family's income in this range – savings, entertainment and even tools can only be obtained by cutting down on food and so sacrificing energy and decreasing resistance to disease. As landlords can only raise rents when the tenant changes and can only evict for non-payment of rent or for rebuilding, a high proportion of slum tenants are paying much less than the newcomer must pay: a resident of seven to ten years' standing will be paying no more than a quarter of the rent that his new neighbour will have to pay for an identical dwelling. Rising land values, an increasing demand for the lowest-priced accommodation and decreasing returns on slum property, pressure landowners to maintain a high turnover of tenants or to evict them all in order to build. Rebuilding, needless to say, never reaccommodates those evicted. The consequences of eviction for all but the most recent arrivals, almost certainly mean a reduction of living standards; slum tenants, therefore, are increasingly insecure and have more reason to fear eviction unless they can get a home of their own. The security factor for this sector of the urban population is predominant.

If the representative family has a property of its own, its expenditures can be kept to a minimum in times of crisis – as it no longer has to pay rent – and it is no longer threatened with eviction and the loss of identity that can so easily follow. And, besides, the property can be an additional source of income, either directly through sub-letting in part or by taking in lodgers or indirectly, through its use as a shop or work shop. For the family that has no other form of security, no social insurance, no convertible capital or no skills in assured and constant demand, inalienable tenure of their own home is essential for their peace of mind,

117

Above top A primitive shelter on a newly set-out lot; the beginning of a new *barriada* or squatter-settlement site.

Above A squatter family, recently arrived, erecting their shack. The woman is pregnant with her third child. They were renting a room in a *callejon* before moving out to this *barriada*. The second man is a relative.
(Photos: John Turner)

and often for their very existence. In such a mild climate as Lima's and with such cheap public transportation, it is easy to understand why this sector is so much less concerned with structures and why so many are prepared to live in relatively distant and isolated locations if, by making these sacrifices, they can achieve residential stability and the economic security that goes along with it.

I have not yet mentioned the other principal source of security which the underemployed and underpaid can and often do have: membership of a large family which extends itself into and binds it up with a local community. As recent studies in London and Lagos have pointed out, the growth of community-wide ties which are strong enough to provide mutual support takes time. Unrelated families with young children must, obviously, live together for a generation at least before many of them become blood relatives.

The representative immigrant family will not be losing this kind of security unless, of course, it has moved into an enclave of its own kith and kin within the city. Whether this happens with any significant frequency or not in Lima, I do not know. It is safe to assume, however, that many of the numerous city-born-and-bred families – who are also threatened with eviction – do live in such local communities; their loss, when they are evicted and cannot relocate themselves locally, is redoubled. This may be one of the reasons why established slum dwellers are so reluctant to move even when they can afford to do so financially, and why such a high proportion of the marginal settlements established by ex-city centre dwellers are of provincial origin. It is also tempting to speculate on the possibility that one of the strongest motives for becoming a home owner, and the extraordinary respect that squatter settlers have for one another's property, is the search for the kind of stability – or security – essential for the cultivation of a meaningful community.

The third clearly different and distinct situation I will describe is that which readers will be most familiar with: the middle-class situation. A qualified Peruvian professional's life in Lima is far nearer that of his North American counterpart than the North American factory worker's life is to that of a factory worker in Lima. Many middle and upper-class Peruvians work in the United States and in Europe and their greatest adaptation problems are with the weather rather than with cultural differences. I will not, therefore, be straying too far from the truth if I refer to the metropolitan middle-class in general rather than to our Peruvian colleagues in particular.

Both in the 'urbanizing' and the already 'urbanized'

countries the qualified professional – whom I am taking as the representative of the middle class in general – is extremely mobile, horizontally or geographically speaking. Residential stability may even undermine the security of the professional which lies, not in his property, but in his intellectual capital and in his freedom to apply it – anywhere. An adequate security of tenure even the most mobile professional must have – he is unlikely to take a hotel room which he can use for only half a night or a house for his family for such a short time that the effort of moving their belongings (however many or few they may carry around) is too great in relation to the duration of their stay. But security of tenure, a minimum of which he must have under any circumstances, is very much less important to the professional and his family than the quality of their shelter. If he does not live in a house that is acceptable to his peers the professional will have no clients and the family will find it difficult to make friends. In fact, the image and comfort that the dwelling offers is far more important for the middle class in general – and the mobile professional in particular – than its security or location functions. If the middle-class family has at least one car, a telephone and a refrigerator it can be as far from its friends, shopping centres and schools as the efficiency which its personal communication systems permits. In principle, as Melvin Webber has pointed out, this can be world-wide.

The Diagram

The diagram summarizes the above interpetations in graphic form. The functional pattern at each level is radically different even though, in each case, the same subject is in view – the residential location, security and shelter of the family or household group. The material components and their shapes – the objective appearance – of each environmental model are as radically different as the changes in the pattern and priority of the functions lead one to expect. If the material environment is analyzed in terms of land, facilities and houses, the correlations between the preferred models at each level and the patterns of functional priority are logical and seem perfectly natural.

The explanation which follows must be preceded, however, by definitions of the material components which I have chosen for the purpose. By *land* I mean, literally, the surface of the land on which the dwelling is placed and which is subject to use and property divisions. A *facility* refers to equipment that eases the performance of an activity necessary for and complimentary to domestic life – work, shopping, education,

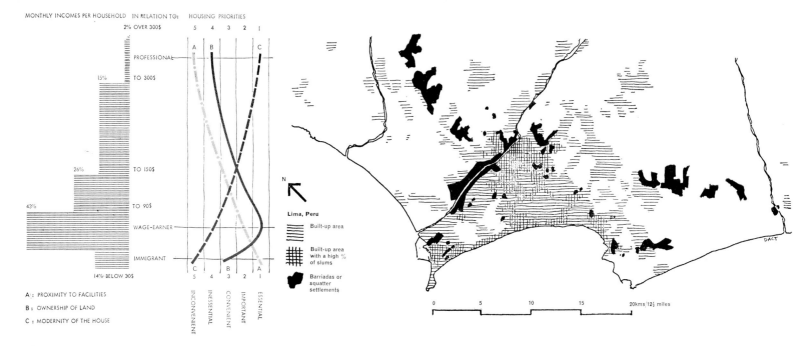

2% OVER 300$ 5   4   3   2   1

PROFESSIONAL

15%   TO 300$

26%   TO 150$

43%   TO 90$

WAGE-EARNER

IMMIGRANT

14% BELOW 30$ 5   4   3   2   1

A : PROXIMITY TO FACILITIES

B : OWNERSHIP OF LAND

C : MODERNITY OF THE HOUSE

INCONVENIENT   INESSENTIAL   CONVENIENT   IMPORTANT   ESSENTIAL

N

Lima, Peru

⊟ Built-up area

⊞ Built-up area with a high % of slums

⬛ Barriadas or squatter settlements

0   5   10   15   20kms/12½ miles

religious ritual and so on. *Housing* refers to the equipment required for domestic living itself – the building with its installations. The figure summarizes my present interpretation of the orders of priority between these material components in relation to income levels and with particular reference to the sectors described above. The degrees of priority, however, have to be seen in different terms: *land* is shown in terms of priority of *ownership* (or any other form of inalienable possession); *facilities* in terms of their *proximity* to the immediate neighbourhood of the dwelling; *housing,* on the other hand, is interpreted in terms of material standards and its *modernity*. In other words, a low priority for land indicates an acceptance of short-term residence while the highest priority indicates a demand for ownership; a low priority for facilities implies that there is little or no demand for them to be in or even near the residential neighbourhood; and the higher the priority the closer they need to be to the household's dwelling; the house varies from the lowest priority indicating the acceptability of a shack (anyway as a relatively temporary measure) to the highest which indicates the demand for the most modern standard of comfort (which, among sophisticated people, may be modified by aesthetic or status

value).

The functional priorities shown in the diagram, interpreted in the material terms, indicate the characteristics of the most typical residential environments of the sectors already described: the immigrant's *shantytown,* the wage-earner's *squatter settlement* and the professional's *garden suburb*. The classic 'shantytown' – known as a *corralon* in Lima – is a densely packed and chaotic but small collection of shacks usually located within a mile or two of areas of intensive and diverse commercial and industrial activity. A classic 'squatter settlement' of the kind which has developed around Lima during the past fifteen years is entirely different. It is large, with populations normally between ten and fifty thousand; regularly laid out on desert land belonging to the State; between five and fifteen miles from the central city and – most important of all – barriadas of this kind are in the process of developing. Almost all dwellings, which are sited on regular lots, are in some stage of permanent construction in brick or reinforced concrete and they are occupied by their possessor-builders – many of whom are still living in temporary shacks within incomplete structures.

The immigrant's shanty-town provides poor shelter

and little security but it is very well *located* for his special needs. The recent immigrant, searching for work and economic stability, spends little time at 'home', and as little cash as possible; and, in any case, his home is likely to be regarded as temporary. The wage-earner's squatter-settlement, in its earlier stages of development, also provides poor shelter but it provides excellent *security* once the squatters have consolidated their possession – without which investment and physical development are unlikely to occur. The peripheral location of the settlement may be inconvenient but it is a tolerable limitation for those who can afford public transport; community facilities are established in the settlements as soon as possible – public transport, markets and primary schools are frequently installed immediately after the initial invasion of the land has taken place and even before the squatters have been allocated their own lots.

My own observations and investigations of squatters' preferences indicate that the great majority – when given the choice – opt for the completion of community facilities *before* the completion of their own homes. Many – according to their declared preferences – would also choose to complete their dwellings *before* the installation of public utilities although, in practice.

they have no option. The degrees of 'modernity' of the single-family house types commonly built in Lima today can be observed in the more advanced *barriadas* which present a clear sequence: the *choza*, a primitive and temporary shack made from woven cane mats supported on bamboo poles; the *cerco*, an enclosing wall surrounding the possessor's lot and within which the household will continue to live in *chozas* while the carcase (i.e. walls, structural floors and roof) of the permanent house is being built. Once the carcase of the first stage of the house has been built, however, the family will use it – even if it has a temporary roof (in many cases the carcase of two or three rooms, built before the *cerco*).

The entire ground floor of the house is usually completed before the second storey is started and it is at this stage that domestic water supply and drainage are in urgent demand; electric light normally precedes water and drainage, partly because of its importance for social and cultural life, street security and domestic appliances – TV, refrigerators and so on. The final stage, the finished house of the successful squatter settler, is essentially the same as that of the middle-class professional and is, in fact, a perfectly acceptable modern dwelling.

The professional's preferred location, however, is in a low-density suburb with large gardens and open space or, especially if there are no children, a high-density down-town apartment block. These are the most 'modern' or highly developed types of housing but they are usually either physically detached or relatively distant from community facilities; it is also relatively unimportant whether or not the properties are owned or rented.

Qualitative versus Quantitative Views of Housing Deficits

If these observations are reasonably accurate and if the interpretations are correct in principle, some widespread and influential assumptions must be modified. In the first place, the argument implicitly rejects quantitative-standard value judgments on local environmental conditions. The proposition that there is a functional relationship between social needs and environmental forms and, furthermore, that these needs are set in a cultural continuum, precludes the moralistic condemnation of physical conditions *without reference to the values underlying the situation which they reflect.*

If my argument is correct in principle, the orders of priority between the functions of housing vary radically: the immigrant's and the wage-earner's housing priorities are, I argue, the reverse of those of the middle-class. While the middle-class family cannot maintain its situation without a modern house, the immigrant – and even the wage-earner – may well be unable to progress if he is burdened with the cost of even the cheapest possible modern standard house. The latter, poorer sectors – which make up over half the urban populations of Lima and considerably more than half in the provincial cities of Peru – cannot progress and the poorest cannot even survive without immediate access to community facilities. This function, however, has the lowest priority for the wealthier classes and for many in this sector physical proximity to workplaces, market-places and even to schools may damage their social position and the value of their property.

The proposition that there is a functional relationship between different life-situations and environmental needs and, furthermore, that these life-situations are set in a cultural continuum, precludes the condemnation of physical conditions without reference to the values underlying the situations which they reflect. The 'housing problem' however, is generally – if not universally – defined in terms of quantitative deficits of housing units. And with few exceptions – such as the very significant statements of the UN Ad Hoc Committee on Housing and Planning – 'housing units' are defined in middle-class terms, with only partial concessions to differences of need. The differences that are most frequently recognized, however, are the quantitative differences of material resources – mainly incomes – and not the qualitative or functional differences which I have described. The universal official image of 'housing' is, essentially, that of the privileged minorities. It is, perhaps, a fair definition of what housing *should* be and, maybe, what it can be in the future; but as a guide for the improvement of existing conditions, the notion that a house is a house only if it approximates the housing standards of already urbanized and industrialized countries, is certainly useless and probably self-defeating.

An analysis of a quantitative 'housing deficit' is not more – and no less – useful than one of an automobile or a refrigerator deficit. All such deficits are indicators of the levels and distribution of wealth but, unless the State possesses the major part of the wealth of the country or has control over its distribution, nothing can be achieved by setting these otherwise unattainable targets – except, of course, the reinforcement of the attitude of those who are satisfied with the status quo. The only alternative courses of action in the face of an apparently insoluble problem are to forget about it or to try to cover it up with a facade. What is the politician supposed to do when his technical advisors tell him that – as in the case of Peru in 1957 – 89% of the Nation's housing stock is sub-standard and that, in addition to this, there is an increasing annual demand for the growing population which far exceeds actual housing production? It is not surprising that housing policies, in underdeveloped countries with so-called 'free' economies, tend to oscillate between *laissez-faire* and somewhat desperate – or cynical – attempts to do something that will create the impression that progress is being made.

Below Alternative suburban low-income housing; a government project 20 kms from the central city, available to families selected from a narrow income range and sold on a 20-year heavily subsidised mortgage. Built in 1961-2, delinquency on payments by the mortgagees was reported to be over 65% in 1965.

(Photo: Alberto Rojas; courtesy Ministero de la Vivienda, Lima, Peru)

The hypothesis that I am presenting also goes some way towards explaining the difficulties which governments so often encounter in the administration of low-cost housing programmes in the recently urbanizing countries. From my own observations and studies, I am convinced that orthodox low-cost government housing projects are, with few exceptions, extremely costly in relation to their real economic value and, whether the financial cost is born by the State or by the 'beneficiaries', the latter are usually dissatisfied and constitute a political as well as economic liability for their 'benefactors'. This, as I see it, is the predictable result of failure to harmonize the goods and services provided – or imposed – with the life-situations of those for whom they are intended.

According to my analysis, the typical wage-earning Lima slum-dweller who has to move or who may even want to move to the periphery of the city, wants, above all, an absolute security of residence in a place of his own; one which, without financial strain or undue risk, he can convert into a modern standard dwelling, in his own way and in his own time. It is hardly surprising, therefore, that he should resent having to pay through the nose – or, rather, through the stomach – for a heavily mortgaged and expensive house; a house, for instance, which is far too small but, at the same time, unnecessarily luxurious in its construction, finishes and equipment. The typical beneficiary will be lucky if there are functioning schools and markets in the new location, anyway initially, and if there is an adequate transportation service to his workplace. From the orthodox angle, the whole question of popular housing is pretty disheartening for the politician and administrator; the problem seems hopelessly vast and efforts to serve the biggest population sector apparently lead to more headaches than progress.

If, on the other hand, the problem is restated in terms of the relationship between changing life-situations and the developing environment, then the whole panorama changes. If, to take the Lima example, the solution is seen to lie not in the construction of tens of thousands of housing units, for which there is neither the financing nor the repayment capacity, but in the provision of land and community facilities, then projections come down to earth. On the reasonable assumption that the majority of the wage-earning sector that want or will be forced to move out of the slums, are motivated in the way that I have described, then at least half the actual housing problem of Lima can be solved at a realistic per capita cost.

Even if privately owned land has to be expropriated at market values, the initial unitary cost of land and facilities would be between a quarter and a fifth of the typical low-cost minimum housing project. On State-owned land the cost would, naturally, be much less but in either case, though by different schedules, the complimentary elements with lower initial priorities could be provided progressively. The Peruvian Junta Nacional de la Vivienda is experimenting with progressive development projects of this nature: with an initial investment of the equivalent of $100 and monthly payments of $3.70, a family, starting with land and a communal water supply, would be living on a fully equipped building lot after six years. The monthly quota is sufficiently low (about 5% of the average income) to enable the family to continue saving for building; without credit they would be able to complete a 7,500 square foot house in about fifteen years without spending more than 15% of their income on building. Assuming a monthly income of $100: six years paying (monthly) $5.00 for the land, services and facilities, plus $10.00 for the house and nine years paying an average $15 for the house, the total spent for the building would be $2,345.00 – more than enough for the materials and skilled labour of a 7,500 square foot house. This also assumes, of course, that wages keep up with building material costs, that the owner acts as his own contractor and that the family provides most of the unskilled labour.

By substituting this type of project for the more orthodox ones actually being carried out, the supply of housing for the popular sector could be increased

Left Project Valdivieso, Lima; temporary dwelling units are built at the bottom of the lots, leaving the fronts vacant for families to build additions. The disadvantage is that many temporary back-to-back units became permanent houses; e.g. those with stucco and white painted fronts.
Below Detail showing family adding on to the temporary unit in the correct form.
(Photos: John Turner)

122

enormously. If the popular housing supply were in fact increased by this much, and providing that its form and administrative procedures were aceptable and properly adjusted to the demand, then there would be several results: a large number of families would immediately improve their living conditions; these families would concentrate their savings efforts – many of which would be greatly increased – on purchases from the local building industry (instead of on manufactured goods most of which are imported); the gross overcrowding of the shrinking supply of slum accommodation would be relieved and rents would tend to stabilise. Finally, and perhaps most important of all, a major cause of squatting – the lack of land – would be eliminated and another – the lack of very low-cost accommodation in the central areas for the very poor and recent immigrants – would at least be reduced. The major urban development problem and an important aspect of the housing problem – uncontrolled and squatter settlement – would, therefore be at least partially solved.

Conclusions

The foregoing is a detailed and, perhaps, a rather roundabout way of saying that the 'housing problem' can be solved in accordance with local demand with locally available resources for housing. This statement carries two obvious implications. First and one which is difficult to substantiate with direct evidence, is that people, especially the relatively very poor sectors that we are discussing, do not demand more costly housing than they can afford. (If this means purchase then, of course, it is reasonable to assume at least short-term and relatively low-interest credit.) The other implication is that urban development will be of relatively low density (30–50 persons per acre) and that it will develop by stages – that it will, therefore, be materially incomplete for a number of years, even a decade or more, after settlement has taken place.

The evidence for the acceptability of these conditions and for the hypothesis that the mass of the people demand no more than they can economically support by themselves is the existence of the squatter settlements and the relative satisfaction that their inhabi-

123

Right Project Valdivieso; a sewer and manholes are being installed; further priorities must be electric power, and paving of main roads, since in this dry climate the dust from buses and occasional trucks and cars is a considerable nuisance.
(Photo: John Turner)

tants express with regard to their housing situation – facts which investigations carried out in Lima, as well as others in other cities, have clearly shown. The objection to low-density development frequently raised by physical planners needs to be more thoroughly examined; I very much doubt that the extension of public utilities is very significant, especially when their installation is subsequent to settlement. In any case it is far less serious than the waste involved in unused speculative subdivisions of very low density indeed; and in having to provide services to the very much more scattered squatter settlements – both of which are the result of failures by governments to control land-use and speculation. Furthermore, by careful initial planning, by planned land-use change and development (guaranteed by the retention of at least part of those areas which are most likely to change in value and use by the authority) the intensity and diversity of land-use can be encouraged – normal changes that should take place in the course of its absorption into the growing city. This, however, is a problem of the particular illustration chosen and, therefore, lies outside the scope of this article.

The main point I want to make, which is independent of the particular form which a solution might take in Lima, is that the housing problem – stated in the terms which I claim to be correct – is not a problem of resources which do not exist but, rather, of the proper use of existing and immediately available resources. There is a housing problem, in other words, when resources available for housing are not being spent on housing or are not producing a reasonable return. Different life-situations are, therefore, as significant or even more significant than the physical condition of the dwelling, its tenancy or, even its rent.

Take, for instance, the cases of two neighbouring families in a Lima slum court of the cheaper and more inferior type: one household is extremely poor, since the bread-winner is un- or semi-employed and the other has a regular income although it is a typically low and rather uncertain wage. Both pay the same rent, which will be high for the poorer family but relatively low for the less poor. I would suggest that the better-off family have the more acute housing problem as they are suffering unnecessarily from the physical conditions of the slum and would suffer most acutely if evicted; the poorer household are less concerned with the state of their dwelling and a great deal more concerned with the problem of filling their bellies. Also, they are probably less worried by the threat of eviction, as they are prepared to put up with extremely primitive conditions – unlike the wage-earning family which would be demoralized by any worsening of their already near-intolerable living conditions – though this might well happen as a new house of the same type might now cost more than they could afford. The regular-wage family would be feeling acutely uncomfortable and insecure and would, therefore, seize any chance of obtaining a property of their own, even if it were on the periphery of the city. The others, however, are dependent for survival on their immediate access to casual work and, in any case, are less able to afford the extra cost of living at the periphery. While one family have the resources and motives for moving as well as the desire to move, the other family do not. So, while both households may live precisely under the same conditions, they could well have exactly the same composition – one has a *housing* problem and the other an *employment* problem. By the terms of the orthodox definition, of course, both families are suffering from the same deficiency and both should be moved into new housing. But this, I argue, is to confuse the issue and would, in fact, be both anti-social – by further reducing the poorer family's chances of economic progress – and uneconomic by subsidizing that family to no useful purpose. But, providing that the services offered were appropriate, the wage-earning family would be greatly helped through resettlement in their own dwelling and the money that they previously spent on rent, television sets and diversions compensating in part for their intolerable housing conditions, would be invested in building – one of the main employers and distributors of wealth. Public investment in housing should, as I see it, be determined by its ratio to the private capital which it diverts into locally productive channels. By differentiating between tensions or problems arising out of the lack of opportunity to *invest* and those arising out of the opportunity to *produce,* the division between 'social' and 'economic' problems – which always seemed to be more theoretical than real – tends to disappear anyway in the housing field.

One final observation – which is by way of acknowledgement – the redefinition that I propose and the action which it implies is clearly stated and demonstrated by the popular sectors in Peru and, if I am correctly interpreting the documentary material I am now studying, in many other parts of the urbanizing world. There is nothing new in what I am proposing – on the contrary, it seems to me that current thinking about housing, as I have interpreted it, is a modern invention and that what I am trying to point out is entirely traditional.

124

Opposite and on pages 149, 172 and 216

Recent posters published by the American Institute of Architects to draw attention to serious urban problems.

125

FROM SEA TO SHINING SEA.

Who dumps old tires into our bays? Who picnics at our beaches and leaves litter for the tides to wash away? Who runs factories that pump refuse into our lakes? Who pours sewage into our rivers? Who throws all those beer cans overboard? Who's going to unpollute it all?

America, the beautiful. Our America. The crisis isn't in our cities; the crisis is in our hearts. With a change of heart, we can change the picture.   AIA/American Institute of Architects

Send this page to your Congressman and ask him to support Federal efforts to control water pollution.

ANN AND GORDON KETTERER

This is an analysis of the modern Mayan house site. It necessarily includes the relation of the modern Mayan site to that of the ancient Mayas, since one is a direct derivative of the other; and an attempt is made to show the evolution of the modern Mayan house site, its function, and its method of construction.

Our field work was done in the town of Pustunich, Yucatan. Pustunich is a small Mayan village that is just on the threshold of the twentieth century. Through the centre of the town runs a paved road. This road connects Merida with Chetumal, but is only paved as far as the border of Quintana Roo. There is not much traffic from Merida to Chetumal, but in the future, when this road becomes entirely paved, there will be quite a lot. Therefore, Pustunich is experiencing some contact with modern civilization now, and can expect much more in the future.

Two house sites were studied in Pustunich: the Mejia household and the Duran household. These two house sites were completely surveyed and recorded in measured drawings. In addition, we made a photographic record.

The Mejia family consists of Don Mech (Demetrio) Mejia and his wife, Dona Aida; a married son, Moises, with three children; and seven other children.

The Duran family consists of Don and Dona Duran,

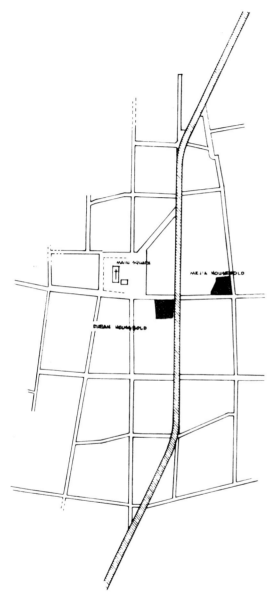

Plan of Pustunich

a married son with one child, and two other children. An attempt was made to analyse the Mayan thatched hut. This was necessary because of the importance that it plays in the form of the Mayan house site. It is the arrangement of these huts that determines the form and function of the site proper. The form of the site as seen from afar is a pyramidal shape very similar to the roof of the thatched hut. It is a very organic form seeming to grow from the landscape, which is almost flat. The site takes a form that is low at the walls surrounding it and builds up to a focal point at the living area where the buildings are clustered. It then diminishes again to the height of the wall. Like a mountain rising from the plain, it creates an immediately evident centre of interest. Yet it is not antagonistic to the land, but blends in perfectly.

The house site

Historically, the Mayan house site was a walled enclosure containing several buildings, usually grouped around a rectangular court. The walled enclosure was, in all probability, an irregular one. Dr Andrews[1] maintains that the walls enclosing house sites at Dzibilchaltun had no order, and this irregularity is also evident in the walls studied at Mayapan.

The Mejia and Duran house sites shown in the accompanying drawings are enclosed by fairly regular and ordered walls as are most modern house sites. The rectangularization of the house site walls is a recent innovation, the result of colonial and twentieth century surveys and title registration.

The modern site is a rectangular enclosure, completely surrounded by dry stone walls. It contains the major house or houses, some outbuildings, and areas of many domestic and agricultural activities. The houses are arranged about a courtyard or outdoor space, which acts as the main centre of activity. If there is a well or running water, it is in or close to the courtyard. The courtyard is usually well defined by the buildings surrounding it, and acts as an outdoor room. Since the buildings surround it, and in most cases enter directly into the courtyard, it becomes the major outdoor space and focal point. The houses clustered around the courtyard are not normally interconnected. The courtyard itself becomes the connecting link for circulation from one building to another, and it naturally lends itself to purposes other than circulation, since there is a tendency to stop to perform some activity here. It acts as a pleasant contrast to the buildings themselves, for it is a different type of space—sunny, roomy and out of doors.

Paths radiate from the central courtyard to various parts of the site. One such path, little more than a trampled-down section of the underbrush, leads to the sascab pit. Sascab is a type of limestone which is used in place of sand in making mortar. It is soft and crumbles when dug from the ground. It is quite often found in Yucatan in small deposits lying close to the surface. As the sascab is mined and used, a cave called the sascab pit is formed under the ground. It is used for storing and weaving palm fibres into hats and other articles, the dampness of the cave allowing the palm fibres to retain their flexibility. Another path leads to the toilet area, which is in some cases walled in and used exclusively for this purpose. In other examples it is simply a portion of the yard into which garbage is thrown, where fruit trees are grown, and which is generally not used for other activities.

Circulation into the modern Mayan house site differs markedly from that of the ancient sites. In the ancient sites, entry was effected at an arbitrary point in the wall surrounding the site. The wall, as mentioned above, was not a regular one, and entry through it was irregular also. A somewhat formalized entry may have been created by trees or perishable materials; however, all evidence of this has been destroyed by the ages. Although entry into the site itself was simply through an arbitrary opening in the wall, entry into the courtyard through a corner was very regular and traditional. The buildings surrounding the courtyard are not connected. The corner, which is open between buildings, provides an entry in which the observer is immediately aware of the total courtyard. The tradition of entry through the corner was a mainstay of Mayan architecture, and is evident throughout the Mayan area.

In the modern Mayan house site, the entry through the wall is normally on axis with the entry to the courtyard. The route of travel is through the wall, up a path, and into the major building, which then opens into the courtyard. Of the two sites studied, the Duran household is the best example of this. Here, entry to the site is also entry to the major building, or sala, now the house of the son. The formalizing of the entry into the site was probably brought about with the squaring off of the site itself. This may have evolved from the architecture of the ceremonial centres where, in the stone buildings, entry is often formalized in this manner. Though the buildings are still not connected at the corners, there is a formal (probably ceremonial) entry through one of the buildings directly into the courtyard. Here, the entry experience is very much like that of the modern Mayan house site where one has a formal entry to the courtyard directly on axis with the buildings.

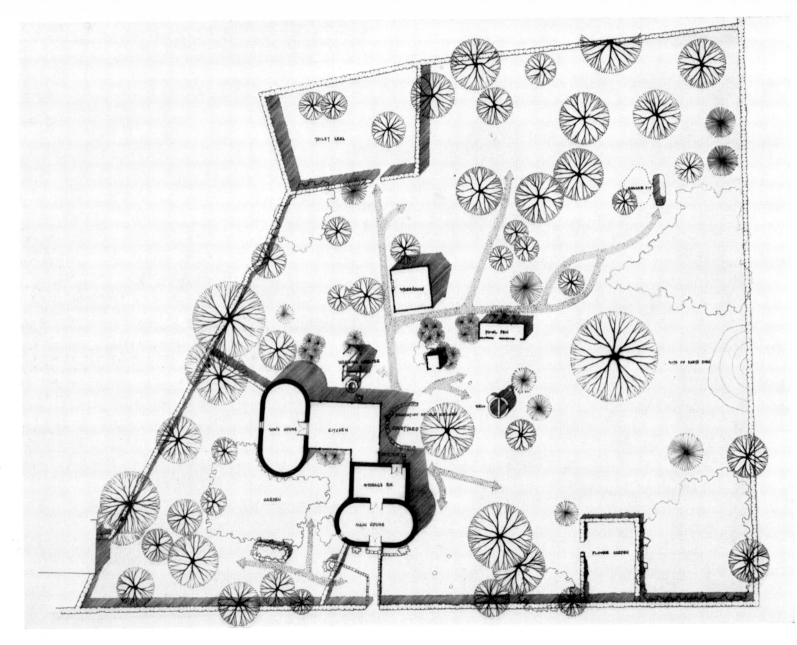

Mejia house site

The Mayan house site is almost a self-sufficient community in itself. Each part of the site is used in some way, whether as the dwelling, or to keep animals, grow trees, wash clothes, or weave hats. This self-sufficiency has one exception: the primary sustenance of the Maya, corn, is not grown on the site. The corn field or milpa is in some other part of the countryside where there is more room. The corn is stored on the stock while it is drying: the ears are bent over when they are ripe, and allowed to dry out in place. The corn is then harvested as needed. Therefore, only that corn which is immediately necessary is stored on the house site.

Every Mayan house site is the equivalent of an orchard, dotted with banana, orange, lime, papaya and other types of fruit trees. These trees serve a double function: they are also used for shade. Other types of trees may include the jicara, producing a large gourd-like fruit that is used for bowls and containers; palms of various types, useful for their fronds; and ramon which is used as feed for horses. The Mayan house site also contains a vegetable garden providing protein-rich beans, spices, and medicinal herbs.

Mayans invest in animals. All families have chickens and turkeys; other livestock includes pigs, dogs and cats. Horses are usually kept on the site, but cows are allowed to roam loose through the countryside. A prize cow or bull (such as Casabell, the Mejia bull) is often kept tied in a conspicuous place on the site for others to admire.

The evolution of the house site follows a fairly traditional pattern. It is directly related to the income level of the particular family in question. After acquiring the land, a site free of rock outcrops and reason-

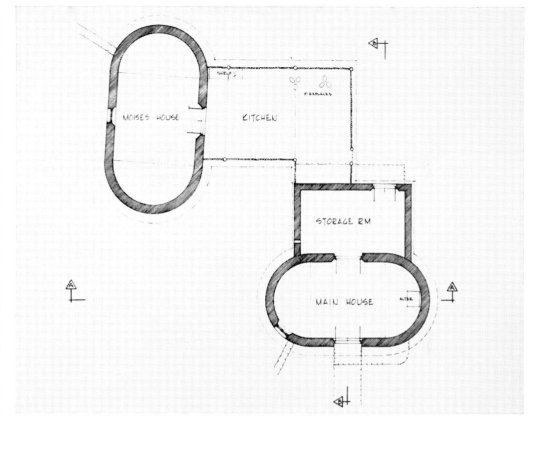

Right Plan of house group

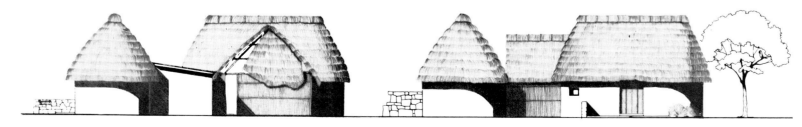

North Elevation   East Elevation

ably level is chosen for the major house. The position of this house determines the position of the rest of the buildings. In the more modern villages, the position of the house is often prescribed by the grid plan of the streets. The house is normally placed so that it is facing the street. After the main house has been built, various additions are made depending on the family income. These are in the form of separate buildings. The kitchen may first take the form of a lean-to connected to the main house. It may later assume the space of the major house or an entirely new kitchen might be built. If the kitchen has taken the space of the main house, a new and more elaborate sala is built, but if the main house is adequate to begin with, the other buildings will take the form of new structures.

These are always placed around the courtyard, which thus assumes its form. The remainder of the site is used as the need arises. Other requirements are placed wherever they are functionally most useful. The site evolves in this way until an organic whole is achieved, comprising in its final form the living area or the courtyard surrounded by the buildings, the garden and agricultural areas. The living area contains the main house, other houses, the kitchen, the washshed, and the storehouse. Fowl pens and structures for the animals are not normally a part of the living area, but are set apart in other sections of the site.

Building functions

The main house acts as living, sleeping and work room combined. Typically, its furnishings are sparse but adequate. There are hammocks for sleeping hung from the walls. During the day these are rolled up and

130

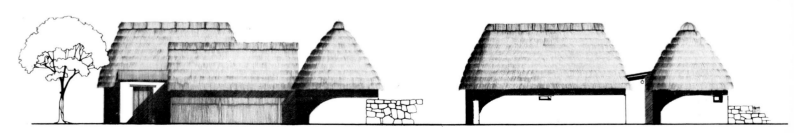

West Elevation   South Elevation

hung out of the way or simply tossed up on to the rafters while still attached to the hooks. They then may be pulled down to serve as seating when needed. Hammocks are not native to Yucatan. They were probably imported from some of the Caribbean Islands either by the Spanish or by earlier trade. The original bed of the Mayas was a frame construction topped by a pliable mat woven from palm fronds or cloth. The wealthier families had built-in beds which were platforms let into one side of the house: these were used as beds during the night and as sitting or work areas during the day.

At one end of the Mayan house is an altar: a permanent fixture. Its appearance changes frequently since it is decorated for major holidays and religious functions. The final basic piece of large furniture is a chest used for storing clothing and other odds and ends. This often begins life as a kind of 'hope chest' for the Mayan woman. Depending on the economic situation of the family, extra household articles may include a store-bought wardrobe and a sewing machine. The sewing machine is today becoming a 'must' for the Mayan family since it provides a large source of income.

The kitchen is also a multipurpose area. The main activity is, of course, food preparation, but it is also used as a work room and a sleeping space. For sleeping, hammocks are used and again present no storage problem.

Various tools which are often used such as saddles, agricultural implements and so on are stored in the kitchen. The major furnishings are, however, cooking implements. The centre of the Mayan kitchen is the fireplace. It is traditionally made of three stones upon which a kettle may be set. Three is the number thus

131

Left Kitchen of the Duran family

Above Washing clothes in a *batea*

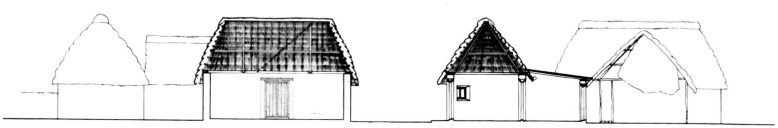

Section A-A

Section B-B

related to woman and woman's work. Man and man's work is associated with the number four, for the four corners of the field. Other kitchen furniture would include the *metate* and *mano* to grind the corn (though today most Mayan women take their corn to the miller). There would be several small benches and a *banco*, a hollowed-out log on which the *metate* is placed when grinding corn. There are various other kitchen implements such as buckets, pottery, water jugs, and storage gourds.

The kitchen is a light and airy room, constructed in a manner similar to the house. The walls are made of small sticks placed close together and left open. This type of wall allows the smoke from the fire to escape, while still giving a feeling of privacy and enclosure. In addition, it creates a fantastic play of light on the inside since there is a highly contrasted figure-ground relationship. The light outside shimmers through the silhouette of the stick walls making the kitchen a very gay, attractive space.

The wash-shed is simply a thatched roof supported by posts. It has no walls and contains only a *batea* supported by posts or masonry posts. The *batea* is the washtub of the Maya. Originally, it was hollowed out of a single mahogany log into the shape of a dugout canoe. However, with the shortage of mahogany and the waste involved, the government has outlawed this and cement *bateas* are becoming common. The function of the wash-shed is simply to provide protection from the sun (and rain) to the person who is washing the clothes. Often a tree or some other form of protection is substituted. Close to the washhouse is a stone or *mamposteria* trough for storing water. This is necessary, since in most cases there is no running water on the site. The source of water for most of the house sites is either a well or a public faucet somewhere in the town.

The storehouse is another familiar building, serving as a general shelter for corn, tools, and anything which needs a roof. For very large families, it may afford a further place to swing a hammock. The storehouse is built in the same manner as other Mayan buildings, with a thatched roof supported by posts. The walls can be wattle and daub or simply sticks placed close together similar to the kitchen. Sometimes, it is an old house that has been replaced by a newer or larger model.

The fowl pen is rectangular with walls also similar to those of the kitchen. It normally has a shed-type roof made of thatch and is used to house turkeys and chickens. Occasionally dogs and pigs may be placed in similar structures though normally dogs are allowed the run of the land and pigs are penned

Duran House Site

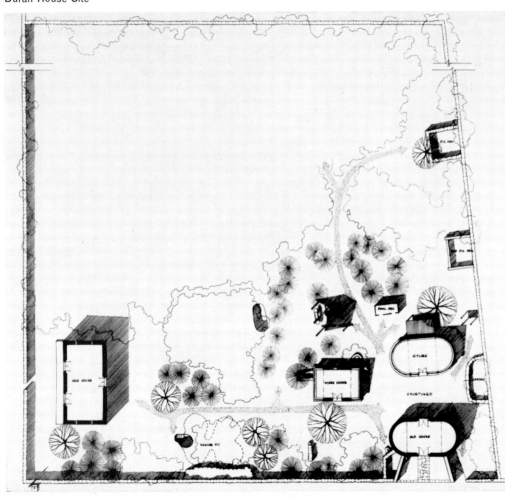

in stone-walled enclosures.

Characteristics of the Mayan house structure

The Mayan hut has a long history. It has not changed essentially in 1,500 years. It was probably the first improved type of dwelling used by the ancient Maya and is obviously the prototype for their later stone buildings. The house prototype appears on the 1,000 year old façade of the Nunnery Quadrangle at Uxmal in essentially the same form as it is constructed today all over the Yucatan peninsula. The interior vaulted spaces of the stone buildings are transpositions of the interior space of the thatched hut into the more permanent material of stone.

The Mayan house varies in size considerably, but the proportions remain the same. It would be interesting to determine why the size varies – because of function, size of family, size of materials or because of physical size of the occupants. It would also be interesting to determine in what way the proportions are kept constant. In all likelihood, there is a module from which all parts of the house are proportioned. We feel that the basic proportion of the Mayan house is the radius of a circle whose diameter is the width of the house interior. Using this radius as the basic module gives the basic proportions indicated in the diagram. These proportions are almost exactly those of the buildings studied on both sites. In the buildings measured, this radius was normally five feet two inches (plus or minus several inches) which is, according to Morley[2], approximately the average height of the Mayan male.

The Mayan hut is a uniquely functional building for the tropics. The height of the ceiling, the reflective quality of the thatch, and the ability of the thatch to dissipate heat rapidly all combine to keep the building cool. The slope of the roof is exactly that necessary to retain a watertight construction with little repair. It is an extremely well thought out design.

The Mayan house has very distinctive spatial characteristics. The rounded corners contain the space in a very soft and human manner. A sense of spaciousness is given by the towering peaked roof overhead, but a human scale is retained by the walls which end at the spring of the roof. The constant height at human scale (for the Maya; a little low for gringos) of the top of the wall keeps the space down to a comfortable level. The height of the roof above, in contrast, gives the feeling of spaciousness needed in so small a multi-purpose area and also gives the space a church-like dignity. Warmth is added by the thatch used on the roof construction much in the same way that a Japanese house is made to feel warm

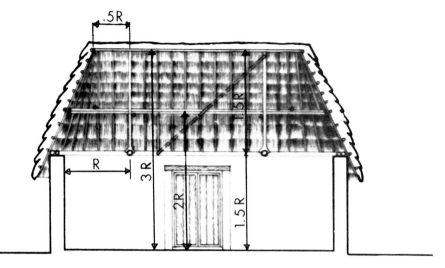

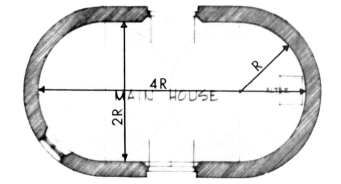

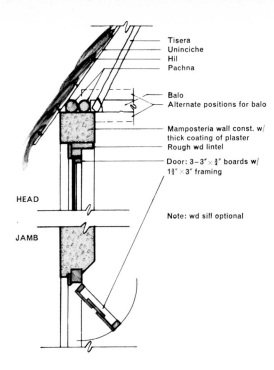

Tisera
Uniniche
Hil
Pachna

Balo
Alternate positions for balo

Mamposteria wall const. w/
thick coating of plaster
Rough wd lintel

Door: 3–3″ × ¾″ boards w/
1¾″ × 3″ framing

HEAD

Note: wd sill optional

JAMB

134

Above Typical detail

by the tatami mat on the floor. The interior walls are whitewashed, which helps to reflect the natural sunlight and to brighten the interior during the day. The Mayan house is definitely a very gracious place.

The house is normally built upon a raised platform, which helps to divert water and keep various animals from the door. This platform, which in the past has been built out of earth, has naturally assumed the pyramidal shape. The ancient floors were either beaten earth or earth covered with a thick layer of extremely hard plaster. Today this platform is of concrete. Concrete is much more expensive than beaten earth, and the platform has shrunk to the size of a simple concrete slab—about six inches. In the past these platforms were sometimes two or three feet in height and were reached by small stairways.

Four posts support the corners of the house. These are erected first and then the major beams and rafters are placed and roped fast with vines. Small sticks are tied to the rafters, and the thatch is looped over these sticks creating an extremely regular pattern on the interior. The wall, the last part of the house to be constructed, is made of wattle and daub (mud applied to small sticks tied side by side). In the more modern houses, the walls are made of *mamposteria,* a type of masonry construction. *Mamposteria,* incidentally, was used by the ancient Maya also but was probably less common. Finally, the walls are whitewashed inside and out. All wood members are tied together with vines which are used green, when they are pliable. As the vines dry, they tighten up and retain their shape, drawing the members together very tightly.

Construction of the Mayan hut is a very specialized procedure. Each part of the building has a name. Each part is carefully chosen for functional reasons.

The corner posts (replaced by *mamposteria* walls in some modern houses) are of a strong, durable wood because they must carry the load of the roof, and must withstand the insect and dampness problems inherent in wood connecting with the ground. The major beams are also of a hard wood, which not only enables them to carry a heavy load with comparatively slim members, but also makes them virtually fireproof a most important safeguard in a thatched house. These hard woods must be transported over long distances and are difficult to obtain: one reason for the rising incidence of *mamposteria* buildings in Mayan villages. As the thatched houses become more expensive to build, the *mamposteria* houses become more popular.

In recent times there has been a general change from the thatched hut which satisfied the needs of the Maya for the past 1,500 years. Difficulty in acquiring materials is one reason for this. A touch of the twentieth century has filtered down to the Mayan community, bringing with it twentieth-century problems and breaking down the traditional conservatism of the Maya. He has begun to acquire 'things' in the struggle for status which is associated with the twentieth century. *Mamposteria* houses, electricity, furniture and Western clothes are immediately-evident examples. The Maya has realized that the thatched hut with its rounded corners is not easily adaptable to twentieth-century appliances, furniture, windows, electricity and, in general, the rectangularity of twentieth-century society. It is a case of an organic human structure competing with a machine concept. The rectangular *mamposteria* building is much more easily adapted to wiring problems, square-cornered furniture and rectangular windows.

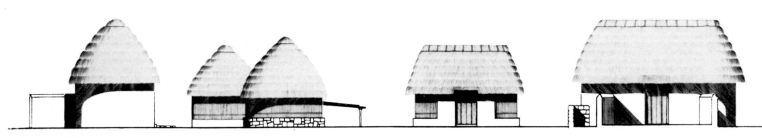

South Elevaton

West Elevation

As the land becomes more cultivated and the jungle moves further and further away, materials to build the thatched houses will become even more difficult to find and more expensive. Perhaps as it becomes more expensive to build, the thatched hut will convey more status and become popular again. This is doubtful, however, for the thatched hut does not answer the problems posed by modern civilization.

The Mayan thatched hut has, through the years, assimilated some characteristics of the cultures through which it passed. The doors are modern. Until the coming of the Spanish, there was no need for a door. Entrances were covered by cloth, usually only for privacy. Theft was rare, probably because of severe punishment. *Mamposteria*, however, is a Mayan invention. It can still be seen in the ruined buildings as a concrete core. In fact, *mamposteria* dwellings have been found at Dzibilchaltun. Windows also came with the Spanish. They have never been completely incorporated into the thatched hut, probably because there are only two natural places for rectangular openings in the hut – on the two straight sides. These are normally used for doorways.

Conclusion

The two house sites studied conform to the above picture of the typical Mayan house site in most respects. The Mejia site has acquired a new kitchen, the foundation of the old one being indicated on the plan. This new kitchen connects to the son's house, and one must now enter the son's house through the kitchen instead of directly from the courtyard.

The Duran household has felt the effect of the new road which passes through Pustunich. A new *mamposteria* house has been built facing the road, with no relation to the other buildings on the site. The older house has been given to the son.

The Duran site also has running water. Both sites have electricity, Western-type articles of furniture and other superficial evidences of twentieth-century culture.

The Mayan site and its buildings will undergo considerable changes in the next ten years. The thatched hut is probably on the way out. With it will go many phases of present Mayan culture. It is to be hoped that the void will be filled with a design as organic and well thought out as the thatched hut it replaces.

Notes

1 Andrews, E. Wyllys, Field Director of the Middle American Research Institute of Tulane University.
2 Morley, Sylvanus G., *The Ancient Maya*, Palo Alto, California, 1946.

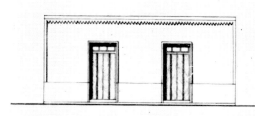
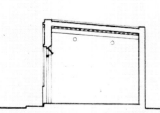

North Elevation and section of *mamposteria* building

CONCENTRIC TOWNS—THE VALLEY OF THE MZAB

DAVID ETHERTON

It became usual to expand towns simply by rebuilding the fortifications further from the centre, although the invention of gunpowder resulted in important changes in the shape and construction of the city walls to make full use of cross-fire by cannon from projecting ramparts. Paris, for example, continued to extend her city walls in a series of rings, the last of which was an average of 5 km from the 'Ile de la Cité' in 1845.

By this time it became obvious that there were many disadvantages to the uncontrolled concentric expansion of cities; a fact which had been clear to Leonardo da Vinci when he proposed ten cities of 30,000 each to the Duke of Milan. These, he said, would 'separate

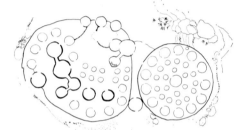

138

The magic of the ring has given more than purely geometrical security to circular settlements and towns. Ancient rites, witchcraft and tribal dances are remembered in the stone rings of places as far apart as the Sahara and the English South Downs. In many cities whose form originated as a circular fortress, later concentric developments continued long after security and convenience demanded.

The successive powers of Church, State and commerce radiated their influence over the growing town, but once the advantages of land speculation were established, there was no longer any magic in indiscriminate expansion close to the centre of cities.

The contradictions which arise out of fitting orthogonal rooms or buildings into a circular enclosure have always been clear, and the best plans seem to depend on adjustments made to the shape of both the buildings and the perimeter. The built 'diagrams' of the 'ideal' Renaissance cities push the contradictions to the limit, compared with the more relaxed arrangement of streets and spaces inside the roughly circular walls of medieval cities.

In the fourteenth century Paris and Venice were exceptionally large, each with a population of around 100,000. But the typical medieval town rarely held more than 500 people within a radius of less than a kilometre.

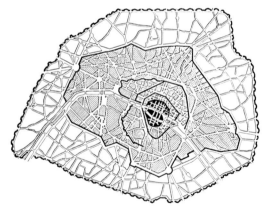

Top Site plan of a chief's compound, North Cameroons. Left are living quarters; right are kitchens and granaries. (Source: L'Habitation au Cameroun, l'Office de la Recherche Scientifique Outre-Mer, Paris 1952).

Above The development of Paris. Central core, early Middle Ages: black line boundaries are c.1180, 1370, 1676, 1784, and 1841–45. (Source for this and of Vienna: Rasmussen, *Towns & Buildings*).

Top & above Vienna. A Roman nucleus with later fortifications against Turkish invasions in the 16th and 17th centuries. Polygonal fortifications and bastions, and a 600 metre 'green belt' isolated the central areas from new suburbs which grew up outside the belt in the 17th and 18th centuries. The fortifications were destroyed in 1809 by Napoleon and the area surrounding the centre city was not developed until after 1857.

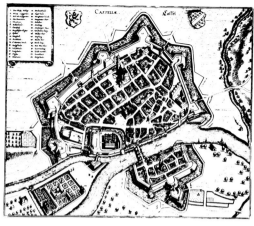

139

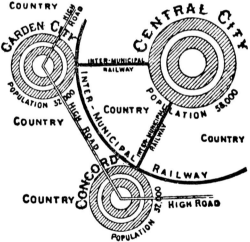

this great congregation of people who herd together like goats on top of one another filling every place with foul odour, and sowing seeds of pestilence and death'. In 1900, Ebenezer Howard refined and tested the idea of a 'planetary' system of town planning where diagrammatically circular satellites of 32,000 were connected to a larger 'central city nucleus'.

The seven to tenth-century towns of the Valley of the Mzab in the Sahara are unique in combining the organic qualities of vernacular hill towns with the idea of controlled satellite expansion. They represent the culmination of human effort and enterprise in the Sahara and their original social and physical structure can still be identified.

The rocky plateau which divides the eastern and western 'erg' is known as the 'chebka' (Arabic: net). Rising once every thirteen years, the 'oued' Mzab traces a dry course through this eroded maze of clefts and ravines. One thousand years ago the Valley of the Mzab was chosen by the Ibādites as the site for seven new towns.

The towns have more in common with the modern artificial environment of the oil companies than with many traditional oases. The 'chebka' is an unfavourable site from almost every point of view; water is far below ground level and communications are difficult. Rain falls on an average of twelve days a year, and in the hottest months temperatures reach a maximum of 45 degrees Centigrade.

The Ibādites were descendants of the Kharijites (Kharij: dissenter) whose fundamentalist brand of Islamic puritanism led to their expulsion from Iraq in the ninth century. Ibn Rustem, the leader of the Ibādites, had a quick following of sympathetic Berber tribes when he arrived in the Maghreb. He founded the kingdom of Tiaret and as its theocratic ruler advocated an austere life devoted to study and trade. As his popularity grew so also did the opposition from orthodox Muslim fanatics, and in 909, Tahert, the capital, was destroyed, and the Ibādites fled to Ouargla.

Sedrata was built nearby, as the first new Ibādite town. It was well situated for trade and quickly attracted other persecuted Ibādi communities. However, it was unprotected, and the need for expansion demanded a new site located away from the main caravan routes (Sedrata was destroyed by Berber tribes in 1071). Of the seven Mzab towns, five are situated in the Valley itself. El Atteuf was founded in 1011 and the other four Valley towns before 1052. Guerrara and Berriane were built in the seventeenth century, 50 km north of the Valley.

Almost half the total population of 38,000 live in

Left Plans for ideal cities by Buonaiuto Lorini, 1592 (above) and Vincenzo Scamozzi, 1615 (below). (Source: Rasmussen, *Towns & Buildings*).

Top Kassel, *c.* 1646, with Unterneustadt (new town) below. (Source: Howard Saalman, *Mediaeval Cities*, New York 1968)

Above Planetary town system suggested by Ebenezer Howard in 1898.

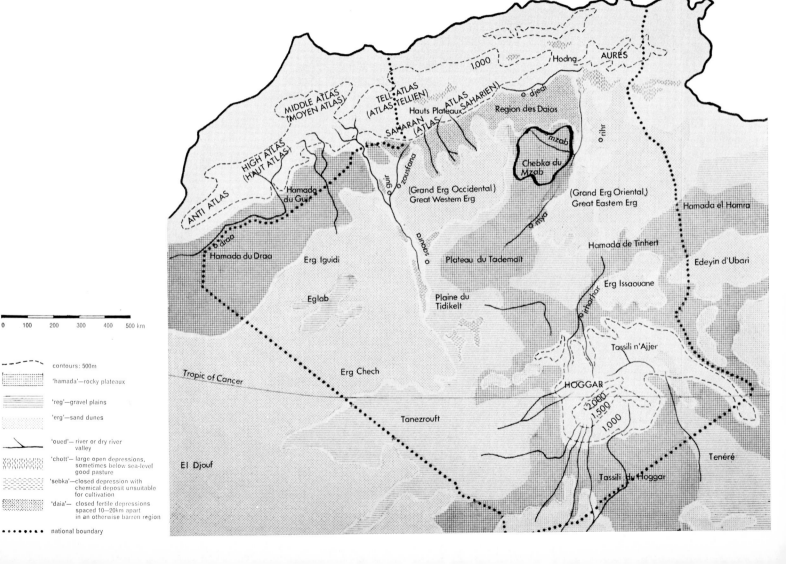

140

Legend:

- – – – contours: 500m
- 'hamada'—rocky plateaux
- 'reg'—gravel plains
- 'erg'—sand dunes
- 'oued'— river or dry river valley
- 'chott'— large open depressions, sometimes below sea-level good pasture
- 'sebka'—closed depression with chemical deposit unsuitable for cultivation
- 'daia'— closed fertile depressions spaced 10—20km apart in an otherwise barren region
- •••••• national boundary

Scale: 0 100 200 300 400 500 km

Map labels:

MIDDLE ATLAS (MOYEN ATLAS)
TELL ATLAS (ATLAS TELLIEN)
ATLAS SAHARIEN
SAHARAN (ATLAS)
Hauts Plateaux
Region des Daïas
Hodna
AURÈS
1,000
o djedi
o rihr
mzab
Chebka du Mzab
HIGH ATLAS (HAUT ATLAS)
ANTI ATLAS
Hamada du Guir
o guir
o zoustana
(Grand Erg Occidental) Great Western Erg
(Grand Erg Oriental) Great Eastern Erg
Hamada el Homra
o draa
Hamada du Draa
Erg Iguidi
o saoura
Plateau du Tademaït
Hamada de Tinhert
Edeyin d'Ubari
Eglab
Plaine du Tidikelt
Erg Issaouane
o mya
o irharhar
Tassili n'Ajjer
Tropic of Cancer
Erg Chech
HOGGAR
2,000
1,500
1,000
Tanezrouft
Tenéré
El Djouf
Tassili du Hoggar

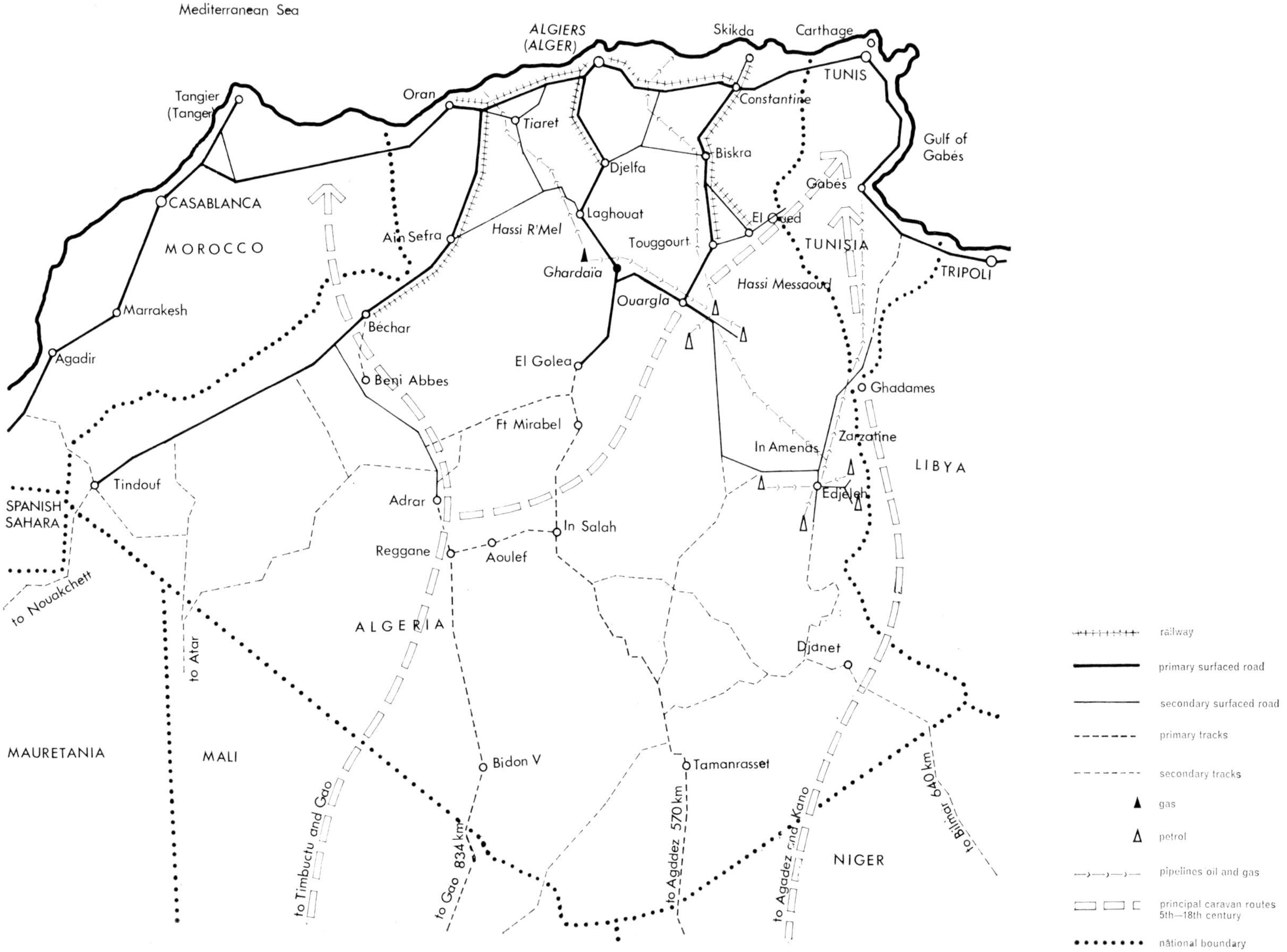

Mediterranean Sea

ALGIERS
(ALGER)

Skikda

Carthage

Tangier
(Tanger)

Oran

TUNIS

Constantine

Gulf of
Gabès

Tiaret

Djelfa

Biskra

CASABLANCA

Gabès

MOROCCO

Laghouat

El Oued

Aïn Sefra

Hassi R'Mel

Touggourt

TUNISIA

Marrakesh

Ghardaïa

Hassi Messaoud

TRIPOLI

Agadir

Ouargla

Béchar

El Golea

Beni Abbes

Ghadames

141

Ft Mirabel

Zarzatine

Tindouf

In Amenas

LIBYA

SPANISH
SAHARA

Edjeleh

Adrar

In Salah

to Nouakchett

Reggane

Aoulef

ALGERIA

Djanet

to Atar

MAURETANIA

MALI

Bidon V

Tamanrasset

to Timbuctu and Gao

to Gao 834 km

to Agadez 570 km

to Agadez and Kano

NIGER

to Bilma 640 km

	railway
	primary surfaced road
	secondary surfaced road
	primary tracks
	secondary tracks
▲	gas
△	petrol
	pipelines oil and gas
	principal caravan routes 5th—18th century
	national boundary

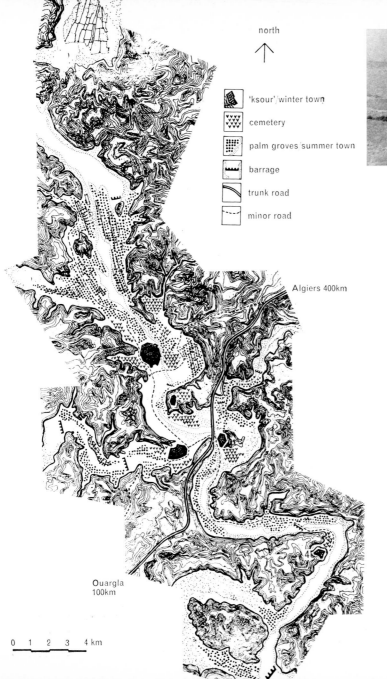

north

↑

'ksour'/winter town

cemetery

palm groves/summer town

barrage

trunk road

minor road

Algiers 400km

Ouargla
100km

0 1 2 3 4 km

Left The valley of the Mzab. The area shown on this map was given protective classification by the Algerian government in 1967.

Above The valley of the Mzab looking north. Beni Isguen, 'the Holy Town', in the foreground; Melika, 'the Queen', to the right; and Ghardaia, the capital, in the background. Each 'ksour' is dominated by the tower of its mosque. The dark patches of date palm conceal the 'summer' towns.

Ghardaia, the capital, 13,000 in Guerrara and Berriane, and 4,000 in Beni Isguen. Metlili, Bon Novra and El Atteuf each have a population of about 2,000.

The physical planning of the Valley follows a consistent pattern. Each of the five towns is made up of the same three elements: a fortified 'ksour' or winter town, an oasis and summer town, and a necropolis. The five town groups are linked by an elaborate hydraulic system which follows the course of the 'oued', but they are separated visually by rugged open areas of desert.

The hydraulic system consists of barrages built across the 'oued' to create surface and subterranean reservoirs. Rainwater is guided from the barrage into the crevices of the 'chebka', sometimes 80 - 120 metres deep, or straight into the gardens through an ingenious network of irrigation channels—'souagui'. Over three thousand wells are connected to the underground reservoirs and the above-ground structures supporting the well pulleys are a characteristic feature of the Mzab.

Except in the common need for fortification, the 'ksour' of the Mzab differ fundamentally from the Berber 'ksour'. Whereas each Berber town was occupied by blood relations of the same tribe or clan, and was dependent on a higher authority, the Mozabites founded each town with a number of family groups. Whilst retaining their individual identity these groups surrendered juridical and executive

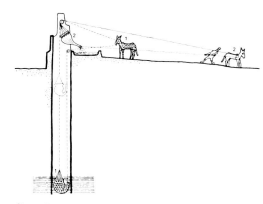

Above Diagram of well operation. The 'tirest' (skin containers holding 10–13 gallons of water) are drawn in rotation by two donkeys. A pull on the cord releases the neck of the 'tirest' and discharges water into the 'segguia' (irrigation channel).

Right The 'blind' northern slope of the 'ksour', Ghardaia. The 'growth rings' of the original town are still visible but later expansion has destroyed the clear separation between the 'summer' and 'winter' towns.

Far right Children collecting water, Beni Isguen.

Below right A 'koubba' (sanctuary or tomb of a saint) on the edge of a necropolis. (Photo: Manuelle Roche)

power to a common higher authority, the 'Quaba il'. Elders elected from the 'Quaba il' of each town in the pentapole formed a higher assembly which held its meetings in the Mosque. The Church was supreme and had the power to excommunicate clans or individuals.

All five 'ksour' are built on high ground with concentric bands of courtyard houses falling away from the central Mosque and its dominant tower. Originally the limits of each town were set by a fortified outer wall. The close texture of streets, ramps and steps is broken only by an open market and alcoves sheltering the public wells.

There is hardly any vegetation in the 'ksour'. Their location on high ground leaves the flat areas close to Oued free for cultivation. The whole Valley has about 200,000 date palms grouped in separate plantations around each town. These are less productive than the palms of most oases, but they play an additional role in protecting the summer towns and their gardens from the sun. At the hottest time of the year it was the custom for most of the population to leave the 'ksour' and to move to the summer towns. During these months the 'ksour' remained silent and parched, and the new life of cultivation began in more pleasant surroundings. Today, the annual exodus is less marked and summer towns are treated more as a second home for prosperous Mozabite traders.,

Shaded by the foliage of apricot, pomegranate and date palm, the streets and houses of the summer town are cool, and the sense of refreshment is heightened by splashing water in open channels. Until the beginning of this century, the life of the Mozabites was centred on the agricultural exploitation of the Valley, and today there is still enough fruit and wheat grown to serve local needs.

Each town has its own necropolis, in the open desert area near the winter town and occupying about twice its area. Separate burial grounds for each clan are grouped around the tombs of famous saints. The individual gravestones are unmarked and large whitewashed areas are left open for prayer meetings.

The physiognomy of the Mzab towns was achieved during the first forty years of their existence—the time taken to build all seven towns. The original conditions imposed two guiding principles, of speed and economy, and these formed the basis for construction and planning. A clear policy for the expansion and growth of the towns anticipated the steady influx of population during the first half of the eleventh century. The best use of land dictated that when one winter town reached its optimum size, a new one should be added on high ground.

There was no hierarchy of buildings in the Mzab. The same materials and methods of construction were used for hydraulic work, houses, public buildings and the Mosque. The size of family determined the size of house, and public buildings were no more than a number of typical houses joined together to provide extra space.

The individual house plan reflects a pattern of life which has hardly changed since the Ibādites first settled in the Mzab; an austere and secret life proud of its early hardship and achievements, and highly regulated in every detail. Until 1878 no stranger had set foot in the Valley, and even today, visitors to Beni Isguen, the Holy Town, must leave before sunset. Women remain locked in their houses, and are forbidden to leave the Valley. Only women, children and old men remain in the towns for more than a few months at a time. The traditions of Mozabite trading go back to the days of Sedrata, and today they are the

Above Two views of Beni Isguen. The upper photograph is taken from the cemetery hill opposite the town, across the dry river bed which connects the 'summer' town and palm groves to the left. The lower photograph is from the opposite direction.

Right Plans and a section of a typical Ghardaia well house. From top to bottom: ground floor or basement; first floor; terrace; section. 1 entrance; 2 living areas; 3 kitchen; 4 rooms; 5 toilet on first floor, collection chamber at ground level or basement; 7 stair; 8 terrace.

Opposite page General view of Ghardaia from the market.

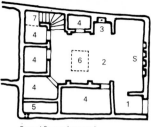

Ground floor or basement

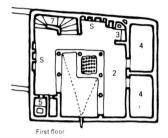

First floor

Terrace

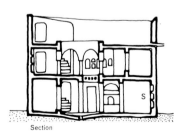

Section

1 Entrance	6	Light well
2 Living area	7	Stair
3 Kitchen	8	Terrace
4 Rooms		
5 WC on first floor		
collection chamber at GF level		

0   5m

144

Top Ghardaia market.

Above Detail of the northern edge of Bou Noura, the 'town of Light'.

most astute and successful merchants in the Maghreb. A Mozabite general store will be found in almost every town and village in Algeria. Boys are sent from the Mzab to learn the trade with relatives and return home to marry at the age of fourteen to sixteen. They leave the Valley again, and only settle permanently in the Mzab when enough capital has been made to retire and continue house-building.

The implacable blind walls of streets and narrow alleys express only the secrecy and austerity of the Mzab. Seen from above, the buildings take on a new meaning, and the subtle organism of courtyard dwellings becomes clear. On all but the south facing slopes of the winter towns, houses are open at the top with a central courtyard diminishing in area through two or three storeys to a small roof-light over the lowest floor. This is either at ground/entrance level, or one floor below ground. It is the coolest part of the house during the day and consists of a large living space bordered by small rooms on two sides. The next floor provides a more open living area with arcades around a central court. After sunset a violent drop in temperature changes the function of the roof terrace from parasol to sleeping area.

On the southern slopes of the winter towns, the walls which usually surround the terrace on all four sides are left open to the south. The arcades efficiently cut off the vertical rays of summer sun and admit winter sun.

There is evidence of Andalusian ornament in the ruined town of Sedrata, yet no applied decoration appeared in the buildings of the Mzab. The only feature which is repeated is the semi-circular arch and the four-pronged termination of the Mosque towers. Otherwise the shapes and sizes of walls and openings were determined by orientation and privacy, and the irregularities of the site.

Building materials and constructional details were the same for all buildings. A hard, quick-drying plaster ('timchent') processed from river silt was used for making building blocks, for mortar and for rendering. The external rendering of buildings is still applied in the traditional way, with palm branches, giving an energetic surface texture to the wall. Stone was used only as rough reinforcements for wall openings, arches and vaults, and for foundations. Wood work was limited to the ingenious use of palm; large planks sawn from the trunk for doors and shutters, branches cut in two as initial support for vaulted roofs, and the nervure bent and tied to form permanent centring for arches.

Discussing the ways in which dwellings can be tailored to suit the particular requirements of the

individual whilst at the same time satisfying agreed common criteria, Christopher Alexander makes a distinction between 'mass' and 'fine adaptation' (to the environment).[1] In the Mzab, a common solution is found in building for climate and for privacy, and at the level of 'fine adaptation'; the interiors of houses are literally moulded to suit the individual family. This is achieved partly by carving out a variety of storage alcoves from thick walls, and also by taking advantage of the speed at which 'timchent' partition walls can be dismantled and rebuilt within the basic plan.

It has been suggested that Le Corbusier's work and thinking were deeply affected by visits which he made to Algeria in the 'thirties. There are similarities in the forms of several buildings in Ghardaia and the chapel at Ronchamps, and it is true that Le Corbusier's interest in curved planes dates from the time of these visits. This attitude to indigenous buildings underestimates the fact that their forms are an unselfconscious and inseparable product of social, geographical and climatic conditions. Of an aeroplane flight which he made over the Mzab Valley in 1935, Le Corbusier himself wrote, '. . . every house a place of happiness, of joy, of a serene existence regulated like an inescapable truth, in the service of man, and for each'.[2]

Recently, through the influence of industrialization, under political pressure and through a slackening of religious practice, Mozabite society and its environment show signs of change, which began in the early days of colonization. Ghardaia became the military centre of an area stretching about 600 km from Djelfa in the Hauts Plateaux to El Golea on the edge of the eastern 'erg'. Gradually the effects of an alien culture took shape in a variety of administrative buildings, missions, a military camp and hospital, and schools. One of the most damaging effects was the introduction of waterborne waste disposal. Traditionally, naturally decomposed waste provided a useful fertiliser and was regularly collected from each house for this purpose. However, due to the infrequent rising of the 'oued', a large area outside Bou Noura has become silted up, resulting in a vast stagnant pond of accumulated waste from Malika and Ghardaia.

The discovery of oil at Hassi Messaoud 250 km east of Ghardaia, has had a profound effect on the whole region including the Valley of the Mzab. The trunk road from Algiers branches at Ghardaia making it an important relay town for traffic on the Tamanrasset route and for the eastern oil towns. There is an airport 12 km from Ghardaia, and the Valley is beginnnig to attract a large number of tourists.

The extent to which the fabric of the Mzab towns can

accommodate change is significant. Since the arrival of the oil companies the desert interstices between the towns have become disorderly with the abandoned wrecks of trucks, makeshift workshops and other debris, but the untouchable cemeteries around the 'ksour' have helped to retain some of their original legibility.

MASTER PLAN, 1963

André Ravereau first visited the Valley in 1958, and towards the end of the War of Independence he returned to make a planning study of the seven towns. The study includes an evaluation of the original planning principles which form the basis of a master plan for the whole valley, detailed proposals for a central administrative area, and a residential extension to Beni Isguen.

The master plan attempts to deal with the uncontrolled development which has already taken place on either side of the road linking Beni Isguen and Ghardaia, and limits further expansion of the area by re-routing through-traffic.

The master plan similarly places restrictions on traditional areas. The ancient 'ksour' (the 'winter' towns)

Left diagram The existing situation.

'winter' towns or 'ksour'

'summer' towns (palm groves)

cultivable land close to the river valley between the 'ksour'

existing individual and cluster housing

necropolis

existing vegetation

existing secondary roads

river valley or 'oued', usually dry

regional amenities:

1 administration, civic, public works, chamber of commerce, post office etc., sited at the centre of gravity of the pentapolis.

2 education, higher education, sited on vacant land.

3 recreation, sports fields, adjacent to open desert area.

4 new medical centre, to replace present inadequate hospital, next to regional road to serve wider area.

5 international cultural institute on high ground overlooking entire valley.

C commercial areas; existing buildings and activities to be consolidated, and existing secondary road to become a service road.

H clusters of new housing on open hillsides or isolated hills, in areas where scattered existing housing will be drawn together as part of the new development.

rocky hillside suitable for future high density housing expansion.

Right diagram Proposals

'winter' towns or 'ksour'

river valley or 'oued'

trunk road, constructed in 1966, to avoid the five towns

proposed feeder road in the valley

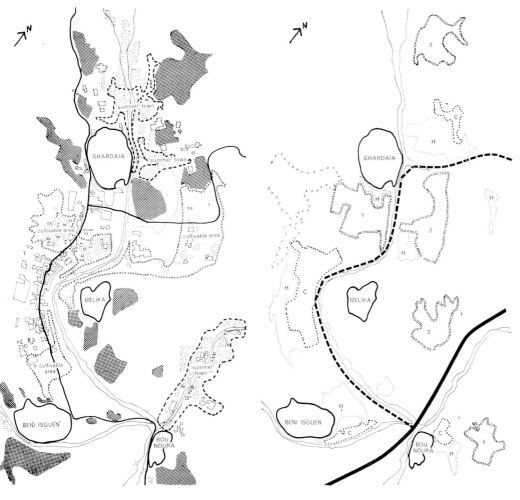

—Ghardaia, Melika, Beni Isguen, and Bou Noura—are to be carefully preserved, along with their traditional burial grounds or necropoli.

In the agricultural areas, tourist accommodation and low density housing may be added to the housing clusters already there, with additional generous planting. In the desert areas or 'chebka', which occupy the areas on each side of the valley and are essential to its character, no development will be permitted.

The fact that the new road has been built and that the entire Valley has been given 'protective' classification by the Government holds out some hope for the implementation of Ravereau's plan and a planning office has been set up in the Valley to bring the proposals up to date. Although the general principles of the master plan still hold good, it is doubtful whether the visual 'stage set' approach suggested for the central administrative area can be given such high priority. A thorough appraisal of the likely scale of expansion in the Valley and the aspirations of the Mozabites themselves must be the first concern of the new planning office.

The future of the Valley depends largely on the reaction of the Mozabites to the economic restrictions imposed on them by the Government since Independence, and, in turn, on the Government's attitude to their continued monopoly of trade throughout the country. Now that it has become more difficult for the Mozabites to invest money abroad they may well be forced into the same position which brought them to the Valley nine hundred years ago.

147

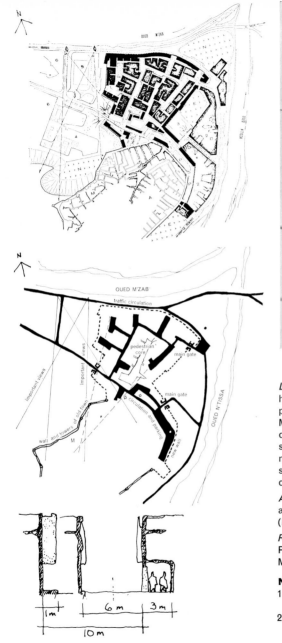

148

Left Extensions to Beni Isguen. Most new buildings have public cloisters to provide shade for pedestrians and are built according to traditional Mzab principles. 1 administration buildings; 2 commercial activities; 3 existing schools; 4 new schools; 5 sports; 6 low density residential (see master plan); A old town; M minaret; P parking serving old town; N new cemetery; E existing cemetery.

Above Model showing lower part of central administrative development of Ghardaia extension. (Photo: Manuelle Roche)

Right View of Ghardaia from roof of Ravereau's Posts and Telecommunications building. (Photo: Manuelle Roche)

Notes
1 'Thick Wall Pattern', Christopher Alexander, Architectural Design, London, July 1968.
2 'Aircraft', Le Corbusier, The New World Vision, London, 1936.

149

OUR GROSS NATIONAL PRODUCT.

Outdoor signs and billboards that are so grotesque. so poorly placed or spaced — so many miles of ugly. We've learned to live with it, even laugh about it. Until, one day, it's our oak tree they're chopping down. Our view that's being blocked.

America, the beautiful. Our America. The crisis isn't in our cities; the crisis is in our hearts. With a change of heart, we can change the picture.

Send this page to your local authority and ask him to support sign control laws.

AIA/American Institute of Architects

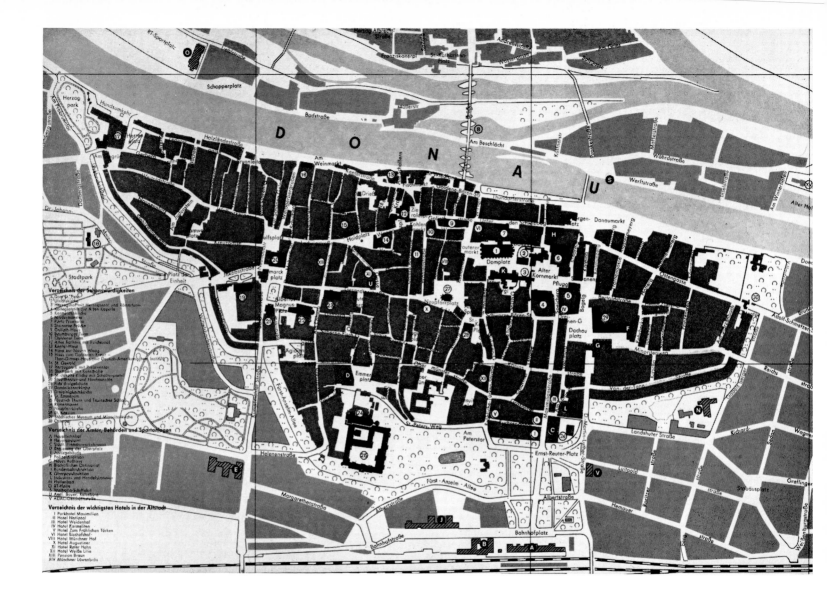

THE REGENERATION OF REGENSBURG

MARGRIT AND DECLAN KENNEDY

In 1964, the attention of the Cultural Circle of the Federation of German Industry was drawn to a series of crises facing Regensburg, the only surviving medieval German city. In addition to the decay of its 800-year-old buildings and the growing pressures of commercial and suburban expansion, Regensburg was threatened by a traffic proposal which showed two six-lane highways cutting through its central core. The interested industrialists set up a research foundation to establish a seminar of planners, lawyers, economists, engineers, historians, and architects to look into the problem: 'What will happen to our historic towns and cities?' Regensburg was chosen to be the example.

The fundamental breakthrough in this study was that it was not concerned with the preservation of single buildings, but with the whole urban organism. For in Regensburg, quite apart from their importance as historic buildings and landmarks, the value of even the most impressive of the medieval houses or churches exists in their being part of a still almost intact and continuous urban structure. This structure is evidence of a time when every activity in a town had its proper place and proportionate size.

The Cathedral **1** occupies the central position in the old city. It is one of the masterpieces of the thirteenth century. Adjoining it, are the palace of the bishops **7** and another church for the worldly governing body **2**. On a square of its own, the town hall **12** was the seat of the 'Eternal Parliament' (the first 'House of Lords' in Germany, which met here until 1812).

Numerous patrician houses **9, 10, 11, 13, 14,** with beautiful interior courtyards and dominating house-towers demonstrate the power and wealth of Regensburg's medieval merchant families. Next to them the splendid houses and inns **15, 25,** for the nobility (or later their representatives) attending the 'Eternal Parliament' provide an unparalleled high density of regal living.

Several monasteries **5, 6, 19, 22** and quarters for smaller merchants and craftsmen occupy the east and west extensions of the originally rectangular medieval town. All these are interconnected by a tight network of narrow lanes and streets which widen out into the 'corn' market near **6,** the 'fish' market near **13,** the 'coal' market near **10,** and the 'herb' market near **1.** The 'Stone Bridge' **8,** which spans the Danube with sixteen arches and is more than 1,000 ft long was finished in 1135 and took ten years to build.

Inside the town walls of Regensburg only one part of the city, in the south-eastern quarter, has been rebuilt in the nineteenth century, and very few houses are new.

Regensburg is situated on the northernmost point of the Danube, where the rivers Regen and Laaber meet. In the middle ages it was one of the richest and most powerful cities in Europe, and was 'Urbs Germaniae Populissima' with 70,000 inhabitants. At the junction of merchant routes from France to the Balkans and from Italy to Russia it was, to use a modern term, an international trade centre in the thirteenth and fourteenth centuries. Personal connections with powerful Italian trade centres were so close that merchant delegates from Regensburg regularly attended the Venice town council; and the existence of these relationships is reflected in the numerous patrician towers found in no other city north of the Alps. By the middle of the fifteenth century Regensburg began gradually but irretrievably to lose its central political and mercantile position. Today it is relegated to the periphery of western Europe, approximately fifty miles from the Czechoslovakian border, where it serves as the centre of only a small region. In looking at the demographic development of Regensburg over the last 130 years the real threat becomes obvious. In 1830 the number of inhabitants was 16,300. In 1900 it had risen to 45,000 and by 1965 it had grown to 125,000.

Many urban structures in Germany were razed to the ground by the bombs of World War II. Now the population growth of surviving urban centres, the need for commercial expansion, and especially traffic demands, are destroying what was spared. Is there any middle ground between radical 'bulldozer renewal' and an 'open air museum'? Can we recreate a livable environment for coming generations in what has been viable for eight hundred years?

These are the questions to which the town planning seminar addressed itself. If the renewal proposals which the seminar produced are realistic in this extremely problematic case, they may well be applicable in modified forms to other old cities.

In trying to answer these questions for survival, it soon became clear that a renewal of the old town would affect not only the adjoining new parts of Regensburg, but also the region for which it is the cultural and economic centre. This meant a greatly enlarged physical study area, with comprehensive interrelationships in several fields, such as sociology, economics, law, and traffic planning.

Over four years, the time which the seminar required to finish the study, a completely new approach to solve the problems of a historic city was developed. The seminar worked on different scales of planning simultaneously. That meant constant interaction between sociological, economic and legal findings. The order of this summary of the study is therefore no indication of its methodology.

A The Old City
B The Core Extension
C The Urbanized Area
D The Region
E The Future of Regensburg

A THE OLD CITY

Renewal categories

The usual objective criteria — density and use of buildings, day and sun lighting, sanitation, accessibility, tax base and market value, and so forth — are not sufficient in assessing the qualifications of buildings for rehabilitation in old cities. Historic, cultural and aesthetic values which a building possesses as part of a conservation area are critical. These are difficult to define objectively. Their assessment requires a high degree of technical and artistic understanding.

In some cases we must renew, even if objective criteria point to demolition. In others, where important parts of buildings should be preserved, particularly to retain historic-environmental continuity, sympathetically scaled infill will be required. In yet others, conflicts between modern use patterns and old buildings will need careful resolution. In exceptional cases, whole blocks will need a completely new structure. But just as aesthetics or scholarship should not be exclusively decisive, neither should monetary economics settle the issue.

The first survey of the old city, an area over one mile long and half a mile wide, was carried out in 1964. Maps were drawn up showing:

— conditions and uses of buildings
— heights of buildings
— open spaces
— land ownerships
— trends in shopping habits
— population fluctuation
— traffic
— social conditions etc.

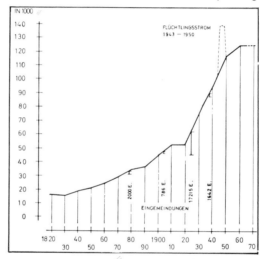

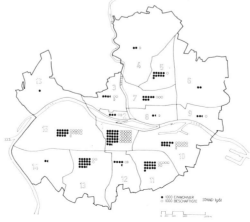

Far left Three examples of traffic congestion on the narrow streets and open spaces.

Above left Increase in population 1820-1970 (peak shows number of refugees after World War II)

Below left Black dot = 1000 inhab. White dot = 1000 employees demonstrating the strong concentration in the central old town area.

152

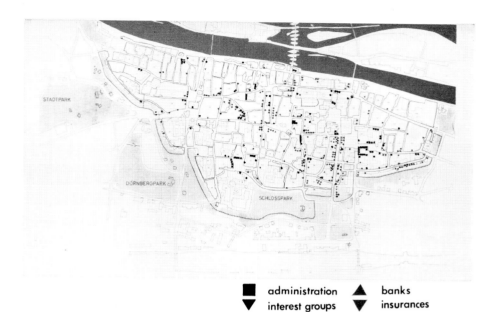

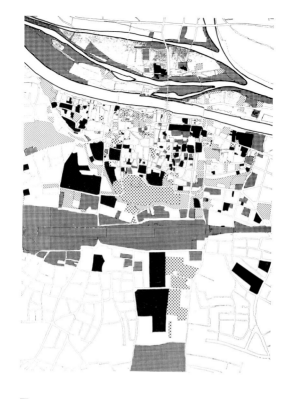

administration   ▲ banks
▼ interest groups ▼ insurances
✚ church admin.   ▨ indust. admin.

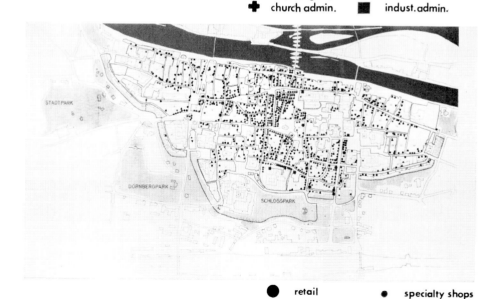

● retail   • specialty shops
▲ wholesale   ◉ departm. stores
▼ warehouses   ▪ rest. & coffeehouse
                    ■ hotel & restaurant

■ church
▒ prince
▦ state
▨ city
□ private

Above and below left Commercial uses 1 and 2 another indication of the importance and central function of the old town.

Above Land ownership pattern indicating barriers (Prince's park and railway tracks) between the old town and the southern parts of the city where the new university is located.

The mapping of historic buildings showed how historic building monuments are knitted in the overall urban structure. It also demonstrated the extent of the task confronting the citizens of Regensburg.

These maps showed how the old city retained its traditional character through the variety of its land uses. The close physical interrelationships of living, shopping and workshops, and administration, have hardly changed over the past decades. However, this does not mean that they are still functioning in the same way. Transformation is due to two main trends:

1 An ever-increasing proportion of the traditional population, especially the economically stronger sections, have left the old city to settle in 'high quality' decentralized housing districts. In their place have come poorer immigrants, mainly old age pensioners (now approximately 40% of the inhabitants of the old town), independent craftsmen and retailers (approximately 15%) and sub-tenants, i.e. apprentices, young employees, restaurant and hotel personnel (approximately 15-20%).

In 1961, 80% of the buildings were declared to be in need of renewal: 75% had no bathrooms or toilets within dwellings.

2 Through the exodus of middle and higher income inhabitants small retailers continually lose customers, and many have been or shortly will be forced to close. Meanwhile productive businesses which have to expand are forced to move out to satisfy their need for space.

Many of the developing administrative offices have remained in the old city in spite of space difficulties, but several are now located in the south-eastern part of the old city where a number of sizeable villas were built in the nineteenth century and have become available.

Above Regensburg building monuments are tightly knitted into the overall urban structure (black—building monuments, dark grey—important buildings, grey—important details).

Below These maps demonstrate the desperate need for improvement and the results of years of neglect.

154

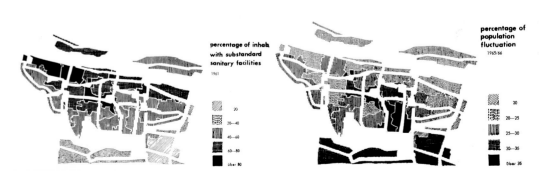

percentage of inhab. with substandard sanitary facilities 1961

percentage of population fluctuation 1965/66

percentage of popul. decline 1965/66

A recommended land use plan

The seminar worked out a new land use proposal for the old city to counteract these trends and provide a stimulus for new development. Some of the more important recommendations are summarized below.

Housing in the old city is to be upgraded to retain and increase population and to attract economically stronger groups.

The main shopping area in the old city remains as existing but will be extended to the north towards the Stone Bridge and to the south towards the railway terminal expansion area.

Mixed uses of buildings are encouraged — housing on upper floors, commercial uses and some non-noxious workshops on ground floors.

Traffic-and-noise generating industry and workshops are located on the easterly Danube islands.

New office and administrative buildings are sited mainly within the central expansion area at the railway station.

Three schools are expanded to double their present size; one is to be demolished.

Student hostels and suitable institutes are accommodated in rehabilitated old buildings to increase mixes of use and density for the old city's benefit. Other present educational institutes remain. New complexes are sited between the new university and the core extension to form a further educational precinct.

Cultural activities: a new theatre, museums, and a new congress hall are recommended.

Churches remain substantially unaltered.

Parking is almost exclusively multi-storied, and that which is shown on the land uses recommendation map is public.

Private garages within buildings are mandatory in the housing areas.

New large hotels, one at the easterly Danube foot-bridge and one next to the 'deck' alongside the park can supplement the smaller, restored hotels in the historic areas.

Open spaces: the existing park around the old city is connected over the railway to the university green belt on the hill.

Sports and other recreation facilities on the islands are to be extended and water sports located on the river banks which are no longer commercially used because of the Rhein-Main-Danube canal by-pass.

Market gardens: the banks of the Regen and Danube, where the two rivers meet, will remain gardens for the famous Regensburg radishes.

The central expansion area is ensured almost limitless east-west growth by use of the air-rights over the railway.

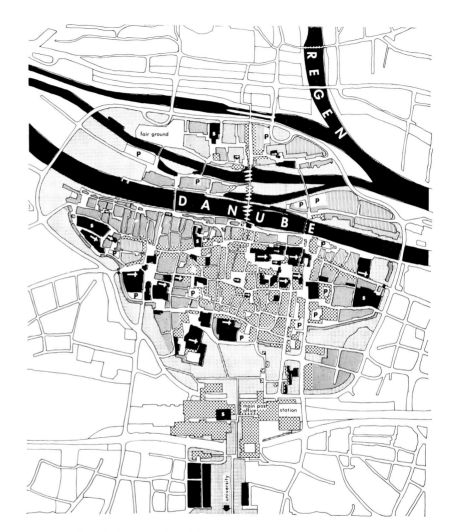

PROPOSED LAND USE

- ▨ residential
- ▦ commercial, administrative & multi-use
- ▥ industrial
- ■ cultural & institutional (s→school, t→church)
- ▧ open space (p→parking)

Historic buildings

To supplement the block survey, to check initial design proposals, and to provide detailed historic and structural information, a second assessment was made of all 1,200 buildings individually in the old city in December 1966. As the information came in, it was categorized and transferred to maps and overlays.

A series of five renewal or restoration categories were suggested in the seminar's report, *Regensburg zur Erneuerung einer alten Stadt*.[1] The authors have somewhat more rigorously redefined the five categories to explain the type of action needed for each particular block or building.

1 *Maintenance*. This category refers to buildings which, whether of historic value or not, need no radical repair or renewal but must be retained as components in important environmental sequences and therefore must be kept in good condition. An example is the St. Emmeran Monastery.

Below Part of the cloisters of St Emmeran's Monastery.

Right Plans for the restoration of the old city inn.

156

5th floor

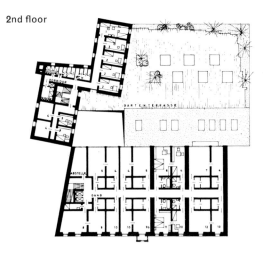

2nd floor

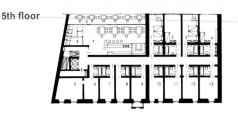

1st floor

2 *Restoration*. This is by far the largest category. A number of historic buildings need extensive repair and restoration if they are to be preserved. An example is the old city inn, which was operated as a hostelry from the sixteenth to the end of the nineteenth century. In 1898 its use was radically altered to house small tenements. The seminar survey demonstrated however that, with little structural change to the original building, fifty-three hotel rooms with bath could be installed in four upper floors, over spacious ground floor reception and restaurant areas. On its south side the hotel would open on to the Haid Square, a pedestrian area which would become the centre of the university students' town facilities. Rear delivery access is provided from the alley bordering the west side of the building.

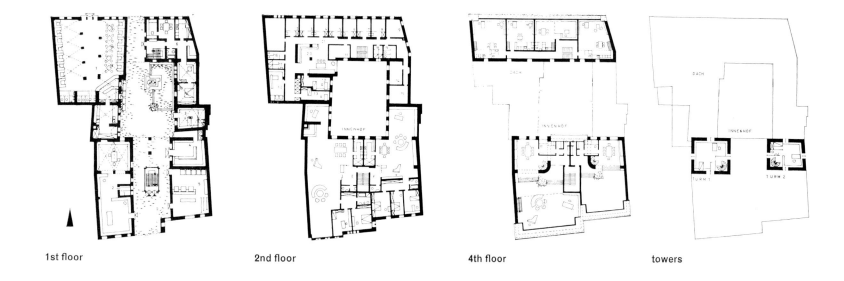

1st floor   2nd floor   4th floor   towers

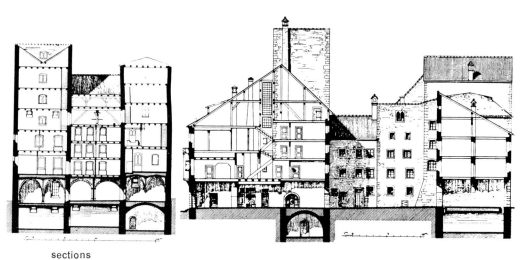

sections

3 *Renovation*. Some historic buildings require extensive internal renovation and restoration of façades; others require major, and extremely careful, conversion for modern use if they are to be preserved with economic reality and yet retain their important historic characteristics. A good example is the Gravenreuther house, one of the old town's most interesting patrician houses, with an interior court and two towers. The seminar recommended:

Ground floor. Small shops and a café-restaurant; small library with ancillary rooms, and a bookshop for the university.

First to third floors. Apartments for lecturers and students.

The very strong facades of the courtyard and lane elevations would not be altered by the new arrangement of the interior.

4 *Infill*. This category refers to the replacement of a single building within a historic sequence. In making each recommendation for this category, the seminar attempted to define square footage, use(s), access,

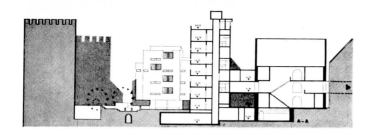

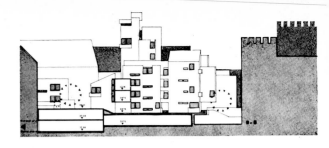

GROUND FLOOR

2ND FLOOR

urban context and scale. For example, with the foundation of the Fourth Bavarian State University at Regensburg, the construction of student living accommodation has become necessary. Some hostels are being built in suburban districts. But in the opinion of the seminar, living quarters should also be provided in-town, to allow students to have close contact with urban life and to contribute to the activity of the old city.

To attract alternative solutions for the reconstruction of free or derelict sites within the historic core of Regensburg, a competition was initiated for students and young architects. To give one example: the derelict site chosen for the largest hostel (120 student rooms) was about 2,500 square metres in size, irregular in shape, and allowed a fairly free arrangement of building masses and open spaces within certain givens in scale.

The prizewinning schemes, of which that awarded the first prize is shown here, had these points in common:
— differentiation of building masses in plan and height;
— ingenuity of spatial arrangements to enable connection to surrounding buildings;
— retention of the stone character and scale of the historic urban setting.

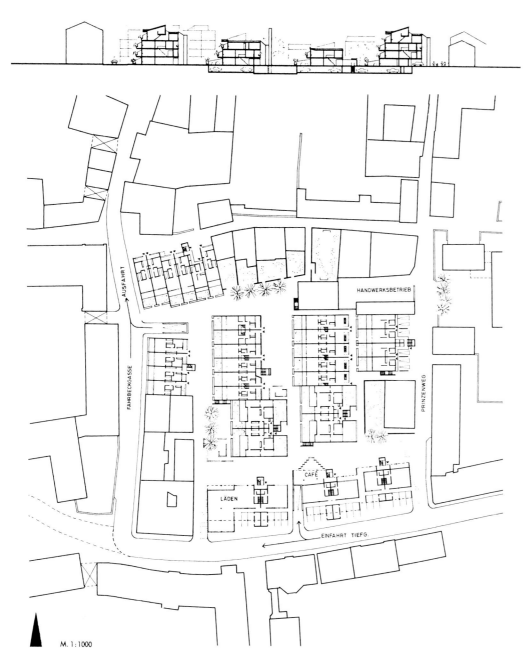

AUSFAHRT

FAHRBECKGASSE

HANDWERKSBETRIEB

PRINZENWEG

CAFÉ

LÄDEN

EINFAHRT TIEFG.

M. 1:1000

5 *Restructuring*. This category refers to those sequences of buildings which can be entirely or in some major way restructured, either through the dereliction of historic sequences beyond recall or where sequences of buildings are in poor condition and are of little or no historic or economic importance. One example is a site occupied at present by haphazard and valueless buildings whose structural condition is poor and with sanitation well below standard. The site is, however, very favourable for a central housing precinct, somewhat detached from the main shopping area but near the green belt and the banks of the Danube.

The seminar's recommendation for the site is a row of stepped-back apartment buildings, arranged in such a way as not to exceed four storeys, with some small service-type shops and boutiques, a cafe, basement parking and a workshop court at ground floor level.

Left Plans for restructuring the main parts of a block in the south-eastern parts of the old town.

Below Photographs of the model block described on the next page.

A renewal action plan

To test the applicability of these five renewal and restoration categories, the seminar selected a centrally-situated and, as far as possible, representative block in the most densely built-up part of the old city; and replanned it in detail in physical terms, and in terms of the political, legal and economic means for historic urban renewal. The following measurements were applied:

floor/plot ratio 3.5;
living space for 146 persons totalling approximately 77,000 sq ft;
commercial space approximately 90,000 sq ft.

The photographs show both the beauty and decay of restored and neglected courtyards. It becomes immediately apparent how the five renewal and restoration categories can be independently implemented once programmes for them have been established. At the same time they will provide in total a right and meaningful solution within the overall renewal proposals for the city.

Instead of the pedestrian being forced to move about the block on the present narrow and dangerous sidewalks beside narrow streets with heavy traffic, the seminar's proposal recommends a radical change. Shops are oriented towards the inside of the block. Entrances to the interior square are created through the beautiful existing doorways, halls and courtyards. Within the block a rich sequence of spaces can be developed revealing the old city's variety and capacity to surprise. In this way historic spaces may be opened to the pedestrian public and used to intensify commercial activity. The surrounding streets may be turned over to delivery and access for residents' cars as part of the overall traffic system for the old city, while the narrow Gesandtenstrasse becomes part of a subsidiary loop.

160

Model block   1st floor existing

Model block   1st floor planned

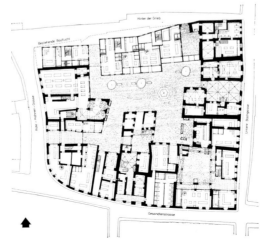

Model block   2nd floor existing

Model block   2nd floor planned

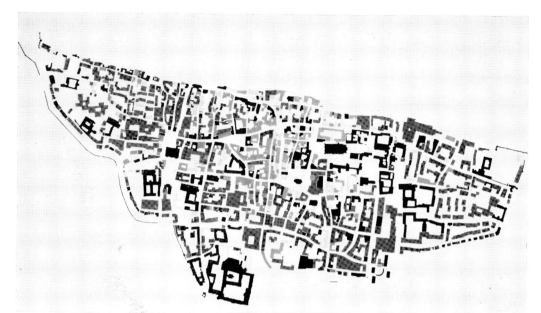

161

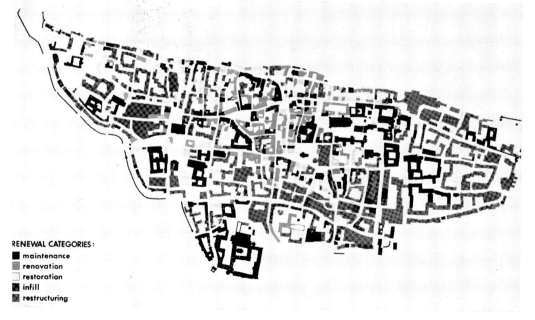

Main proposals
The seminar set the five renewal and restoration categories in two master plans for action, so that the necessary information showing what may be altered and what is to be conserved is at hand at all times. These were the main proposal and the variant.

In the first, conservation of all types of historic buildings is emphasized as far as practically possible. In the second, only the more important monuments and the general medieval urban structure are preserved. Between the two extremes the actual renewal process finds its place, allowing the overall plan to remain flexible and responsive to important changes and decisions on a building-by-building basis and ensuring the incorporation, through time, of the most up-to-date economic, social and legal requirements.

RENEWAL CATEGORIES:
- ■ maintenance
- ▨ renovation
- □ restoration
- ▨ infill
- ▨ restructuring

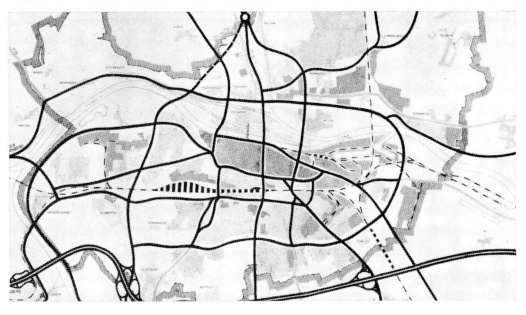

Traffic

In 1952 a traffic plan by Regensburg's municipal authorities was made and passed. Although it cuts the historic city into three pieces by four- or six-lane highways and separates it from the riverside recreational area, this plan is being executed day by day. When it is completed it will bring local and through traffic of all types indiscriminately into the middle of the old city, with junctions too closely spaced and too small to cope with the volumes and their destinational complexity. The inadequacy of the municipal plan is increased by the fact that in 1952 the decision to add a new university for 4,000 to 10,000 students had not been made (a catalyst now so critically important for the renewal area) nor was pressure for the new city extension so acute.

To counteract the inadequacies of the municipal plan, and to avoid more demolition of the historic urban structure of Regensburg, the seminar proposed:

1 to increase the proportion of public transport by
— a regional rapid-transit system
— an improvement of local short-distance public transport through the use of smaller units (minibus) with high frequency schedules;
2 to by-pass the old city, the Danube islands, and the bridge-head town by means of a ring road which would connect with the regional pattern by tangential roads, and to the core by main and subsidiary loops;
3 to effect thereby a separation of local and through traffic before the old city is reached, and to achieve, within the old city, the highest possible degree of pedestrian and vehicular segregation.

Thus within old Regensburg all main loops are one-way streets in the seminar's traffic plan, with public multi-storeyed parking. The system uses narrow lanes and alleys, which run parallel to pedestrian streets, for delivery and access. Concentrated small units of garages are adjacent to housing.

Minibuses are the only form of through traffic in the old city. They are permitted to use pedestrian areas and will stop by request for tired, old, or walk-shy people. Pedestrian connections to areas outside the dense old city environment are important and these are either by bridge or underpass where traffic volumes demand it.

Above left Municipal traffic plan.

Below left The seminar's proposal.

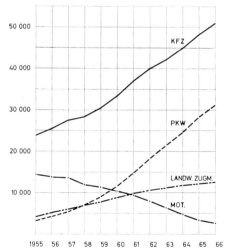

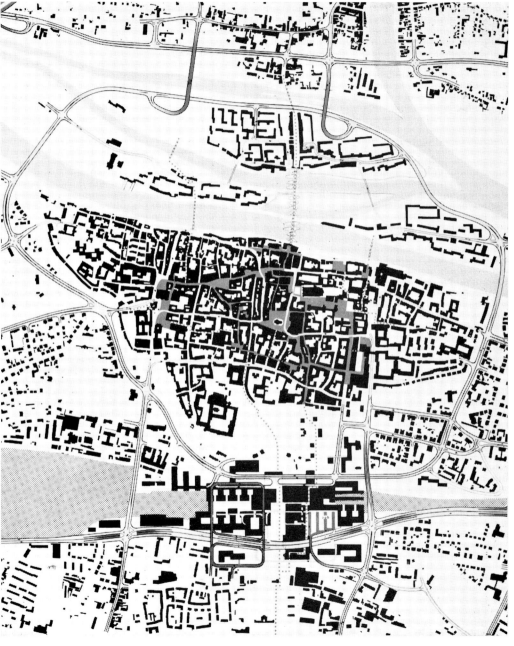

Above Increase in traffic in Regensburg and vicinity.

Right The seminar's proposal showing ring road around the old town and pedestrian access (dotted).

B THE CORE EXTENSION

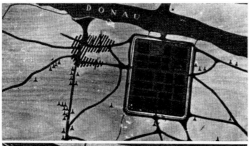

The growth of the old city

City extension has always been a means of coping with new demands or with incompatible uses. The four historic maps of Regensburg show:

Map 1—the Roman Camp, Castra Regina, which was completed in AD 179, a rectangle 1,780 × 1,485 ft with walls 23 ft high and four *portae* which are partly preserved to the present day.

Map 2—by about AD 930 the extended camp, Ratisbona, had become the most important Carlovingian fort in southern Germany.

Map 3—by 1300 the free Imperial city of Regensburg was in its most glorious days. Yet to the west and east new town extensions parallel to the Danube were necessary to accommodate increases in population.

Map 4—by 1860 Regensburg had become a Bavarian provincial town, an intellectual and economic 'sleeping beauty'.

Had Regensburg continued the original pattern of its physical and political growth it would have become a very important metropolis. Since 1930, after a long lull, the city has once again been on the move. Already the old core is running the risk of having to absorb metropolitan functions which are spatially incompatible with its scale.

The seminar studied in depth the following options for the growth of the city:

A In the old city the main shopping district forms a NW-SE axis. The seminar studied the continuation of this axis to the south-east, outside the old town walls; but this proved difficult due to fragmented land ownership.

B As an alternative the seminar studied the siting of the extension on a new island created north of the Danube by the by-pass Rhein-Main-Danube canal. This would provide Regensburg with two new activity poles, the new university and this new core-expansion area, with the old city between them. However foundation problems and the distance (2½ miles) to the new university made this site unpractical.

C Many considerations supported the third possibility which the seminar studied — that of using air-rights over the railway.

—The land for air-rights development is in one ownership;

—the 300 yds wide railroad barrier between the old city and the new university would be bridged;

—projections based on recent escalations of land value in Regensburg demonstrate air-rights in such a central situation for high intensity usage to be feasible.

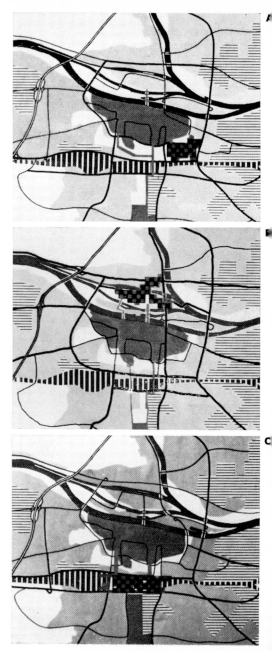

Core extension land uses

In major cities throughout the world, the rapid nineteenth-century growth of railroads has left as its legacy a wasteland of tracks in central areas where today sites are scarce, expensive, and extremely difficult to assemble. Thus decking over railroad tracks in large cities has become an increasingly common and attractive means of obtaining big undeveloped sites, offering opportunities for comprehensive development and high returns while retaining railroad movement unimpeded underneath. Although air-rights developments of this kind have been implemented mainly in larger cities, they can be equally realistic for smaller cities where land restrictions place a similar premium on sites for high density expansion. Regensburg is certainly a case in point.

For quantitative purposes the seminar made a series of assumptions. One of these was that in comparable modern European cities, 40% of the places of employment are in downtown areas. For the old city, a desirable but not too high quota of 20,000 employees was assumed. This left 16,000 employees to be accommodated in the core extension. Working with Federal rail planning technicians an overall zoning was worked out to demonstrate the site's potentialities, and alternative land uses, vehicular access, and the economic and architectural feasibility of superstructures were tested in a model.

The seminar determined that the first phase of development would bridge the station, and that further phases would extend the new core east and west. The height of the buildings in this central portion of the deck is purposely kept low to enable a two-way view between the historic core and the new university. The deck connects at the south with the hill coming down from the university, and drops on the north side of the station slowly to the level of the main shopping street. The design of the first building phase was governed by the need for the uninterrupted use of the lines and the station during construction. Platforms, local bus stops, parking, and delivery, are at ground level. The main deck, with a regional bus terminus, department store, shops, and passenger concourse, is 32 ft above ground level.

The seminar declined to endorse housing within such a centre, assuming the location to be too noisy because of the trains. However Place Bonaventure in Montreal and the Bern project in Switzerland have successfully overcome noise problems by keeping the main deck continuous and by treating noise-generation at its source. The authors believe that it would be a grave mistake to omit housing in the programme for the core expansion area.

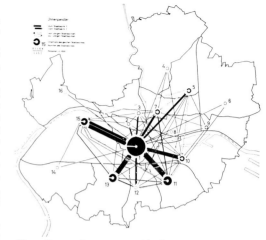

Above Commuter movement in Regensburg.

Left A. City extension south-east of the old town.
B. City extension north of the Danube.
C. City extension using air-rights over railway.

Below View over railway tracks and model photo of city extension using air-rights over railway tracks.

C THE URBANIZED AREA

Town and region

Before the decision to locate the new city expansion area over the railway had been made, it became clear that the only way to solve the problem of growing traffic congestion in the old city would be to improve public transport for the whole of Regensburg and its region.

Rapid and mass transit

The most direct way to do this would be to increase the effective capacity of existing railway lines through introducing a rapid transit system. This could be done in small stages. At first there would be a higher frequency of services on short distances. The second stage would be an improvement of the quality of service. Finally regional coverage would be accompanied by zoning policies leading to settlement concentration around stopping points.

In this system, the main regional station becomes the point of interchange between rapid transit, national rail, and municipal and regional bus services. It serves as shopping centre, administrative centre (with multi-storey office space), recreation centre (for indoor sports), and parking centre for the old city. In due course similar subcentres would be developed at regional stopping points, as catalysts for the concentrated growth of new or existing settlements along the rapid transit line.

New settlements

This is not as difficult as it may seem at first sight. The seminar established that the turnover from old to new housing during the last thirty years was 35%, and could be expected to rise above 50% in the next generation. The seminar developed a relocation and settlement strategy for the urbanized area of Regensburg which assumed a minimum of 33% and a maximum of 66% of existing housing. In addition to this, surveys of the agricultural districts of the region and of other towns nearby showed population increases of 1% per annum or 33% per generation.

At present in the Regensburg area a decentralized pattern of housing is accentuated through a government subsidy of one-family houses. This policy results not only in wastage of agricultural land, but also in tenuous and uneconomic public transport services, leading inevitably to steady increases in private car ownership. The assumption that everyone enjoys driving a car overlooks the fact that people in the first instance simply want to be conveyed from one place to another quickly, cheaply, and in a dignified way.

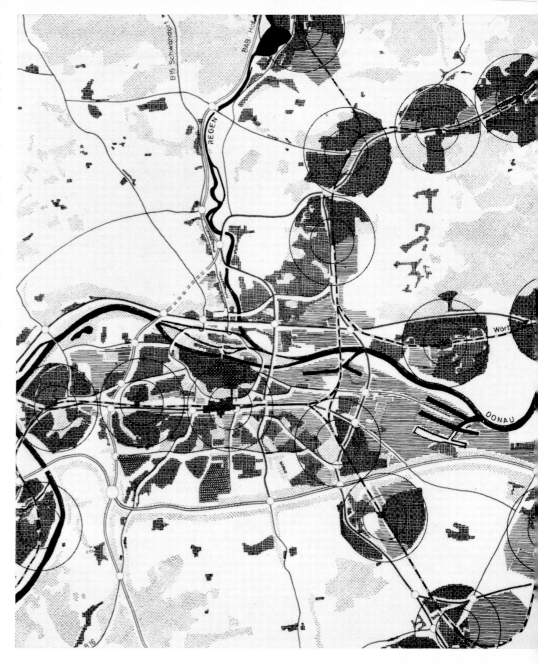

The seminar therefore recommended changes in subsidy policies which would encourage new settlements to cluster rather than to disperse, resulting in a series of concentrated settlements in the Regensburg region, linked by transportation systems and economic interdependence.

167

Variant II

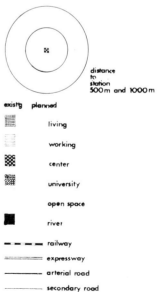

distance
to
station
500 m and 1000 m

existg	planned	
		living
		working
		center
		university
		open space
		river
		railway
		expressway
		arterial road
		secondary road

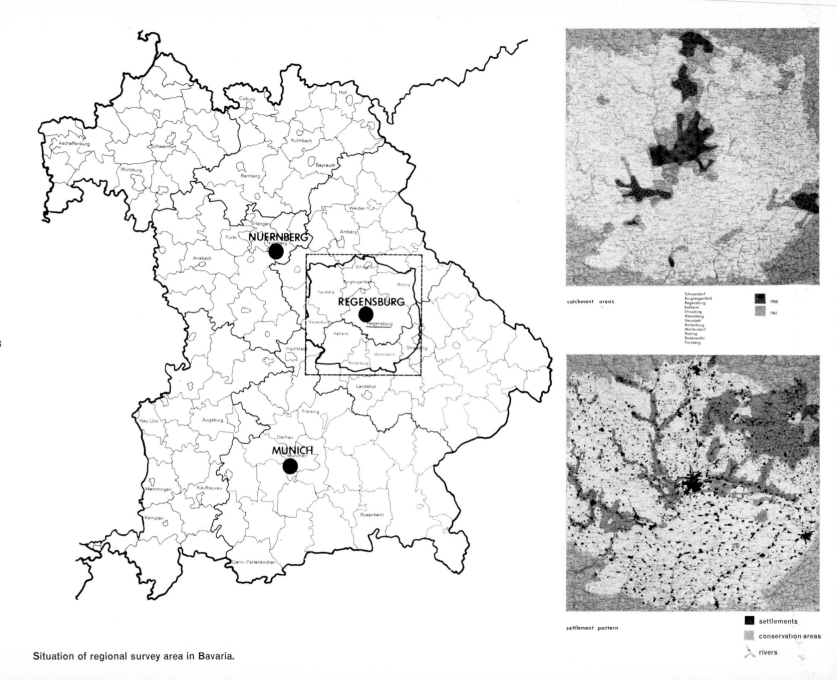

168

catchment areas

Schwandorf
Burglengenfeld
Regensburg
Kelheim
Straubing
Abensberg
Neustadt
Rottenburg
Mallersdorf
Roding
Bodenwöhr
Parsberg

■ 1950

▦ 1961

settlement pattern

■ settlements

▦ conservation areas

⋏ rivers

Situation of regional survey area in Bavaria.

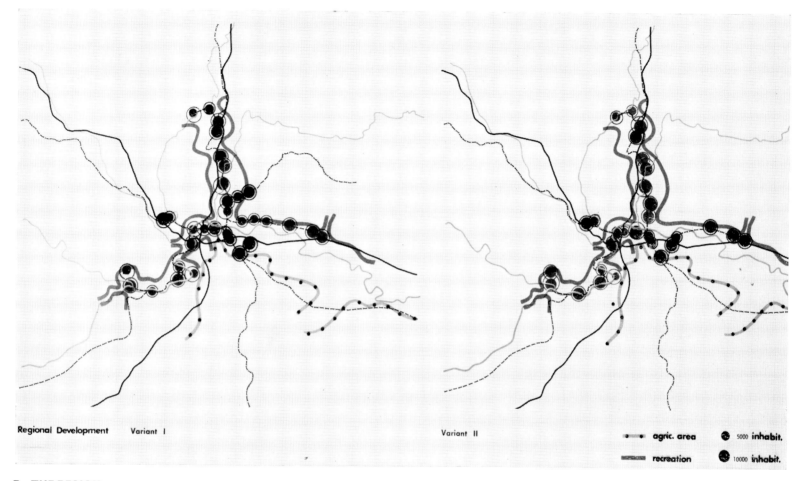

Regional Development   Variant I

Variant II

- ···•··· agric. area
- ▓▓▓▓ recreation
- ⬤ 5000 inhabit.
- ⬤ 10000 inhabit.

D THE REGION

A regional plan for Regensburg
There is at present no regional plan for Regensburg. Yet obviously the development of regional economic and transportation policies call, for a regional planning unit alongside the municipal planning authority. The seminar defined a regional survey area as a zone which could be reached from the centre of Regensburg in approximately forty-five minutes by car or rail. The resultant zone covers an area of some 48 × 48 miles and includes all or part of eleven counties.

Industrialized zones
Within this region industrialized zones were defined as follows:

1 the non-agricultural population is more than 60% of the inhabitants;
2 more than 50% of the earners are commuters to the catchment area's centre;
3 the maximum distance to the centre is less than fifteen minutes.
Through insisting that all three criteria had to be met, the seminar established five zones in a coherent pattern of linear development mainly along the existing railway. The seminar then worked out two strategies,

or variants, to underline the model character of their regional proposals:

Variant 1. This variant has two major phases. In the first phase, settlements are concentrated on the three-arm existing railway (rapid transit) lines; and in the second phase, the growth of these settlements is encouraged as linear infill.

Variant 2. This variant calls for a ribbon development on the north to south-west axis during the same period as the first and second phases of Variant 1; and in phase three the third arm would be developed, with an additional six miles of track to serve the harbour areas.

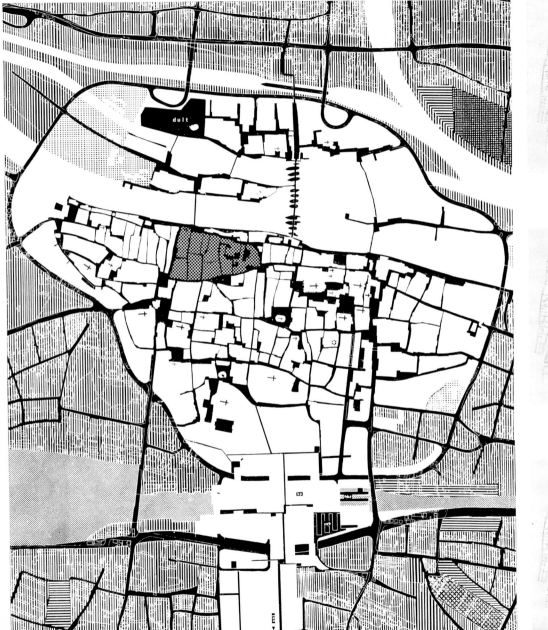

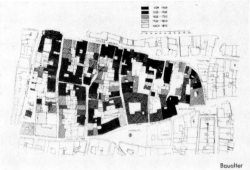

Baualter

Bauzustand

Geschoßzahl

COST OF RENOVATION AND
RESTORATION IN REGENSBURG'S
PRESERVATION AREA I

1958	280 000 DM
1959	671 000 DM
1960	350 000 DM
1961	310 000 DM
1962	375 000 DM
1963	1 225 000 DM
1964	1 326 000 DM
1965	2 010 000 DM
1966	1 568 000 DM
Total	8 115 000 DM

Far left Map of Regensburg indicating preservation area I.

Left top Age of buildings in preservation area I.

Left middle Building conditions.

Left bottom Height of buildings.

Below Renovated houses and towers in area I.

E THE FUTURE OF REGENSBURG

Sociological, economic and legal aspects
As in all European countries, the greater portion of the people of Federal Germany will have more time at their disposal at the end of this century than today, and more purchasing power to make use of it. A considerable amount of this time and purchasing power will be used in educational and artistic pursuits.

Although the suburban areas of Regensburg have grown since the war, the old city has not been recognized as having an economic potential. Even today its renewal appears to its own citizens as an almost intolerable burden. Yet it is clear that this great urban work of art can support itself economically in the immediate future if only we can conserve it now, and in doing so, prepare it intelligently for its future rôle.

It would be of great advantage to Regensburg's economic development if an organization could be formed to perform full and detailed planning, without simply leaning on existing regulations. Such an organization would face a complex task, and would need to work like modern business management. Even the seminar was unable to determine precisely how many hundreds of million D-Marks would have to be continuously available to thoroughly renew an old city such as Regensburg. But one thing is certain: the overall sum must include a high proportion of non-returnable investment.

From a legal point of view it may be argued that the task is one for a national preservation authority. At present, in Germany, there is no such national authority; and the protection of historic urban areas can be guaranteed only if the town council issues the necessary local regulations and backs them with its own funds. Regensburg certainly has no such funding base. For this reason, a ruling similar to the French *loi Malraux* would be very important for the German Federal Republic. According to this law, conservation areas in cities are seen as part of national cultural history rather than as local preservation. Conservation areas in old cities are both protected and designed in detail for renewal, backed by national funds. In content, the *loi Malraux* is comparable with the British development-plan law, but here private initiative is encouraged in the execution of the renewal (similar to the proposed German Urban Furtherance Law) and local authorities and public bodies are included with wide legal powers and control over the distribution of large amounts of public expenditure.

The on-going planning process
It is important to see the work of the seminar, not as a final plan, but as a clear demonstration of the possible.

1 Much of the information on which the Regensburg study was made was out of date before the study was completed. This needs not imply a halt to action; but confident long-term programmes should not be launched without the continuous up-dating of base-line information.

2 The rapid transit strategy is only one element of a comprehensive development plan. It must be interlocked with other elements before action at the regional scale can be taken.

3 The central expansion area proposals for siting and general land use, though correct in theory, require comprehensive study regarding costs and detailed design.

4 The renewal proposals must be accompanied by detailed studies of squares, streets, and buildings in continuous urban environment, and with cost-benefit analyses, before specific action is taken.

5 The seminar's process of survey and analysis was forced to use many sets of information and to make assumptions which were untested. These must be progressively improved if decisions based on the study are to remain valid and become more accurate over the years. Programmes must be drawn up for further detailed studies, and these need to be pro-rated for content and urgency. New proposals must then be made to answer the requirements of these studies, within a continual planning process.

6 Over and above official action of this kind, there must be new opportunities for individuals and local groups to play a decisive rôle in the planning process. Independent bodies can focus attention on major issues in town planning and architecture through meetings, conferences, projects, citizen task forces, and reports. In this way the interested citizen of an historic city can have an important and creative say in the bureaucratic — but not always democratic — renewal of his urban heritage.

Conclusions
If, as architects, planners and citizens, we feel the need to evaluate the aims and achievements of our own time, it is salutary for us to understand the aims and achievements of other ages. But keeping in touch with the past, which is so powerful a means of renewing the present, becomes more and more difficult as material evidence disappears.

Regensburg, like so many old cities which we destroy every day bit by bit, expresses the ability of the human being to give form, beauty and meaning to his social structure. Since we seem to be in danger of losing this ability, perhaps we should conserve our heritage in order to relearn.

1 Econ-Verlag (publisher), Düsseldorf/Vienna, 1967.

THINE ALABASTER CITIES GLEAM.

Clouds of smog hover over our cities. Cities once crowned by canopies of stars. Grime on our windowsills and soot in our eyes no longer surprise us. And we bring tiny babies out of sterile hospitals into an atmosphere so polluted, plants choke on it in a matter of weeks. With America, the beautiful. Our America. The crisis isn't in our cities; the crisis is in our hearts. With a change of heart, we can change the picture.   AIA/American Institute of Architects

Send this page to your Congressman and ask him to support enforcement of our air pollution laws.

OBSERVATIONS ON THREE AEGEAN ISLAND TOWNS

CONSTANTINE E. MICHAELIDES

173

Introduction

The following are some general thoughts which have resulted from observation and study in the Aegean Islands during 1970, as an initial stage of what will become in due course a long-range comparison of the form, growth, and content of Aegean Island towns. Hydra, Astypalaia and Kalymnos share the common historical and cultural background of the Aegean Islands, the origins of which can be traced back to at least Minoan times. The present forms of the island towns, however, belong to stages of development which date from the decline of Byzantine power in the area in the early thirteenth century. The establishment of the Latins in the Aegean, followed by the Turkish conquest and finally Greek Independence in the early nineteenth century were the major historical contexts within which the development occurred. Throughout this time, piracy was a constant and significant threat in the Aegean and lack of safety on or near the sea dictated the formation of settlements whose character was primarily defensive.

Warring among the Latin feudal lords and against the Turks and corsairs of every origin had devastating effects on the islands, some of which appear to have

Aegean Sea

Right Aegean Sea.

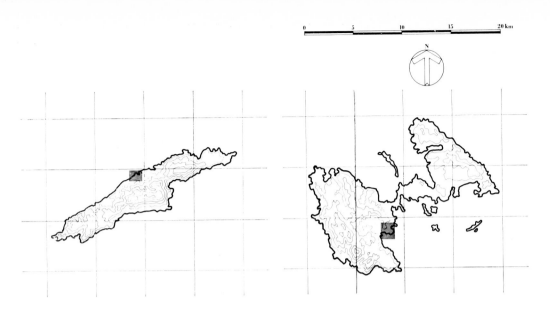
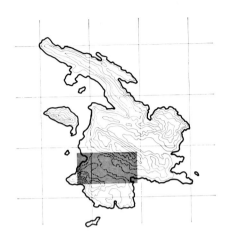

Above Hydra, Astypalaia, and Kalymnos. Contours shown at 100 metre intervals: shaded areas are enlarged on the following page.

become completely depopulated during the fifteenth century. As control of the sea lanes passed to the Venetians and Genoese, the islanders' contacts with the sea diminished and the ancient art of seafaring became all but lost to the native population. As a result, the island towns were deprived of their importance and shrank in size.

Turkish expansion in the eastern Mediterranean and the final wresting of the Aegean Islands from the Latins at the end of the sixteenth century brought in an era of relative security which, together with a considerable degree of autonomy under Turkish rule, allowed a gradual rebirth of seafaring and commerce in the area. A rise in population and nautical power, strongly accelerated after the middle of the eighteenth century, resulted in the expansion and opening up of the earlier defensive settlements, a trend which continued for most islands following national independence.

In this context, island towns 'moved' physically to accommodate themselves to the circumstances. This 'movement' of a town within its immediate natural site can better be observed today in some of the smaller islands such as Hydra, Astypalaia, and

Kalymnos, rather than the larger ones such as Naxos or Rhodos, where land available for extensive agricultural use reduced the dependence of the island on the sea and made it less susceptible to outside pressures.

Hydra

Of the three towns discussed here, Hydra is the one with the most recent history of development, since apparently no settlement of significance existed on the island before the 1650s. The original and later settlers were villagers fleeing upheavals on the mainland. Collective response to external danger guided the building of the town. The product, Hydra I, was what one might call a 'populist' overall form, as opposed to some older Aegean examples such as Astypalaia where the form of the town was dominated by the central position of the local prince's castle. This 'populist' collective form was by no means unique to Hydra, neither was it in itself new, as its constituent elements (the individual house, open spaces, streets, their interrelationship, etc.) were those traditional to the area. But in its present application it expressed, in good measure, the political autonomy enjoyed now by the islands, and in a stronger more significant vein the new spirit of the people.

That high ground with a commanding position over

sea approaches was an essential requirement at this time for the survival of an Aegean town, was recognized by the builders of Hydra.

The defences of a town like Hydra were primarily meant to withstand a surprise attack by a relatively small raiding band, rather than a staged siege by regular troops or naval forces. At the same time, the scale of such a settlement did not call for the building of an enclosing wall as a separate structure, which after all was an undertaking beyond the financial means of the islanders. Instead, an age-old device was used by which an external row of houses built on a party wall system with minimum and minimal openings towards the outside, provided the required defence perimeter. Access to these houses was through an interior street, while flat roofs served also as ramparts in times of need. The interior of the town was reached only through a limited number of controlled gates. Streets were narrow and irregular, and spaces both interior and exterior were rather tight, producing as a total a minimal defence perimeter.

Population increase which was both natural and a result of the influx of additional refugees went hand in hand with expansion of Hydra's commercial and sea power, and caused successive transformations in which the initial defensive enclosure was ruptured as the town expanded downhill and towards the sea in a

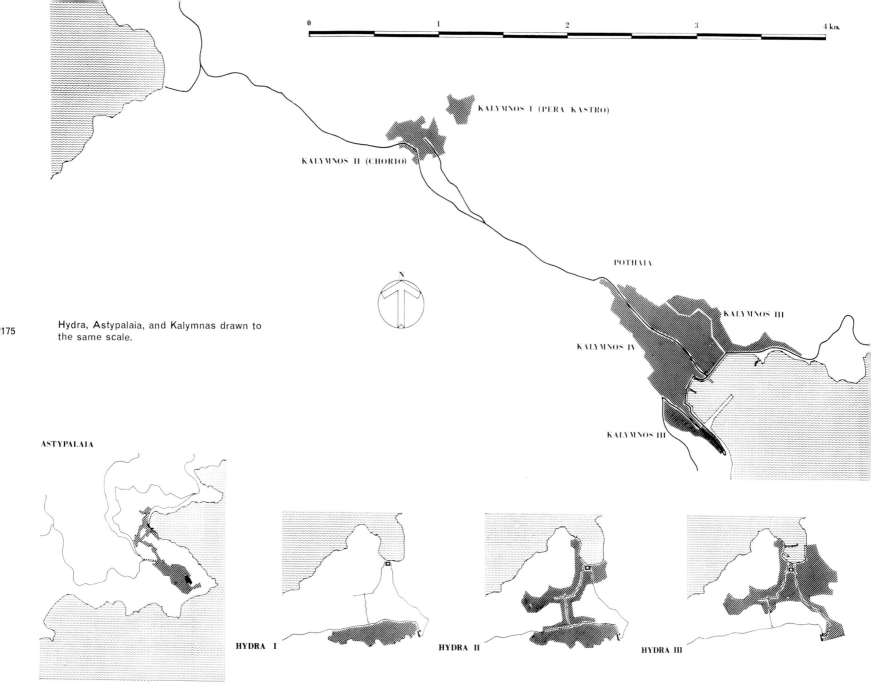

0   1   2   3   4 km.

KALYMNOS I (PERA KASTRO)

KALYMNOS II (CHORIO)

POTHAIA

N

KALYMNOS III

KALYMNOS IV

KALYMNOS III

175   Hydra, Astypalaia, and Kalymnas drawn to
the same scale.

ASTYPALAIA

HYDRA I   HYDRA II   HYDRA III

Left View from heights above Hydra I.
Above Hydra, aerial view.
Right Kastro on Siphos. Note the 'commanding' position of the town over the sea approach down below.

dramatic show of self-confidence. European events culminating in the Napoleonic wars supported and accelerated this development which formed Hydra II, and which was finally arrested just before the Greek revolution of the 1820's. Following the inclusion of Hydra into the newly independent Greek state and the return to normalcy in the Mediterranean the population of Hydra declined sharply. During the latter part of the nineteenth and early part of the twentieth century the original uphill site of the town was gradually deserted in favour of a location near the port, Hydra III, which together with a good part of Hydra II makes up the present town.

Tourism has revived Hydra since the end of World War II, and has brought the island back to international fame; this time, however, on an entirely different basis from that of the eighteenth and nineteenth centuries. It is significant that a dignified and powerful form such as the town of Hydra has managed to absorb this radical change in content.

Above left Kastro on Siphos. The external row of houses forms the defence perimeter; large openings and balconies are 'contemporary' additions.

Left Town of Naxos on Naxos. External row of houses making up the defence perimeter.

Above Flat roofs from Chora on Patmos.

Right Astypalaia. Quirini Castle.

Astypalaia

Today the town of Astypalaia, in terms of population, is the smallest of the three under discussion. Although the number of its inhabitants has shrunk somewhat during the last sixty years (a trend which is noticeable in most Aegean Islands) it has not in its past history experienced an era of great prosperity or population rise as the other two islands have.

The castle, which physically dominates the form of the town, was rebuilt on existing fortifications in pretty much its present form by John IV, one of the Quirini family of Venetian nobles who ruled the island as a personal fief, with some interruptions, from early thirteenth century up to the middle of the sixteenth century when it passed under Turkish rule. During this time Astypalaia returned briefly to Byzantine control, was raided and completely devastated by a Turkish corsair in the 1340s and apparently remained un-

inhabited for a period of almost seventy years before the Quirinis attempted to repopulate it with immigrants from the island of Tenos.

Turkish rule from the sixteenth century onwards afforded Astypalaia, as the rest of the islands, a period of recovery. Sponge fishing produced during the latter part of the nineteenth century a reliable source of income which, combined with the small agricultural production of the island, provided for a life slightly above marginal level. In more recent times Astypalaia became part of Greece after World War II, following about thirty-three years of Italian administration.

The geographic location of Astypalaia, along the sea lanes to the East and to the Black Sea, together with its sheltered bays made it a better known entity than its size would normally warrant. In this sense, the pointed shape of the promontory on which the town is built easily invited both fortification and settlement. Although all the constituent elements used in building the town of Astypalaia are again those traditional in

Above Astypalaia, aerial view.

Below Astypalaia; the old town on the right, the 'port' at the lower left, the spine connects the two.

180

the Aegean milieu (individual house, open spaces, streets, etc.) their application indicates a complete reliance on the Quirini stronghold, into which the islanders apparently retreated and defended themselves whenever the need arose. The repeated ring-like arrangement of houses on the north-west side of the castle is an apparent response to the topography of the hill site rather than an indication of early attempts to organize the defence of the town in the Hydra fashion.

Eradication of piracy contributed to the partial dilution of the defensive character of the town. Strict adherence to the rule of building only on high ground, and in this particular instance near the fortification, was relaxed as the natural bay north-east of the promontory gradually began to assume the rôle of a 'port' settlement serving Astypalaia. A natural path

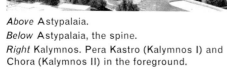

Above Astypalaia.
Below Astypalaia, the spine.
Right Kalymnos. Pera Kastro (Kalymnos I) and Chora (Kalymnos II) in the foreground.

connecting the two developed following the principle of minimum effort. Over the years, both sides of the path were built up and produced a 'spine' as a new and separately identifiable part. While they physically support one another, each of these three elements, the old town on the hill, the 'port' facility, and the spine, has retained its own identity.

Kalymnos

The population of Kalymnos today is almost seven times (14,000) that of each of the other islands while the island in size (about 110 sq km) is comparable to Astypalaia and almost twice as large as Hydra. There is one settlement on each of Astypalaia and Hydra, while more than two-thirds of Kalymnians reside at the major island town also called Pothaia. The rest inhabit Chorio and perhaps half a dozen other smaller places.

Kalymnian recorded history by far predates the 'Pera Kastro' which is the oldest example of a habitation on the island still in some partial use.

Pera Kastro is a natural fortress, a huge rock in the middle of the largest and most agriculturally productive valley of Kalymnos stretching diagonally across the island in view of the sea at both the south-east and

Above Kalymnos. Pera Kastro (Kalymnos I) and Chora (Kalymnos II) in the foreground.

north-west sides of it. This combination of natural stronghold and strategic position had apparently invited settlement and fortification through the ages. The Knights of St. John who in 1309 occupied Rhodos and gradually stretched their control over the neighbouring islands came to occupy Kalymnos and chose to rebuild and improve the existing Byzantine fortifications which enclosed the medieval town of Kalymnos. The walls of the fortress still survive today in good shape and offer a breathtaking view to the visitor who gathers up enough courage to climb them. They also enclose the remnants of the town, completely uninhabited now, while the ruins of houses and public buildings still stand in heights of 5 or 6 ft. Eleven small whitewashed churches in perfect repair and still functioning dot the area of the old town underlining the continuous interest of the islanders in their past.

It was the middle of the seventeenth century and after the expulsion of the Knights, when conditions described in the preceding pages caused a population increase so serious that the tight enclosure of the castle could no longer accommodate the growing numbers of the inhabitants. As a result, and at approximately the same time when Hydra I came into being, Kalymnos II began to form on the gradually sloping ground right under the foot of the rock which held Kalymnos I. The islanders again, as in the case of Astypalaia, relied on Pera Kastro and on the considerable distance between Kalymnos II (which is today known as Chorio) and the sea at both ends of the valley for their defence. Consequently in Chorio, although houses are clustered closely together, the tight defensive organization of Hydra I is absent. Prosperity, however, did not arrive for Kalymnos until the middle of the nineteenth century when, still under Turkish rule but enjoying complete autonomy, it began developing a fleet for sponge fishing which took Kalymnians all over the Mediterranean and

secured for the island a steady and plentiful source of income.

With their future by now substantially identified with the sea and a large fleet to care and support, Kalymnians had to move closer to the water and establish a port. The natural features (size, southern exposure, etc.) of the bay at the south-east end of the valley made it an apparently better choice over the outlet at the other end for satisfying the need for a port. Perhaps, however, beyond the obvious, there was a subtle reason for this choice which becomes clearer when one notices the rather unexpected way in which Kalymnos III was formed: houses, rather than being built on the flat piece of land where the valley empties into the sea, were erected on the steep inclines facing one another and defining the width of the bay. These steep inclines were also a distinct feature of the south-east, but absent from the north-west bay.

Two possible explanations for this start from different points, but are mutually reinforcing. The first is that the traditional notion of the house in the minds of the islanders was that of one built above another in an image which was handed down from a long tradition of building on inclined sites for defensive purposes. This image was also meaningful in daily terms because it provided for a better view and better opportunities for each individual unit to catch the all important late afternoon breeze. The second indicates that despite the newly found prosperity at sea, reliance on the products of the land was not to be completely rejected; consequently fertile land was not to be easily sacrificed for building. This attitude prevailed until quite recently, that is the end of World War II, when Kalymnos IV came to be built right over previously cultivated land. This building came as a response to new pressures developing from another transforma-

Below Houses, northern section of Kalymnos III.

tion of the island's economy from a declining reliance on the sponge industry to an increasing one on merchant marine service and immigration (there is another Kalymnos in Australia and a third in the US, and in terms of family ties the three work together). Unfortunately, however, this latest building development does not do justice to that of the earlier Kalymnos, but a discussion of this belongs perhaps elsewhere.

Review

In reviewing the 'movement' of each of these three towns the following points can be made: Astypalaia 'moved' the least of the three. Because of lack of pressures from the outside and within, the town essentially reformed itself on the same site; while responding to the need for connections with the outside world it extended an arm towards the sea. In this it has retained by and large its medieval form insofar as the later additions (spine and port) are clearly articulated and identifiable elements. In a parallel sense, the topographic limitations of the site have also restrained the scale of development. It is interesting to compare Astypalaia with the very similar example of Patmos where the distance between the old town (Chora) and the new port (Scala) is substantial. As a result, Scala developed into a small town of its own at the expense and complete absence of a con-

necting 'spine'. Today a new road, recently completed, assumes the role of 'spine' with very different physical dimensions.

Hydra underwent a dramatic change in a very short period of time (that is the forty years preceding the conclusion of the Napoleonic wars) and a slower one in the following one hundred years. During this span of time it shifted its centre of gravity from the high up the hill defensive enclosure down to the centre of the port, literally rolling down the hill. However, this shift occurred in a continuous manner and the newly developing parts of the town grew in adherence to older sections.

Kalymnos 'moved' over a much longer time span than Hydra and in a very different manner: except for the last stage which developed contiguously, it leaped from stage to stage over a considerable distance. But despite this apparent fragmentation, images and forms were carried from old to new with a degree of consistency, ensuring continuity in the development.

In a broader sense, Aegean towns as represented by the examples of Astypalaia, Hydra, and Kalymnos, have demonstrated their capacity and adaptability as open ended forms. In all stages of development, however, one basic topographic feature prevails, that of a sloping site, which becomes instrumental in producing variety within the overall unity of town form. This variety is perhaps basic to the positive

response of today's visitor to the Aegean Islands and in this light one cannot help hypothesizing that the central issue with Habitat (Montreal, Expo 67) as with all similarly inspired student theses of recent years, is the substitution of this topographic feature by technological means, which once more allows 'irregular' juxtaposition of visually identifiable individual units within the unity of the overall form.

Above Kalymnos III and IV.

Below View of Kalymnos III and IV from Pera Kastro. Note the cultivated parcels of land over which Kalymnos IV has been built, mostly since World War II.

GOVERNMENT-BUILT CITIES AND PEOPLE-MADE PLACES

JULIAN BEINART

'And the Black Man keeps moving on, as he has always done the last three centuries, moving with baggage and all, forever tramping with bent back to give way for the one who says he is the stronger. The Black dances and sings less and less, turning his back on the past and facing the misty horizons, moving in a stream that is damned in shifting catchments. They yell into his ears all the time: move, nigger, or be fenced in but move anyhow. They call it slum clearance instead of conscience clearance – to fulfil a pact with conscience which says: never be at rest as long as the Black Man's shadow continues to fall on your house.'[1]

Ezekiel Mphahlele's writing, that of the poet and participant, is, if less anodyne than official statistics, no less accurate a description of a centrifugal process that has given a special shape to contemporary cities in Southern Africa. The constant shifting of Africans and other non-white peoples outward from the centre of the city has kept them on or close to the periphery, pushed out from a position of enclosure to one of isolation; from a condition of choice, however limited,

SOPHIATOWN

WESTERN NATIVE TOWNSHIP

NEWCLARE

Right Aerial view of the expansion of Johannesburg.

in the private market to the optionless environment of authority housing. While the developers' market has enticed white suburban expansion in the direction of high land, water and view, black growth has been forced away from all natural amenity on to land owned by government and into houses built by government.

Epidemics and civil disturbance were often the *raisons d'etre* for immediate action but in general the rate of black expulsion has been dictated by the political pressures of a white electorate on the one hand, and by the weight of non-white urbanization on the other. Throughout, the process has been underpinned by a constant belief by authority in the value of geographical separateness: a belief which, if naive at first, came to be explained by more sophisticated rationales later. (A minute of the Johannesburg City Council of 1904 suggests that 'the advantages of keeping the native quarters completely away from the white population will be obvious to everyone, whether one considers the interests of the Native or those of the poorer class of European.') [2]

Black urbanization and white reaction not only produced new methods to explain old attitudes but changed an administrative framework from one characterized by a lack of regulation to one which today superintends almost every aspect of non-white urban life and which sees to the application of these laws with increasing rigidity and efficiency. A lecture by the Chairman of the Non-European Affairs Committee of the Johannesburg City Council in 1966 blandly lists ninety-six separate acts passed since 1945 'affecting the administration of Non-European affairs' and adds that 'in addition to the Acts, knowledge is required of the regulations framed under the various Acts'. [3]

In sum, at the cost of non-whites being kept outside the matrix of urban life and without their having taken part in the making of any of the decisions that shaped the process, inner-city slums have been cleared and non-white people have been provided with hundreds of thousands of new houses on vacant land outside the city. Thus have South African cities been built: white, rich and free on the one side; and black, poor and imprisoned on the other.

The purpose of this article is to look at one small part of this urban situation; to see how a community, allocated an environment by a remote political decision, transformed these utterly anonymous surroundings into an intensely personal piece of city-building. Western Native Township was the first African township built by the Municipality of Johannesburg. In 1918 the City Council, stimulated by the high mortality

186

Above The core of Western Native Township, around Hay Avenue.

rates of an influenza epidemic, decided to house Africans on the outskirts to the west of the built-up area of the city. To the Council it must have seemed an extremely straightforward, if expensive, decision. Africans lived in slums and needed houses: building a small township away from where white people lived would solve the problem. No official could foresee that such an isolated and modest response would soon have to give way to a policy structured to cope with pressures of quite a different scale and requiring a vast legal mechanism to impose patterns of segregation on to the highly integrated economy of a modern city. The budget for housing 1,100 Africans in the township was about $110,000 (including the cost of extending the city tramway system); and for an administration whose annual expenditure on Africans and on the zoo had for a long time coincided, the decision to build WNT must have caused greater econo-

mic concern than concern about the kind of environment they were about to create.

The houses were designed and built by the City Engineer's department, almost all consisting of two small rooms with narrow, cross-barred windows: there were no bathrooms and no separate kitchens, only an outside toilet. Houses had no external or internal finishes, no fittings, no ceilings or internal doors, no individual water-supply, no waterborne sewerage or electricity. Under no conditions could inhabitants own a house. The first inhabitants were Africans who had either migrated directly from rural areas or moved from shacks or backyard rooms closer to the centre of the city. They, and those who came to WNT later, reacted vigorously to their surroundings, organizing themselves to provide a wide range of social services and shaping their houses and streets to counteract official facelessness. WNT became an important and particular place in the city.

After twenty years of effort by the inhabitants to maintain Western Native Township as a viable community, the City Council were again contemplating a political decision: one which would this time destroy the community and disperse it to various positions outside the now-grown city. It took another twenty years before the City Council could carry out its decision and in 1961 the inhabitants were moved out to new townships twelve miles from the city centre. By now the scale of African residence in cities had generated a governmental policy aimed not only at destroying settled communities but at maintaining urban Africans in as insecure a capacity as the needs of a white-dominated economy could tolerate. This insistence that Africans could never find a permanent residence in the city but ultimately belonged to some tribal homeland informed a policy aimed at keeping tribal affiliations as strong as possible among those that had to be in the city. Thus the people of Western Native Township, where many tribes had jelled into a tight non-racial community, were now rehoused in separate areas based on major tribal groupings. A political decision had not only disenfranchized a community from its geographic place but split the co-operative nexus that it had built up over forty years.

Western Native Township has now become a Coloured township (Coloured in South Africa refers to non-white people of mixed descent). Some of the original houses in the township have been replaced

Above and far left Houses and people of WNT.

Left The endless extensions of new townships south-west of Johannesburg, housing three-quarters of a million people.

187

but the majority of the old houses still stand, now housing people who neither chose them nor find them suitable to their needs. Even now some of them attempt to better their surroundings; but the township has never been theirs and in this form it never will be.

Before examining Western Native Township in more detail, it is important to understand its position over time in the pattern of African residence in Johannesburg.

Gold was discovered on the Witwatersrand in 1885 and Johannesburg was founded as a temporary mining-camp a year later. The diggings needed labour and Africans, Malays, Coloureds, Indians and Chinese poured into the town. Ten years after its foundation Johannesburg had a population of 102,000 within three miles of Market Square and half of these were non-white.[4] There was no legislation to prohibit non-whites from living wherever they could find a place but already social pressures were such that most lived in separate 'locations' on the west side of the town. (These, the 'Natives', 'Kafir' and 'Coolie' locations, are in Zone 1 of the figure on the next page.[5])

Conditions in these locations were primitive but slum clearance was impossible: a white electorate refused to allow Africans to be moved out and rehoused on land adjacent to white areas. It took the plague of 14th March 1904 to force the City Council to act. It burned the Coolie location the same night and shifted its inhabitants as far out as possible to a site (later called Pimville) next to a large sewerage works about ten miles from the town's centre (Zone 3).

The decision to move so far out is explained by the Council as follows: 'We are convinced that the public interest requires not only that the location should be placed outside the town but that it should be as far as possible removed from any neighbourhood inhabited by the Europeans.'[6] On the top of a small hill temporary huts were built and land leased to Africans for private house-building. To this day Pimville has remained a problem for the City Council: in 1929 the infant mortality rate was reported to have been 958 per 1,000.[7] Its history is a rich one, however, and among its products is the singer Miriam Makeba, still affectionately known as Pimms No. 1!

Above People attempt to better their surroundings by modifying and decorating their red brick Government-built shacks, but the houses will never be theirs and they will always risk being made to move on by the authorities.

Right A Western Native Township family waiting with their possessions after being forced out.

188

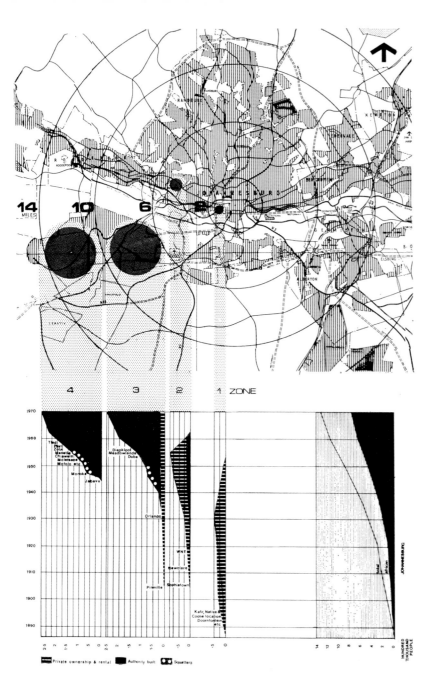

For a long time Pimville remained an isolated village separated by mine workings and dumps from the inner city, and its attractions, whatever they were, were not enough to prevent Africans from returning to the inner city. But the city was spreading and in the last years of the South African Republic, the owner of a farm called Sophiatown, about five miles from the centre of the city, offered his land to the Government for use as a location.[8] Some white people settled there but its natural attractions – it also adjoined a municipal sewerage and depositing site – soon caused it to become a non-white suburb. Here, and slightly further to the south adjoining the railway line (Newclare), Africans became landowners and tenants of privately built housing and backyard rooms (Zone 2).

It took another disease, this time influenza, to stimulate the City Council once again to try to clear the innermost area. Now it built Western Native Township, between Sophiatown and Newclare, thus consolidating what became known as the 'Western Areas' of Johannesburg. Zone 2 was now established as the major area of African residence in the city and here between the mid-thirties and fifties the synthesis of a new African urban culture took place; one of physical poverty but intense community; of crime and deprivation, but one celebrated with a new music, journalism and writing. It had, in Nathaniel Nakasa's words, 'a heart like Greenwich Village or Harlem'.[9]

The innermost zone was still full, Zone 2 was filling up and Zone 3 was open land except for Pimville. Alexandra, a freehold area, and Eastern Native Township, a much smaller version of WNT, had appeared in the east but the next important development was again in the west. After a long period of indecision during which various unsuccessful attempts were made to move inhabitants out of the innermost zone, the City Council, now with their responsibility placed upon it by the Natives (Urban Areas) Act of 1923, built another location, Orlando. Orlando was close to Pimville and these were the precursors of the vast developments that were to take place later in Zones 3 and 4. Having built new houses the Council could now legally clear slums close to the city centre but this forced people to move, not to the new houses far out of town, as the Council may have hoped, but to the much closer 'Western Areas'. If poor people have to move they will move as short a distance as possible, especially if this move coincides with their preference of the private market over the discipline of municipal housing. Thus while Africans in Zone 1 diminished, Zone 2 swelled and townships in the outer zones remained distant villages.

But the war made choice for Africans academic.

Industries stimulated by war production needed labour and there was as yet no control on African influx. Soon even Orlando was packed. As happens when there is neither public nor private supply, people built their own houses. Seven squatters' movements arose as a spontaneous exodus of sub-tenants from crowded houses in Orlando, Pimville, Newclare and Alexandra. The City Council, unable to find houses for the squatters, responded by screening them (there were well over 60,000) and transporting them to camps of 'controlled squatting' provided with elementary services only (Moroka and Jabavu). The former, erected on an area of 1,534 acres, was over twelve miles from the city's centre and the furthest Africans had ever had to live outside the city (Zone 4).[10]

After riots in Moroka in which three white policemen were murdered, the investigating Commission was sympathetic to the squatters' cause, interpreting the position of movement leaders Mpanza, Ntoi and others as follows: 'By applying the segregation provisions and not setting aside any land on which we (the Africans) may build ourselves, the Municipality has taken on itself the duty of providing us with houses. But it has not carried out that duty; there are no houses for us. Very well, then, we shall go and sit down on municipal land and wait for the Municipality to come and put a roof over our heads.'[11]

But such blame was not enough to impel the City Council to build more houses. The demand was far greater than the Council's resources could supply: and to add to the Council's problems, white pressure was now insisting on the Africans being moved out of the 'Western Areas'. Already in 1939, as a result of agitation by white ratepayers in the neighbourhood, Councillor S. J. Tighy 'had begun vehemently to urge the total removal of all Non-European settlements in the Western Areas as a solution to the problem'.[12] Most of the inhabitants of the 'Western Areas' were living in housing provided by the private market. They would now, according to official policy, have to be rehoused almost entirely in public housing.

The resources of determination, capital, organisation and labour needed to rehouse the squatters and make possible the removal of the 'Western Areas' were however to come. A government elected in 1948 on a policy of absolute separation of black and white now gave priority to legislation and finance for getting non-whites out of the city. With the additional help of low-interest loans from the mining industry, Johannesburg could now embark on a vast housing programme for Africans. Spreading outwards from and including Orlando and Pimville an unstructured and undifferentiated carpet of single-storey units was laid over nearly thirty miles of farm land: the apotheosis of the physical form of suburban sprawl but a mindless caricature of its democratic intent. Here, in Soweto, as it is now called, half a million people[13] live at a density of thirty per acre. (Unofficial estimates place the population at much higher, some as high as a million.) It is, according to the publicity of the City Council of Johannesburg, 'perhaps the biggest housing project (sic) in the world and an achievement of which the Johannesburg City Council and the South African Government can be justly proud'.[14]

The development of Soweto meant an end to squatting and the 'Western Areas'. The squatters' camps were dismantled and first Sophiatown (replaced by a white suburb grotesquely called Triomf) and then Newclare were cleared, bringing to an end African ownership of land in the city. Finally in 1969 the people of Western Native Township were removed and with them the last obstacles in the way of a policy ruthlessly determined to keep white and black apart. Except for domestic servants and a few temporary anomalies, the inner circles of the diagram were cleared. Johannesburg was now all white and the land beyond the mine dumps to the south-west all black.

The patterns that emerge over time in a city such as Johannesburg as a consequence of the imposition of changing modes of racial discrimination (changing from social convention to legal institution) can be summarized as follows:
1. In the first place there is a *fine-grained distribution* of small pockets of non-white residence throughout the city with very few separate commercial, civic or recreational facilities, short journeys-to-work and little distortion of loads on existing transportation services. Virtually all the housing stock is supplied privately.
2. A second phase follows of *greater concentration but enclosure* within the city of fewer but larger non-white residential areas. More than half the population still live in private housing; the rest is supplied by the government. Some separate facilities are provided such as small shops, schools, playing fields and clinics. As the shops are in a position to have a market area which includes shoppers of other races as well, there is a better service than the non-whites alone can support. The communities rely heavily on the environment they create for themselves: self-help creches and churches, illegal drinking and gambling houses, gangs, clubs and societies; but because of their location are still able to tap some of the resources of the city around them. Autonomous improvements to housing contribute to these self-created surround-ings, the styles for such changes coming in part from contact with other groups in the city. Workplaces are now generally outside walking range, causing the city's public transportation to be stressed and special services to be introduced. Residents can however choose between bus or train and if necessary will walk.[15]
3. The third phase is one of *total isolation* outside the city of vast non-white settlements built on vacant land for which the white market has shown little demand. Now non-whites are allowed no ownership of land and all the housing is authority housing. Commercial facilities are of a low order relying on the support of the poor residents of these areas only, who, tied to the city's Central Business District by a fixed-line rail system, prefer to use the CBD for their major shopping. (Shops are among the few facilities that whites cannot yet afford to segregate.) Thus while both whites and non-whites live in decentralized situations, non-whites help to maintain an abnormally strong shopping component in the CBD. Some civic, recreational and educational facilities are provided and attempts are made in the direction of autonomous administration of the non-white areas. The scale and nature of the environment is such that community integration is weak and autonomous attempts to improve housing and the surroundings are sporadic and have little impact. The journey-to-work consumes both time and money leaving few resources for such activity. (The daily return rail fare is over 300% and the monthly 100% greater than the commuting cost

in the second phase areas described above). There is now no choice between public transportation modes (nor the alternative of walking) and the enormous loads placed on the completely inadequate rail link to the city result in congestion and the frequent collapse of the system. Despite poverty car ownership rises, pointing to greatly increased future vehicle congestion along the route connecting the white city with its far-flung black appendage.

The 'Western areas' of Sophiatown, Newclare and Western Native Township were the most important second-phase ghettoes of Johannesburg. In an eighty-year history of white decision-making and forced African movement, they represented fifty years of relative stability. Each had its own character ('WNT was the place to go home to, Sophiatown a place to have a ball').[16] The whole was a viable mixture; the relatively peaceful WNT in the middle between the 'inflammable' Sophiatown on the north and the 'lusty' Newclare on the south, Indian and Chinese shopkeepers along the seams between them and the 'prim and pretentious' [17] Coloured people's township of Coronationville on the east. To the north and east lived whites. For those Africans who came to live here, particularly for those straight from the

country, it was where they learned the urban life; where they were fashioned by what was around them and where they in turn responded by attempting to match their surroundings to their own developing physical and spiritual needs.

It is difficult to distinguish exactly which qualities or which combination of qualities of time, people and ghetto-place itself could account for the generation of such response; but nowhere was it as energetic and organized, at both personal and social levels, as in Western Native Township. Certainly a generally benevolent municipal administration, individual home rentership and reasonably secure tenure marked WNT from Sophiatown and Newclare, and were all given by residents as reasons for having been satisfied there. People called the place 'Thulandisville' ('OK, I heard you') referring to the fact that the Municipality responded to their requests; they sang a song about a city councillor, Mr. Ballenden:
'Siya mbongu Ballenden
Ngokusikhuph 'e dolbeni'
'We thank Mr. Ballenden,
For having taken us out of town.'
They also mention liking the ethnic composition ('a gay mixture of all tribes') the low rent, the low costs of transportation to town, the inexpensive and wide

range of goods ('from a candle to a beer') available from the many stores in the area, and all the social amenities within walking distance.

The table (over) attempts to summarize some of the patterns of action and response that occurred over the four decades of Western Native Township's existence. The first was a period of immigration and organization of a village environment that must have resembled in many respects the rural background with which the residents still had an active intercourse. The thirties faced the community with the problems of ordering a society suddenly swollen and made more complex by the filling of the 'Western Areas'; and if the response was still tentative, by the fourth stage when a generation had already been born in the township it had become confident enough to challenge authority wherever the community felt threatened. Time had replaced the residents' natural insecurity of rentership with a sense of permanence and optimism which the alteration of their houses and the symbols on them reflected. By the last years of the township's life the community, with its constantly increasing commitment to urban life, had changed a limited and personal environment into one which, if still overcrowded, dangerous and poor, nevertheless contained much that was rich and special.

STAGE ONE 1918–1930	STAGE TWO 1930–1940	STAGE THREE 1940–1950	STAGE FOUR 1950–1962
HOUSING:			
Township established but little demand for houses. About 2,000 houses built in five stages: first single rooms, huts and two-roomed houses, and after 1930 three-roomed houses. Houses have no plaster, ceilings, floors or internal doors. Houses built at costs ranging from $156 to $226 per unit; house rents from $3.50 per month upward.	Population pressure builds up (population about 12,000 in 1933) and township crowded. Municipality allows residents to house sub-tenants on application but demolishes outbuildings and shacks built by tenants in backyards. Municipality recognizes pressures on space and at end of this stage adds an additional room for tenants who request more space and are willing to pay increased rental.	Municipality considers temporary porch enclosures health hazards and orders them removed after fires. Building of additional rooms by Municipality suspended until after war: tenants may still do so at own expense. Illegal outbuildings still being removed by Municipality. Municipality first adopts resolution to remove **WNT**.	Rents increased: now range from $2. to $9.00 per month. Municipality acts against permane porch enclosures but after test co case and in loco inspection allows su construction on approval of plans superintendent. No more municipally built room ad tions after 1957. Municipality begins negotiations wi tenants about removal but refuses compensate tenants for any improv ments.
Tenants use cowdung on floors, mud on walls, hessian for ceilings and curtains as interior doors. First decorations by people of Bakwena tribe consisting of patterns and animals scratched in mud and dung.	Tenants build shacks in yards and enclose front porches with wood or metal ceiling panels (Mr. Duda the first of these builders) to make more enclosed space. Tenants try painting decoration on brickwork (Ben Ngqaza the first). Tenants complain and rents reduced.	Tenants build porch enclosures (Mr. Stahlo the first builder) generally for living space but sometimes for shops. First decorations (family Sithole) on permanent porches and front walls. A few tenants make major alterations to houses at own expense.	Demonstrations against rent increase Decorations on plaster walls becon very popular with many variations limited number of themes. Agitation about removal and especial lack of compensation begins but by 19 township almost completely remov and 'Coloured' people move in.
SERVICES:			
People walk, cycle or use horse-drawn public transport. Municipal tram service extended to WNT; fare 3c to town. Houses have no individual water supply; only two communal taps per street and bucket sewerage. Municipality erects fences and plants some trees around township and in three streets.	Street-lighting installed and later electricity also available to tenants at own expense (20 years later only 5% of households had installation). Municipality erects fences around individual house plots. 1937: African newspaper calls WNT 'dingy, dirty, and ill-kept but is impressed by what some of our people are doing to improve their conditions that are anything but conducive to noble living'.	Tram fares increased to 4c and after tram boycott, service is withdrawn. Railway extended to Newclare (within walking distance of WNT). Individual water supply and waterborne sewerage installed. Roads improved and stormwater drains installed.	Public Utility Company Bus Servi introduced with terminus in centre WNT: fares now 4c to town.
Women form organization to prevent people from throwing dirty water into streets.	Tenants plant trees and hedges in front of houses.	Strikes, riots and boycott of trams after fare increase. Space in front of house developed as outdoor living space with decorated gateposts and letter-boxes.	Residents boycott buses because fares. A few cars appear in township, oft derelict, and taxi and car repair servi in vacant lots adjoining certain houses
COMMUNAL FACILITIES AND SOCIAL ORGANIZATION:			
Municipality builds administrative and police station. First schools (American Board Mission	Communal Hall built by Municipality. Two more schools (one high school) and six churches erected.	First African library built. Two more schools (second high school) opened.	New creche opened by Native Council African Women from money rais from residents.

STAGE ONE 1918–1930	STAGE TWO 1930–1940	STAGE THREE 1940–1950	STAGE FOUR 1950–1962
and Wesleyan Methodist Mission) opened. First churches (Presbyterian and Congregational) built. Municipal clinic and later first private hospital built (Nokuphila hospital).	'Talitha House' girls' reformatory opens. Municipal Beer Hall opens after continuous police raids on houses where women brew beer illegally in back yards.	Two more churches built. Old-age home and YMCA opened. Playground equipment installed by Municipality as well as additional sports fields. Co-operative society goes bankrupt and replaced by seven privately owned shops including 'Abyssinian Fish and Chips' shop. Municipality offers prize for best gardens at WNT.	At end of this stage, WNT has seven schools, ten churches and ten shops.
First residents arrive either from areas nearer city centre or from country: wide variety of tribes take up residence. Occupation of residents almost all unskilled or domestic workers: average annual household income about $170. Witch-doctors provide some medical and magical services. Before 1923, control of village in hands of 14 men, 'Iso Lomzi' (Eye of the Village) replaced by Advisory Board and Vigilance Committee, with chairman considered as mayor, to work with Municipality: annual elections with parties choosing colour, e.g. the blue party, to distinguish themselves.	Economic level of residents remains static: average annual household income about $180. First African co-operative society founded with 166 members and four shops (tearoom, grocer, butcher and baker). Wide variety of social, sporting and entertainment organizations formed: WNT Ladies' Civic Society, Unemployed Young Men's Club, Hungry Lions Benefit Society, Philharmonic Society of WNT, WNT Pioneers' Club, Children's Picnic Committee, etc. Sporting clubs: Transvaal Jumpers Football Club, baseball, tennis, cricket, etc. Jazz and dance bands: Merry Black Birds, Harmony Kings, Jazz Maniacs, Japanese Express Band, etc. 1937: first report of crime at WNT to appear in *Bantu World* newspaper.	War stimulates growth of new industries and average annual income rises to about $340. 'Rising tide of lawlessness' and hooliganism (tsotsis) reported in African newspapers. Civic guards and later Civic Protection Society (CPS) formed to combat thugs and gangs. Gangs: 'Corporatives' and 'Young Americans from New Orleans' said to have been formed and stove pipe trousers worn after showing of film 'Orchestra Wives' in local cinema. Shebeens: 'Green House' and 'Shepherds' offer illegal liquor and 'Stokfels' system instituted (rotating parties with host supplying liquor). Saloons in houses offer illegal gambling particularly 'fah-fee': lady decorates her house with lucky horse symbol. Political parties active: mayor of WNT decorates his house with African National Congress symbol.	Population still almost entirely working class with small percentage of professional and clerical workers: average annual household income now about $560 but still far below Poverty Datum line (about $700). Fairly static population with high proportion of widows as female heads of families and pattern of interchange with rural areas less frequent than before. Riots at Municipal Beer Hall because of police raid. Boycott of schools organized by African National Congress and residents open their own school, Mohlomo Community School: Mayor expelled from ANC after having been accused of sabotaging boycott. Gang warfare between WNT 'Corporatives' and Sophiatown 'Berliners'; also clashes between 'Russians' and Civic Guard. Jazz singer Dolly Rathebe stabbed and famous reporter Henry Nxumalo killed by thugs. Witch-doctors ('nyangas') still operating and consternation caused by appearance of 'tokolosh' (magic animal) in WNT. After failure of continued representations to Municipality, people accept being moved out: Mayor addresses residents: 'This is the saddest day of this township ... this is the oldest township of Johannesburg and people of this area in Johannesburg have made the greatest contribution in building Johannesburg.'

193

The remarkable scenario of the WNT community's organization and maintenance of their society was acted out on a stage set by a passive and patronizing administration. Left to itself the community could go far in extracting comforts out of an environment constantly being eroded by the effects of poverty and repression.

The physical matrix given to the community was equally bland and their reaction to it just as energetic. A straightforward grid-iron of streets was easily understood raw material which could take the community's improvizations and yet suffer little loss of imageability. The whole township was compact and grey enough for even modest changes to have impact. All the communal facilities which the community could not affect were grouped in a central area away from where they could interfere with the insistent rhythms of small lots and streets. (See opposite page, upper site plan: land use and growth.) The rough two- and three-room (plus open porch) houses were so incomplete in space and appearance that their occupants felt impelled to involve themselves. Houses were small enough not to suggest obstacles beyond the capacity of their occupants. Narrow lots meant that occupants could not remain unaffected by what their neighbours did. Thus individual inventions produced new streets; and rows of smiling new streets in turn blew away the pall of a government-built military camp (see street elevation drawing).

This communal face-lift depended ultimately on each person being allowed and able to act on his own. Within the constraints of poverty, what the authorities would allow, and the nature of the house object itself, individuals had only two freedoms; to adapt the space inside and outside the house, and to alter its facades.

1. *Space adaptation:*

Space could only be added to the house through horizontal extension and here the alternatives were limited either to infill or extension backwards away from the street. (See opposite page, lower site plan: space changes.) There were in fact only three ways in which tenants could achieve more space inside their houses; and choice depended on what they could afford and the method of payment. All required scrutiny and were consequently a constant source of friction between tenants and authority.

The first method, the enclosing of the front porch of the house either with temporary or permanent materials, was the most obvious and cost the least. The idea of providing a front porch in the design of the house seems to have come from a desire by the authorities to reproduce the outdoor sitting area apparently

common in tribal dwellings.[18] The reasons the porch seems to have satisfied residents in African townships are somewhat different however: a survey in Orlando showed that over 90% of residents wanted one because 'a house doesn't look like a house without a stoep, Europeans generally have verandas and people like to sit on stoeps in the evenings and during the weekends'.[19] Certainly the porch was luxury in Western Native Township; in almost all the houses it occupied approximately one-eighth of the area of the rest of the house and in the earliest two-roomed houses as much as three-fifths. Consequently over 80% of tenants altered their porches, almost all enclosing them completely to make additional interior space which most used as sitting rooms, some as bedrooms and others as kitchens. (A handful were also used as storerooms and in a few cases as either tailors' or cobblers' shops). The porch also had to serve as an entrance, the houses having been equipped with only one door and this always opened on to the porch.

The addition of the porch was too small to make a fundamental difference to the life-style of the family;

Above Axonometric projection of original house and space in front of house.

Right Four axonometric projections of decorated houses showing relationships between wall

treatment and floor of forecourt; various solutions to the problem of relating street gates to entrance doors; and use of front space (a car may be permanently enclosed within the space and used as an outside room).

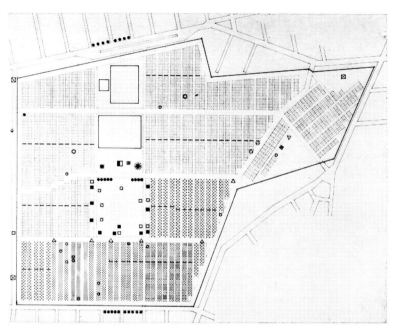

195

Above right Western Native Township: land use and
growth.

Below right Western Native Township: space
changes.

Left and above Shortage of space inside the basic houses caused over 80% of the residents to close their porches and add the much-needed space to an inside room. Closed-in or open, they become a key to decoration. And outside sitting is still essential, a tree providing shade and enclosure when the porch is gone.

in almost all the houses a family size of six (the average for the township was higher) still meant that every room was also a bedroom sleeping at least three. To get a significant increase in space tenants had either to build themselves, or have the Municipality do it and pay an added quarter to their rents. The Municipal addition was always built on at the back of the house and this together with the enclosed porch meant an additional area half again that of most of the houses. An existence below the Poverty Datum Line however meant that few could afford the increased rent and only 5% of tenants availed themselves of the Municipality's offer.

Even fewer (about 1%) could afford to make permanent structural alterations themselves but those that did spent an average of $650 on these, about four times the original cost of the house itself. Sometimes these

alterations expanded the existing rooms (from 9 ft × 9 ft to 12 ft × 12 ft) instead of adding another room, this being a solution which favoured the arrangement of furniture over the need for privacy. A letter from a tenant to the superintendent explains this preference: 'Now, Sir, if I have one extra room it will mean that I must divide my bedroom suite as well as my dining room suite according to the number of rooms. As for instance, I will have to store few chairs in this extra room and other furniture for the bedroom too, which is no good ... I cannot put the whole Dinning Suit in, and I have two pieces of three pieces of Chesterfield Dining r. Suit left at the store for want of space. Organ and piano are also in the kitchen, all which things ought to be in the Dinning Room.'[20]

This method of expansion was allowed only in the case of the few three-roomed houses standing on bigger plots of land; in all other cases four-foot side spaces had to be maintained. As houses had no back doors and the kitchen was always in the front, the area at the back of the house was seldom used and never improved. The space in front of the house however was treated with as much concern as was the house facade itself. Here was an opportunity to make an outside living area to replace the enclosed porch, to furnish it with gardens, paving and pergolas and surround it with hedges, gates and sculptured gateposts cum letter-boxes. (See axonometric drawings; the car in the garden is stationary and an outside room, another way of adding space!)

If the amount of space that these people could add for themselves was limited by their poverty, it achieved size for them through being so indistinguishably connected with their general struggle. Thus when the Municipality refused to compensate them on the grounds that they had been warned that they had improved their houses at their own risk and that they were being given indirect compensation through better housing in the new townships, it did not satisfy them. Neither did it when they were not allowed to take the improvements away with them or sell them to the new 'Coloured' immigrants. One of the officials showed some understanding of the problem when writing in a memo: '... It must be remembered that the sentimental value of their houses is really more important than the intrinsic value....'[21] A resident of twenty years in WNT understood it much better: '... originally we were handed these houses in their base and barren constructions and structures, in consequence of which all of us started from scratch, plastering, pounding the floors and pulverizing the walls, as well as applying some paintings ... this incredible decision of "penalising" the Natives against compensations is that WE HAVE MADE USE OF THE GROUND AND DERIVED COMFORT OF THESE IMPROVEMENTS.'[22]

2. Decoration

The drives behind changing the surface appearance of the house were not toward as straightforward a goal as increased space; nor were they constrained by lack of money. It was cheaper to buy appearance than space and in 1961 three-quarters of all the houses in the township (see below) had street-facing façades which were either decorated or plastered only. The original house was built of cheap red bricks and residents considered the appearance so 'unfinished' that it forced them to do something to make it look 'beautiful'. In the first days of the township, residents did this by mixing cowdung with red clay soil and scratching *litema*[23] patterns in it. These early decorations were attributed to the first decorators, people from the Bakwena tribe, who drew animals and figures 'like the Bushmen paintings' or the chevron and grid patterns common in tribal mud-wall decoration. Then the township was still empty and cows grazed among still unoccupied houses.

By the forties and fifties however the decorations had changed as much as the township. The materials were now bought in the hardware stores of Sophiatown, and the designs complex enough to warrant the commissioning of a builder. There were over twenty such builders working in WNT and each claimed that his work carried his own stamp. The builder of house No. 1347 describes his way as follows:

'I plastered the whole wall first, smoothed it, left it to dry for about two days. Then I used a string dipped in oxide powder with a nail tied to one end, knocked the nail in at one end of the wall, and then stretched the string (I asked somebody to hold the other end taut) and then proceeded to make the straight lines by pulling the string in the middle, leaving an imprint on the wall. Then I chipped out the marked area with a hammer. I sprayed the chipped part and while wet, applied the rough-cast by hand, using a trowel to

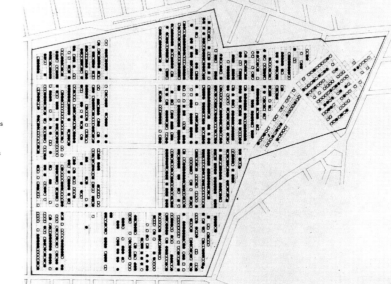

Decorated houses

Plastered houses

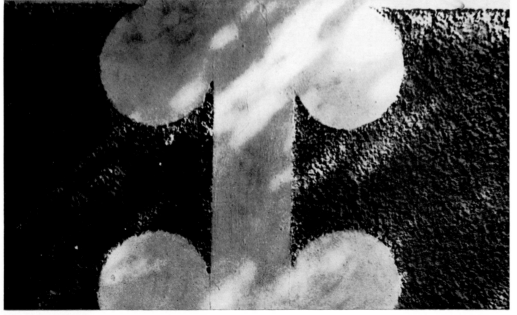

even it out. Having done the solid portion at the bottom and the sun's rays I then worked on the sun by drawing a circle with an ordinary food plate.'

Only the street-facing façade was treated in this way. A few tenants claimed that it was too expensive to do the rest (the average cost of a decoration was about $50 or one month's household income) but most felt anything else would not be seen. For some the façade was a way of directing visitors to their houses; for others a way indicating their position in the community ('I was a school teacher and so wished to enhance my status'), but for most it had to do with a less specific extroversion: 'wanting my house to be admired' or 'wanting to please my neighbours'.

In a highly other-conscious community the façades were thus a way of both satisfying outsiders and at the same time receiving the gratification of their approval. Never stepping beyond certain tacitly approved norms ensured against displeasing others and trying your best to be different within this framework meant maximizing your own wellbeing. Herbert Gans suggests a similar process of competition within conformity in Levittown:

'I heard no objection among the Levittowners about the similarity of their homes ... Aesthetic diversity is preferred, however, and people talked about moving to a custom-built house in the future when they could afford it. Meanwhile they made internal and external alterations in the Levitt house to reduce sameness and to place a personal stamp on their property.'[24] But while Levittowners could move out when they could afford it, WNT residents could not. It is one thing to wait until you can achieve your goals, it is another to know you can never achieve them. Then you have to compress your frustrated ambitions into what you have now and you make your possessions look like those you will never possess. Thus the houses of WNT are imagined versions of houses in white suburbia – decorated WNT houses were called 'Parktown', after the wealthiest suburb in Johannesburg – decorated with all the intensity necessary to make a shelter live up to a dream.

Certain areas within the township seem to have been regarded as better than others and people moved within the township to suit their environment to their position. The area of three-roomed houses in the north-east corner was considered the best, and the oldest houses on the southern fence the worst. The distribution of income however does not reflect this pattern nor does the distribution of house occupancy rates. Neither of these show significant clusters of income or density.

The diagram showing the intensity of decoration (right),

however, clearly indicates a zone of intense decoration in the middle of the township just east of the
central area. While residents here were neither
wealthier nor their houses less overcrowded than
others, this was the central and enclosed area of the
township and the area through which most residents
had to pass en route from the main gate in the north-
east corner. The elite area in the north-east corner on
the other hand was an isolated pocket. The houses
were difficult to decorate because they had no dominant wall which faced the street and it was, in spite of
its being an apparently wealthy area, an area with very
little decoration. (The bar-charts below show that
decoration occurred in a pattern unrelated to the
particular income of the household or the number of
people living in the house.)

The process of people using the designs of others as
the basis of their own spontaneously set limits to the
language of decoration in the township. While none
was identical, all the decorations were really variations

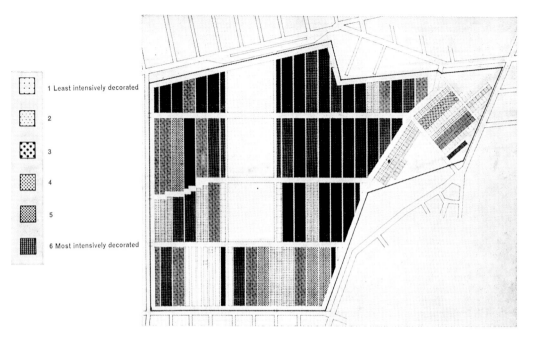

1 Least intensively decorated

2

3

4

5

6 Most intensively decorated

Right Intensity of decoration; each bar represents
the ratio of decorated houses to all houses on two
facing streets.

199

Below Population distribution, space changes, and
decoration by household income and house
density.

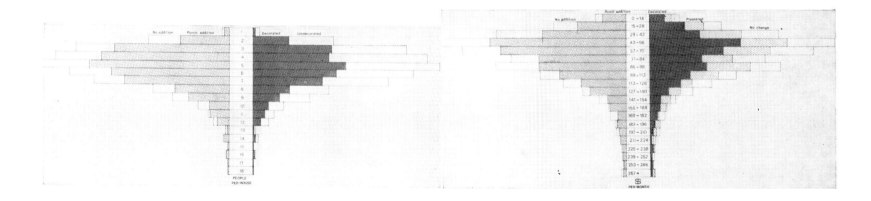

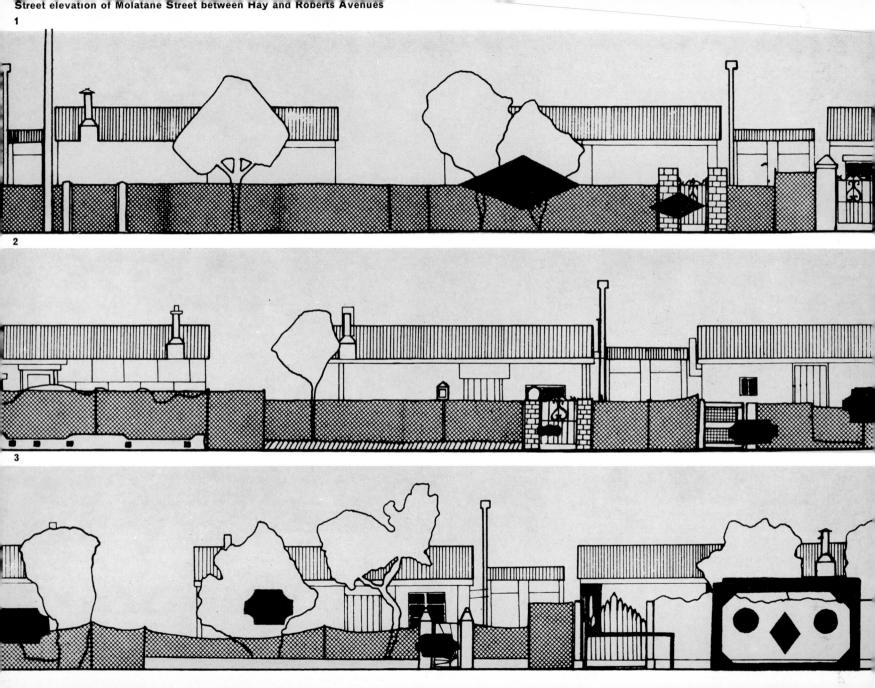

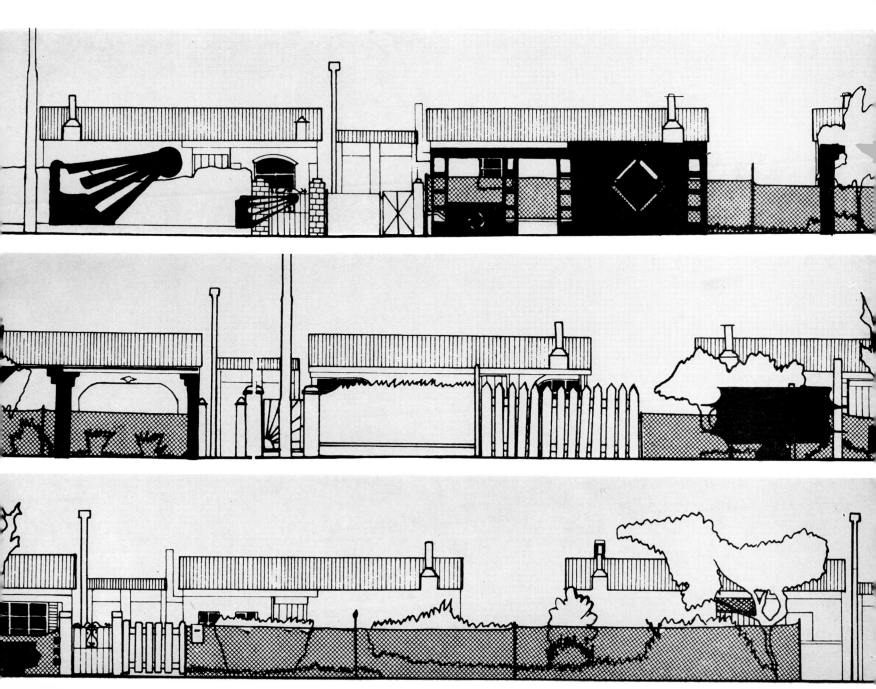

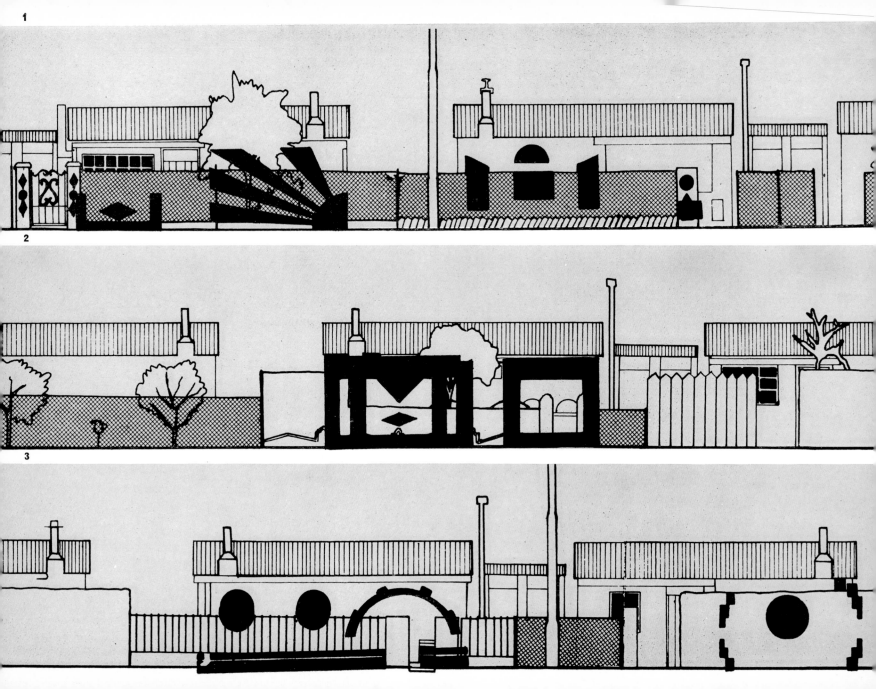

of about half-a-dozen basic shapes. By manipulating these and adding colour and texture residents could make surfaces which conveyed either a purely architectonic impression or recognizable images: the razor-blade, for instance, made by inserting three circles into an indented rectangle or the sun made by adding triangular wings on either side of a half-circle.[25] (The distinction between abstract decoration and obvious imagery is likely however to be stronger in the mind of the uninitiated than it was in the community: some residents, for instance, clearly identified certain circular or semi-circular shapes as having to do with the sun, an interpretation unlikely to have come from an outsider to the society.)[26]

Certain shapes were explained by their creators as advertising the activities inside the house: a tree shape on the wall because religious meetings were held inside or a horse shape because the house was a gambling saloon; but most were less specific. In fact there seems to be a dichotomy between a set of explanations which suggest a primordial, tribal derivation on the one hand and a more urban, rather banal one on the other. Some, for instance, suggested that 'these are our traditional drawings and white people do not know anything about them' or 'I wanted to show typical Tswana designs'. One Tswana woman even claims to have been sent back to the reserves specifically to learn the designs; but another resident, on the other hand, admits to seeing the design in a geometry book and another in a book on architecture. One resident in fact says that she specifically 'wanted something that would look modern instead of the decorations we do on the farms'.

The pattern of relationships between the decorations and the various tribal groups in the township helps to clarify this ambiguity. Had decorations been linked to tribal affiliations one might have expected certain tribes who have a strong decorative tradition, particularly in respect of mural art, to have played a significant role in the township's decorations. This was not so. Of the major tribal groups in the township, the great majority were either Nguni (Xhosa, Zulu, Swazi) or Sotho (Twsana, N. Sotho, S. Sotho) and were distributed randomly throughout the township No tribal group decorated much more frequently than any other: all decorated more or less in proportion to their

Above Wall decoration based on a sun motif is continued as floorscape.

Below left Sun rays.

Below right A razor blade motif is capped by a motif based on a house gable.

203

numbers in the township, Swazi and Northern Sotho (together only 10% of the township) being the only groups who tended to be more active than others.

If some tribes did not decorate more frequently than others, certain tribes however seem to have preferred certain modes of decoration (right): the Nguni group of tribes, for instance, seems to have preferred the circle as the basis for their decoration while the Sotho-speaking group inclined towards the sun family. These preferences could perhaps be explained in terms of cultural differences between these tribes; they cannot be explained by looking for coincidences between the WNT decorations and those in the rural areas from which these tribes emigrated to the city. In the first place the WNT decorations are generally so different from those of tribal decorations that it is difficult to establish a basis for comparison. Secondly, the characteristics that distinguish one mode of tribal decoration from another are not those of shape. Bantu parietal art is essentially architectonic and geometric and the distinctions between tribal expressions are generally less qualitative than quantitative.

Right Distribution of tribal groups by categories of decoration.

204

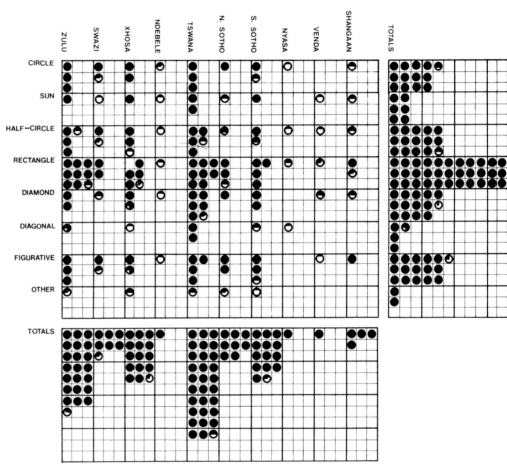

EACH ● REPRESENTS ONE PERCENT

Ndebele decoration, for instance, is really only the more intensive and relentless use of forms which are common in Sotho and other decoration. In addition rural decoration is not static and does not remain unaffected by frequent interchange between city and country. So the Ndebele incorporate a wide range of urban symbols in their later decoration and the Pedi of the Northern Transvaal use symbols from playing cards (as did the people of WNT).[27]

The people of Western Native Township kept in contact with their rural homes and in the early forties residents were said to have spent long periods in the country every three years.[28] If this interchange affected the way some thought of decorating their houses – and probably the way their rural relatives felt about theirs – it was only one of many inputs into the stock of ideas available to them. For this is the key point in explaining the context of these decorations. The people of Western Native Township were exploiting what is uniquely available in a city, even a city with as many barriers as theirs: the chance to pick up new stimuli that only density and diversity offer. Thus their choices ranged back and forth overlapping what they brought with them from the country with what they found in the city.

Those who belong to the culture of wealth shape their suburban environments through a different process of selection: they generally make two sets of choices. First they choose their house styles from the pre-digested and often diluted range that their professional or semi-professional advisers provide. When they find many others have made similar choices they then choose ways of differentiating their own, extending and elaborating their original choice. Their efforts at personalisation tend to be much more naive and direct than the styles of their houses.

In WNT there was no choice of house, only the choice between ways of changing it. Here people spent the same resources in relation to their income and the cost of their houses as do people in suburbia.[29] Their choices were much more naive and indiscriminate however and their applications more direct and intense. In suburbia merely being there means respectability: in a township when your street-facing wall may be all you have with which to achieve the approval of others, you have to do more. Naive and yet sophisticated, the decorations had the combination that gives a particular power to popular art: spontaneity and unselfconsciousness mixed with composition and completeness. In one sense the

shaped outside floor and wall of a house are patterns of stoep polish, in another they are the architectonic tricks of the masters. The overall impression of the township streets was one of humour, smiling, staring faces and funny flags.[30] What can be more naive – or sophisticated – than treating a ludicrous environment as if it were a big joke?

The Coloured people who now live in Western Native Township have remained indifferent to it. For some even the forty-year old houses were an improvement on what they had come from. Others could not wait to get out, but most seemed passive with little conviction about what one resident described as 'the forlorn atmosphere of the place'. They liked WNT for similar reasons to the Africans': its location in the city and the cheapness of transport, but could not understand why they should be paying twice the rent Africans had paid.

When interviewed a year after coming to WNT, there was a strong consciousness among the Coloureds of the African overtones of the townships. There were still Africans left in WNT, determined to stay there, had used their lighter skins and change of name – from the Bantu to the Afrikaans equivalent – to con the authorities into reclassifying them as Coloured. (An official race classification index is a necessary tool of a system that uses the law to discriminate.) Some Coloureds found 'certain African neighbours objectionable,' and saw the wall decorations as another aspect of the township's Africanness: 'African people always got something funny.' One man did a new painting on his house 'as a joke to imitate the Bantu custom'. They thought the decorations 'looked stupid' or were part of a legacy of 'witchcraft' which the Africans had left them. Soon after they had moved in this report appeared in the local newspaper:

'A Coloured family of fourteen has fled from its newly-acquired Western Native Township home because of eerie and mysterious happenings that have left the children sick and half-witted and the father with blue scratchmarks on both his arms. The family had occupied the house for two days when the youngest member Dolores, whose age is two, went limp and her eyes rolled back. Immediately after that fifteen-year-old Eveline complained of a splitting headache and collapsed. While the parents were being interviewed, Eveline lay reading in a bed as if delirious and could not speak. A few minutes after Eveline had collapsed, Ivan whose age is twelve said he had seen a short man in the house and pleaded with his mother to take him away. Ivan also collapsed and when a neighbour was

called to pray for the children Noel collapsed outside. The eldest brother Kenneth, twenty-one, picked him up but was seized with an attack of giddiness. As all the family had become ill a doctor was called in from the Western Native Township clinic but could not diagnose their sickness. A little later in the afternoon of the same day the father, Mr. Henry Ahrens whose age is 46, received scratches on both his arms which turned blue. The children vomited the whole day.'[31]

Those who felt strongly about the wall-decorations either painted over them or cancelled their effect by using one colour over the whole wall. Most however did not have such strong feelings. They merely accepted the walls of their houses and when repainting them followed the African pattern but with different colours. Two years after the Africans had left about 40% of the houses had been repainted or had small structural changes made to them. A handful had new designs, mostly freehand paintings of ships, flowers, trees or designs based on new house names such as "Little Green Gate' or 'Hoyton' (Houghton is another wealthy white suburb).

When interviewed six years after their immigration into Western Native Township the Coloured residents

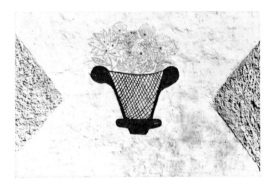

were less conscious of the people who had been there before. Their major concerns were now with the degraded quality of life in the township and the danger of living there. Adults spoke of keeping their children inside lest they be molested; staying indoors themselves so as 'not to mix with the drunks in the street'. Crime and the lack of adequate police protection had become their major problem: people being interviewed spoke of 'the little girl next door who is in hospital' and 'my husband who was stabbed to death outside the house'. Few changes had been made to the walls in the intervening six years.

Despite many attempts to keep together various vigilance groups to combat crime, the African community of WNT had also been helpless to protect themselves. In the thirty years before 1960, one-third of all reports dealing with WNT in the major Johannesburg African newspaper had been about crime. Towards the end of their stay residents constantly spoke of the hopelessness of their plight, that 'lately it has become tough and ugly and gangsterism rules the township with an iron hand'. Local self-organized resistance had become meaningless in relation to the scale of the social problems that now faced non-white living in South African cities. A newspaper report of this time is typical:

'An attempt to sever a man's private parts was made by thugs, among them some girls, in WNT recently. The 36 year-old victim, Mr Patrick Mofokeng, now lying in the Coronation Hospital fighting for his life, said the thugs demanded money from him. When he told them he had none they sat on him. A life and death struggle followed . . . '[32]

Where the people of WNT now live crime is still pervasive. Despite larger houses (at double the rent) they are far from the city and transportation is much more expensive, limited and time-consuming. There are fewer shops, the range is less and residents claim foodstuffs cost more. They miss the density of their social life at WNT. Of those interviewed less than half wanted to decorate their new houses and of these less than half wanted to stick to their WNT design. One had 'become a Christian and did not consider the designs suitable any more'; another wanted to do 'something new in a different town' and another could not repeat his design because it had been 'spontaneously drawn on to the wall and I don't think I could equal it again'. Of those who wanted to repeat the same design one wanted to 'hand the design down as a family heirloom', another because of 'memories'. Half of those who thought they would do nothing to

the walls felt it 'wasn't necessary as the bricks do not look ugly': the rest because it was too expensive or no longer fashionable. All over the new townships however people do improve their houses and there are some decorations but the government-built surroundings in which they live are too diffuse and the few decorations have little impact.

One wonders how much it matters now. The second-phase city seemed so intense by comparison, so full of a strange, if difficult to understand, hope. Perhaps this was only the hope of the liberal: that Africans still being in the city meant some kind of contact, and while there was contact there was hope. Perhaps the reading of the walls of WNT as an optimistic assertion in the face of a repressive system – as a set of symbols of this hope – is equally romantic. But there is a lingering feeling that the end of those walls meant the end of one kind of city and the beginning of a new one: one with a new and lifeless world for Africans and one in which few retain much hope.

If this is the third-phase, what then of the fourth-phase city? Will it be two cities even further apart, more different, each staring at the other across a no-man's land of gold mine dumps? Can it be that one will keep on getting richer and the other poorer, the one with bright lights and the other with candles? Or will it change; and will it change slowly, or will it suddenly burst apart for the pieces to fall where they might? No one knows; but some say that 'nearly every African speaks of the intolerable frustration in the townships, the consciousness that there must be, before long, a massive explosion. They can sense it in the packed buses and the trains, the barometers of African opinion. . . .'[33]

1 Ezekiel Mphahlele, *Down Second Avenue* (Faber, London 1959).

2 Minutes of the Johannesburg City Council, 1904.11. 855-90.

3 Patrick R. B. Lewis, *A 'City' within a City—The Creation of Soweto* (University of the Witwatersrand, Johannesburg, 1966) p. 38.

4 Peter Randall and Yunus Desai, *From 'Coolie Location' to Group Area* (South African Institute of Race Relations, Johannesburg, 1967) p. 1.

5 The population graphs are compiled from official census statistics for 1921, 1936, 1946, 1951 and 1960 as well as a wide variety of other sources.

6 Minutes of the Johannesburg City Council, 1904.11. 866–80.

7 Figures quoted by John P. R. Maud, *City Government* (Oxford University Press, 1938) p. 135, with the following footnote: 'This figure was given by Dr Bernstein after making a scientific study of conditions there. In part, but only in part, it can be explained away by the fact that the machinery for registering native births is so defective that the official number of recorded births is considerably smaller than the number of actual births.'

8 J. Lewsen, 'The Relationship of the Johannesburg City Council to the Western Areas' in *The Western Areas—Mass Removal?* (South African Institute of Race Relations, Johannesburg 1953) p. 3.

9 Nathaniel Nakasa, 'Writing in South Africa', *The Classic* Vol. 1, No. 1, p. 58.

10 Ellen Hellman, 'Urban Areas' in *Race Relations in South Africa,* (Oxford University Press, London, 1949) p. 248.

11 H. A. Fagan *et al., Report of the Commission of Enquiry into the Disturbance at Moroka, Johannesburg on the 30th August, 1947,* Pretoria, 1948, p. 23.

12 J. Lewsen, *op. cit.,* p. 4.

13 Ellen Hellman, *Soweto, Johannesburg's African City* (South African Institute of Race Relations, Johannesburg, 1967).

14 Non-European Affairs Department of the City Council of Johannesburg, *Thousands for Houses . . . ,* Johannesburg, 1961.

15 City of Johannesburg Non-European Affairs Department, *Report on a Sample Survey of the Native Population residing in the Western Areas of Johannesburg,* 1951, p. 173.

16 From an interview with an ex-WNT resident, Campbell Gwidza.

17 Descriptions taken from Cosey Motsisi, 'Riot', *The Classic,* Vol. 1, No. 2, p. 71.

18 D. M. Calderwood, *Principles of Mass Housing* (S.A. Council for Scientific and Industrial Research, Pretoria, 1964) p. 63.

19 Jacqueline Eberhardt, *Survey of Family Conditions with special reference to Housing Needs in Orlando Township, Johannesburg,* quoted in D. M. Calderwood, *Native Housing in South Africa,* p. 24.

20 From File No. 192/1/4, Non-European Affairs Dept., Johannesburg City Council.

21 From File No. 71/4/3/3, Non-European Affairs Dept., Johannesburg City Council.

22 Letter to *The Star,* Johannesburg, 14th October 1961.

23 From the Sotho word meaning 'the furrows of a ploughed field'.

24 Herbert Gans, *The Levittowners* (Allen Lane, the Penguin Press, London, 1967) p. 171.

25 This process is called 'forcing mere abstractions into becoming iconic symbols' by one commentator: see *The Listener,* 1st April 1965, p. 499.

26 For a story of how outsiders perceive these decorations, see J. Cohen and C. Kessel, 'The Effects of Racial Attitudes on the Perception of Wall Decorations in Western Native Township', unpublished paper, Dept. of Psychology, University of the Witwatersrand, 1964.

27 Example cited in James Walton, 'Mural Art of the Bantu', *S.A. Panorama,* April 1965, p. 35.

28 Ellen Hellman, 'The Native in the Towns', in *The Bantu Speaking Tribes of South Africa,* ed. I. Schapera (Maskew Miller, Cape Town, 1946) p. 429.

29 Julian Beinart, 'The Process of Urban Participation', in *Proceedings of the Conference: Focus on Cities* (Institute of Social Research, University of Natal, Durban, 1969).

30 For such an interpretation, see 'Suns, Flags, Eyes, Clocks' in *Society of Industrial Artists Journal* No. 144, February 1965, p. 23.

31 The *Bantu World,* Johannesburg, 6th January 1962. Similar reports on superstition appeared while Africans were still living in WNT; for example this one of 28th August 1954:

'There was wild excitement in Johannesburg's WNT on Sunday. Word got round that a ngaka had captured a tokolosh. Soon people were streaming from meetings, sports grounds and homes to Ntsala Street in WNT. A big crowd gathered in the street and Police arrived to keep order. Fearing that the crowd would get out of order, they escorted the ngaka, Jackson Paledi, and the body of the tokolosh to the Newlands Police Station. A growing crowd followed them. Ahead of them, people ran for safety. Mothers dragged their children into the houses and windows and doors were locked and bolted. A few brave men ventured out to meet the procession, but they kept their hands at their throats. They were afraid Tokolosh would strangle them . . . The beast was found hiding on the veranda of No. 1915. For a year there had been trouble at this house. The children complained of noises at night and could not sleep. Mrs. Evelyn Mokoena of No. 1924 Ntsala Street is a professional ngaka. She was called in. She was away on Sunday . . . Her daughter Caroline is also an ngaka. She called in Jackson Paledi. He went to house No. 1915 and sought out the brown furious animal with the human-like fingers. He killed it with a medicated stick . . . Next day the *Bantu World* brought a scientist from the Zoo to look at it. "It is a magnificent specimen of a large otter", said the scientist. "It lives along rivers and only comes out at night to look for food. This one might have come from the Vaal or Jukskei river. It is a miracle how it could get into such a built-up place. It must have left the main river and travelled along tributaries in search of food." '

32 *The Bantu World,* Johannesburg, 8th February 1957.

33 Anthony Sampson, 'Behind the Black Curtain', in *The Observer,* 19th April 1970.

CHURCH STREET SOUTH HOUSING IN NEW HAVEN

CHARLES MOORE AND GERALD ALLEN

Businessmen, casual tourists, and occasional students who in the past came to New Haven, Connecticut, travelled there more often than not aboard the New Haven Railroad. Some still do, and they arrive at a terminus some three-fifths of a mile away from the centre of the city near what used to be the edge of the New Haven harbour.

'The first impression of most visitors to the city will be gained on emerging from the station; this impression may be followed by others, but the first impression is a lasting one, and upon it will be largely based the opinion of the city as formed by its visitors.' This first modest impression will soon be made by the façade of the Church Street South housing development, though the new buildings will no doubt appear directed more towards caring for the city's own people than impressing its visitors.

Whether or not this fact represents what is called a change in priorities since 1910, when the sentences we have quoted were written, and whether Cass Gilbert and Frederick Law Olmstead, who wrote them, would have been pleased by the result, are both problematical matters. What is clear and therefore worth noting is that the stretch of land between the railroad station and the centre of New Haven has been regarded in the minds of the great and less great as an urban 'problem' for well over fifty years, and that they have from time to time exercised themselves over it. For this reason the Church Street South area and its new buildings are moderately felicitous illustrations of the ways in which we do (and do not) change our surroundings, and of the curious fashion in which ideas and ideals of design play hide and seek among the exigencies and practical energies of the city.

Seventeenth-century planners laid out the town of New Haven in a pattern of nine squares with a central common or green, and thereby they demonstrated a comely taste for order that has been less than apparent in more recent development. The larger square formed by the nine smaller ones was connected to the harbour by a diagonal road running from its southern corner, and to the road to New York at the south-west side. As the town grew the southern and south-western parts became predominantly commercial areas, while with some exceptions residential neighbourhoods and Yale College expanded in the other directions. When the railroads arrived in the nineteenth century tracks were put down on the flat land between the town and the harbour and in the then abandoned canals on the south-east side of the town.

The first station was built near the southern corner of the large square close to the businesses and industries. By 1900 the population, swollen by foreign immigration as well as by the usual increases, had reached 108,000. The city had sprawled far beyond the original nine squares, and the existing station, along with other public facilities, was becoming inadequate. It was therefore decided to move it slightly more than half a mile west to what is now its present location, which was then an area of hinterlandish markets and houses. The decision to move the station, which was an important one for the city, appears to have been made entirely by the railroad company for compelling operational reasons such as the increasing length of trains, the governing grades, and the need for additional sidings.

In 1907, however, a group of citizens who styled themselves the New Haven Civic Improvement Committee raised $10,000 by subscription and hired Cass Gilbert and Frederick Law Olmstead to prepare plans and comprehensive recommendations for the future development of the city. In their report, which was published in 1910, Gilbert and Olmstead pointed out that the new station, as it was then being planned, had no proper site and no straight line of access to the centre of the city. This, they felt, was bad, and so they proposed first a station building of suitably

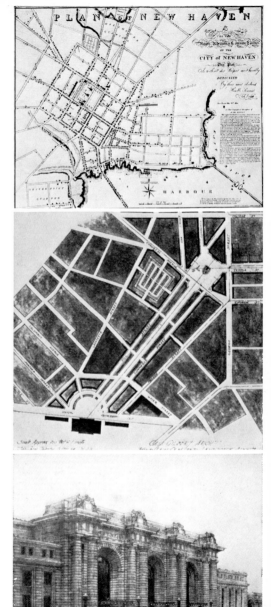

grand and important scale and, to connect it to the centre of activity, a broad avenue leading diagonally from the Station Plaza near the harbour up to the edge of the nine squares. Gilbert and Olmstead seem to have reflected clearly that, whatever the importance of the land (now Church Street South) between the station and the town centre, it was not of the same kind as those two nodes of public activity. And they saw with similar clarity that it would be desirable that the two nodes be connected.

Their avenue, nevertheless, was not built, and during the next half century the land between the station and the Green slowly became a nowhere between two somewheres. Or, since Gilbert's station was not built either, it slowly became a nowhere between an almost nowhere and a somewhere. The area served the functions of arrival and access, at the scale of the city, and, at a smaller scale, the functions of marketing and to a lesser extent living. It never seems to have done any of these things really well, and maybe for this reason it had few of the qualities of place that are memorable in a variety of other parts of New Haven. The rest of Gilbert and Olmstead's plan for the city was also in the course of time forgotten, and this fact is worthy of passing interest since, even though it was sponsored and read by men of élite tastes and apparently finite energies, it was as a whole calm and handsome, and in its details it contained a good many of the precepts which we please ourselves by thinking are our own.

Planned development sponsored by the city, or redevelopment, as it came to be called, did not begin in earnest in New Haven until 1941, when the languishing planning office was revitalized and Maurice Rotival was hired to prepare a new comprehensive plan. In the early 1950s the city was faced with the imminence of a large system of new highways in its midst, financed under the Interstate Highways programme and planned by the State Highway Commission. Thus Rotival was asked, with traffic engineering

209

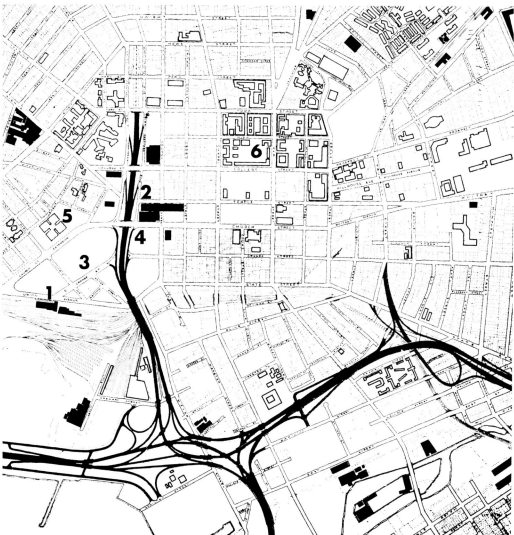

Above left In contrast with the station building designed by Gilbert and Olmstead, see the previous page, this is the station as ultimately built.
Above The highway plan for New Haven, developed in the 1950s and still being implemented, virtually put an end to the original Gilbert and Olmstead plan.

1, the railroad station; 2, the site of the focal square at Temple Street and Congress Avenue, envisaged in the Gilbert and Olmstead plan as the axis of their broad diagonal avenue; 3, site of Charles Moore's Church Street South housing; 4, site of the Knights of Columbus building by Kevin Roche; 5, Lee High School by Kevin Roche; 6, the university.

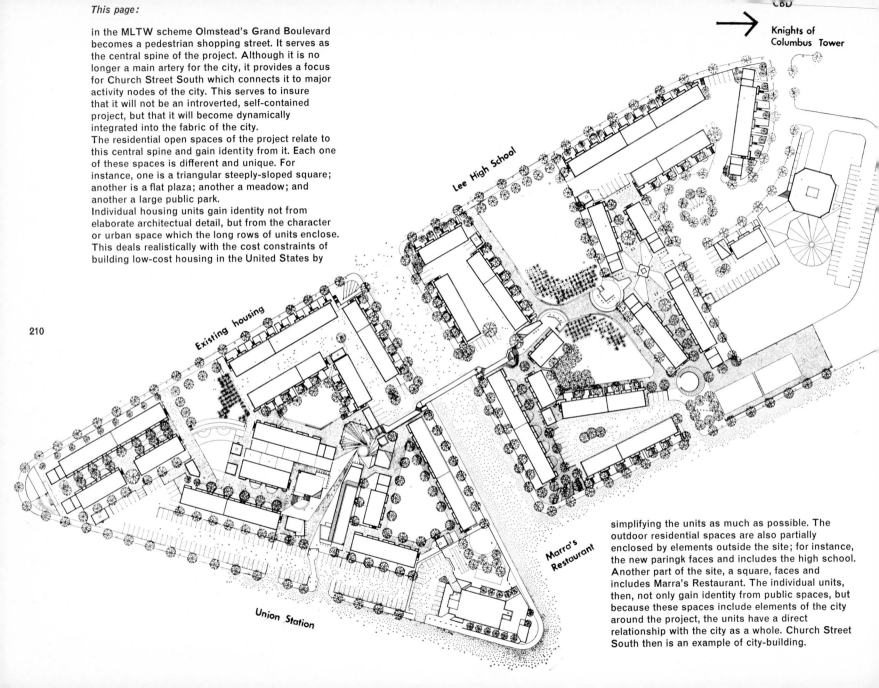

in the MLTW scheme Olmstead's Grand Boulevard becomes a pedestrian shopping street. It serves as the central spine of the project. Although it is no longer a main artery for the city, it provides a focus for Church Street South which connects it to major activity nodes of the city. This serves to insure that it will not be an introverted, self-contained project, but that it will become dynamically integrated into the fabric of the city.

The residential open spaces of the project relate to this central spine and gain identity from it. Each one of these spaces is different and unique. For instance, one is a triangular steeply-sloped square; another is a flat plaza; another a meadow; and another a large public park.

Individual housing units gain identity not from elaborate architectual detail, but from the character or urban space which the long rows of units enclose. This deals realistically with the cost constraints of building low-cost housing in the United States by

210

Knights of Columbus Tower

Lee High School

Existing housing

Marra's Restaurant

Union Station

simplifying the units as much as possible. The outdoor residential spaces are also partially enclosed by elements outside the site; for instance, the new paringk faces and includes the high school. Another part of the site, a square, faces and includes Marra's Restaurant. The individual units, then, not only gain identity from public spaces, but because these spaces include elements of the city around the project, the units have a direct relationship with the city as a whole. Church Street South then is an example of city-building.

consultant Lloyd Reid, to make another plan which would show the desirable placement of the new highways in relation to the city's future development. This plan was finished in 1953, the State was brought to substantial agreement with it, and accordingly New Haven's large highways were built during the next ten years. Mayor Richard Lee first took office in 1954 and in turn put Edward Logue in charge of the redevelopment programme. The city was possessed by an energetic new administration, federal financing was available, and the Great Phase of New Haven redevelopment began.

Whereas the 1910 plan showed, in the tradition of the City Beautiful, an overriding sensitivity to the residential amenities and to the visual qualities of public places, the plan engineered by Logue and his staff of professional planners was, at least in its first stages, subtly and shrewdly aimed at the dynamics of commerce and the revitalization of Downtown. A first consequence of their plan on the Church Street South area was that the railroad station, and the land where the Church Street South housing now is, was further disassociated from the central city by a wide high-speed connector from the Connecticut Turnpike at the shore to the downtown area. A second consequence was that virtually all buildings in a band from the southern tip of the Green to the station were demolished.

Though the redevelopment of the cleared land beyond the connector was not of the highest priority, efforts were made ultimately to reassociate it with the city. Church Street, which runs along the southeastern edge of the Green, was, in a faint echo of Gilbert and Olmstead's plan, extended across the connector around the edge of the cleared land, where it finally met Union Street and led to the station. Various residential and commercial uses for the area were considered, and by the mid-1960s Mies van der Rohe had been hired to make plans for a complex of houses and an elementary school. Mies's housing scheme was never completed, and his school had to be abandoned because of financial difficulties; though Lee High School, designed by Kevin Roche, was finally built on the west side of the Church Street extension.

The discontinuous threads of intention and execution which run through the history of the Church Street South site continued to run when, after Mies's

Above This recent photograph of New Haven's renewal area shows the still incomplete highway loop. In the upper right is the traditional 'Green'

which formed the middle square in the original laying out of the town. On the left of the photograph the dark tower is the new Knights of Columbus by Kevin Roche. Between this building and the Green is the new enclosed and air-conditioned shopping centre, and the famous parking garage by Paul Rudolph; below it is the site for a major indoor sports arena, including professional ice hockey. Beyond the 'Green' are the quadrangles of the old university, which are gradually becoming surrounded by new buildings, towers of offices, housing and education.

Right the Green.

scheme came to nothing, the present architect, Charles W. Moore of MLTW/Moore-Turnbull, and the Development Corporation of America were engaged. It was proposed that the site be developed as three separate projects: Church Street South housing under a Federal government — FHA 221(d)(3) — programme[1]; a public housing facility for the elderly; and a second high-rise building for the elderly sponsored by the Jewish Community Council with financing from the Federal Department of Housing and Urban Development.

The programme for the first project called for 400 housing units, 100 of which were to be financed at market interest rates and 300 at below market interest rates by the Federal Housing Authority. The rents for sixty of these 300 units were to be supplemented by the city, and thus the whole project would provide housing for people of varying incomes and would be, as Mayor Lee desired, 'vertically' integrated. The Redevelopment Agency felt strongly that the units should take the form of three and four-storey walk-ups with covered parking. But since the buildings were in the city's fire zone they still had to be fireproof. On the other hand, the project had to be economical enough to qualify for financing under the 221(d)(3) housing programme. So in one of a multitude of efforts to keep costs low, the developers suggested a system of long span precast planking on precast walls, with which they had worked elsewhere.

Below The Church Street South housing site is across the expressway between the Knights of Columbus building and the railroad station. Immediately opposite the Knights of Columbus building Charles Moore has placed his octagonal apartment tower for the elderly.

In design the scheme was later modified to a system which produced long rectangular blocks of apartments with planking spanning from front to back between identical precast façades.

The Redevelopment Agency gave relatively few specific instructions for developing the site, except that Columbus Avenue, which runs east-west through the centre, had to be preserved, since it was to become a part of an inner ring road. In the first site plan not only this street was maintained, but a second street was added running from the station up to the connector, almost where the avenue proposed in 1910 would have been built. On either side were stores on the ground floor, and apartments above and behind. This arrangement did not please the city authorities, who objected to an additional intersection on Columbus Avenue, nor the FHA, who felt that apartments above stores were undesirable. It became clear, in fact, that the FHA would not accept even the mixing of market interest rate and below market interest rate units. Thus the idea of vertical integration had to be sacrificed in favour of horizontal contiguity — a sacrifice that became in the fullness of time beside the point, since financing for the 100 market interest rate units could not be found anyway, and those apartments were not built. When they are built they will be financed at below market interest rates; for the immediate future their place on the site will remain vacant.

After some thirty-two site plans were developed a final one was chosen. In it what was originally the street can be seen as a pedestrian way from the bottom to the top, passing over Columbus Avenue in the middle on a bridge. With only a few exceptions all the dwelling units are made up of only two basic pieces, a condition that was suggested by the necessity of economy and demanded by the precast system that was to be used. One of these pieces is three storeys high and consists of two- and three-bedroom duplex on top of a three-bedroom apartment. The other is four storeys and contains the same duplexes over a two-storey, four- or five-bedroom apartment and garages for all three. There are also a few one-bedroom apartments on the ground floors and, with them, special two-bedroom apartments with terraces. That there are four-storey units with garages and three-storey ones without, but within an easy walk of a parking place, represents a compromise between the Redevelopment Agency's insistence on covered parking and, again, economy. That the matter was not compromised altogether may have been unlucky, since it is possible to think of a garden next to an apartment as more desirable than a garage.

Above This view of the model shows the central pedestrian spine (echoing the old Gilbert-Olmstead axis) and the pedestrian bridge crossing Columbus Avenue.

FHA Minimum Property Standards dictate the rules under which a project must be designed in order to qualify for financing, and these rules include, for example, minimum square footages for bedrooms to be occupied by two people. The equally strict rules of economy in Church Street South, however, tended to cause minimums very closely to equal maximums, and this circumstance produced typical plans that are perhaps most notable for their conventionality, but that are nevertheless capable of being made Home. The *coup de théâtre* in this enduring drama of Finance and Art occurred at Church Street South when, the designs having been nearly completed, it became apparent that, in New Haven at least, it would be cheaper to build the buildings not of prefabricated units but of concrete block. So they were built out of block, thereby becoming unprefabricated prefabricated housing.

At the time when the first designs for Church Street South were begun, Le Corbusier's dreams of high towers set in large and verdant parks had fallen somewhat into disrepute as a solution to the problem of public housing. Thanks in part to the eloquence of townsfolk like Vincent Scully, this reversal was felt in New Haven by the Redevelopment Agency. Consequently it began to seem desirable to maintain the intimacies and vitalities of the street and, wherever possible, to allow houses to face the street and open to it. It appeared similarly important that each of the apartments along the row should not be an anonymous cell. With prefabricated units, however, it was out of the question to make each one different and thereby the centre of its own world. So another way had to be found.

A first step was to try to arrange the buildings across the site in a way that would emphasize not so much the specialness of each unit as the specialness of its location. A series of physical addresses was made, and each was given a name. If the designers in the office could not after a few weeks remember the name it was changed, and if they could remember the name but not where it was then the design was changed. These metamorphoses of addresses were also continued outside the office by the authorities, and by this process the 'X' was expunged from the name of Malcolm Court. A second step was to use the resources of concrete block and paint to make each front door memorably discrete, if not different, from

its neighbour. In order to sweeten somewhat the bare surfaces of the outside walls rusticated blocks were used on the top floors except where, at windows and corners, special blocks would have cost too much and smooth coigns were excusable.

It was important to have among the series of smaller addresses a larger and more memorable neighbourhood place along the central pedestrian way. To this end the Redevelopment Agency and the FHA were persuaded to upgrade what had originally been a minimal programme for commercial buildings in the development, and to include other buildings such as a store, a small community centre, and a laundromat. Since, moreover, the developers could not afford the niceties of landscaping, the city was persuaded to

take over parts of the site as a public park. When the new street which was originally to have been built through the site had to be abandoned, along with the shops and apartments on either side, it was necessary to move the commercial buildings which could be built to a tiny scale and to special shapes along what became the pedestrian street. These buildings then work alongside the large billboards and the fountains, benches, lights, paving, and all the other lively accoutrements of Urban Design to make a somewhere. Thus a worthwhile progress can be made through the development from the station and the stores at the south up to the Jewish Community Council elderly housing, which begins to rise to the scale of the central city and, bereft of its corner

houses to wide thoroughfares like the Church Street South extension. Maybe on the whole it would be much better to turn away from them. Inside the site itself, it has not yet been possible to build the pedestrian bridge across Columbus Avenue. This link between the two parts of the site is critical, but it has been delayed because of the extended controversy in New Haven over the proposed inner ring road, of which Columbus Avenue would be a part. Thus it is a curious irony that people must oppose what they do need in order not to seem to encourage what they do not need.

cylinders, saucily greets its elegant neighbour, the Knights of Columbus building, like a poor relation.

One intention which has not been executed perfectly was to make Church Street South the opposite of a 'project' limited by its own walls and much more a part of the fabric of the city itself. The fact that it was not possible to mix housing units of different costs militates against this goal, as does the regularity of the façades which seemed to be demanded by the building system which was proposed, though not by the one finally used. When one walks through the development there is considerable variety and liveliness, but at the scale of the streets around it, and of the automobile, the buildings are more consistent and form more of a package than might have been wished. The ugly colour of the unpainted concrete block, too, during the many months of construction will remain in people's memories for a long time.

The streets around and through the Church Street South housing still, in fact, bring up two problems, one of design and the other of politics. On the basis on what has been built it now seems questionable whether any comfort can be gained from opening up

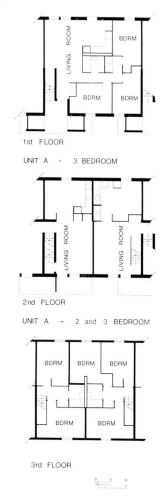

1st FLOOR

UNIT A - 3 BEDROOM

2nd FLOOR

UNIT A - 2 and 3 BEDROOM

3rd FLOOR

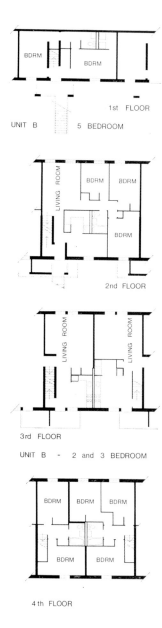

1st FLOOR

UNIT B   5 BEDROOM

2nd FLOOR

3rd FLOOR

UNIT B - 2 and 3 BEDROOM

4th FLOOR

RAT TRAP.

When you have to live in one as a kid, you learn a lot. About killing. And about violence. Not that you ever get used to sleeping in the same room with rats. America, the beautiful. Our America. The crisis isn't in our cities; the crisis is in our hearts. With a change of heart, we can change the picture. AIA/American Institute of Architects

Send this page to your Congressman and ask him to support decent housing for our poor.

HOUSING AND URBAN GROWTH

RAYMOND L. GINDROZ

Each month American weekly news magazines announce a new national crisis – Vietnam, youth, drugs, the generation gap, the environment. The crisis for May 1970 magazines was the housing crisis. Figures were quoted to demonstrate that while US housing need has drastically increased the capacity to provide housing has not. In fact, labour problems, difficulty in financing, and bureaucratic complexities have made it increasingly difficult to build any housing at all, but most especially low-cost housing.

Not mentioned in articles on the 'housing crisis' (but heavily covered a few issues earlier when 'our environment' was the crisis-of-the-month) is the waste resulting from uncoordinated urban growth. The fact that the two problems were not related in the news magazines is typical of the problem. Instead of being the key element in a coordinated programme of urban growth, housing is viewed as a commodity, as accomodation, and independent from other problems.

The housing industry in the US generally functions independently from other organizations involved in urban growth, and responds to its own market analyses. Realtors and developers respond to large-scale changes in urban growth such as the construction of new highways and interchanges, but there is little comprehensive communication between the housing industry and planning agencies, zoning boards, or other potential vehicles for coordination. As a result home-builders in the US, most of whom are small contractors, tend to construct in a climate of opportunism, when land and money become available at the right price, and where there are fewest controls and constraints to complicate the building process or raise costs.

This is as true of the inner city as it is of the suburbs. In the suburbs new subdivisions are frequently built far removed from public transport, schools, and other amenities. In the inner city, where new housing is desperately needed to replace slums, developers and contractors generally insist on similar opportunities. Large inner city projects are usually considered impossible until sufficiently big areas have been totally cleared and populations are dispersed. In both cases there is little or no understanding that housing is more than accommodation: it is city-building.

In recent years there have been a few somewhat isolated attempts, in the private sector and in various levels of government, to face the challenge of providing low-cost housing and of coordinating housing with other types of development. Four such attempts will be discussed in this article:

Co-op City, in New York, the world's largest housing project, successfully provides housing at extremely low cost. It was developed as a co-operative, which not only makes it possible to lower the consumer's cost, but also gives him a sense of ownership. As a result the project's 15,382 units were sold out years before the construction of the project was scheduled to be complete. It is being built at the extreme outer edge of the city, beyond the reach of existing infra-structures of services, transportation, and development. In the absence of a comprehensive framework for metropolitan expansion, Co-op City has been forced to become a semi-independent city-within-a-city, relying on conventional building and environmental forms rather than developing new forms in dialogue with New York's comprehensive development.

Operation Breakthrough is an attempt on the part of the US Government to develop co-operation between government and private industry to solve the housing problem. Unfortunately, the primary emphasis of this programme is focused on the technological problems of mass industrialized building rather than on establishing the rôle of housing as a key element in coordinated urban growth and evolution, particularly of the inner city.

Morrisania South is a proposal for the Morrisania

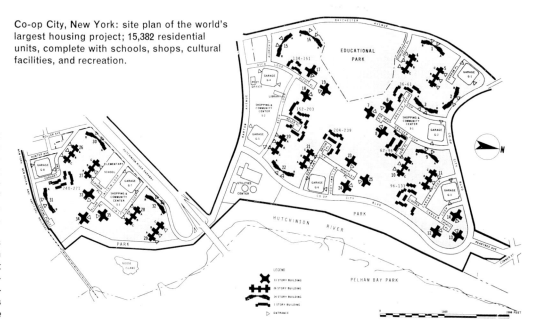

Co-op City, New York: site plan of the world's largest housing project; 15,382 residential units, complete with schools, shops, cultural facilities, and recreation.

section of the Bronx district of New York. It provides 1,000 units of public housing coordinated with commercial uses and community facilities. Part of a comprehensive planning study which identifies a series of opportunities for building housing, it uses innovative technologies in such a way that new housing construction serves to eliminate major land use and traffic conflicts. The proposal is a response to the need for housing, and also to the serious urban problems of that area. It is tragic that this scheme lacks the support of a development organization such as Co-op City has, and is dependent upon the cumbersome, contradictory, and self-defeating bureaucracy of New York City government for its realization.

Local community groups as developers have recently begun to emerge, and today they promise to become an important new direction in providing low-cost housing as part of urban growth. By joining forces with local banks, institutions and industries, community groups are working with urban planners, architects and city officials to find ways of co-ordinating public and private development. Setting themselves up as major clients for planners, architects and builders, these groups, who know the problems and aspirations of their own community better than anyone else, are attempting to ensure that the building of housing and other facilities are a direct response to their problems. One such community project, in the Sunset Park section of Brooklyn, New York, is discussed in this article.

CO-OP CITY

Perhaps the most difficult place in the United States to build housing is within the City of New York – so difficult in fact that in the past 5 years the number of new housing units completed decreased by 75%. This is in spite of the fact that the City's vacancy rate of 5% indicates the desperate need for new housing. A significant percentage of these few new housing units is concentrated in one single project. Co-op City, the world's largest housing project, is now being built at the outer edge of the city in the extreme northeast corner of the Bronx. 15,382 units with a total population of 55–60,000 people will be housed in 31 high-rise towers varying in height from 24–33 storeys, and in 236 three-storey townhouses.

The 300 acre site located in a former swamp along the Hutchinson River includes 240 acres of open space, park and recreation space, two elementary schools, one middle school, and a comprehensive high school complete with planetarium, four shopping centres, eight parking garages, housing a total of 10,850 cars, its own power plant, and numerous community facilities. It is a larger community than most American towns and small cities.

Although it satisfied the intention of its builders to provide middle-class housing within the City limits,

Opposite This aerial view of Co-op City, New York, from the north, shows clearly how this huge housing co-operative is built as a self-sufficient island, a city within the city (*Photo: Thomas Airviews*)

Below Built on reclaimed marshland, Co-op City appears from the outside to be a series of sterile institutional towers, but for its 40,000 inhabitants it is a secluded self-contained world, happy in its introversion away from the harsh problems of the big city.

it is in fact a development far removed from urban New York City. Since there is no subway line near Co-op City, the trip to Manhattan requires a transfer from bus to subway and takes a minimum of one hour and fifteen minutes. When Co-op City was under construction, there were solemn predictions by both the architectural press and the American Institute of Architects that this isolation from the City coupled with the impersonal scale of its architecture would produce an unlivable environment with severely negative social and psychological consequences for its residents.

By the summer of 1970 with 20 of the 35 towers occupied, all the units for the total development had been sold and the waiting list for 1 and 2-bedroom units numbered 3,000. A great many of the people now living in Co-op City work in midtown Manhattan and willingly endure the long commute in order to live there. The response of most residents to the quality of life in Co-op City is extremely positive. In spite of the opinions of the architectural profession, it is clearly an enormous success. In order to understand that success, we must both look at what it offers the residents and at the way in which it was built.

A Sense of Ownership

Co-op City is a co-operative. Every resident buys equity in the co-operative and becomes a 'co-operator'. He pays $450.00 or £188 per room, which means a 6-room apartment would cost $2,700 or £1,125 to buy. When he moves out, he sells his unit back to the co-operative. In effect then, he owns his unit for an extremely low price. Although he signs an agreement with the co-operative which is in many ways similar to a lease agreement between tenant and landlord in a rental situation, the co-operator as part-owner is no longer at the mercy of an exploiting landlord.

To the inner city resident this is extremely appealing. New York has a terrible problem with absentee landlords who, because of rent control policies, cannot afford to maintain their buildings properly. And because of absenteeism, tenants are unable to contact the landlords to register complaints or to request repairs and maintenance. The tenant feels that he has no control over his housing unit and can in no way influence the owner. In Co-op City there is a large full-time staff for repairs and maintenance, under the administration of the co-operative.

Because all profit from the development is turned back into the co-operative for the benefit of the community, each co-operator has a voice not only in the management of his own housing unit, but also in the destiny of his community. As a result there is a remarkable sense of community identity in Co-op City, in spite of its enormous scale and impersonal architecture.

The elimination of a developer's profit, together with the remarkable skill of Co-op City's development team, have produced housing at an amazingly low price. The monthly payment to the co-operative for maintenance payments and mortgage payments is approximately $30.00 or £12.10 per room. For a 6-room apartment the co-operator pays $180.00 or £75 per month, which is less than half the monthly rent for a comparable unit anywhere else in the City. In fact, Co-op City offers the only available new, low-cost middle-income housing in New York City. In a market where people are desperate for housing, it is immediately sold out.

How Co-op City was Built

Even more impressive than its commercial success is the fact that Co-op City was built at all at this time in New York City and that it has been built so quickly. It began in 1964 when the United Housing Federation, an organization that has built many housing co-operatives in New York City since the 1930s, first went to the State of New York with the idea. The proposal to the State was to provide 15,000 units of housing in a co-operative development with a rent in the range of $23.00 per month per room. The State Housing Finance Agency through its Mitchellama Program is empowered to provide guaranteed construction loans for up to 90% of construction cost at a tax-free borrowing rate. Because of UHF's past experience and because of the size of the project the State tentatively agreed to endorse the programme.

The next step was for the United Housing Foundation to acquire the property and to obtain both zoning approval and an agreement for tax abatement from the City. After much difficulty and rapid reworking of site plans both zoning approval and the tax abatement were granted. At that point with their 6 months option on the property almost gone, the UHF did not have any capital to supply the 10% of the land cost as equity in order to obtain the site. Gambling on their ability to raise the money quickly, the directors of UHF committed themselves to buy the land.

The land cost was approximately $15,000,000. The required cash equity was therefore $1.5 million. The United Housihg Foundation hurriedly announced the project and began to accept applications for new housing units. There was some advertising, but for the most part, news of the project circulated by word of mouth. The United Housing Foundation has a wide-spread reputation for being able to produce housing and, in fact, had a waiting list of applicants for other projects. In a few short months 4,000 people had filed applications each with a deposit of $500.00. This total of $2,000,000 was more than enough for the developer's equity, and the land was acquired with the 90% loan from the State Housing Finance Agency. The programme then received approval from the State and the City. At that point the Riverbay Corporation, a subsidiary of the UHF organized specifically to develop Co-op City, was able to accept the full payment from the people who wanted to buy housing units in Co-op City. The total of all the individual equity payments became the developer's cash equity in the project. The State supplied the other 90% with a 40 year loan at $5\frac{1}{2}$% interest. The total of all the monthly payments contributed by each resident is used to pay off this mortgage.

In effect, the developer, without major capital investment of his own, served as the administrator for 15,000 families to acquire popularly desirable and new housing units at a price far lower than they would be able to get as individuals in New York City.

This very simple formula becomes an inevitably complex and daring venture at the scale of Co-op City. In order to be successful, 15,000 people had to invest an average of $2,000 (£800) long before construction began. Only an organization like the United Housing Foundation, which has a well established reputation for building successful housing co-operatives, could have the confidence of so many people. This reputation is for housing developments which offer more than just accommodation. The co-operatives have come to represent a kind of community self-determination and social organization which has evolved in a very dynamic way over the past 40 years.

The Co-op Movement in Housing

This housing movement began in the 1920s with the Amalgamated Garment Worker's Union establishing a co-operative to build a few units of housing on the Lower East Side. As time went on numerous other projects were developed and co-op services expanded to include commercial, recreational, and community facilities.

In 1951 the United Housing Foundation was organized by existing consumer co-operatives to act as a continuing organization offering assistance and guidance for the construction of housing co-operatives. An affiliated organization, Community Services Inc., acts as general contractor and builder. For each co-operative development, a separate corporation is organized. In the case of Co-op City, it is the Riverbay

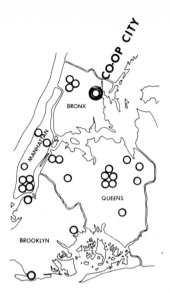

Above The enormous number of housing units provided by co-operatives in New York City is generally unappreciated. This map shows United Housing Foundation member co-operatives.

Corporation which has primary responsibility for planning, administration, and management. Initially its Board of Directors is composed of prominent people in the City interested in housing and members of the UHF. As Co-op City is occupied, residents elect representatives to the Board of Directors. The co-operative eventually becomes an independent, self-governing community. The UHF's role is to initiate, sponsor, and provide general direction until the co-operative is established. After that point, the co-operative decides what the UHF role will be.

Although this basic formula has been the same for all the co-operatives developed by UHF, it has evolved and developed to accommodate many communities of widely different size, scale, type, and location. Since it is a flexible programme, and the UHF itself is adaptable to new institutions, it has become a dynamic and effective catalyst for building new communities rather than a dead formula for building housing projects.

Co-op Urban Design

The first housing co-operatives were established to provide an alternative to the oppressive life of New

220

221

Below The upper photograph shows 1930 co-operatives on Grand Street in Manhattan; the lower photograph shows the Warbasse co-operatives in Brooklyn. *Right* The East River Co-operative as seen from the East River.

York's slums. The people who built them were reacting against the crowded 5–6 storey walk-up tenements which had inadequate ventilation, light, plumbing, or privacy. There were no recreation facilities, no public open spaces except the hot asphalt streets. In these neighbourhoods there was no relief in the dense pattern of block after block of walk-up tenements.

The co-operatives offered a dramatically different environment. It is one which resembles Le Corbusier's visions of a *Ville Radieuse* more closely than it does the old streets of New York. Elevator high-rise towers set in a landscaped park provided for the first time fresh air, light, and green space to every resident. They represented a release from the oppression of inner city life. In addition to eliminating many of the evils of the overcrowded, old urban environment, these complexes offer very tangible, visible amenities, such as open space with grass and trees, playgrounds, recreation areas, and parking.

However, where this same urban form of high-rise towers set in an open park has been used for public housing and other non co-op housing developments, it usually results in a barren and hostile project. Rarely does this form generate the kind of communities which the co-ops are. It is clearly the co-operative's organizational and community structure which has made these communities successful, and not the architectural environment.

Over the years this environmental form has developed and evolved in response to the reactions of people living in the co-operatives and to the constraints

222

Above Garment workers' union co-operatives (photo: Burton Berinsky) and the Rochdale Village co-operative, New York City, from the air.

Right Inside Co-op city.

imposed by changing governmental regulations. For the most part, these changes have been minor ones related to matters of detail. For example, the complaints of people living on the ground floor about noise and fear of street crime resulted in eliminating ground floor units. The basic *Ville Radieuse*-like form has not changed. Even the design of the towers themselves has not substantially changed. Whether the projects are built in the middle of a dense urban community or out in the undeveloped fringe of the city, the form is the same.

In view of the constraints imposed on the project by the need to appeal to a mass market; the lack of effective co-ordination between planning agencies in New York; and the lack of interest in the problems of low-cost mass housing on the part of the architectural profession, this unchanging and rigid physical

design formula is not surprising. It is however in striking contrast to the very flexible, ever-changing *organizational* policies of the UHF which respond sensitively to new situations.

Co-op City's Design Appeal

The design of Co-op City is based on the usual environmental concept. Its tall towers stand in a large landscaped park. The result is an environment which seems, when seen at a distance from the expressway, to be overwhelmingly over-scaled and barren. What is most striking about walking around Co-op City, however, is that there is nothing overwhelming about it. It is quite an ordinary environment. Because of the landscaping and the openness of the towers' ground floor, the large scale of the buildings is relieved. The variety of textures and materials on the building façades tend to take attention away from their hugeness and to dissolve them into a textured background for the activities and facilities which take place between them.

The principal focal points of the design are a series of very visible amenities and facilities. All of these amenities are ones which are not provided in most inner city neighbourhoods in New York. They include:

over 200 acres of continuous traffic-free open space;
tennis courts, basketball courts, gigantic sand boxes for young children, and other recreation facilities;
parking spaces for £17.00/month in 8 clearly visible, separate parking garages;
co-operatively-owned commercial facilities housed in bright new shopping-centre buildings;
spacious and well-built housing units, with large areas of glass and full air-conditioning;

the first Education Park in New York City. Instead of relying on the very slow School Board to build the project, Co-op City has built the buildings to turn over to the School Board upon completion. The campus includes two primary schools, one middle school and a comprehensive high school complete with theatres, art studios, a planetarium and large recreation areas. This means that brand

new schools will become ready at the same time as the residential occupation of Co-op City. This Education Park is a separate, easily identifiable complex;

the power plant which provides central air-conditioning and emergency power in case of another east coast blackout and is Co-op City's most monumental structure and a source of great pride.

It is almost as if the architecture makes a set of symbols which represent what the inner city *does not have.* To the resident of the teeming overcrowded Bronx, with overcrowded vandalized schools, no parking, no recreation space, and rundown dilapidated apartment buildings – the appeal of Co-op City's design is obvious and immediate.

The lingering question is, however, whether a new city made up of built symbols of what the old city lacks, will ever function as a city, or as an effective part of the city. Will the less visible but important qualities of the old city such as the close relationship of a wide variety of different activities, convenient transportation, and the vitality of street life, be lost? Will there be the most important quality of urban life – a wide variety of options for every resident?

Social Consequences

Whether or not Co-op City is a sufficiently rich environment to provide a maximum number of options for its residents and whether its effect both psychologically and socially on residents is positive, will, of course, only be known after many years.

The developers and administrators of Co-op City hotly deny the frequently-made charges that the barrenness and lack of scale of the high-rise towers will cause social alienation. They claim that bricks and mortar do not cause alienation, but that the social structure of a community does. They further claim that the nature of the co-operative system stimulates a new sense of openness and community identity. As a result, Co-op City offers a much more open and free environment than does the old city.

A basic goal of the UHF is to build communities rather than housing projects, in order to provide a well-balanced and active living environment. To accomplish this a concerted effort was made to appeal to a wide range of people. Median family incomes range from $3,000 or £1,200 year to $20.000 or £8,330 year. The ratio of non-white is about 20%. UHF had some difficulty in attracting a full range of age groups and family types. The opportunity to escape the ills of the central city appealed most to the elderly people; and there is now a 3,000-person waiting list for the one and two-bedroom units which reflects this appeal. To overcome this problem, advertising has been aimed at younger families with children; particular emphasis has been placed on the safe play areas and the Education Park.

The UHF administrators claim that in Co-op City the many different classes, races, and age-groups of people can associate with each other much more easily than they could in the old city. Since from the outside the identity of each housing unit is de-

emphasized, visible signs of social class and wealth are not evident. The dominant social as well as visual elements are not the individual units, but the foci of community activity and identity–the shopping/community centre, the play areas, the schools, etc. Major social activities take place on the ground. The lack of streets and traffic creates an openness which makes it possible to get easily to various activity programmes and to come in contact with many more people than in the old city. There are a great many programmed activities, all of which have a remarkable following. The evolution of the co-operative into a self-governing community is a vital and exciting process which actively involves a great many people. In addition, there are over 150 social organizations related to a wide range of specific interests such as fishing, music, ecology, black power, etc. A social director and staff is employed by the co-operative to co-ordinate all these activities.

Most of these social activities are programmed ones, more like the kinds of social activity on a ship or in a resort than in a city. Whether the spontaneous activity, interaction, social options, and vitality of city life will take place in Co-op City remains to be seen. Certainly a walk through the shopping/community centre on an autumn afternoon, offers many hopeful indications of vitality. Crowds of people of all ages were out walking, talking, playing, shopping, fighting, and enjoying the activity of the place.

How Residents Feel About Co-op City

Some insight into the attitudes residents have about Co-op City, what they like and dislike about it, and the type of social life that takes place there can be gained from reading its newspaper.

Each week a new issue of the *Co-op City Times* is delivered to each resident. In it are many articles of concern, such as progress of construction, problems with the City administration, investment of monthly payments, etc. Co-op City's many activity groups and community organizations advertise and publish articles describing their programmes. There are also a series of articles about residents of Co-op City with their opinions of life in Co-op City as well as on specific issues.

The following are reprints of selected articles from the *Co-op City Times* which may help to provide some understanding of Co-op City's appeal, its people, and their life there, as well as some of its problems: Co-op City is being built in stages with a new apartment tower being completed and occupied every month or two. The opening of each new tower is a major event and is covered by the *Times*.

Co-op City Times

Co-op City's official
publication/serving
15,382 member families
in the world's largest
cooperative community.

Volume 4, No. 8   November 22, 1969

WELCOME BUILDING NINE

First Happy People Move into Bldg. 9

The first couple to move into Building 9 when it opened on Wednesday, November 18, were Mr. and Mrs. Jack Barshop, who had been living in Hewlitt, Long Island.

They arrived at the administrative office shortly after 8 a.m. and patiently waited until 9 a.m. to receive their keys saying, "After waiting so long, what's another hour? We had been impatient to get here and now we are all around happy to be here. Even before moving in we like it."

The reason they like it is because they feel right at home. They have many friends who living here already, more who are coming and have spent every weekend here. On move-in day they had at least ten invitations to dinner, which they did not accept, but said one of their friends as soon as possible.

Mr. Barshop, a retired foreman carpenter said, "There will be no complaints from me. I know there are always things to be adjusted when buildings are mass produced. It takes time, in every trade, to iron

out and instead of calling the service department, I will fix things myself."

They are looking forward to visits from their son and daughter and a granddaughter who will be married soon.

The second couple to arrive were Mr. and Mrs. Isaac Weinberg, who moved from Grand Avenue. They said they were very optimistic and expect to be very happy here.

Mr. and Mrs. Irwin Rothholz and their three children moved into 9B - 23F, a three bedroom apartment. Mr. Rothholz, who is president of the executive board of Sedgewick Houses, said, "You have no idea how happy we are to be here. We hated to leave our old friends but we were very overcrowded and the neighborhood is starting to change. We will probably have all the executive board members of Sedgewick here eventually."

Things do not always go smoothly when dealing with 15,000 housing units. The buildings have not been built in the same order as they are numbered. For instance Building 6 was not ready as soon as Building 9 was. This letter indicates a kind of depersonalization resulting from the project's size, but it also demonstrates how people respond to the problem.

Disapointment Doesn't Dampen His Humor

By coincidence, two families with the same last name have somewhat similiar addresses. One family is scheduled to move into Building 9, the other into Building 6.

The move in notice intended for the Building 9 family was delivered to the Building 6 family.

It was returned to us with the following letter, written by a man who was able to smile through his tears.

Dear Whoever:

This was delivered to me by mistake (unfortunately). The Goldberg this was intended for has moved to Queens.

My address is ––– so that is why it was probably delivered to me in error.

Please forward it as soon as you can. I know how these people are waiting with baited breath for their notice.

We are going into Building 6, God and the "high speed" elevators willing. So who cares if the elevator runs slow to the 22nd floor as long as I'm in there and out of this horrible neighborhood.

I'll tell you what ––––– you let me move in to 22K in Building 6 and I'll use the elevator to 18 and consider it a 4th floor walkup.

Help!
Jerry Goldberg

On the first anniversary of the opening of Co-op City, Don Phillips, the Director of Social Activities, looked back to the first days of Co-op City and to the community spirit which developed. At least in the first few days it seems the statements that this was an inhuman environment which would cause social alienation were not well founded.

December 10th Marks Our First Birthday

By Don Phillips

It was a very cold day on Tuesday, December 10, 1968. Sand and snow carried by a strong Nor'easter funnelled through the portico of Building One, stinging faces. Movers leaned against the bitter cold wind, sometimes being pulled backward by pressures on mattresses which became more like sails. Considering the wind factor, the temperature stood at near zero degrees.

It was a terrible day just to perform normal tasks, but consider the problem of moving. Sixteen families did! And so did scores of other families, on similar days, as New York

munity began to rally to the need. Old and young gave unselfishly -- food, time, money. And before the snow ceased more than 300 strangers were fed and housed. Some lives

shivered through the worst winter in many years.

On that first day -- one year ago -- hot coffee tasted good in the administration office. Those who worked there managed to keep warm in their coats and boots, since work in the office had not been completed. Not even the heaters. We were a determined lot -- setting a precedent -- as the world's largest cooperative community became a home for families who had waited so long for a new apartment.

It wasn't long before "community life" began The weather, the common problems -- everything worked toward bringing new cooperators together. Before furniture stood in place, before unpacking was finished, people, once strangers, sat together around tables drinking coffee and getting acquainted. Almost every evening lights burned in the administration office as children, teens, young adults, and older folk began laying plans for cooperative community life.

The "big" affair came the night of February 8th. Those who had shared their move-in hardships watched the traffic on the New England Thruway grind to a halt as snow piled up. Co-op City youth brought the first storm victims from the highway and the new com-

were saved.

One cannot pass this first anniversary without reflecting on what's happened to the "pioneers." There have been moments of tragedy, joy, disappointment, and fulfillment. All these have contributed greatly to Co-op City's future. From the early buildings have come the largest number of community leaders. Leadership in our Day Camp, Nursery School, play groups, teens, handicapped, schools, Mr. and Mrs. Club, young adults, Scouts, and many other groups have formed through these pioneers. The foundation of our community is laid in the determination and mutual efforts of cooperators who faced the Nor'easters of the first winter. They braved the sand and snow, they worshipped and held parties, sang and danced, fed stranded victims, spent countless hours fashioning community programs, and have not slackened in their hope and aspirations.

On this anniversary month we salute and pay special tribute to both the early cooperators and to the scores of staff who have continued to run the power house, clean our halls, bring our mail, develop our landscaping, maintain our facilities, and to assist our efforts in becoming what we hope to be.

Each week in the *Times* a biography of a Co-op City resident appears with statements about Co-op City.

Alex and Ida Levin have one of the most beautiful apartments in Co-op City. Exquisitely decorated, Alex says of it, "My wife and I did it together. We do everything together and all that we dreamed of when we filled out the application has come true."

They had owned their own home in Sheepshead Bay and their neighbors were all professional people. "I'm a plain man," Alex said, "and I felt sick and lonely. No one spoke to me except to say "Good morning" or "Good evening" and I had no friends there.

"Then I had a heart attack and had to retire from tailoring. I couldn't work around the house anymore, doing repairs, up and down stairs, shoveling snow and everything else a house entails, so we decided to sell the house and move to Co-op City."

The literature he had read about Co-op City appealed to Alex and he pictured a friendly community with plenty of activities to fill his retirement years. A naturally friendly, gregarious man, he

has found his niche as president of the Senior Citizens, the largest, fastest growing club in Co-op City.

"Now," he said, "I am surrounded by so many friends every day is a holiday to me. I became involved a week after I moved here last March. Don Philips had called a meeting for senior citizens and I went just out of curiosity. He asked for a volunteer to organize a bus ride to Lakewood, N.J. and I offered to do it provided I had a secretary to help and Lillian Isaacs volunteered."

From this initial meeting and the successful bus ride, the Senior Citizens Club evolved and was formalized. Alex was elected president and has an executive board consisting of V.P. Sylvania Avent, Secretary Bertha Lorber, Treasurer Sol Nettboy and Chairlady of bus rides and outings Pauline Chessler. The club now has more than 300 members and plans are complete for their third bus trip on October 23rd.

If, as Alex says, everyday is a holiday for him now, life was not always such.

He was born in Poland and when he was ten years old his father apprenticed him to a tailor to learn the trade. For the first two years his father paid the master for Alex's training and Alex says that in addition to learning he had to act as "maid" to the family, doing housework, carrying water, baby sitting and doing everything he was ordered to do.

The third year his father no longer had to pay, and Alex worked just for meals. "That was the worst thing to happen to me," he said. "The food stuck in my throat and even though I lived at home I still had to go there on Saturday and Sunday for my meals, because my family was poor, and my pride was hurt."

Then World War I broke out and his family had to flee the town they lived in and all during the war years they were hounded from place to place. In 1919, after the war ended, they returned to their home town and Alex started working to help support his family.

He came here in 1923 and he and Ida were married on Thanksgiving Day in 1926. They had two sons, Robert who now lives in Poughkeepsie with his wife Janice, and two children, Shari and Bruce, and Herbert who is a Bachelor.

An active member of the ILGWU, one of the pioneering organizations in the cooperative housing field, Alex remembers the bitter years of struggle in the union. A five month general strike in 1926 left the union split into two factions the lefts and the rights, as Alex calls them, and the lefts got control.

Things were bad until 1932 when President Roosevelt was elected and started the NRA. David Dubinsky was elected president of the union and succeeded in overthrowing the leftists and obtained the best union contract ever, one which established the 35 hour working week.

"During those years of struggle I regret that I neglected my family," Alex said. "Many families split up but I had an understanding wife. She never stood in my way even though I was so involved with the union that I was seldom home.

"I never made an easy penny and the only things I had going for me were ten fingers and a wonderful wife. She's a lovely women," he added simply.

Now in his new home and social life Alex is gloriously happy. "Please," he said, "at the end, tell everyone that I wish my family and friends and all here should be healthy and enjoy life for many years to come."

The Failure of Co-op City

The failure of Co-op City lies not so much in its design as in the lack of co-operation between the planning agencies of the City of New York and the developers

of Co-op City. The major impact of the Planning Commission has been to block innovations rather than stimulate them.

As a result Co-op City, the largest single construction effort in the US, is an end in itself. It does not fit into the urban structure of New York City in such a way that an orderly sequence of future developments and expansions can take place. It is a separate island and does nothing more for the city than provide housing. At this point in New York's history, that in itself is a great achievement. It seems wasteful, however, that instead of becoming a part of a larger city with all its amenities and vitality it must synthetically create its own urban environment, and derive its major form determinants from the need to appeal to a mass market. The concept of building new housing in such a location so that it will stimulate large-scale social change is not new to the developers of Co-op City. They have in the past built many projects in the centre of the city. Some of these have achieved major social objectives beyond that of providing housing. For example, Rochdale Village in Queens is built on the site of an abandoned race track in the centre of an all-black community. Rochdale Village, a co-op development, brought in thousands of white families. It also provided three new schools, serving not only Rochdale Village, but also the surrounding black community. The resulting integrated school system had a ratio 50% black, 50% white. Thus the development of Rochdale Village served as a catalyst for integration and for the construction of new facilities which serve the existing community.

Unfortunately, the City School Board has enforced a 'busing program' on Rochdale Village which sends white students into black ghetto areas. This was done in Rochdale Village in spite of the existing integrated local situation. As a result, the white population is moving out of Rochdale Village because of the low quality of education in ghetto schools. The effect of the School Board's policy of large-scale integration has been to destroy a successful experiment in local integration.

In Rochdale Village as in Co-op City, however, the project was developed as a separate one rather than as part of a coordinated programme of growth for the metropolitan area. This lack of coordination makes it less surprising that the larger social goals of the project were defeated by the planning of an indifferent agency of city government. The physical form of Rochdale Village is the same as other co-op developments. It is a generalized solution to high-density housing rather than a specific response to Rochdale Village's location.

What problems Co-op City will have are not yet known. Now that it is partly built, its administrators are very concerned with the way in which it relates politically and socially to the rest of the Bronx. They see it as a city-within-a-city rather than an independent city and are working very hard to bring about co-ordination and interaction between Co-op City and the metropolitan area. They are attempting to maximize the catalytic effect of the influx of 15,000 families to that location. For example, they are attempting to get a subway extension to Co-op City which will serve more than Co-op City, and they are hoping to get students from outside Co-op City into the Education Park which they are building. In effect then, Co-op City, an isolated construction effort, is forced to respond to the need for comprehensive planning in a piecemeal way in order to ensure its own survival. If it fails on these terms, the fault will be not with Co-op City's developers, but with the planning and governmental agencies of New York City who have no workable programme for metropolitan expansion.

The Housing Industry and the Design Professions

In addition to the separation between the developer and the planning agencies, there is a huge gulf and bitterness between large-scale developers and the design professions. Co-op City administrators have repeatedly said that they like 'good' design, but cannot afford it. Good design seems to mean pretty façades and fancy detailing. They tell with relish of an encounter with an architect who is known all over the world as a good designer. When his design was criticized because of poor unit plans, his reply was to turn over responsibility for the design of the interior to another architect. All he cared about was the façade.

In order to overcome some of the objections which the Planning Commission had raised about the design of Co-op City, the developers and their architect chose to provide a variety of building types all within the same basic vocabulary of tall towers in a park. The variations increased construction cost since the alternate building types are more expensive than the basic tri-core building which they were accustomed to using. There is little change in the quality of environment as a result of this 'fanciness', but the same expense spent in developing new relationships between the towers and ground floor uses could certainly have provided a more diversified and rich environment. Because of the very tight schedules for design and construction, and because of the need to provide a known marketable commodity, it was deemed necessary by the developer to rely on the

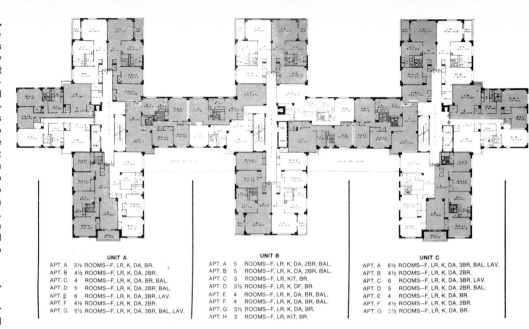

UNIT A		
APT. A	3½	ROOMS—F, LR, K, DA, BR.
APT. B	4½	ROOMS—F, LR, K, DA, 2BR.
APT. C	4	ROOMS—F, LR, K, DA, BR, BAL.
APT. D	5	ROOMS—F, LR, K, DA, 2BR, BAL.
APT. E	6	ROOMS—F, LR, K, DA, 3BR, LAV.
APT. F	4½	ROOMS—F, LR, K, DA, 2BR.
APT. G	6½	ROOMS—F, LR, K, DA, 3BR, BAL, LAV.

UNIT B		
APT. A	5	ROOMS—F, LR, K, DA, 2BR, BAL.
APT. B	5	ROOMS—F, LR, K, DA, 2BR, BAL.
APT. C	3	ROOMS—F, LR, KIT, BR.
APT. D	3½	ROOMS—F, LR, K, DF, BR.
APT. E	4	ROOMS—F, LR, K, DA, BR, BAL.
APT. F	4	ROOMS—F, LR, K, DA, BR, BAL.
APT. G	3½	ROOMS—F, LR, K, DA, BR.
APT. H	3	ROOMS—F, LR, KIT, BR.

UNIT C		
APT. A	6½	ROOMS—F, LR, K, DA, 3BR, BAL, LAV.
APT. B	4½	ROOMS—F, LR, K, DA, 2BR.
APT. C	6	ROOMS—F, LR, K, DA, 3BR, LAV.
APT. D	5	ROOMS—F, LR, K, DA, 2BR, BAL.
APT. E	4	ROOMS—F, LR, K, DA, BR.
APT. F	4½	ROOMS—F, LR, K, DA, 2BR.
APT. G	3½	ROOMS—F, LR, K, DA, BR.

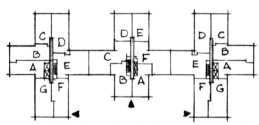

Above and left Typical plans of triple core building.

same building forms they had been using since the 1930s. They felt the need to use the same forms which had been successful in the past rather than generate environmental forms in response to Co-op City's rôle as a semi-independent city-within-the-city. In the absence of either a comprehensive framework for New York's metropolitan expansion, or the time and capacity to generate new forms, the developers had no choice but to use traditional housing project forms in an attempt to create an urban environment.

It is unfortunate that so brilliant an entrepreneurial effort and social experiment should result in a mediocre environment far removed from an ailing city crying out for new development and regeneration. It is

226

clear, however, that no better environment can be produced unless we have a more effective collaboration between planning authorities and builders, and unless the design professions become more involved in the technological, political, social and marketing problems of mass housing.

OPERATION BREAKTHROUGH

In response to this very problem, the major effort of the Nixon administration to deal with the housing crisis is an attempt to establish a collaboration between private industry and Federal government in order to bring the housing industry up to the level of efficiency of industries like the automobile industry. The major thrust of this programme is Operation Breakthrough. Towards the end of 1969 private corporations were invited to submit proposals to the Federal government for developing housing with mass-produced systems. The Government agreed to help overcome zoning and code problems while the developer was expected to find increasingly efficient methods of mechanized housing production. When the proposals came in, most of them were for prefabricated trailer-like boxes —the emphasis being on industrialized techniques. The equally critical problem of how housing construction can become a catalyst and key element in a co-ordinated programme of urban growth was a side issue.

The response of the Aluminum Company of America (ALCOA) to the Operation Breakthrough programme was singularly different. ALCOA assumed that enough systems are already on the market. The question was not to invent yet another system but how to use those which already exist. ALCOA therefore proposed a kind of grab-bag of building systems; they did not want to impose a single system on all of the situations which required housing construction, but rather wanted to develop a repertoire of systems which could then be adapted to local and specific situations.

Urban Design Associates, consultants to ALCOA, developed a series of prototype sites in a high-density but decayed and troubled urban community in order to demonstrate how ALCOA's building systems could be used to provide not only housing, but also to resolve urban problems.

Pittsburgh's Lower Northside is an inner city neighbourhood directly across the Allegheny River from the Central Business District. Sites were selected on the basis of their availability and their suitability to respond to the acute problems of the area. In an historic conservation area with spot clearance, a system of low-rise apartments consisting of building elements at a similar and responsive scale to the existing old houses was used to create a series of pedestrian urban spaces and parks and to provide a dynamic focus for an area which currently has none.

Below The U.S. is today following Europe's lead in looking to industrialized modular systems to solve the problems of the national housing shortage through mass-production. In the process the local and unique nature of the city is lost. In response to this situation, the Aluminum Company of America (ALCOA) selected a high-density section of the inner city of Pittsburgh to demonstrate how housing systems can respond sensitively to unique social, political, and physical configurations without massive clearance of the old city. *Below left* is the site plan for Pittsburgh's Northside; *below* is the site plan and sketch perspective of Christian Frey's suspended truss system applied to a hillside and the elevation of townhouses and apartments by John Holten of the Perkins and Will Partnership.

227

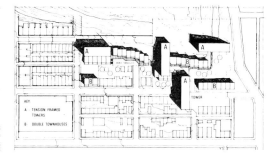

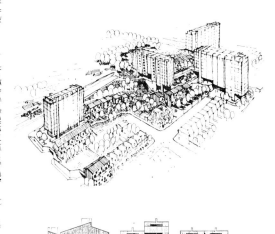

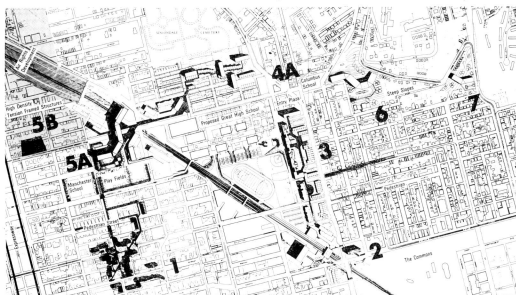

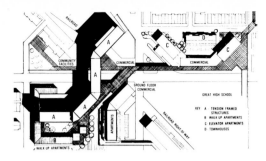

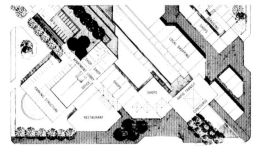

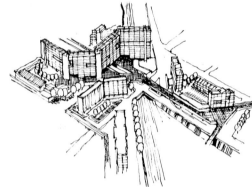

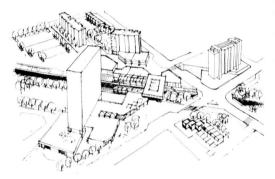

in the heart of existing communities. They are being deliberately designed as islands, independent from the communities in which they are located. As a result, the prototype sites can in no way demonstrate how building systems can be used to transform housing construction into city-building.

MORRISANIA

An example similar to ALCOA's Operation Breakthrough proposal, but which was done independently, is a project for the neglected Morrisania section of the Bronx. The Bronx office of the New York City Planning Commission commissioned Weiner & Gran to do a planning study to identify areas for redevelopment and to develop a phased programme of renewal. The result is a long-range scheme which attempts to remove major causes of decay by replacing incompatible land uses or poorly used land with new housing and community facilities. It was also considered important to minimize relocation by building first-phase projects where there was no housing.

A major wound in the community is the main line of

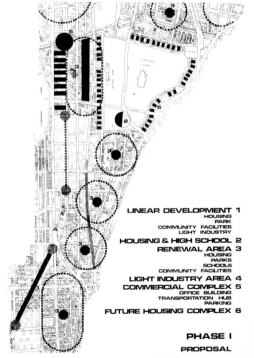

LINEAR DEVELOPMENT 1
HOUSING
PARK
COMMUNITY FACILITIES
LIGHT INDUSTRY
HOUSING & HIGH SCHOOL 2
RENEWAL AREA 3
HOUSING
PARKS
SCHOOLS
COMMUNITY FACILITIES
LIGHT INDUSTRY AREA 4
COMMERCIAL COMPLEX 5
OFFICE BUILDING
TRANSPORTATION HUB
PARKING
FUTURE HOUSING COMPLEX 6

PHASE I
PROPOSAL

Above Like many old cities, Pittsburgh's urban neighbourhoods are often traditionally separated by barriers such as railways, highways, and strip industry. ALCOA demonstrated how industrialized modular systems may span railways or highways using Christian Frey's tension framed structures for high-rise apartments, or using long-span truss systems for a combined concourse and commercial bridge.

This insertion of new construction would do more than just provide housing: it provides an identity for the community which can stimulate other development including rehabilitation of the old historic houses.

Another sustem in ALCOA's proposal was Christian Frey's suspended truss structures. With this system concrete slip-form towers 200–400 feet apart support a clear-span bridge. From this bridge steel straps are hung. Prefabricated apartment units are then raised into place and are suspended from the steel straps. Because it uses steel efficiently and because of its ordered construction sequence, this is an economic

way to build high-rise structures with few foundation points, enabling air rights housing spanning across other uses such as railway lines, roads, industries, etc. In the ALCOA proposal the Frey system was used to cross railway lines which historically have been barriers isolating two urban communities from each other and from community facilities.

Thus each system in this proposal was used to provide housing which responded to the local context of each site, and which also replaced negative elements in the urban environment with positive foci for new development. In this way the new construction would serve as a catalyst for large-scale and open-ended regeneration, instead of being an end in itself as in Co-op City. How these ideas will finally be realized as Operation Breakthrough proceeds is not clear. ALCOA's proposal was one of 22 out of 560 responses to win a Government contract. But the Government has now declared a series of prototype sites on which not one but several housing producers will build prototype units. Unfortunately the sites are seen primarily as showcases for the different building systems. Because of the hordes of visitors expected to see these sites, it will be difficult to integrate them comprehensively

NORTHERN SITE

MIDDLE SITE

SOUTHERN SITE

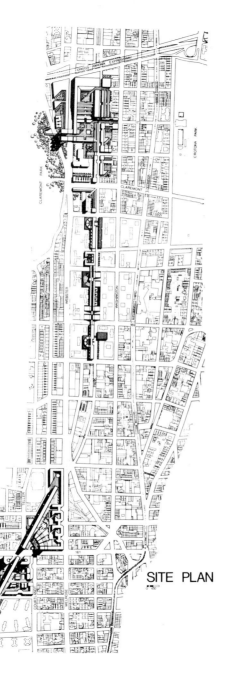

SITE PLAN

the Penn Central Railroad which rips through the middle. It creates an extremely unpleasant environment and serves to cut the community into a number of small pieces. By developing air rights housing over these railway tracks it is possible to both eliminate the most negative element in the area and provide 1,000 new housing units without any demolition of existing units.

The proposal includes a long 10-storey slab apartment to be built continuously over the railway tracks. This is to be penetrated at existing street levels by pedestrian and vehicular streets. Along it are a series of low and high-rise structures which create a variety of spaces against the long building.

This long element is intended to serve as a unifier for the fragmented and dissimilar elements in the community. Another reason for building it as one continuous element is that it guarantees the railway tracks will be completely covered for the full distance.

The problem then was to find a structural system

Left In their proposal for the Morrisania section of the Bronx in New York City, Weiner & Gran also use the air rights over railroad tracks to bridge between two neighbourhoods and to create a spine for the phased and sensitive renewal of the old city. *Below* is the southern site.

SITE PLAN

capable of building low-cost housing without any cost penalty for building over the air rights of the railway. The building system selected is called the 'staggered truss system' which uses 10-ft high, 60-ft long trusses to span between column supports on the periphery of the building. It was originally developed as an economic way of building housing. In fact, it has been considered by the architect for United Housing Foundation's most recent project. In addition to being economic, it needs no intermediate supports for its 60-ft span.

Since the railway cutting is 60-ft wide, the solution is to build the housing with the staggered truss system over the tracks at virtually no increase over the cost of building on land. The proposal includes covered parking in the construction cost as well as a $4.00 per sq. ft air rights fee. Even with those penalties, the cost is only $1.00 per sq. ft more than building public housing on normal land with conventional construction. If a new law, which would enable air rights to be used without fee, is approved, the cost of this project would be substantially less than building on land.

This project recognizes the rôle of housing construction as city building rather than merely accommodation. It responds to the major ills of an area by removing the primary cause of decay and makes it possible to stimulate the regeneration of a much larger area.

Because of the transient community in that part of Morrisania, the Bronx Planning Commission discouraged the architects from active involvement with the residents of the area. The project, one year after completion of the study, was still being considered by the bureaucratic machine of New York City. Although it is an innovative concept developed in response to both a technical innovation and to an urban problem, it is unfortunate that the project was created and proposed independently of either a development power or a local community group, and therefore has every chance of being lost in the maze of New York City bureaucracy.

LOCAL COMMUNITY GROUPS AS DEVELOPERS: SUNSET PARK, NEW YORK

A project whose very beginning was stimulated by both the concern of city government and of a local community is currently being developed in Sunset Park West, Brooklyn. In the centre of Sunset Park, a traditional Brooklyn neighbourhood with a large low-income population, is a hospital, the Lutheran Medical Centre. Because its old facility is extremely obsolete, the hospital's administration looked for new space. Across the Gowanus expressway in Sunset

230

Park West is a mixed-use area of decaying industries and housing.

Conflict Between Industries and Housing

Conflicts between industrial and residential uses, as well as inadequate industrial access, have brought about the decline and deterioration of both uses. The southern part of the industrial area has in recent years lost two major industries. One of these, American Machine & Foundry, found it so uneconomic to operate in that location that the least costly course of

Below and right This large project in the Sunset Park section of Brooklyn in New York City was catalyzed by a proposal to build a new hospital in an abandoned foundry building (the AMF) in a rundown industrial /residential area near the waterfront of New York Bay. Using the hospital as a springboard the existing community set in motion a renewal project involving over 2,000 new residential units in the action plan area alone.

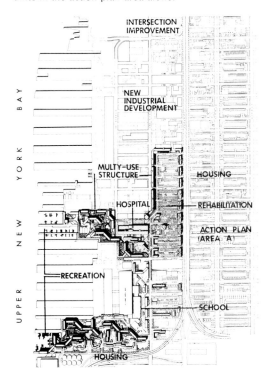

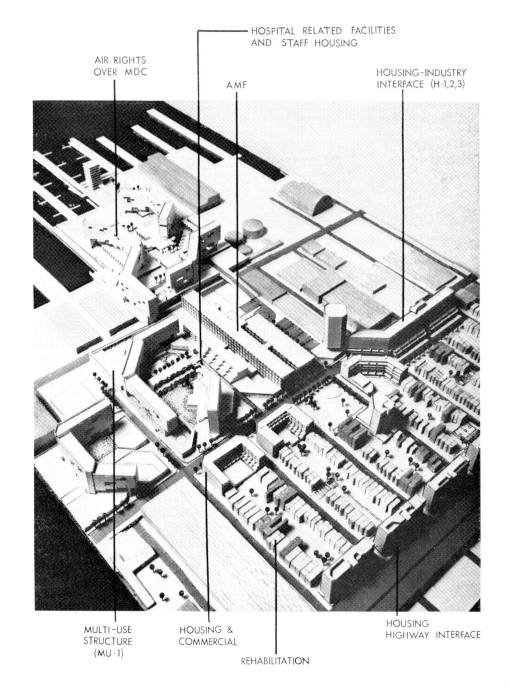

action was to give their $8 million building to the City.

The Lutheran Medical Centre approached the City with a proposal to convert the foundry building into a hospital. The main problem was not the suitability of the building itself, but how a community-based hospital could survive in an industrial wasteland.

At the same time, the City was searching for somewhere to relocate a Meat Distribution Centre. Across the street from the foundry building is another abandoned industrial site, the old Bethlehem Steel yards, which the City chose as the location for the meat market.

The community, which is largely low-income Puerto Rican, and which had enthusiastically endorsed the relocation of the Lutheran Medical Centre, was horrified with the idea of an adjacent meat market, and felt that it would destroy any new development around the hospital. They vowed to prevent the meat market from moving in even if it meant lying down in front of the bulldozers. This confrontation between the City administrators and the local community became the mainspring for the formation of a citizens' redevelopment committee.

The City agreed to a planning study to resolve conflicts between these facilities, and to develop a master plan for the regeneration of the area. In the months that followed, the community group developed a series of planning and urban design proposals in close collaboration with the City administrators and the urban planners who were selected by the community but paid for by the City. The planners were Urban Design Associates, the same group which had been appointed by ALCOA for Operation Breakthrough.

In response to the need for insulation between industrial and residential uses traffic and land use plans were developed. First-stage development parcels were identified and located at critical points along the seam between residential and industrial uses. These are proposed as multi-use structures using innovative structural systems to build housing over industry economically.

As in Morrisania South the overall form of these structures was a response to large-scale urban problems. The more detailed design, such as relationship of shops to housing, the form of gathering spaces, types of housing, type of recreation facilities, etc. are to be developed in the next phase of design in close dialogue between the architects and the community. Both the large-scale form and the detailed design are developed in direct response to the needs of the area.

Because of this process, the project has a much

Below In the past the industries and residential streets of Sunset Park suffered from being side by side. Industrial traffic found access difficult through narrow neighbourhood streets, and the neighbourhood was harmed by trucks and noise. Working with the community the architects, Urban Design Associates, using Christian Frey's system, designed townhouses and apartment buildings, with shops and offices, on air rights over loft industries. This enables an industrial traffic loop to be separated completely from the residential streets where only occasional local traffic will interrupt pedestrians and playing children.

greater chance of being realized in spite of the lack of collaboration from City government. The community group, which was so much a part of the design process, has now become chartered as a development corporation and has increased its strength as a developer through its local bank and local industry. In addition, considerable political support has been rallied behind the scheme simply because so many different political, social, religious and ethnic groups have been involved in its evolution. As a result, the project has built up a momentum of its own.

The next step is for the housing industry to respond to this situation, and build housing according to the programme developed by the community planning team.

This is a major turn of events. Currently the housing industry locates and builds housing which responds only to a generalized need and which rarely relates its product to the urban problems of the city.

In Sunset Park, in Harlem, and in other urban communities, local community groups, as part of large interdisciplinary and inter-agency teams, have become prime movers in developing and realizing projects which are part of an overall co-ordinated scheme of growth for the metropolitan area. What is needed to fully realize the potential of this process is a serious commitment on the part of government, both local and national, to stimulate and foster such efforts, and even more importantly to provide the administrative, fiscal and planning framework needed for coordinating them into comprehensive programmes for urban growth.

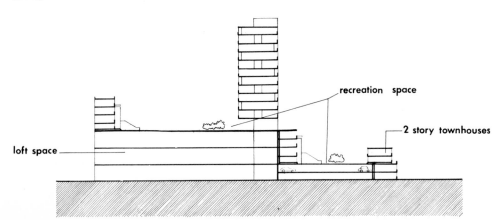

loft space

recreation space

2 story townhouses

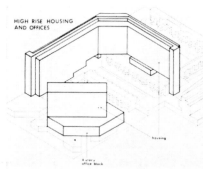

HIGH RISE HOUSING AND OFFICES

housing

THAMESMEAD

JOHN CRAIG, ALEXANDER PIKE, AND
JOHN A. McCARTHY

PREFACE

Thamesmead, now under construction, lies within the metropolitan area of Greater London; yet it is to be a new town of 60,000 people on a 1,700 acre site.

In terms of metropolitan growth it is at once an extension of London to the east, and also to a considerable extent a self-contained urban unit with its own shopping, schools, recreation, and industries.

This is very much in the tradition of London, which has been described as a large collection of villages.

The site lies on the south bank of the Thames about twelve miles east of central London, and has a three-mile frontage to the river. It is flat and low-lying, much of it marshland with high water-tables, but it also contains many fine groups of trees and moated earth-works which provide great opportunities for imaginative development.

Although the London County Council had owned most of the Thamesmead site for some time, the decision to go ahead with housing on a large scale was made only after plans to build a big new town at Hook, in the south of England, were abandoned in the early sixties. A preliminary attempt, in 1962, to plan and develop the Erith section of the Thamesmead site as a city of slender 31-storey towers with clusters of town houses, schools and shops at their base, to be built on platforms raised above the marshland, was described by Kenneth Campbell in AYB 11, *The Pedestrian in the City.*

Water is therefore a great feature of the site. Dykes and canals flow through the area, fringed by tall reeds and grasses. Within the site one is hardly conscious of the river because of a 20 ft high embankment constructed against flood; but from the top of this embankment the river views are very dramatic. Great industrial installations face the site across the wide river to the north, and large ships move to and from the docklands further upstream to the west.

Apart from the characteristics of the site itself, one major proposal has an important impact on the project. This is the Ringway Two motorway which will circle London at approximately twelve miles radius from the centre. Ringway Two will pass through the

The map below shows the relationship of the Thamesmead site to central London, and compares equivalent lengths of river frontage.

Thamesmead site and under the river in a tunnel. This motorway with its intersection with the main spine-road of the development has been a great formative influence in the design of the new town, for it requires substantial areas of land, it generates noise, and has a scale which is akin to the scale of the river and the huge industries to the north.

The site therefore calls for bold architectural solutions, responsive to the dramatic opportunities and constraints of the site. The illustrations and the three descriptions of the new town in the following pages — its basic principles of planning by John Craig, a report on its first phases of construction by Alexander Pike, and a description of traffic access and circulation by John A. McCarthy — show how a design has been developed in which two long spines of tall buildings on the northern edge of the site echo the river embankment and command sweeping views of the river reaches, while providing shelter from north-west and north-east winds for the smaller scale developments within: the human and pedestrian scale of housing, schools, and neighbourhood shops.

This is therefore a truly large-scale situation. The decision to design Thamesmead to match this scale is the basic philosophy behind the project, into which all the other requirements have been fitted. For example, not only the two high-density residential spines and the multi-level town centre, but also the use of water, have been conceived on a large scale and linked with an extensive open space system. Together they will provide urban and recreational facilities of regional significance, as well as serving local needs.

THAMESMEAD: PLANNING

JOHN CRAIG

Thamesmead is a new comprehensive town development on a 1,690 acre site, along a three and a quarter mile stretch of the river in south east London. Mainly river marshland, much of it formerly belonged to the Ministry of Defence and formed part of the great munitions complex known as the Woolwich Arsenal.

In the early part of the Second World War raids on the Royal Arsenal showed that it was too vulnerable to enemy attack to retain its predominant status in the country's chain of armaments manufacture. As a consequence, much of the work and many employees

were transferred to other factories. Nearly 1,000 people died or were injured here in enemy raids during the war, and by 1945 only 15,500 were engaged as against 32,500 in 1940.

After the war other work was found to maintain a reasonable establishment but by 1952 it was clear that the Arsenal was a 'white elephant'. A Select Committee on Estimates in 1952 asked the government to look at the whole question of rationalization of activity and release of lands at Woolwich. The Hutchinson Committee appointed in 1959 to consider the future of the Arsenal recommended the release of about 700 acres of land. The Armament Research and Development establishment was to stay and about 130 acres retained for other government purposes. Their one positive suggestion for alternative redevelopment concerned the old cartridge filling station area. They thought this might be suitable for a power station. The Committee said that owing to the deficiencies of the site, it appeared unlikely that anyone would be prepared to undertake comprehensive redevelopment. This observation clearly reflected the opinions of the local planning authorities, the London County Council (LCC) and Erith Borough Council, and perhaps their lack of interest and enthusiasm calls for some explanation.

The LCC already owned a large portion of land adjoining the Arsenal in Erith. They acquired it in connection with the construction of the high level sewer and the outfall works at Crossness in the last years of the nineteenth century and the early years of the present one. Modernization of the sewage treatment works in the 1950's meant that some of this land was no longer required by the Main Drainage Committee.

In 1953 the LCC decided to build a housing estate for 9,000 people on 240 acres of this land (between the railway and the sewer bank, west of Harrow Manor Way), now known as Abbey Wood estate. They also acquired over 100 acres of Arsenal land to build an industrial estate. The land east of Harrow Manor Way, which became available a little later on, was more problematical from the building point of view. It was low lying with areas of open water. Erith Council, who were responsible for buildings in the area, had a bye-law in force which stipulated that no habitable room should be built below 8 ft 6 ins Ordnance Datum Newlyn. The area was also poorly connected by road to the adjoining districts. Clearly development here was going to be extremely costly and difficult.

The LCC was, of course, continually harassed by the problem of finding suitable land for house building after the war, but the first offer by the government of this land at Woolwich came at a peculiar moment in time. In the mid-50s the LCC had decided to concentrate on building up a programme of new and expanded town developments outside London, and in 1957 they were given permission to go ahead with a really big new town and a site. Hook in Hampshire was selected and a plan drawn up. In 1959 when the Hutchinson Committee approached the LCC about the Arsenal, Hook was very much on the cards, and it represented a sizeable financial commitment. The Council did not feel able to undertake another big development.

In the event Hook was dropped and the Council, faced with even more pressing housing problems and needs in their area, were left in a most difficult position. The Council, and of course, the Ministry of Housing and Local Government, who had special responsibilities towards London in the absence of any responsible regional executive or planning body, were prepared to consider almost any area of land on offer for housing within reasonable distance of London. Government departments and public bodies of every kind were approached and asked to reconsider their operational needs for land, and to offer as much as possible of the surplus to local housing authorities. The Railways Board, for example, a big central land owner, was able to make a useful contribution in this respect. Unfortunately many of the sites, being small and awkward to develop certainly did not present the kind of opportunity which everyone was seeking to make a significant contribution to the problem.

The LCC, after Hook, reviewed every possibility within their own area and the extension of Abbey Wood estate assumed a new significance. The Council's architects set to work to devise a scheme which would overcome many of the problems, such as marshland, previously mentioned. It was proposed to construct great decks, 12 ft above the ground, and to place the bulk of the housing on them. Between the platforms, slender towers of thirty-one storeys connected up the platforms and provided elevator access to them. Six or seven platforms were grouped together into a 'village'. Three villages were to be linked to a new secondary road connecting with the existing Abbey Road between Woolwich and Erith. The 'town-on-stilts', as it was affectionately called, and which was described at length in *The Pedestrian in the City* (AYB 11), was to house around 25,000 people on 500 acres. In 1962 the LCC almost reluctantly announced their intention to develop the site. In the preface to the brochure outlining the proposed development Norman G. N. Pritchard, Chairman of the

Housing Committee at the time, sounded a note of warning about its status. He said 'the Council has not yet decided, indeed cannot yet decide, whether this scheme — technically brilliant though it is — is a practical proposition.'

The government's second attempt to interest the LCC in the Arsenal lands came right in the middle of the further evaluation of the Erith project. It was gradually realized that the Erith scheme was impracticable. In the first place it was based on a mixture of tall and low buildings. It was soon discovered that the atmosphere above the site was heavily polluted, ruling out any dwelling space above 200 feet from the ground. The reduction in densities which would have followed from a shortening of the tall blocks made the whole proposition 'uneconomic'. Secondly, the size of the proposed community was such that the town could not support a shopping centre of any size and communications to the adjoining town of Erith were very poor. Road improvements on the scale required once again made this a prohibitively expensive development. Since the problems which had been iden-

tified bore directly on the question of the scale of the proposed development, for instance the problem of the heavy infrastructure costs in relation to housing gain, the prospect of more land for building was immediately attractive.

During the many months of negotiation between the LCC, the Ministry of Housing and Local Government and the Ministry of Defence which followed, the Council's original intention, to develop just so much of the Arsenal land as might be necessary in order to make the Erith scheme viable, was transformed into a more radical proposal to build a new town on the combined Arsenal and Erith lands. Even after agreement had been reached in principle, some issues remained which had to be resolved before the LCC would finally agree to buy the Ministry's land. First there was a proposal to build a mammoth electricity generating station near the town which the LCC said should be dropped on amenity grounds. Second, even more land had to be released by the Arsenal in order to ensure the success of the new project; and third the LCC said that the government should

agree to co-operate closely with them in the matter of local employment.

By the middle of 1965 agreement was reached and the land acquired for £6,800,000 ($16,320,000) by the newly formed Greater London Council (GLC)

The plan for Thamesmead

The next stage was to draw up an inventory of needs and a provisional layout of the land for various occupations and uses. In the case of Thamesmead, the larger planning issues of density, of land occupancy and urban structure to some extent arose out of the constraints and possibilities on site. Because of atmospheric pollution, tall blocks over 200 ft high were impossible. Sizeable areas of land could not be used for housing, for instance the headlands of Tripcock Point and Crossness which had to be kept clear for navigation, and an area around the sewage works which could not be used for obvious reasons. These lands were therefore set aside for parks and open spaces. The sewer bank could not be removed and presented a formidable barrier to communications. The old Abbey Road could not support the level of traffic which would be generated by even a modest development like the town-on-stilts. The only answer in the case of the new giant Thamesmead was a new major road. This 'spine road' as it is called was routed as close as possible to the existing east-west linear barriers, the sewer bank, railway and road. Even so the influence it was to exert over the planning of the site in terms of noise was considerable. To meet the stringent quiet standards which were set for residential areas, residential development had to be pushed quite close to the river. To tame the vast quantities of water in the area, an imaginative scheme of canals and lakes to channel and store it was proposed. Once again the technical requirements and possibilities in these considerations played a profound part in influencing the disposition of housing, shops and schools. This then, broadly speaking, was how as planners and architects, we went about the task of designing the new Thamesmead. Behind all this discussion of the limitations and potentialities of the particular site we were carefully examining the town's effect on the region and the metropolis of which it is a part, and trying to realize some of our planning and policy goals for London as a whole.

Regional implications

Housing

It was important, first of all, to get as much as possible out of the site in terms of relief for the

housing needs of Central and Inner London. This is not as easy as it seems. In Inner London people often live 300 or 400 to the acre, but in Woolwich and Erith, this would seem very crowded where the average is not much above fifty. It would be quite unacceptable to build a new community too dissimilar in this respect.

People are notoriously unwilling to move far from their existing areas. To persuade people, even those badly housed in Central London, to go and live at Thamesmead, would be a public relations exercise of some magnitude. The gain in housing for Inner London from Thamesmead is encouraged by what is known as the 'rippling out' process. People from areas close to Thamesmead, especially Council tenants, are moved (of their own free choice) to Thamesmead, and the accommodation that they have vacated used to help people in housing need from nearer the centre.

Thamesmead in this way is not likely to attract Inner London dwellers directly in large numbers and therefore to some extent the town must measure up to the tastes and aspirations of those in the natural catchment areas, i.e., areas immediately adjoining it or within a reasonable distance north and south of the river. Therefore very high densities were out of the question. It cannot be stressed too much that the Council has no power to compel people to live at Thamesmead and the influence of even slum conditions on people's choices of a new place to live and work is less powerful than most of us imagine. To provide homes for 60,000 Londoners would in itself be a significant contribution to London's housing needs — but to benefit from such an opportunity Thamesmead has to be considered as a first stage in a cycle or urban renewal around London enabling other large areas in London to be redeveloped.

Broadly speaking the present plan provides for a total population of around 60,000, housed at an average figure of 100 persons to the acre (ppa) and ranging between 140 and 70 ppa. There will be approximately 17,000 dwellings grouped into ten neighbourhoods each with its own local schools, shops and public houses.

Employment

One of the lessons which the former London County Council learned from building large estates in outer London after the war, was that the new residents often experienced difficulty either in retaining their old employment in Inner London (owing to the cost, time or inconvenience of transport) or alternatively in finding local or intermediate area employment.

Clearly this situation must not recur at Thamesmead. The Council, therefore, decided to provide a certain amount of employment in the new town itself. Apart from offices and shops, about 170 acres of land have been allocated for industrial development. Twenty acres will be in small two acre lots placed close to the residential areas throughout the development (especially to cater to the needs of women workers), and 150 acres in large industrial estates at the eastern and western extremities of the area. This it is hoped, taken together with the job opportunities in the surrounding districts and a small number in Central London, will prevent the town from becoming yet another central area dormitory with all the inconvenience and wasted efforts the name implies. Seventy acres of the 170 are held in reserve, since it is recognized that the precise level of employment to be provided at Thamesmead needs to be related to changing circumstances and developing plans and policies for the region.

At the time when the plan was drafted, a fairly rigid policy of office and industrial decentralization was being effected and no overall increase in employment within the London area was acceptable. To meet this requirement it was decided to use Thamesmead to resettle industries, which were tied by their function to London but which had been either displaced as a result of the Council's day-to-day activities or as non-conforming users of land. The GLC today is concerned about London's capacity to export employment indefinitely and intends to bolster up some parts of its area which show signs of running down.

The flexibility built into the plan has proved extremely valuable in this respect. In recent times several big firms in the Woolwich and Erith area have shut down, throwing thousands of workers on to the local labour market and, whilst most of these have been absorbed, the longer term prospects are more worrying.

In fact the relationship between employment and homes at Thamesmead is likely to be an indirect one, and the Council now see the question of Thamesmead employment rather as a contribution to the total pool of opportunities in this section of London than as jobs for Thamesmead dwellers alone. Seen in this light, Thamesmead's industrial areas and the improved communications pattern (Ringway Two and

Below This diagrammatic traffic plan, although since revised, shows the hierarchy of circulation systems on which Thamesmead is based. The Ringway Two motorway, planned to encircle London on an approximate 12-mile radius, passes through the western part of the site before crossing the river in a tunnel. The site is also bisected by a major east-west limited-access spine road. The first three stages of construction are the shaded area. On the next page is a more recent master plan.

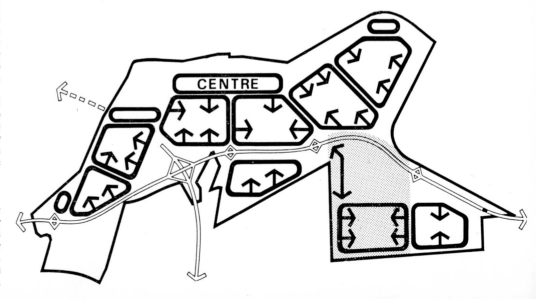

238

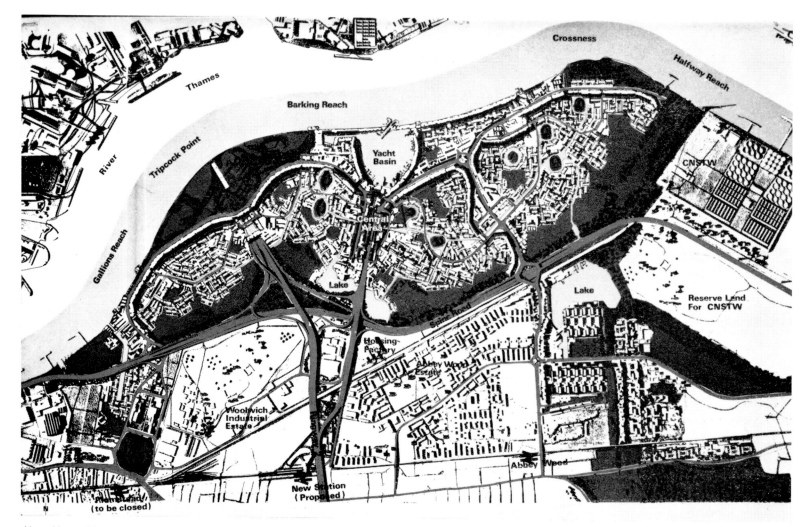

239

Above Master Plan for Thamesmead. Note the
central areas and yacht basin; and also how the
spine road and major secondaries define the new
city's neighbourhoods. Each neighbourhood will have
local shopping and employment centres, schools,
and facilities for recreation, linked by traffic-free
pedestrian networks.

spine road) may prove to be a most significant contribution to revitalizing a rather run-down and somewhat depressed part of the metropolitan region.

Communications
Reference has been made above to the poor communications in this area. This challenge has been met but not without cost. The railway which borders the site in the south is part of the busy south-eastern portion of the Southern Region rail network. It is heavily overloaded in peak hours with traffic to and from the central area. Whilst some improvements are being made now, such as new colour signalling and station renewal, more radical steps may be necessary later on to cope with the build-up in Thamesmead traffic.

The principal weakness, however, is in the existing road system. Fortunately for Thamesmead a major new road, Ringway Two (which will circle London at about a twelve mile radius from the centre) crosses the river at Woolwich and passes through the western half of the Thamesmead site. A new principal road is to be built between Woolwich and Erith, running along the north side of the sewer bank and connecting up with the new Ringway close to the entrance to the tunnelled river crossing. The form of the river crossing has been fairly controversial, but from the point of view of the new Thamesmead community, a tunnel is by far the better solution. A bridge, although cheaper, would have towered over the town, engulfing areas in intolerable levels of noise and fumes. Although one sage recently said 'why should I do anything for posterity – what has posterity ever done for me', future generations of Thamesmead dwellers will surely appreciate the courage of the Minister who bent the grant rules and agreed to put up the rather large sum of money for the tunnel.

Thamesmead as a late twentieth century town is planned to cope with the car. One of the most important principles underlying the town's structure is that there should be the most complete vehicle and pedestrian segregation possible. A network of high level walkways is being provided in the medium and high density areas and at ground level elsewhere, quite separate from the network of main and secondary distributor roads throughout the development. An independent system of cycleways is also planned, since this low flat area is excellent cycling country. Extensive car parking facilities will be provided both in the housing areas and the community centres.

The provision of adequate public transport has been catered for, however, and the main and secondary distributor roads have been specially designed to provide convenient and economic routes for buses.

Private and public development
There is a tendency for new towns and extensive municipal housing developments to accommodate one class, that is mainly industrial workers, because these are most in need of new houses. This tendency relates to the age groups of the immigrant population, so that parents of the age group 25–35 years with growing families tend to predominate. This leads to imbalance, on the one hand with few old people, on the other with young people who reach maturity only to find that there is no housing for them. They leave to find work and residence elsewhere and this aggravates the problem of imbalance in the now middle-aged new community.

To redress the imbalance, at any rate of the class structure, research for Thamesmead indicated that a split of 35% in favour of private enterprise housing for sale and 65% of municipal housing would go far to alleviate the problem.

Private development helps to relieve the burden fall-

Above An early study model for the central areas and yacht basin of Thamesmead.

ing on the national exchequer and on the rates but is not entirely beneficial because it usually means lower densities and fewer people, which may significantly alter the total population figure and the economic justification for some of the community facilities it is hoped to provide.

Town centre and shopping
Almost in the middle of the whole area will be a town centre, Y-shaped in form, with its arms embracing the proposed yacht basin for 5,000 – 6,000 vessels. In the words of a 1967 brochure on Thamesmead the 'aim is to create an excitingly varied but compact area in which residents will be able to combine shopping trips with visits to the cinema, going to evening classes or a stroll around the yacht marina or along the river to watch the ships'.

The extent of the shopping to be provided is at present restricted to 200,000 sq ft. This is in deference to the views of the local borough councils who con-

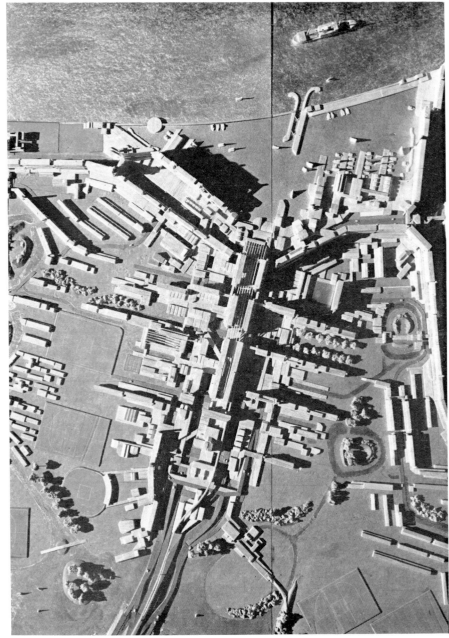

241

sider that parts of Thamesmead lie within the natural catchment areas of the existing centres at Woolwich and Erith. Erith in particular, has always been concerned about the provision of rival facilities since they undertook the construction of a new major shopping centre in 1966. The Greater London Council believes, taking into account the growth potential of the wider area, that there is room for both.

Cost and change

This, then, is the plan and some of the reasoning which lies behind it. How much will it cost and how long will it take to build? We live in times of monetary inflation, so that the apparent cost of Thamesmead is always rising. There does not appear to be any very large increase in real terms but, of course, any statement of accounts must allow for this inflationary effect. In 1968 it was calculated that in '68 prices, the total cost would be around £200 million ($480 million) shared between the principal authorities, in the following way: GLC 50%, Borough Councils $3\frac{1}{2}$—4%, ILEA 7%, Central Government 5%, other developers, i.e., private house builders, statutory authorities, etc., 34%. Some items which benefit and are related to Thamesmead but which cannot strictly be said to be required because of it — such as Ringway Two and the river crossing and the railway improvements — are excluded from this calculation.

The plan itself is subject to change and in the four years since the first draft master plan was published there have been many alterations and doubtless there will be many more. Some of these are dictated by changing social and economic circumstances or by a broadening appreciation and understanding of Thamesmead's situation, and yet others arise out of the difficulty of staging the project itself. The broad outline invested with statutory authority, however, is not likely to alter and, disaster apart, should be realized in time. The whole project from start to finish is expected to take around fifteen years and should be completed by the early 1980s.

Acknowledgement

John Craig acknowledges the great assistance of Mrs W. Lamberth who prepared the draft of this section.

Left Model of the central areas.

THAMESMEAD REPORT

ALEXANDER PIKE

The project

The Thamesmead site is a flat and featureless stretch of land on the south bank of the Thames with a three mile frontage to the river, but a number of fine trees and moated earthworks provide great opportunities for imaginative development. The scale of the landscape is large. Facing the site, across a broad stretch of river, are Dagenham Docks and the Ford Works. Within the site, the proposed Ringway Two motorway is planned to pass through the area and under the river in a tunnel. This motorway, with its intersection with the main spine road of the development, has been a great formative influence in the design. It requires substantial areas of land, generates noise, and has a scale comparable with the natural landscape.

As already mentioned, the decision to design Thamesmead to match this scale is a basic philosophy behind the scheme, into which all other requirements have been fitted. Thus the use of water has been conceived on a large scale, and linked with an extensive open space system; together they will provide

Right Site plan for Stage 1.

Next page Model of Stages 1 and 2.

242

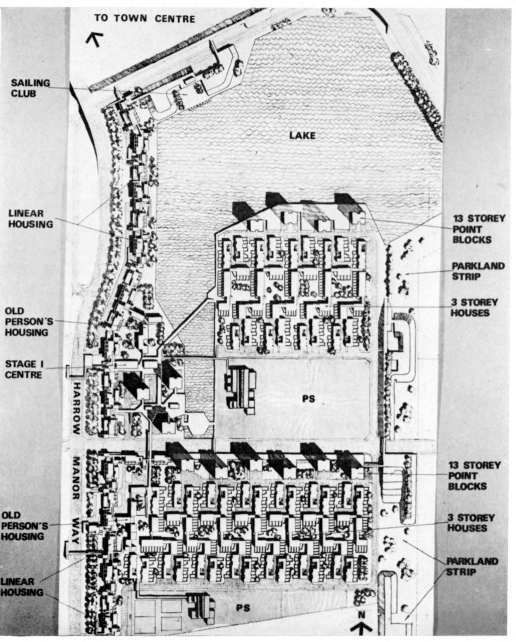

Playing fields and landscaped embankments can be located to act as a buffer between dwellings and major road.

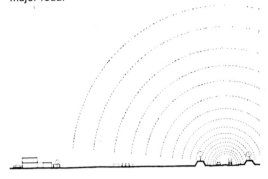

Where orientation toward the sun permits, continuous terraces of single aspect dwellings can be located adjacent to major roads, so that they shield both themselves and areas beyond from traffic noise.

244

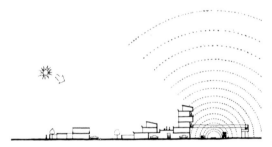

Where dwellings must face the traffic noise source in order to get proper sunlighting, non residential buildings can be used as a noise barrier.

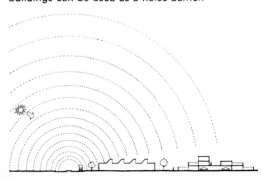

Below Model of Stage 3

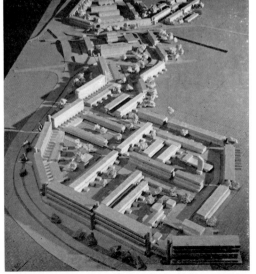

facilities which, apart from local needs, will be of regional significance.

The other principles on which the scheme is based are:

Thamesmead will not be a dormitory area. It is intended to provide a complete environment with employment and full educational, communal, commercial and recreation facilities.

Within the relatively high average net density as many families as possible will have gardens or an outdoor living space. Density will be used as a design tool and will vary from housing areas with large family dwellings at seventy persons per acre to parts of the town where the density will be at about 140 persons per acre and provide dwellings for the small family and single persons.

Movement about Thamesmead for both pedestrians and vehicles will be along routes carefully designed to be safe and convenient. Communications between the new development and the neighbouring areas of London have been planned to ensure that the development will become integrated as part of Greater London.

It has been accepted that landscaping makes a major contribution to the quality of urban environment and the designs of buildings and open space have been considered as a single problem.

The resulting design has a pronounced and coherent form, with a line of tall buildings which in general run along the river frontage and a further high density leg of development running north-south from just north of Abbey Wood Station to the central area.

The centre is planned at right angles to the river, with a yacht basin at the northern end and a lake at the southern end, and is linked with the high density limbs of the housing areas.

The movement structure of the plan consists of a road network for vehicles and a footpath network for pedestrians (and possibly another for cyclists). These are planned to operate independently and are complementary to each other. Provision is also made in the plan for the introduction of public transport. The road network contains the main east-west spine which forms a major feeder route to the Ringway Two motorway. There will be a system of main distributor roads running from this spine road along high density housing areas and these roads will in turn serve a system of secondary distributor roads on to which will feed culs-de-sac giving access to the dwellings themselves.

The routes for pedestrians are being planned as carefully as the routes for vehicles. They will run independently of the roads, through open space, over

245

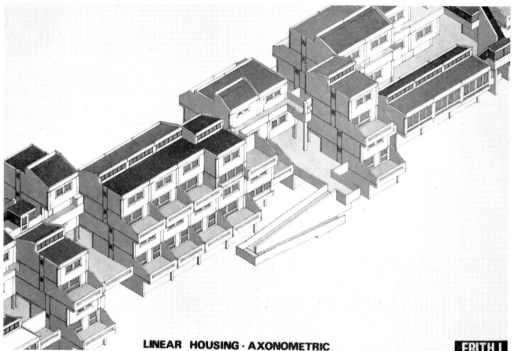

LINEAR HOUSING · AXONOMETRIC ERITH I

Above This part of the model of Stage 1 shows a number of residential options including tall blocks, townhouses with private gardens, garden apartments, and maisonettes. The model also shows the linear housing along a man-made lake on one side and a major distributor on the other. Accommodation provided in Stage 1 is as follows:

1 person dwellings (Old People)	50
2 person dwellings (Old People)	65
2 person dwellings	288
3 person dwellings	296
4 person dwellings	416
5 person dwellings	335
6 person dwellings	44

The total number of dwellings is 1,494, housing 5,245 people. In addition to residential units, each Stage or neighbourhood will include shops, schools, recreation, and employment. A system of canals links the lakes, and within each Stage are a network of traffic-free landscaped pedestrian pathways.

VIEW OF LINEAR HOUSING ACROSS LAKE ERITH I

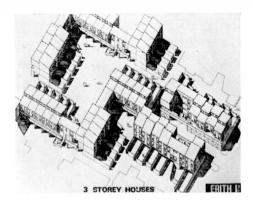

3 STOREY HOUSES   ERITH

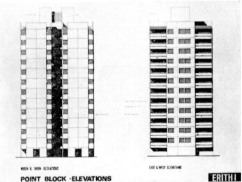

POINT BLOCK ·ELEVATIONS   ERITH

area uses.

The central area will contain shopping, office employment, community, recreational and educational facilities including a comprehensive medical centre and an ecumenical centre. The design of this area provides for a number of dwellings and a high main concourse with vehicular services, parking and a public transport interchange at natural ground level. The main concourse will provide access to, and views of, the river at the northern end and the lakes at the southern end. It is suggested that important educational buildings should be placed at this end of the centre, to overlook the lake and also to form an interesting approach to the centre for those using the main road over the lake.

Building system chosen

The Master Plan was prepared in 1965–66 and followed by a Second Master Plan later in 1966. Considering the exceptional scale of the project, one of the fundamental objectives was to start building as quickly as possible. It was decided that to achieve this aim an Industrialized Building (IB) system should be employed, but that this should not be regarded as a restriction of the design. Previous experience had shown that the use of IB systems had produced overall costs that were slightly above those for traditional construction and revealed little or no indication of the profit margins.

The design team decided that the correct approach would be to design a good project without reference to a specific IB system and then apply the use of a system to the scheme.

By the spring of 1966 design work on Stage 1 was sufficiently advanced for a cost plan to be established by the Council's quantity surveyors. This was intended to cover the first two stages and was based on normal traditional construction. Advice was then sought from the National Building Agency for their opinions on which combinations of contractors and IB systems could show suitable production and management capacity for the project. After initial discussions with a number of possible combinations, three national building firms were invited to prepare submissions to the Council, showing how they would propose carrying out the work with their particular system within the cost targets.

The contractor finally chosen was Cubitts, whose submission was based on the use of the Balency &

and under roads, and also at an upper level through the high density development to link with the top of the river bank and the main level of the centre. These footpaths will serve schools, shops and playing fields so that movement on foot throughout the entire project will be pleasant and safe for all users.

The scheme will provide about 17,000 dwellings grouped into neighbourhoods which vary in size from about 1,500 to 2,000 dwellings. In general these neighbourhoods are designed with tall buildings on their northern or eastern edges and lower buildings within. They will contain their own primary schools, local centres for day-to-day shopping, churches, pubs, and some employment for local workers. The specially designed tall buildings will protect the central part of the housing areas from traffic noise and wind. Beyond these areas the major school playing fields and public open spaces will serve to separate the lower density housing from the main road of the development.

The plan makes extensive use of water throughout

the site. Two lakes will be created, linked by a canal forming part of an entire system running through the town. These canals will run alongside the secondary roads serving the housing and will act as a barrier to crossing the road at unsuitable positions. Thus it will be possible for pedestrians to move across the roads and canals only at selected points where footpaths go over the canals and under the roads, which will be slightly raised at these points. The excavated material from lakes and canals will be used to create differences of level within the open space system.

The lakes will form part of the general open spaces in the project and these, associated with extensive tree planting, are already well in hand.

It is anticipated that the main element of the recreational provision will be the yacht basin. This is proposed to be of international status and aims to bring to the centre of Thamesmead, and to this part of London in general, a facility and colourful activity to add greatly to the attractions of the area. The basin will be flanked by high density housing and central

Top Stage 1, 3-storey houses.

Below Stage 1, point blocks.

Schuhl system, which the company has already used on the extensive Ballymun housing project in Dublin.

The Balency system

The Balency system has been used on the Continent for over fifteen years and is claimed to be one of Europe's best-tried IB methods. It is based on the use of precast concrete wall panels, but differs from almost all other 'heavy' concrete systems in that it normally employs an *in situ* concrete floor slab construction. Both the internal and the external wall panels are designed as load-bearing elements, precast in highly sophisticated steel moulds. The height of the wall panels is constant for any one contract, but considerable latitude is possible in the length of panels.

The basic principle of the system presupposes that each building will have a total dead weight sufficient at all times, whether during construction or completed, to resist the lateral wind load forces without inducing undue tension in any of its constituent parts. Each precast wall is designed as a load-bearing unit to carry its own weight together with all the super-imposed weights and a proportion of the horizontal wind load.

All internal walls are cast vertically and have electrical conduits and outlet boxes cast in. Special wall units, known as 'technical blocks', have pipework for hot and cold water services and drainage cast in, with kitchen outlet points on one side and bathroom outlets on the other; a technique claimed to reduce the site work required for the installation of piped services.

External wall panels are cast horizontally and consist of a 3 in. outer skin of concrete with exposed aggregate finish, a 1 in. thick expanded polystyrene insulation membrane and a 5 in. thick internal structural concrete skin. The two skins are tied together by metal ties which pass through the insulation membrane.

The standard method of floor construction is for all items to be cast in conduit runs, outlet boxes, reinforcement, etc., to be assembled on the ground on a metal frame made up of scaffold tubes. The unit is then lifted up into position ready for the concrete to be poured.

This method was employed throughout all stages of the Thamesmead project but was modified so that the entire floor slab could be precast and positioned as one unit in the three-storey housing.

When all walls for one storey have been erected and supported, formwork is placed in position and the floor slabs cast over the walls. The tops of walls are

arranged to project into the floor slabs ½ in. above soffit level and all protruding reinforcement at the tops of wall panels is bent down for casting into the floor slabs, ensuring rigid joints.

The vertical joints between external panels form hexagonal holes which are carefully hand-filled with dry-mix concrete. A loose tongue of felt-covered expanded polystyrene is fitted within the joint to maintain insulation and to prevent concrete seepage into the front of the joint.

The contract

The exceptional size of the project demanded special attention to the form of contract and in this instance the usual value-cost system seemed to be particularly eligible, in spite of the fact that it had not hitherto been employed for an IB project.

This system was devised in 1920 to meet the need for large housing contracts at a time when prices of labour and materials were constantly fluctuating and conditions in the building industry were unsettled. In essence the contract provides for the building construction to be financed by the Council, the contractor being paid a fee to cover his head office expenses. Tenders may be invited from selected firms of suitable experience and capacity who quote percentage variations to a fixed schedule of rates and prices or, alternatively, schedules of items of work with indicative quantities may be provided for the tenderers to insert their own prices and rates. Sometimes an offer is negotiated with a single contractor to carry out the work on an agreed schedule.

The actual cost of work is compared with a 'value' calculated from the schedule and agreed with the contractor. If 'value' and 'cost' correspond, the contractor's basic fee is computed as a percentage (about 3%) of the 'value'. If the actual cost is more than the 'value' the fee is reduced, but if less than the 'value' the contractor is paid a bonus, representing part of the saving, in addition to his basic fee. The comparisons between cost and value are made at intervals throughout the progress of the work and at the completion of the contract.

The economic advantages of this type of contract increase with the size of the scheme, and costs compare favourably with other types of contract for large-scale schemes. It also enables work to be started more quickly, it being unnecessary for detailed layouts, working drawings and bills of quantities to be available before tendering. Variations and modifications can be incorporated and different types of building can be introduced.

As the Council had previously used this type of

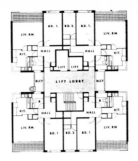

1

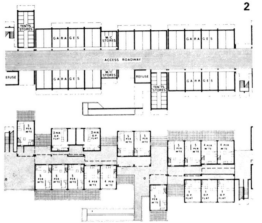

2

3

4

Plans for Stage 1 housing.
1 Typical plan for 13-storey point blocks built in the Balency system.
2 Linear housing, ground and first floor plans.
3 Linear housing, 4 person maisonette.
4 Typical floor plan of 3-storey houses.

contract solely for schemes employing traditional building methods, a subsidiary purpose for its use on this project was to obtain important data on the economic aspects of Industrialized Building, a subject on which comparatively little information is available.

The first phase

The contracts for Stages I and II of the project were awarded to Cubitts in October 1966, for the construction of 4,000 dwellings over a period of five years at a cost of nearly £30 million ($72 million).

Stage I has an area of 85 acres, of which 50.7 acres are to be used for housing and the remainder allocated for two primary schools. The sub-centre provisions will provide approximately 1,500 dwellings in three different housing types; thirteen-storey point blocks; two- to five-storey linear maisonette blocks; three-storey terrace houses. The twelve point blocks are sited in two groups; four on the south bank of the main portion of the lake and eight in the middle of the site. Six of these are on the southern side of the main east-west roadway and the remaining two on the opposite side of the road, directly related to the Stage I sub-centre.

The linear housing runs down the full extent of the

248

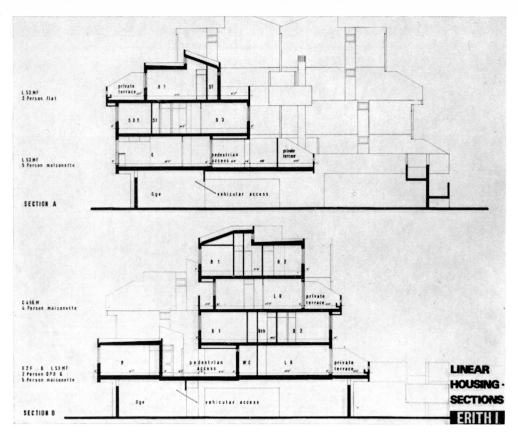

L 53 MF
3 Person flat

private terrace · B 1 · St

S D T · St · B 3

L 53 MF
5 Person maisonette

K · pedestrian access · private terrace

SECTION A

Gge · vehicular access

C 456 M
4 Person maisonette

B 1 · B 2

L R · private terrace

B 1 · Bth · B 2

E2F & L53 MF
2 Person OPD &
5 Person maisonette

pedestrian access · WC · L R · private terrace

SECTION B

Gge · vehicular access

LINEAR HOUSING · SECTIONS
ERITH I

---

western side of the site, following the line of Harrow Manor Way, with extensions of the pedestrian deck to the sub-centre and the line of six point blocks at first floor level. The three-storey terrace houses are grouped to create pedestrian enclosures within the perimeter access road pattern and are sited on each side of the central primary school site.

The five-storey linear blocks are of a type not previously used, and have been specially designed for this project. A ground level access road gives access to the garages, above which the linking pedestrian level route, half a mile through the first stage, gives access to the four floors of maisonettes and the one-storey old persons' flats located at deck level.

Preliminary design studies at the tender stage indicated that the highly modelled form of these blocks made them unsuitable for the economic application of the Balency system, and the first of these units on the site have been built by rationalized in situ cross-wall and floor slab techniques, with non-loadbearing cladding panels. This decision was reinforced by the added advantage that an earlier start could be made on this part of the work without waiting for the completion of the factory for the production of the precast components.

Now that the factory is in production, future elements of the linear blocks will employ the Balency system units.

Site conditions

The site is low-lying with a high water table and lies below the high-tide level of the Thames. The sub-soil is of poor load-bearing capacity with an underlying stratum of peat of varying thickness. Pile foundations will be necessary for all buildings, down in some cases to depths of 30 to 40 ft. The former by-law restricting habitable floor to a minimum of 8 ft 6 ins above Newlyn Datum has been superseded by the new Building Regulations but may be retained in this instance as a planning regulation. The final decision is dependent on the progress of proposals for the Thames River Defences and the possibility of Thames Barrage.

The site allocated for Stages I and II of the development is on the Erith Marshes, which only drain at low tide, and the lake planned for this area will facilitate drainage and act as a flood water balancing area.

The site factory

The on-site factory for producing the concrete units was the first building to be erected on the site. It has an area of 114,000 sq ft, a production line 560 ft long, and using one-shift working has an output of approximately 950 dwellings a year. This could be increased to 1,500 dwellings a year by using two shifts.

The units are produced in fifty steel moulds (twelve vertical, thirty-eight horizontal and special moulds) which can produce approximately 700 different castings. The steel end formers, which make up the side walls of the mould, can be fixed at any predetermined position of bolt holes in the baseplate of the mould, thus allowing the production of a limited number of different sized units from the same mould.

At the present rate of production each horizontal mould produces on average two castings a day and each vertical mould three castings a day. This is achieved by accelerating the initial curing period of the concrete by heating both the concrete mix (to about 120°F) and the moulds (to about 140°F) before pouring. Each horizontal mould is fitted with an hydraulically operated autoclave head which when lowered completely covers the baseplate and the concrete panel. The average initial curing period varies from five hours for the floor slabs and four hours for the external wall panels in the horizontal moulds to three hours in the vertical moulds. These periods vary according to the temperature in the mould, the temperature of the mix when poured, the ambient temperature and the size of the panel.

The special moulds include those designed to produce stairs, balcony fronts, floor slabs (for the three-storey house only) and technical blocks.

Vertical moulds are used to produce internal partition panels. The internal faces of these moulds are constructed of polished steel to achieve a smooth panel surface for direct application of paint or wallpaper after erection. The concrete is injected pneumatically

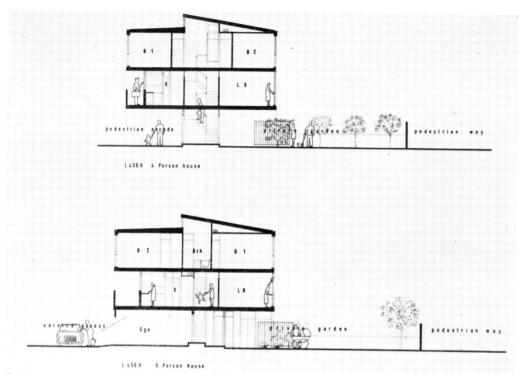

pedestrian arcade   garden   pedestrian way

L 456 H   4 Person house

B 2   Bth   B 1

servi___ access   Gge   garden   pedestrian way

L 456 H   6 Person house

Stage 1, 3-storey houses.

from the bottom of the vertical moulds to give greater control over the placing, to avoid distortion of the steel and segregation of the mix, and to allow for natural displacement of air from the mould.

External wall panels are cast flat in horizontal moulds. The panel is placed with the external facing mix laid on a retarder applied to the baseplate, over which is laid the concrete, reinforcement and insulation. The top (internal) surface of the unit is power-floated twice during the initial curing period (one hour and two and a half hours after placing the mix in the mould) to achieve a finish comparable to that obtained on partition panels cast in the vertical moulds. On completion of casting, the autoclave hood is raised, and all end formers, except that along the bottom edge of the panel, are removed and the baseplate is tilted by hydraulic jacks to allow the overhead gantry crane to remove the unit in a vertical position to the finishing bay.

In the finishing bay the aggregate is exposed by hosing and brushing off the retarder coated surface;

all units are inspected and any necessary minor repairs are carried out.

The finished units are lifted from the finishing bay by tower crane and placed in the stockyard for a minimum period of forty-eight hours before being loaded on to transporters for delivery to the building site.

Costs

The immense scope of the project and the type of contractual system employed make assessment of the overall cost extremely difficult. The initial cost plan was formulated before the introduction of the present Ministry housing yardsticks, and future phases of work will require modifications to conform, in spite of the objective to obtain conclusive data on the cost of Industrialized Building.

The cost of the site factory for manufacturing the components will be written off during the production of the 4,000 dwellings comprising the first phase. Thereafter, the costs will be related merely to general maintenance and replacement of plant and equip-

ment, and production cost for the components will fall sharply, considerably reducing the overall costs of dwellings.

The extent of the scheme and the unusual, and basically unsuitable, nature of the site have, predictably, produced high abnormals in the cost plan. Site development costs are high for a number of reasons: the drainage system is complex and extensive; large areas of site will require building up;[1] piling is necessary everywhere, not only for buildings, but also for the elevated walkways and bridges and even for the sewers of the main drainage system; the cost of high capacity services supplies and long distribution runs is considerable; the lakes, lagoons and canals, necessary in this case for the drainage system, constitute an extra not normally encountered.

In addition to these items certain planning principles — the provision of extensive elevated walkways and the use of single aspect dwellings to contain the noise from major roads — are an inevitable source of increased costs. In mitigation of these abnormals, land costs are low at approximately £170 ($408) per dwelling compared with an average between £1,000 ($2,400) and £1,500 ($3,600) per dwelling for all other GLC housing sites.

The future

The interest of Thamesmead lies not merely in the exercise of urban planning on a vast scale. It seeks to provide solutions to the national problem of increasing the output of building within the limits of the total labour force available.

Of the £225 million ($540 million) estimated to be the total cost of the project, approximately £180 million ($432 million) will be for building work, extended over a thirteen-year period. The present rate of building of £7.5 million ($18 million) a year is already very high, probably exceeding twice the rate ever previously achieved in this country, but even this must be improved if the target programme is to be met.

The estimated figure for the number of operatives on the site is 3,500, but as it is difficult to attract certain types of tradesmen to the area, 2,500 is probably a more realistic figure. The total of 17,000 housing units will be provided by the GLC and private developers in the ratio of about 65% to 35%, giving the GLC responsibility for about 11,000 units, an output well within the capacity of the site factory.

---

[1] The entire fifty acre housing site for Stage I had to be covered with sand for a depth of 2 ft before work could commence. The site for Stage II was treated in the same way, the sand being pumped from barges in the Thames.

THAMESMEAD: TRANSPORTATION PLANNING

JOHN A. McCARTHY

Introduction

In the development of a new community one of the fundamental problems to be dealt with is that of access. Regarding Thamesmead in particular, an important point to bear in mind is the differing responsibility of the architect from that of the director of planning and transportation. The latter is responsible for the design and construction of the proposed metropolitan roads, with the Greater London Council being the highway authority. With other roads, whether principal or non-principal, the London Boroughs of Bexley and Greenwich will be the highway authorities and the architect, through his housing engineer, is responsible for the design and construction of these roads. This he does in conjunction with the local highway authorities who will take over the roads when completed to their satisfaction.

A principal road, which can be metropolitan or non-metropolitan, may be defined as a road which is an essential route for traffic and which has a sufficiently important place in the national highway system to justify central Government interest in its planning and Exchequer assistance towards its improvement.[1] Such a road normally attracts a grant of 75% towards the cost after any other contributions have been deducted, the highway authority paying the balance.

Background

The creation of a new community of up to 60,000 people introduces a major and entirely new factor into the planning of the highway network in this part of London. Although it is intended to make provision for some local employment, the development will need to provide for those workers who wish to travel to other parts of London. It is also important that the new industries should have good communications with the rest of the country.

Thamesmead lies across the route of the proposed Ringway Two, forming part of London's proposed system of primary roads. This road will not only give Thamesmead excellent access to the rest of London, but will also open up the development and its surrounding area to the national motorway system. In doing this it may help to arrest the decline in the existing industrial areas which lie alongside the Thames. Also, by crossing the Thames, it will have a secondary but vital role of providing a link between the mainly residential area south of the river and the large industrial areas to the north

Traffic forecasts

The road network has been tested on the basis of forecasts for travel demand for the completion of the project. These forecasts cover both the peak hour 'journey to work' and off-peak flows. The results indicate that the spine road and the main and secondary roads should be able to cater for the predicted traffic flows on the basis of present assumptions and employment within Thamesmead. They also indicate that the road pattern will be able to cope with traffic flows predicted over a wide range of assumptions about the actual places of work of the residents. It should be noted that the results assume an attractive public transport system which will keep to a minimum the level of car usage within Thamesmead.

Further work has also been carried out into the question of the effect of any possible expansion of the central area. This has been done in conjunction with the firm of Jamieson and Mackay, consulting civil and transportation engineers, who are advising the GLC on the detailed design of the transportation plan for the central area. This work shows that a reasonable amount of expansion can be catered for in the road system feeding the central area, including the link to Ringway Two. A particular problem will be the provision of an adequate amount of car park facilities within the centre and their distribution around the internal road system.

It is important to remember that from the transportation point of view, Thamesmead forms a comparatively small part of London and therefore any traffic studies must be related to London as a whole. For example, if there were no industrial areas within the development, the extra traffic caused by all the work trips having to go outside Thamesmead could overload the surrounding road system.

This forecasting of travel must be a continuing process of evaluation throughout the construction of the development so as to cater for any modifications that might arise during this period.

One final point to be realized is that the design process of Thamesmead is backed by a sophisticated system of analysis and synthesis which is an aid to, but not substitute for, judgement.

Movement to and from Thamesmead

At present there is no one point from which satisfactory access can be made to the whole of the site. However, it is proposed to build a new principal road from Woolwich to Erith, bypassing the existing congested principal road A206 running through Plumstead High Street, etc., south of Thamesmead. The route of this proposed road was carefully related to the design for Thamesmead and in fact it provides the 'spine' on which is hung (if this is the right medical term) the body of Thamesmead. This road, now known as 'the spine road' will be an all-purpose high class route without footways, and with four junctions along its length, all providing access to different parts of Thamesmead. One of these junctions (junction 'C') functions both as a link to Ringway Two and to the central area of the development. Therefore visitors to the shops in the central area will be able to drive into the car parks directly from the spine road or Ringway Two. This particular intersection will be basically a three-level design in which lines of traffic staying on either of the main roads will cross each other by means of bridges whilst the turning movements, including the link into the central area, use a large roundabout or 'gyratory' system.

Junction 'D' (now under construction) takes the form of an elevated roundabout with the spine road passing underneath, the roundabout connecting with an existing road (Harrow Manor Way) on the south side and a new principal road on the north, linking back through the development into the central area. The elevating of the roundabout, rather than the spine road itself, was necessitated by the latter having to go as close as possible to the sewer bank for planning reasons. The forms of the other junctions have not yet been finalized, although they may also take the form of grade separated intersections but with the roundabouts on ground level and the spine road flying over.

Although it is proposed that the spine road outside Thamesmead will be constructed with dual two-lane carriageways, within the development it is basically designed for dual three-lanes with a safeguarding for dual four-lanes between junctions 'C' and 'D'. These extra lanes are required to deal with the traffic generated by Thamesmead, this traffic consisting of vehicles going outside the site and those travelling between the housing areas and the Thamesmead industrial areas.

As to the river crossing, present proposals are that the tunnel will incorporate dual four-lanes. This will enable it to cope with the traffic generated by Thamesmead and the surrounding local areas as well as the through traffic on Ringway Two.

Public transport (rail)

Thamesmead is served by the North Kent line of Southern Region. Trains on this line run to Charing

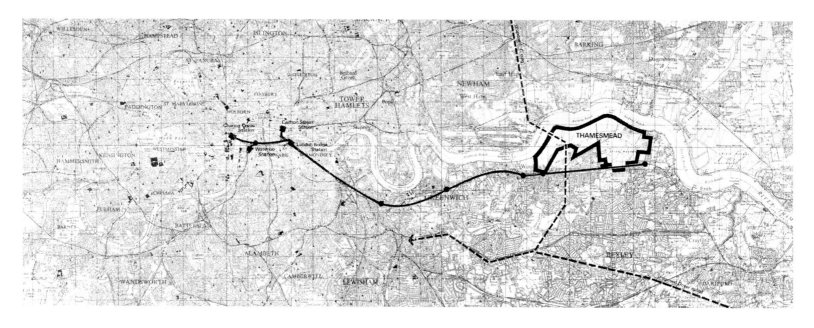

Cross and Cannon Street via London Bridge in the up-direction and to Dartford, Gravesend and Gillingham in the down direction. Three stations give access to the site at Plumstead, Abbey Wood and Belvedere.

The North Kent line forms part of the south eastern division of Southern Region and is one of the most heavily loaded parts of the system during peak hours. Under the 1967 reorganization of the timetable, an additional train on this line was introduced to give relief to overcrowding. In order to improve the reliability of the service and enable the full line capacity to be utilized, resignalling is taking place and little-used level crossings closed.

The traffic forecasts predict that Thamesmead, when complete in the 1980's, could generate around 6,000 – 8,000 persons commuting to Central London, and that by 1976, with about 20,000 residents, up to around 3,000 will wish to travel to Central London by rail.

To deal with this extra traffic, Southern Region propose to provide extra trains calling at both Abbey Wood and Plumstead (or the suggested new station at Church Manor Way) before proceeding to the London termini.

For the longer term additional services would depend on major works being carried out to enable trains to

be diverted into Victoria. Parliamentary powers have already been sought for some of these works and it is confidently expected that the necessary extra trains can be made available when necessary.

With regard to the actual stations, including interchange facilities with other modes of transport, Southern Region have already rebuilt Belvedere Station and have in their programme proposals for reconstructing Abbey Wood Station in conjunction with the replacement of the level crossing by a bridge. The provision of this new bridge is the joint responsibility of the London Boroughs of Bexley and Greenwich, whose boundary runs up the centre of the existing unclassified road, Harrow Manor Way, which links up with the spine road at junction 'D'. As a proposed principal road, the cost of the bridge is being shared between the joint highway authorities, the two Boroughs, the Ministry of Transport and the GLC, the latter making a contribution as the 'developer' of Thamesmead. The bridge design is being closely integrated with that of the new station so as to give direct access from the bus laybys on the bridge to the booking hall. It is also proposed to provide car parking facilities under the structure and this space, together with other vacant land adjoining the railway, should be able to satisfy the ultimate parking demand at this station for about 500 vehicles.

At Belvedere Station it is hoped to close the existing level crossing and that immediately to the east at Crabtree Manor Way, with the construction of a new bridge by the London Borough of Bexley over the railway on the line of Picardy Manor Way (half way between the two crossings). This bridge and its associated road links will give a direct connection from the temporary termination of the spine road at the eastern end of the Thamesmead site (junction 'E') on to the existing B.213 route into Erith.

On the question of the third existing station at Plumstead, in the original published proposals it was suggested that it be closed and a new one constructed at Church Manor Way. However, subsequent discussions with British Rail and London Transport have shown that there may be a case for retaining Plumstead rather than providing a new station and this matter is currently under investigation. Whatever solution is arrived at it is proposed that there will be interchange facilities with buses and cars, with parking space provided for the latter.

Public transport (bus)

Under the bus reshaping plan, London Transport propose to break up many of their existing long routes as traffic congestion at one point can cause irregular running of buses at places several miles

Above and right Stage 1 model, and Stage 1 under construction.

distant. London Transport intend to replace them by short routes based on local centres and Woolwich has been suggested as one of these. With the improved roads planned for Woolwich and Thamesmead, which are being designed to cater for buses, it will be possible to provide a regular and economic service between these two centres. Other routes are planned to connect Thamesmead to Erith and to the area north of the Thames, possibly Barking, via the Ringway Two tunnel under the Thames.

Movement in Thamesmead

The road network

In such a large development as Thamesmead it is necessary to establish a hierarchical pattern of roads. Excluding Ringway Two, first comes the spine road, then the main linear distributor off which the secondary distributors branch into the housing areas; with the actual houses being served by local access and minor service roads. The main and secondary distributors form the framework of Thamesmead, the main flow of traffic within the town being concentrated on the main distributor. This road runs north and east from the spine road at junction 'B', over Ringway Two (where the latter goes into tunnel to pass under the river) through to the central area, where it has an intersection with the link southwards to Ringway Two and the spine road at junction 'C'. From the central area the main distributor continues east then turns south to rejoin the spine road at junction 'D', where it

joins the improved Harrow Manor Way and thus provides a route out of Thamesmead via Abbey Wood.

To this main distributor will be connected at intervals a secondary distributor collecting traffic from the environmental areas. It will take an indirect route *through* the lower density housing area lying behind the high density linear blocks along the line of the main distributor, this giving rise to only a comparatively small increase in journey time. The secondary distributor provides a continuous road for bus routes and purely local movements within Thamesmead. By 'meandering' through the environmental areas it will minimize the distance people will have to walk from home to the bus. Through traffic will be discouraged from using this route by its 'meandering' and by the design of the junctions with the main distributor which will attract traffic on to the latter. It is, of course, essential that the main distributor has ample capacity to absorb without congestion all the through traffic. The secondary distributor will be basically a single two-way road constructed so as to reduce to a minimum any barrier effect between the housing areas lying on either side. There will be no frontage access on to this route and no footpaths alongside the carriageway.

Public transport
One of the fundamentals of the master plan for Thamesmead is an efficient and convenient public transport system that will attract to it the maximum number of persons. By doing this it will enable the road system to be kept to a minimum consistent with an ultimate high car ownership.

As part of the consideration of this, a close and detailed investigation was made into the possible use of an unconventional passenger transport system such as a monorail. However, it soon became apparent that any form of fixed track system had serious disadvantages. One of these was the capital cost of the fixed track, which would have had to cross under or over the roads, cycleways, canals and footways. No other form of transport would be able to use these tracks whilst a bus shares roads which are required in any event. Another aspect is the lack of flexibility in that it must operate in conjunction with the existing extensive bus services in the area and must cater for a project growing over about fifteen years with all its difficulties of temporary routes through areas under construction and possible changes in public demand. Also there was the problem confronting the Council of how to successfully integrate such a system, which in Thamesmead would almost certainly have to be elevated, into the buildings. Moreover there was no fully developed, practical, system on which to base the plans! Consideration was also given to providing a separate bus-way, but this was found not to be justified as adequate capacity should be available in the proposed highway system.

As a result of these deliberations, it was agreed that buses would offer the most practical solution to solving the public transport needs of Thamesmead. However, to operate efficiently and in order that a reliable and frequent service can be provided, the bus must have the use of a suitable road system. This system must be designed to fulfil the following requirements:

(a) There must be two-way roads penetrating through the heart of the residential areas so that ideally no one lives more than a quarter of a mile walking distance from a bus stop. These roads must also provide reasonably direct routes between residential areas, main shop-

ping centre, industrial areas and railway stations.
(b) These roads, i.e., the secondary distributors referred to above, must be designed so that buses can run freely on them; to fulfil this they must not be overloaded with other traffic.
(c) Bus stops must be sited in relation to the system of pedestrian ways so that there is easy access from all parts of the development. Also stops at shopping centres and railway stations must be near to and give convenient access to the destination.

An important aspect of *(a)* is that the development be of a reasonably high density. If the density should be too low then the bus services could be rather diffuse and therefore infrequent or, alternatively, walking distances become too long; in either case the attractiveness of public transport could be seriously diminished.

The design of the road system in Thamesmead means that special bus roads or lanes are unlikely to be required except possibly in the central area to give free access to the proposed bus station.

It is not possible to say in detail what the final pattern of routes will be. As Thamesmead grows, temporary routes will have to be provided to serve each stage and these will tend to establish patterns of movement. However, as an indication the following routes might be included:

(a) A route from Woolwich town centre through the western side of the site and out to the extreme north-east corner via the central area.
(b) A 'panhandle' service around the central area and the housing areas east of it, then southwards across the spine road at junction 'D' and down to Abbey Wood Station.
(c) A service from Central Woolwich to Erith via the existing roads to Abbey Wood Station, then through stages I and II of the development along Yarnton Way to the eastern industrial estates.
(d) A service, possibly peak hour only, from the central area through the existing Woolwich Industrial Estate via junction 'C' to Woolwich.
(e) A service across the river via the Ringway Two tunnel, possibly to Barking.

As to the actual vehicles, it is probable that by the time the project is complete most of them will not be the traditional double deck bus with driver and conductor. It is much more likely that they will be single deck types, one man operated, with an automatic

Right Model of Stage 3

means of fare collection and ticket issuing. Also during this period there is little doubt that advances in technology will lead to other significant improvements.

One final aspect is the thought that a bus service could be provided above the level which would give a reasonable prospect of overall commercial viability. This could encourage people to accept some restraint in their use of private transport and voluntarily leave their cars at home during some of the local trips for which, they might otherwise use them. However, the economic consequences and the means of financing such measures would require examination.

Cycling

The site of Thamesmead being fairly flat and the development of reasonably high density presents practically the ideal conditions for providing a cycleway system. Experience has shown that where they have been constructed as a proper and complete system and not merely provided as a few cycle tracks alongside busy roads, they are well used. In such new towns as Stevenage, extensions are being made and it is of great interest to see the large numbers of workers and school-children, particularly the latter, using them. With regard to school-children, a recent survey carried out by the London Borough of Bexley showed that up to 45% of children attending secondary schools used their cycles.

It has therefore been agreed that a cycleway system be provided, together with cycle parks at such places as the local and main shopping centres, schools, industrial estates, etc.

Walking

As can be ascertained from the above the pedestrian will, as far as possible, be segregated from vehicular traffic. This will be achieved by separating the footwalk system from the road system and, where they do meet, providing subways or overbridges, except for such places as minor access roads.

Safety

One of the cardinal points in the design of Thamesmead is road safety, whether it be for pedestrian, cyclist, or motorist. The road pattern is being designed to keep the number of traffic conflicts to a minimum, consistent with giving access to the development. Cyclists, the most vulnerable to accident and injury, will be discouraged from using the main and secondary roads whilst pedestrians, as far as possible, will be removed completely from these roads. Experience has shown that where the road and

footway systems have been designed from the start with vehicle-pedestrian segregation and vehicle/vehicle conflict paths reduced to a minimum then the accident rate will be substantially lower. Examples of this are the new towns of Cumbernauld[2] and Stevenage[3].

General

As a final note to this rather brief summary to transportation in Thamesmead, I would like to emphasize the element of teamwork in the design of such a large project as Thamesmead. It will be appreciated how various aspects of the plan overlap and thus entail continuous close co-operation. This working together with other disciplines is to me most stimulating and provides one of the great interests in working on such a project. Even the occasional conflict between different ideas helps to sharpen the interest!

This co-operation, however, is not confined to the GLC. It extends (on the transport side) to British Rail, London Transport, the London Boroughs of Bexley and Greenwich and the various Ministries, such as Transport, Housing and Local Government (now called Environment), Defence, etc. In particular on the public transport sections the background has been set by work done by London Transport and British Rail in very close co-operation with the GLC.

References

1 Ministry of Transport Circular Roads No. 1966.
2 'Report on Road Accidents' issued by Cumbernauld Development Corporation (1967).
3 Stevenage Traffic Accident Survey' issued by Stevenage Development Corporation (1968).

Above right Service access and parking for 3-storey houses in Stage 1.
Right Linear housing in Stage 1 with pedestrian ways and parkland.